Examining Cloud Computing Technologies Through the Internet of Things

Pradeep Tomar
Gautam Buddha University, India

Gurjit Kaur
Gautam Buddha University, India

A volume in the Advances in Wireless Technologies and Telecommunication (AWTT) Book Series

Published in the United States of America by
    IGI Global
    Information Science Reference (an imprint of IGI Global)
    701 E. Chocolate Avenue
    Hershey PA, USA 17033
    Tel: 717-533-8845
    Fax: 717-533-8661
    E-mail: cust@igi-global.com
    Web site: http://www.igi-global.com

Library of Congress Cataloging-in-Publication Data

Names: Tomar, Pradeep, 1976- editor. | Kaur, Gurjit, 1980- editor.
Title: Examining cloud computing technologies through the internet of things
  / Pradeep Tomar and Gurjit Kaur, editors.
Description: Hershey, PA : Information Science Reference, [2018] | Includes
  bibliographical references.
Identifiers: LCCN 2017017430| ISBN 9781522534457 (hardcover) | ISBN
  9781522534464 (eISBN)
Subjects: LCSH: Internet of things. | Cloud computing.
Classification: LCC TK5105.8857 .E95 2018 | DDC 004.67/82--dc23 LC record available at https://
lccn.loc.gov/2017017430

This book is published in the IGI Global book series Advances in Wireless Technologies and Telecommunication (AWTT) (ISSN: 2327-3305; eISSN: 2327-3313)

British Cataloguing in Publication Data
A Cataloguing in Publication record for this book is available from the British Library.

All work contributed to this book is new, previously-unpublished material.
The views expressed in this book are those of the authors, but not necessarily of the publisher.

For electronic access to this publication, please contact: eresources@igi-global.com.

Advances in Wireless Technologies and Telecommunication (AWTT) Book Series

ISSN:2327-3305
EISSN:2327-3313

Editor-in-Chief: Xiaoge Xu, Xiamen University Malaysia, Malaysia

MISSION

The wireless computing industry is constantly evolving, redesigning the ways in which individuals share information. Wireless technology and telecommunication remain one of the most important technologies in business organizations. The utilization of these technologies has enhanced business efficiency by enabling dynamic resources in all aspects of society.

The **Advances in Wireless Technologies and Telecommunication Book Series** aims to provide researchers and academic communities with quality research on the concepts and developments in the wireless technology fields. Developers, engineers, students, research strategists, and IT managers will find this series useful to gain insight into next generation wireless technologies and telecommunication.

COVERAGE

- Global Telecommunications
- Digital Communication
- Radio Communication
- Cellular Networks
- Wireless sensor networks
- Wireless Technologies
- Telecommunications
- Virtual Network Operations
- Broadcasting
- Mobile Communications

IGI Global is currently accepting manuscripts for publication within this series. To submit a proposal for a volume in this series, please contact our Acquisition Editors at Acquisitions@igi-global.com or visit: http://www.igi-global.com/publish/.

Titles in this Series

For a list of additional titles in this series, please visit:
https://www.igi-global.com/book-series/advances-wireless-technologies-telecommunication/73684

Advanced Mobile Technologies for Secure Transaction Processing...
Raghvendra Kumar (LNCT Group of Colleges, India) Preeta Sharan (The Oxford College of Engineering, India) and Aruna Devi (Surabhi Software,India)
Information Science Reference • ©2018 • 177pp • H/C (ISBN: 9781522527596) • US $130.00

Examining Developments and Applications of Wearable Devices in Modern Society
Saul Emanuel Delabrida Silva (Federal University of Ouro Preto, Brazil) Ricardo Augusto Rabelo Oliveira (Federal University of Ouro Preto, Brazil) and Antonio Alfredo Ferreira Loureiro (Federal University of Minas Gerais (UFMG), Brazil)
Information Science Reference • ©2018 • 330pp • H/C (ISBN: 9781522532903) • US $195.00

Graph Theoretic Approaches for Analyzing Large-Scale Social Networks
Natarajan Meghanathan (Jackson State University, USA)
Information Science Reference • ©2018 • 355pp • H/C (ISBN: 9781522528142) • US $225.00

Powering the Internet of Things With 5G Networks
Vasuky Mohanan (Universiti Sains Malaysia, Malaysia) Rahmat Budiarto (Albaha University, Saudi Arabia) and Ismat Aldmour (Albaha University, Saudi Arabia)
Information Science Reference • ©2018 • 304pp • H/C (ISBN: 9781522527992) • US $215.00

Routing Protocols and Architectural Solutions for Optimal Wireless Networks and Security
Dharm Singh (Namibia University of Science and Technology, Namibia)
Information Science Reference • ©2017 • 277pp • H/C (ISBN: 9781522523420) • US $205.00

Sliding Mode in Intellectual Control and Communication...
Vardan Mkrttchian (HHH University, Australia) and Ekaterina Aleshina (Penza State University, Russia)
Information Science Reference • ©2017 • 128pp • H/C (ISBN: 9781522522928) • US $140.00

For an enitre list of titles in this series, please visit:
https://www.igi-global.com/book-series/advances-wireless-technologies-telecommunication/73684

701 East Chocolate Avenue, Hershey, PA 17033, USA
Tel: 717-533-8845 x100 • Fax: 717-533-8661
E-Mail: cust@igi-global.com • www.igi-global.com

Table of Contents

Detailed Table of Contents

    Gurjit Kaur, Gautam Buddha University, India
    Pradeep Tomar, Gautam Buddha University, India

Internet of Things (IoT) and Cloud computing are exceptionally different innovations that have become the backbone of the smart world. This paradigm where IoT and Cloud are integrated is anticipated as an empowering influence to an extensive number of smart applications. In this chapter, the integration of Cloud and IoT is explored. This chapter also provides a picture of the integration of Cloud IoT applications. Finally, some future open issues are described.

    Akash Chowdhury, Institute of Science and Technology, India
    Swastik Mukherjee, Institute of Science and Technology, India
    Sourav Banerjee, Kalyani Government Engineering College, India

The various services that are offered by IoT and Cloud Service Providers (CSPs) to the customers today feature a pay-per-use service-charging policy. Customers can choose and avail these services when they want, how they want, and from where they want on demand. Demand for these services has increased drastically over the years among individuals and enterprises worldwide, and thus, it is very important to keep up good Quality of Service (QoS). This chapter highlights the history of internet, the gradual evolution of cloud computing, the reasons behind it, evolution and concepts of the Internet of Things (IoT), CloudIoT and its necessities, and various applications and service fields of CloudIoT. This chapter also precisely highlights various concepts regarding maintenance of good QoS, controversies in

QoS maintenance, different parameters that the QoS depends on, various problems faced in maintaining those parameters, and the possible solutions for overcoming those problems. Possible directions towards future works are also highlighted in this chapter.

Aditya Pratap Singh, Ajay Kumar Garg Engineering College, India
Pradeep Tomar, Gautam Buddha University, India

Cloud computing has proven itself and is accepted in industrial applications. Cloud computing is based on the co-existence and co-working of various technologies and services from different sources that together make cloud computing a success. Over the last few years, the Internet of Things (IoT) has been widely studied and being applied. The blending of these two efficient technologies may provide an intelligent perception about usage of resources on demand and efficient sharing. The adoption of these two different technologies and usage is likely to be more and more pervasive, making them important components of the future internet-based systems. This chapter focuses on the deployment models of cloud computing in relation to IoT. The implications of cloud computing in view of deployment are discussed. The issues for deployment and optimization related to the merger of IoT with cloud computing are raised.

Marcus Tanque, Independent Researcher, USA

Converging Cloud computing with Internet of Things transformed organizations' traditional technologies. This chapter examines the intersection of cloud computing and internet of things in consort with how these solutions often interact on the internet. Vendors develop CloudIoT capabilities to support organizations' day-to-day operations. IoT is a combined platform encompassing physical and virtual nodes. IoT objects comprise device-to-device data sharing, machine-to-machine provisioning, sensors, actuators, and processors. These systems may be deployed as hardware components and applications software. This chapter also emphasizes data security, reliability, resource provisioning, service-level agreement, quality of service, IoT, privacy, and device integration. This chapter also highlights operational benefits and/or security issues affecting CC and IoT technologies.

Chapter 5

Govind P. Gupta, National Institute of Technology, India

Internet of Things (IoT) offers the capability to connect and integrate both digital and physical objects to the internet and to enable machine-to-machine and machine-to-human communication or interactions services. The real-time adoptions and deployments of such systems for different applications such as smart cities, smart grids, smart homes, or smart environments require guaranteed security and privacy-enabled IoT services. This is due to fact that devices in the IoT generate, process, and exchange huge amounts of safety-critical data as well as privacy-sensitive information. In order to ensure secure and safe operation and to avoid cyber-attacks on such systems, it is crucial to incorporate security and privacy measures to countermeasure the different possible attacks. This chapter presents different security and privacy requirements and a taxonomy of security threats in the context of the IoT. In addition, the authors survey the most relevant defense strategies available in the literature related to IoT security with their merits and demerits.

Chapter 6

Yaman Parasher, Gautam Buddha University, India
Deepak Kedia, Guru Jambheshwar University of Science and
*   Technology, India*
Prabhjot Singh, Salesforce Inc., USA

The advent of Cloud computing has acted as a catalyst for the design and deployment of scalable Internet of Things business models and applications. Therefore, IoT and Cloud are nowadays two very closely affiliated future internet technologies, which go hand in hand in non-trivial IoT deployments. Furthermore, most modern IoT ecosystems are cloud-based, as will be illustrated in the chapter. This chapter briefly introduces the main cloud computing and IoT standards.

Chapter 7

Deepak Kedia, Guru Jambheshwar University of Science and
*   Technology, India*
Gurjit Kaur, Gautam Buddha University, India

The integration of Cloud computing and IoT provides the capability of omnipresent sensing services and powerful, efficient storage as well as processing of sensor data beyond the capability of distinct things or devices. The ability of Cloud platform in providing automatic and reliable decision making will boost the development of newer and innovative applications, like smart healthcare, cities, buildings, agriculture practices and buildings, etc. This chapter surveys a few key application areas where Cloud-based IoT technology can mark its impact. The Cloud-based architecture has been proposed for these applications, simultaneously examining and identifying the challenges involved. The salient points identified in this chapter will help researchers and scientists to explore newer applications based on the Cloud-IoT platform.

Chapter 8

Cloud IoT has evolved from the convergence of Cloud computing with Internet of Things (IoT). The networked devices in the IoT world grow exponentially in the distributed computing paradigm and thus require the power of the Cloud to access and share computing and storage for these devices. Cloud offers scalable on-demand services to the IoT devices for effective communication and knowledge sharing. It alleviates the computational load of IoT, which makes the devices smarter. This chapter explores the different IoT services offered by the Cloud as well as application domains that are benefited by the Cloud IoT. The challenges on offloading the IoT computation into the Cloud are also discussed.

This chapter provides an insight into big data, its technical background, and how need for it has arisen globally. The evolution of Cloud technology provides a favorable environment for IoTs to nurture and flourish, creating an exponential increase in the amount of data. The Cloud environment provides easy access to this vast data from anywhere on the globe, but this availability has given rise to some challenges for organizations in managing big data efficiently. The chapter discusses the key concepts and technical and architectural principles of big data technologies that help to curb the challenges in managing big data generated by IoTs in the Cloud environment and identifies the important research directions in this area.

The Internet of Things (IoT) represents the current and future state of the internet. The large number of things (objects) connected to the internet produces a huge amount of data that needs a lot of effort and processing operations to transfer it to useful information. Maximizing the utilization of this paradigm requires fine-grained QoS support for differentiated application requirements, context-aware semantic information retrieval, and quick and easy deployment of resources, among many other objectives. These objectives can only be achieved if components of the IoT can be dynamically managed end-to-end across heterogeneous objects, transmission technologies, and networking architectures. In this chapter, Software Defined Systems (SDS) is described as a new paradigm to hide all complexity in traditional system architecture by abstracting all the controls and management operations from the underling devices (things in the IoT) and setting them inside a middleware layer, a software layer, using a software-based control plane.

Chapter 11

The public cloud Amazon Web Service (AWS) provides a wide range of services like computation, networking, analytics, development and management tools, application services, mobile services, and management of Internet-of-Things (IoT) devices. The Amazon Web Services (AWS) IoT is an excellent IoT cloud platform and is exclusively responsible for connecting devices into various fields like healthcare, biology, municipal setup, smart homes, marketing, industrial, agriculture, education, automotive, etc. This chapter highlights many other initiatives promoted by AWS IoT. The main motive of this chapter is to present how AWS IoT works. The chapter starts with the design principles of AWS IoT services. Further, the authors present a detailed description of the AWS IoT components (e.g., Device SDK, Message Broker, Rule Engine, Security and Identity Service, Thing Registry, Thing Shadow, and Thing Shadow Service). The chapter concludes with a description of various challenges faced by AWS IoT and future research directions.

In the Cloud-based IoT systems, the major issue is handling the data because IoT will deliver an abundance of data to the Cloud for computing. In this situation, the cloud servers will compute the big data and try to identify the relevant data and give decisions accordingly. In the world of big data, it is a herculean task to manage inflow, storage, and exploration of millions of data files and the volume of information coming from multiple systems. The growth of this information calls for good design principles so that it can leverage the different big data tools available in the market today. From the information consumption standpoint, business users are exploring new insights from the big data that can uncover potential business value. Data lake is a technology framework that helps to solve this big data challenge.

The Cloud of Things (CoT) is the multi-domain, emerging, and dynamic technology in today's era. Cloud of Things can perform security services and virtualization with different sensor devices for a powerful and scalable high-performance computing. The author emphasizes the evaluation of various applications used in Cloud of Things. The chapter has been this chapter is divided into two parts which cover the significance of the Cloud and Internet of Things. The chapter focuses on introduction of the Cloud, IoT, and CoT and shows the security and challenges occurring in CoT. It also covers the security issues in IoT with different applications. The chapter will help the academician, researchers, and industry professional to further investigate the associated area of Cloud IoT, and it also helps them find solutions from different perspectives.

Chapter 14

Jayashree K, Rajalakshmi Engineering College, India
Babu R, Rajalakshmi Engineering College, India
Chithambaramani R, Rajalakshmi Engineering College, India

The Internet of Things (IoT) architecture has gained an increased amount of attention from academia as well as the industry sector as a significant methodology for the development of innovative applications and systems. Currently, the merging of this architecture with that of Cloud computing has been largely motivated by the need for various applications and infrastructures in IoT. In addition to this, the Cloud ascends as an eminent solution that would help solve various challenges that are faced by the IoT standard when varied physical devices. There are an excessive number of Cloud service providers the web along with many other services. Thus, it becomes critical to choose the provider who can be efficient, consistent, and suitable, and who can deliver the best Quality of Service (QoS). Thus, this chapter discusses QoS for cloud computing and IoT.

Preface

The Internet of Things (IoT) has drawn great attention from both academia and industry, since it offers challenging notion of creating a world where all the things, known as smart objects around us are connected, typically in a wireless manner, to the internet and communicate with each other with minimum human intervention. Another component set to help IoT succeed is Cloud computing, which acts as a sort of front end. Cloud computing is an increasingly popular service that offers several advantages to IoT and it is based on the concept of allowing users to perform normal computing tasks using services delivered entirely over the internet. Cloud computing is a paradigm for big data storage and analytics, while IoT is exciting on its own. The real innovation will come from combining it with Cloud computing. The combination of Cloud computing and IoT will enable new monitoring services and powerful processing of sensory data streams. These applications alongside implementation details and challenges should also be explored for successful mainstream adoption. IoT is also fuelled by the advancement of digital technologies. The next generation era will be Cloud-based IoT systems.

Recently, IoT and Cloud computing have been widely studied and applied in many fields, as they can provide a new method for intelligent perception and connection from M2M (including Man-to-Man, Man-to-Machine, and Machine-to-Machine), and on-demand use and efficient sharing of resources, respectively. The IoT and Cloud computing are inseparable systems. On the one hand IoT promises to make any electronic devices part of the Internet environment and provide the required information whereas the Cloud computing will help to extract the valuable data from that information. A novel paradigm where Cloud and IoT are merged together is foreseen as disruptive and an enabler of a large number of application scenarios. This new paradigm opens the doors to new innovations and interactions between people and things that will utilize of scarce resources and improve the quality of each individual life. The book identifies potential future directions and technologies that facilitate insight into numerous scientific, smart business, smart cities, smart e-healthcare and smart consumer applications.

The main goal of this book is to spur the development of effective Cloud-based IoT system and identify state-of-the-art research in the Cloud-based IoT systems, its applications, architectures and technologies. It focuses on the integration of Cloud and IoT named Cloud IoT paradigm. It examine various aspects of Cloud-based IoT system, the need for integrating them, the challenges deriving from such integration, and how these issues have been tackled. Various applications like Cloud-based smart cities, smart grids, smart homes, smart farming and smart e-health services, etc. has been described. Different communication technologies and protocols for Cloud-based IoT system has been explored. To help realize the full potential of Cloud-based IoT system, this book addresses the numerous aspects and challenges for integrating them and discusses the conceptual and technological solutions for tackling them. These challenges include the deployment of Cloud-based IoT model, security issues, designing in integrated Cloud and IoT architecture, and the privacy and ethical issues around data sensing, storage and processing.

This book contains 14 chapters authored by several leading experts in the field of IoT and Cloud computing. The book is presented in a coordinated and integrated manner starting with the fundamentals, and followed by the technologies that implement them. The content of the book is organized as follows:

Chapter 1: This chapter shows the genesis of Cloud and IoT systems and their integration. Starting from the fundamental presentation of Cloud and IoT this chapter will discuss the integration part of Cloud and IoT. This chapter will also provide a latest picture of integration of Cloud IoT applications. At last some future open research issues are described.

Chapter 2: This chapter presents the history of internet, the gradual evolution of Cloud computing, evolution and concepts of the IoT and CloudIoT and its necessities. It also discusses the various applications and service fields of CloudIoT. At the end of this chapter various concepts regarding maintenance of good QoS, controversies in QoS maintenance, different parameters that the QoS depends on, various problems faced in maintaining those parameters and the possible solutions for overcoming those problems are discussed. Possible directions towards future works are also highlighted at the end of this chapter.

Chapter 3: This chapter focuses on the deployment models of Cloud computing in relation to IoT. The implications of Cloud computing in view of deployment are discussed in an exhaustive way. The issues for deployment and optimization related to the merger of IoT with Cloud computing are also raised.

Chapter 4: This chapter examines the convergence of Cloud computing and IoT systems and explain how these solutions can interact via the internet. The main emphasis of this chapter is on data security, reliability, resource provisioning, service level agreement, quality of service, IoT, privacy and device integration.

It also underscores the operational benefits and security issues in Cloud computing and IoT technologies pose to customers.

Chapter 5: In this chapter, various security and privacy requirements in the Cloud-based IoT system have been discussed. To solve these security issues the trust management systems has been presented. At the end of this chapter security analysis of IoT-related standard protocols, and security threats at the different layers of IoT has been presented.

Chapter 6: This chapter describes the various standards of Cloud and IoT. A critical survey has been done for the need of standards, standardization bodies, their standards and functions.

Chapter 7: This chapter presents the various applications by using Cloud and IoT. Various applications like smart healthcare, cities, buildings, agriculture practices and buildings, etc. have been analysed from different perspectives, including sensors, data management, Cloud computing, etc. Then Cloud-based architecture has been proposed for these applications which simultaneously examining and identifying the challenges involved.

Chapter 8: This chapter explores the different IoT services offered by Cloud as well as application domains which are benefited by the Cloud IoT. The challenges on offloading the IoT computation into Cloud are also discussed.

Chapter 9: The chapter provides an insight of big data, its technical background and its need for adoption globally. On the contrary, the big data management for Cloud-based IoT system has thoroughly discussed. Its key concepts, technical and architectural aspects, management of big data and its identification is presented in a very simplified way.

Chapter 10: This chapter elaborates the software defined networking for Cloud-based IoT system. The software defined systems is a new paradigm that appeared recently to hide all complexity in traditional system. The architecture of SDN is very well explained by abstracting all the controls and management operations from the devices attached through IoT.

Chapter 11: This chapter introduces the public Cloud Amazon Web Service (AWS) system for a wide range of services like computation, networking, analytics, development and management tools, application services, mobile services and management of IoT devices. Its working principle, design principles has been presented including the detailed description of the AWS IoT Components viz. Device SDK, Message Broker, Rule Engine, Security and Identity Service, Thing Registry, Thing Shadow, and Thing Shadow Service, etc.

Chapter 12: This chapter elaborates the Cloud-based IoT systems the major issue is to handle the data because IoT will deliver an abundance of data to Cloud for computing. Under this situation the Cloud servers will compute the big data and try to identify the relevant data and gives decisions accordingly.

In the world of big data, it's a herculean task to manage inflow, storage and exploration of millions of data files and volume of information coming from multiple systems. The growth of this information, calls for good design principles so that it can leverage the different big data tools available in market today. From the information consumption standpoint, business users are exploring new insights from the big data that can uncover potential business value. Data Lake is a technology framework that helps to solution this big data challenge.

Chapter 13: In this chapter, various applications used in Cloud of Things are presented. Starting from the introduction of Cloud, IOT and Cloud of Things (CoT), it also covers security and challenges occurred in CoT.

Chapter 14: This chapter presents the IoT with significant methodology for the development of innovative applications and systems. It is very much evident that the integration of IoT and Cloud computing enables resource sharing more efficiently. But the research demands the necessity of QoS requirements. These must be capable enough to deliver real time provisions and applications with ensured quality. The basis of Cloud computing, IoT and the survey that was done in QoS of Cloud computing and IoT is discussed in this chapter.

The targeted audience for the book includes professionals who are designers and planners for Cloud-based IoT systems, researchers (faculty members and graduate students), and those who would like to learn about this field. This book is expected to have the following specific salient features:

- To serve as a single comprehensive source of information and as reference material on Cloud-based IoT systems.
- To help those who are interested in exploring and implementing the IoT and related technologies, protocol and standards with recent research and development in the Cloud-based IoT system.
- To deal with an important and timely topic of emerging Cloud-based IoT systems of today, tomorrow, and beyond.
- To present accurate, up-to-date information on a broad range of topics related to Cloud-based IoT systems and its architecture.

Pradeep Tomar
Gautam Buddha University, India

Gurjit Kaur
Gautam Buddha University, India

Chapter 1

Genesis of Cloud–Based IoT Systems for Smart Generation

Gurjit Kaur
Gautam Buddha University, India

Pradeep Tomar
Gautam Buddha University, India

ABSTRACT

Internet of Things (IoT) and Cloud computing are exceptionally different innovations that have become the backbone of the smart world. This paradigm where IoT and Cloud are integrated is anticipated as an empowering influence to an extensive number of smart applications. In this chapter, the integration of Cloud and IoT is explored. This chapter also provides a picture of the integration of Cloud IoT applications. Finally, some future open issues are described.

1. INTRODUCTION

In telecommunication fields there is a new technology called IoT which means "the network of physical objects, buildings, devices, vehicles and other things which could be embedded with software, electronics, sensors and network connectivity and permits these objects to gather and interchange data". IoT technology is at the boom in the new technology advancement sector which ultimately will produce a major changes in the business to get smart. In the next generation networks, millions of devices will be connected and located at different sites and perform

DOI: 10.4018/978-1-5225-3445-7.ch001

their functions to provide information to the decision making devices. This new idea will not only effect the business era but also on the several aspects of the everyday life and behavior of potential users. This IoT will transform individuals and organizations to get connected with customers, partners, suppliers and other individuals. The significant test for associating sensors, actuators and devices to a system was the primary test. In any case, equipment advancements like Raspberry Pi are making it quicker, simpler and less expensive and furthermore help to grow new gadgets organizing guidelines for low power systems. LoRaWAn or Sigfox, make new open doors for interfacing little gadgets to a system new benchmarks. These are being created particularly for IoT utilize cases, as MQTT for informing, or OMA Lightweight M2M for gadget administration. Lastly, a ton of upgrades in information stockpiling, information examination, and occasion preparing are making it conceivable to help the measure of information produced in expansive scale IoT arrangements.

The Cloud computing collects the data from the IoT sensors and compute it according to different requirements. Integration of IoT along with Cloud computing is another worldview which stretch out the degree to manage true things. It can help for conveying new administrations in countless life situations. From one viewpoint, IoT can benefit by the practically boundless abilities and assets of Cloud to remunerate its innovative limitations (e.g., capacity, handling, and vitality). In particular, these two paradigms i.e. IoT and Cloud are altogether different from each other. Such complementarily is the principle motivation behind why numerous specialists have proposed and are proposing their incorporation, for the most part to acquire benefits in particular application situations.

2. CLOUD COMPUTING

Cloud computing provides four different services as follows:

1. **SaaS:** In this, service application can work over the internet and customer can use it on the basis of utilization. Here customer need not to store the data and keep that data on the hard disk. The customer has to pay as he use.
2. **PaaS:** In this service the cloud server gives a platform and toolboxes where different applications can be designed.
3. **NaaS:** It is a totally virtual network for customers. Here, customers can get different quantities of systems as required, with wanted division and approach authorization.
4. **IaaS:** This service gives calculation and capacity benefits on leasing premise. Rather than buying costly machines, servers, and capacity devices,

notwithstanding for little assignments, client can outsource this undertaking to the IaaS specialist. With capacity in IaaS, not just the information is put away by the IaaS benefit, yet in addition, it makes the information generally open over the Internet.

Distributed computing makes another method for outlining, creating, testing, conveying, running and keeping up applications on the internet. Customarily, the application engineer needs to deal with running working frameworks, systems, stack adjusting, switches, capacity and incorporating these things and enabling them to connect with the framework (Zhou, 2013). The engineer additionally needs to assess versatility, or how the application could scale many geologically circulated clients. Distributed computing is an advanced model which can create different processing assets. The Cloud customer can get the benefits over the internet and customer need to pay just for the time and administration he require. The Cloud can likewise scale to help substantial quantities of administration demands. At last, Cloud registering deals with the smaller scale lifecycle administration of utilizations, and enables application chiefs to concentrate on application advancement and observing.

Distributed computing is the conveyance of on-request registering assets i.e. everything from applications to server farms and over the web on a compensation for-utilize premise. In the least difficult terms, distributed computing implies putting away the data over the internet rather than on the laptop/personal computer hard disk. Putting away information on a home or office arrange does not consider using the cloud. Some other real cases of distributed computing are:

- **Google Drive:** This is an unadulterated distributed computing administration, with all the capacity discovered online so it can work on the cloud applications.
- **Apple iCloud:** Apple's Cloud benefit is basically utilized for online capacity, storing and synchronization of your mail, contacts, calendar and photographs etc.
- **Amazon Cloud Drive:** The Amazon Cloud runs on the Cloud since they store a synchronized rendition of your records on the web. Synchronization is a foundation of the distributed computing knowledge, regardless of the possibility that you do get to the document locally.

3. INTERNET OF THINGS

In Internet of Things, the meaning of "Things" has changed as innovation advanced, the primary objective of seeming well and good data without the guide of human interaction. Each and every device is connected with a sensor. These sensors provides the information to the cloud system . Various communication technologies plays their vital role e.g. Bluetooth, RFID, Zig bee, Wi-Fi etc.

The IoT explores new doors and applications, including smart home, smart cities, smart e-health, smart grids to enhance productivity and energy efficiency, intelligent transportation, ecological checking to drinking water resources and urban climates or oversee the transmission of perilous squanders, or e-wellbeing to quicken and organize administration of medicinal data, healing center wards, quiet care, and medication arrangement. Besides that there are many difficulties confronting "Things" related application improvement, for example, end client versatility, information stockpiling, heterogeneous asset obliged "Things", different geographical data sending, or vitality productivity.

4. INTEGRATED CLOUD-BASED IOT SYSTEM

A large portion of the literature have reviewed IoT and Cloud independently and discussed their fundamental properties, highlights, basic innovations and some open issues. Besides that to the best of our insight, these work does not have an close examination of the new integrated Cloud based IoT system, which includes totally new applications, difficulties, and research issues and assume a main part of the future internet. The two worlds of IoT and Cloud are inseparable from applications point of view. From one perspective, IoT can take advantage from the practically boundless capacities and the main assets of Cloud is that Cloud can offer a powerful answer for execute IoT benefit administration and synthesis and also applications that endeavor the things or the information created by them. Then again, the Cloud can get advantage from IoT by stretching out its extension to manage true things in a more dispersed and dynamic way, and for conveying new administrations in countless life situations. The correlative qualities of Cloud and IoT emerging from the diverse recommendations in literature and rousing the word CloudIoT.

The Cloud goes about as widely appealing layer between the things and the applications, where it covers the significant challenges and the functionalities imperative to execute the last specified. This framework will influence future application change, where information get-together, dealing with, and transmission will convey new troubles to be kept an eye on, similarly as in a multi-cloud condition. IoT incorporates gathering, getting to, planning, envisioning, chronicling, sharing, and looking a great deal of data. Offering basically perpetual, negligible exertion, and on-ask for putting away point of confinement, Cloud is the most accommodating and monetarily sagacious response for oversee data conveyed by IoT. This coordinated circumstance open new entryways o develop for data accumulation, settlement and bestowing to outcasts. Once into the Cloud, data can be managed homogeneously

4

through standard APIs, can be guaranteed by applying top-level security, and direct got to and imagined from wherever. IoT devices have constrained handling "Things" that don't permit nearby information preparing. Information gathered is typically transmitted to all the more intense hubs where collection and preparing is conceivable, however adaptability is trying to accomplish without a viable system. The limitless handling abilities of Cloud and its on-request show permit IoT preparing should be appropriately satisfied and empower examinations of extraordinary many-sided quality. This information can do the forecast calculations without using much effort and would give expanding incomes and decreased dangers.

5. APPLICATIONS OF CLOUD-BASED IOT SYSTEMS

Cloud based IoT is relied upon to offer promising solutions for change the operation and role of many existing mechanical frameworks, for example, transportation systems and manufacturing systems. Additionally cloud based IoT can be utilized as a part of numerous applications like in horticulture, food industry, ecological monitoring, security surveillance and pharmaceutics industry (Gil, 2016). The different applications can be named as follows:

- Cloud based IoT can be utilized in healthcare service industry. It is controlled by IoT's identification, sensing and communication capacities. All the objects in the healthcare systems (individuals, hardware, drug etc.) can be followed and observed always.
- Cloud based IoT can be used in Food Supply Chain (FSC) to trace, perceive and control challenges. The supposed sustenance IoT contains three sections: (a) the field devices etc., WSN hubs, RFID labels, UI terminals etc. (b) the backbone system e.g. databases, servers, and numerous sorts of terminals associated by disseminated PC systems and so on.
- Cloud based IoT system can be used for more secure mining generation in order to make early warning and disaster forecasting. Its goal is to make early cautioning, calamity determining, and safety improvement of underground creation conceivable. For instance, the effective communication amongst surface and underground keeping in mind the end goal to track the area of underground mineworkers and break down basic wellbeing information gathered from sensors to improve security measures. Another valuable application is to utilize compound and natural sensors for the early malady location and determination of underground excavators, as they work in an unsafe situation (Jadhav, 2015).

- Cloud based IoT system can be used in transportation and coordinate the movement of physical vehicles from a starting place to the destination.
- Cloud based IoT systems can be used in firefighting to recognize potential fire and give early cautioning to conceivable fire disasters. By utilizing RFID labels, portable RFID perusers, shrewd camcorders, sensor systems, and remote correspondence arranges, the firefighting specialist or related associations could perform programmed conclusion to acknowledge constant natural checking.

6. CHALLENGES OF CLOUD-BASED IOT SYSTEMS

There are a number of challenges of Cloud based IoT systems. Some of them are listed as follows:

- Cloud based IoT framework can do the advancements like reconnaissance cameras or tracker framework that routinely work to track the individual like in the home or in vehicles in which our wants of insurance are inside and out various. In doing this there are various social requests challenges as the "right to be permitted to sit secured" in one's home or private space. For instance an area based sensor tails somebody in an auto and record data about all occupants of the vehicle, paying little heed to whether each one of the inhabitants require their territory took after. It may even track individuals in near to vehicles. In these sorts of conditions, it might be troublesome or hard to perceive, extensively less regard, particular security slants. Also individuals' wants of assurance in spaces they consider to be open (e.g. parks, strip malls, get ready stations) are being tried by the extended nature and level of seeing in those spaces.
- Big data examination associated with amassed singular data starting at now addresses a critical peril of assurance interruption and potential isolation. This peril is opened up in the Cloud based IoT framework by the scale and more noticeable closeness of individual data collection. IoT gadgets can accumulate information about people with an outstanding level of specificity and inevitability; aggregate and relationship of these data can make point by point profiles of individuals that make the potential for isolation and distinctive harms. The many-sided quality of this advancement can make conditions that open the individual to physical, criminal, cash related or reputational hurt.
- The inescapability, acknowledgment, and social handle of various Cloud based IoT gadgets may make a confused impression that all is well and great and urge individuals to unveil fragile or private information without full care

or valuation for the potential aftereffects of doing all things considered. IoT security addresses these insurance issues would test paying little respect to the likelihood that the interests and motivations of most of the individuals in the IoT natural framework were particularly balanced. The data source may see an unwelcome interference into private space, as often as possible without consent, control, choice, or even care.

- Exactly when an IoT device producer or customer is orchestrating the headway of a thing, they need to overview specific arrangement threats of traditions in the change method. Combining existing and exhibited models into thing or system designs can address a lower particular risk stood out from the progression and usage of selective traditions. The use of insipid, open and extensively available gadgets (for instance, the IP suite) as building ruins for gadgets and organizations can bring diverse focal points, for instance, access to greater pools of particular capacity, made programming, and more affordable change costs.

- Absence of measures and archived best practices have a more noteworthy effect than simply restricting the capability of Cloud based IoT devices. Latently, nonappearance of these benchmarks can empower terrible conduct by Cloud based IoT devices. At the end of the day, without principles to direct makers, engineers of these devices now and then outline items that work in troublesome courses on the Internet without much respect to their effect. These devices are more terrible than just not being interoperable. In the event that inadequately composed and arranged, they may have negative outcomes for the systems administration assets they associate with and the more extensive Internet.

- Interoperability institutionalization is a test for new IoT devices that need to interface with systems as of now sent and working. This is important to numerous industry-particular and application-particular conditions that have set up systems of devices. IoT engineers are confronted with configuration exchange offs to keep up similarity with inheritance frameworks while as yet attempting to accomplish more noteworthy interoperability with different devices using measures.

- Customers will confront expanding challenges in overseeing bigger quantities of IoT devices. One such test is the need to rapidly and effortlessly alter the arrangement settings of numerous IoT devices on a system. When confronting the overwhelming prospect of arranging many individual devices, it will be fundamental to have attentive outline and institutionalization of setup devices, techniques and interfaces.

7. OPEN ISSUES AND FUTURE SCOPE OF CLOUD-BASED IOT SYSTEM

Cloud Computing and IoT have been quickly progressing as the two essential innovations of the Future Internet (FI) idea. Different Cloud based IoT systems are planned and executed by the IoT sensors without thinking about the issues of transparency, adaptability, interoperability, and utilize case autonomy (Gubbi, 2013). There are such a large number of open issues to deal with the future IoT systems by making secured models, advancements, arrangements and administrations. It is expected that in future smart cities, an IoT system will play a vital role by using smart implanted devices. There is a need to propose arrangement which can beat the discontinuity of vertically situated closed systems, designs and application zones and move towards open systems and stages that help numerous applications. This is a key prerequisite for smart city systems that can be reused by a plenty of uses in different spaces, for example, transportation systems, vitality, squander administration, ecological checking, structures etc. It is expected that future arrangements will rearrange information exchange by supporting most by far of exchange conventions and will permit compelling use of system abilities for change and gathering of constant information. Utilizing FIWARE administrations will guarantee unwavering quality, measured quality and uniform APIs free of the hidden equipment and it will move past current arrangements that are stage ward, and merchant particular. The outcome will be a dynamic configurable foundation, versatile, interoperable, heterogeneous and secure that could likewise consistently coordinate other existing and future stages and devices. Data can stream among IoT systems in a safe and security protecting route, taking into account removing setting for creating cross-space applications.

8. CONCLUSION

In this chapter, the basic introduction about the IoT and Cloud system is given. Then the integration of Cloud and IoT, their challenges and applications has been described. The Cloud based IoT systems can provide numerous benefits for making smart applications. At the end of this chapter, some open research issues has been discussed.

REFERENCES

Botta, A., Donato, W., Persico, V., & Pescape, A. (2016). Integration of Cloud computing and Internet of Things: A survey. *Future Generation Computer Systems*, *56*, 684–700. doi:10.1016/j.future.2015.09.021

Gil, D., Ferrandez, A., Mora, H., & Peral, J. (2016). Internet of Things: A Review of Surveys Based on Context Aware Intelligent Services. *Sensors (Basel)*.

Gubbi, J., Buyya, R., Marusic, S., & Palaniswami, M. (2013). Internet of Things (IoT): A vision, architectural elements, and future directions. *Future Generation Computer Systems*, *29*(7), 1645–1660. doi:10.1016/j.future.2013.01.010

Jadhav, P. A., & Hammadi, J. (2015). Applications and Architecture of Cloud-Based Internet of Things (IOT). *International Journal of Advanced Research in Computer Science and Software Engineering*, *5*(5).

Zhou, J., Leppanen, T., Harjula, E., Ylianttila, M., Ojala, T., & Yu, C., & Jin, H. (2013). CloudThings: A common architecture for integrating the Internet of Things with Cloud Computing. *Proceedings of the 2013 IEEE 17th International Conference on Computer Supported Cooperative Work in Design (CSCWD)*. doi:10.1109/CSCWD.2013.6581037

Chapter 2
Examining of QoS in Cloud Computing Technologies and IoT Services

Akash Chowdhury
Institute of Science and Technology, India

Swastik Mukherjee
Institute of Science and Technology, India

Sourav Banerjee
Kalyani Government Engineering College, India

ABSTRACT

The various services that are offered by IoT and Cloud Service Providers (CSPs) to the customers today feature a pay-per-use service-charging policy. Customers can choose and avail these services when they want, how they want, and from where they want on demand. Demand for these services has increased drastically over the years among individuals and enterprises worldwide, and thus, it is very important to keep up good Quality of Service (QoS). This chapter highlights the history of internet, the gradual evolution of cloud computing, the reasons behind it, evolution and concepts of the Internet of Things (IoT), CloudIoT and its necessities, and various applications and service fields of CloudIoT. This chapter also precisely highlights various concepts regarding maintenance of good QoS, controversies in QoS maintenance, different parameters that the QoS depends on, various problems faced in maintaining those parameters, and the possible solutions for overcoming those problems. Possible directions towards future works are also highlighted in this chapter.

DOI: 10.4018/978-1-5225-3445-7.ch002

1. INTRODUCTION

The evolution of Internet and then the creation of the World Wide Web (WWW) made people from all over the world, capable of connecting, communicating and exchanging data with each other and thus got rapidly extended. This new revolution led to the business expansion of individuals and enterprises from all over world which showed them a steep growth of their economy. But with the passing time, various kinds of data that are created by the people, for the people and about the people started increasing in an exponential rate. Organizing and structuring this data became very difficult as huge processing tasks are involved. Storing such huge amount of data was a bigger challenge that was faced until new enterprises took to solve this issues by providing services of rented storage and processing units and enabled a pay-per use model regarding rents for those services and thus the concept of cloud and cloud computing evolved, which is described in section 2.2.

With more advancement in technology and increasing demand for better or smarter living standards, new services were started to be created that supported real life scenarios like smart homes, smart cities, intelligent working environments, smart transportation, and smart environmental monitoring systems, etc. This new technology involved the concepts of connecting the real world objects or things to the Internet, incorporating all sorts of infrastructural support required, from the cloud to create Smart Living Services (SLSs). In this technology, things from the real world were made to connect, communicate and share data with other things over the Internet, to create different SLSs and thus named as the IoT. Maintenance of smart living standards depends on the maintenance of good QoS and on the various parameters that the QoS depends on. But maintenance of good QoS is a very big challenge and thus faces many problems regarding different parametric issues, as described in section 3.

2. BACKGROUND

The IoT technology though stands as an independent technology, it depends on the Cloud Computing technologies for its proper implementations. Cloud computing further found its backbone in the Internet Technology.

2.1. Evolution of Internet

In the late 1960s (Cisco.com, 2017) DARPA or Defense Advanced Research Projects Agency, formerly known as ARPA or Advanced Research Projects Agency under the Department of Defense of United States did an experiment by inter-connecting computer networks of different universities and private companies and granting their involvements in the research related works. This experimented network went online for the first time in 1969 having a four node network connected with circuits of 56 Kbps. United States and Europe found proofs regarding this network's reliability and created their own military networks named MILNET and MINET respectively. With the passing years more and more universities and private organizations connected their private networks to this network and thus gave birth to ARPANET or "ARPA Internet". The Acceptable Use Policy (AUP) followed by the ARPANET clearly stated that ARPANET cannot be used for commercial purposes. ARPANET was so heavily used that by 1985 it got vigorously congested and in 1989 it got decommissioned.

The National Science Foundation (NSF) started the development of the first phase of their network named as NSFNET. The structure of the NSFNET comprised of a major backbone which acted as the core of the NSFNET and connected many networked peers and multi-zonal networks (for example, the NASA Science Network). In the year 1986 NSFNET had a tri-levelled communication network. The tri-levelled architecture first connected computers and other devices within a private network. These networks belonged to various universities and research organizations. These networks got further connected to the regional networks available. These regional networks got further connected to a major backbone which comprised of a network of six super computer centers that further got funded nationally. The speed of the links were 56 Kbps.

In the year 1987, Merit Network Inc. and its partner – MCI, IBM and Michigan State received the award of NSFNET competitive solicitation for a faster network for successfully speeding up the NSFNET to 1.544 Mbps links and thus formed the NSFNET T1 backbone. These backbones interconnected 13 sites including Merit, Westnet, NorthWestNet, MIDnet, BARRNET, National Center for Atmospheric Research (NCAR), SESQUINET, SURANet and five supercomputer centers of NSF.

Michigan state, MCI and IBM formed the Advanced Network and Services (ANS) in 1990. The policy routing database and routing consultation and management services for NSFNET was provided by Merit Network's Internet engineering group and a Network Operation Center (NOC) along with the backbone routers were operated by the ANS. By the year 1991 NSFNET T1 backbone network service was upgraded to T3, due to tremendous network data traffic. The NSFNET T3 backbone featured network service links of 45 Mbps.

With the passing years various organizations wanted to connect with each other; Interests for commercial and general purposes started booming up and that led to the growth of Internet Service Providers (ISPs) for serving the purpose. Thus this network surpassed the boundaries of US and made international connections. This made the network connectivity even more complex and pushed its infrastructural growth. In August 1991, the first web browser for accessing this network was made publically available, after the invention of WWW in the year 1989 by Tim Berners-Lee. WWW was medium by which anyone could search about any document or web resource that can be identified by a Uniform Resource Locator (URL). The web resources were in the form of web pages and were linked by hyperlinks. NSFNET got decommissioned in the month of April, 1995.

The Internet today, unlike its core form (NSFNET), follows a lot more complex and distributed architecture connecting institutions, organizations, private and government agencies and societies worldwide, made operational by commercial service providers like BBN and MCI. Till 1980s this network interconnected various organizations and private networks and thus was called 'internet' but this word got capitalized to be 'Internet' when this network connected the worldwide set of internets or interconnected networks.

2.1.1. Internet to Cloud Computing

With the globalization of the Internet, more and more organizations started seeking ways to expand their business by offering their services to distant locations and even worldwide. To do so, they started creating their websites and hosted them to their web servers which are connected to the Internet. Any client at a distant location can connect his computer to the Internet and can access the website through a web browser and avail the services being offered by the organization. But this was possible for those organizations who could actually afford to maintain a web server as physical web servers are very costly. It is even very hard to maintain such a server as anytime the server could crash and can result to immense data loss if all the data aren't backed up.

At times if any client, be it a single user or an organization needed a different Operating System (OS) to run on their computers the only thing possible was to re-install their computers with the desired OS software.

To avail a software application in a client machine the client had to install it manually on his machine thus requiring more storage. The desired software may not be even available for being proprietary or platform dependent.

With increasing technological advancements complex algorithms started evolving which called for more powerful processing units which may not be available in the client computer. In this situation the client needs to upgrade the system hardware configurations of his computer which could be very costly for the client.

A client may momentarily need any software, platform, storage or processing unit. In such cases the client had to buy the software and hardware components permanently even though they are not going to be used for long.

With increasing time the amount of data of an organization that needs to be stored also increases. Companies offering services like online shopping, email, social media, and search engines, etc. has exponential data increasing rates. Thus, very soon it became infeasible for a single server to store all the data.

On listening the market demand and for making a revolution against the aforementioned issues many new companies sprang up who offered services like web hosting for those who cannot afford their own web servers, on demand processing and storage units, software platforms (desired OS), network connectivity with required features like security and bandwidth, and various software applications that can be availed on demand. All this services were made available on receipt of considerable rents and thus the new paradigm of Cloud Computing evolved. Today Microsoft Azure, Google Cloud Platform and Amazon Web Services (AWS) are some of the big names among the CSPs.

2.2. Cloud Computing

Cloud can be defined as an online on demand computing service that features unlimited computational power and storage capacity, data sharing, virtualization, distributed computing, web services and networking by hosting networks, processing and storage units, servers, applications and services.

The National Institute of Standards and Technology (NIST) defined cloud computing (Mell, &Grance, 2011) as – a model for enabling of computation that enables ubiquitous, convenient, on-demand connectivity and accessibility towards a shared pool of configurable computing resources (e.g., networks, servers, storage, applications, and services) that can be rapidly provisioned and released with minimal management effort or service provider interaction. Figure 1 gives an overview to the various aspects of Cloud computing.

2.2.1. Service Models of Cloud Computing

The cloud resources are basically exploited under three service models- IaaS or Infrastructure as a service, SaaS or Software as a Service and PaaS or Platform as a Service (Banerjee, Paul, & Biswas, 2016).

1. **Infrastructure as a Service (IaaS):** Under IaaS the users get access to computing resources, communication resources and storage resources on demand. With the availability of IaaS, clients have no need to host servers, networks and other required infrastructure of their own thus decreasing the establishment costs.
2. **Platform as a Service (PaaS):** PaaS provides a suitable platforms and environments to developers for building various applications and services. Users access PaaS services hosted in the cloud by simple web browsers.

Figure 1. An overview to the various aspects of cloud computing

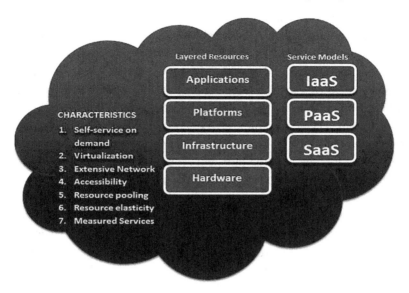

3. **Software as a Service (SaaS):** SaaS is a service that provides users access to various software applications through the internet. Google and Facebook are examples of Software as a Service.

2.3. Internet of Things (IoT)

With the evolution of the Internet people all over the world were able to connect, share data and communicate with each other. Most of the products like data, images, recordings, games, websites, commercials, books, etc. that prevailed on the internet were created by the people, for the people and about the people. People, connected to the Internet, were capable of creating various online on demand services related to these products like online games, online audio and video websites, online television and many others; thus it was the Internet of People and it revolutionized the whole world ("What is the Internet of Things? And why should you care? | Benson Hougland | TEDxTemecula", 2014).

Kevin Ashton gave birth to the term "Internet of Things" in 1998. Since then devices started getting connected to the Internet. In 2008, a new Internet started emerging and it was strongly felt that it was again going to revolutionize the whole world, being the future of the Internet and Ubiquitous computing (Wu, Lu, Ling, Sun, & Du, 2010). This Internet was not about the people but about the real world objects or things getting connected to it and thus called as the "Internet of Things". IoT (Atzori, Iera and Morabito, 2010) comprises of a network of interconnected objects or things from all over the world and does obey certain standard communication protocols (Duce, 2008) having the Internet as the point of convergence. The idea behind IoT was to connect devices and real world objects to the Internet so that they can share their data and information, connect and efficiently communicate with each other to reach a specific goal. Through this new technology real life objects, be it a smart communicating electronic device or a dumb non-communicating object, are capable of talking to each other regarding their jobs and manage themselves to provide a particular service. complex devices and electronic components like mobile phones but also includes things like foods, clothing, furniture, houses, monuments, work of arts etc. (Evangelos, Nikolaos and Anthony, 2011). These objects can be made to act as sensors or actuators so that they can interact with each other for accomplishing a common goal.

The year 2011 witnessed the increased number of connected devices in the internet than the total number of people (Gubbi, Buyya, Marusic, &Palaniswami, 2013). It was estimated that by 2020 more than 24 billion devices will get connected to each other via the Internet. Such exponential increase in the number of interconnected devices made IoT a huge source for big data (Dobre, &Xhafa, 2014). Figure 2 shows the architectural point of view of IoT.

Figure 2. Architectural point of view of IoT
Adapted from [http://bppmalta.com].

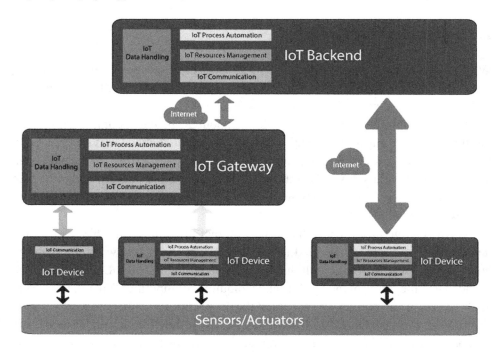

2.3.1. Penta-Layered Architecture of IoT

The penta-layered architecture of IoT comprises of five distinct layers (Khan, Ullah Khan, Zaheer, & Khan, 2012) –

1. Perception layer
2. Network layer,
3. Middleware layer
4. Application layer
5. Business layer.

Figure 3 shows the penta-layered architecture of IoT.

1. **Perception Layer:** It is the lowermost layer and its main purpose is to identify objects, perform data collection and sensing (Uckelamann, Harrison, &Michahelles, 2011). This layer includes sensors, RFID tags, cameras, GPS and labels of bar codes.

Figure 3. Penta-layered architecture of IoT
Aazam, Khan, Alsaffar, & Huh, 2014.

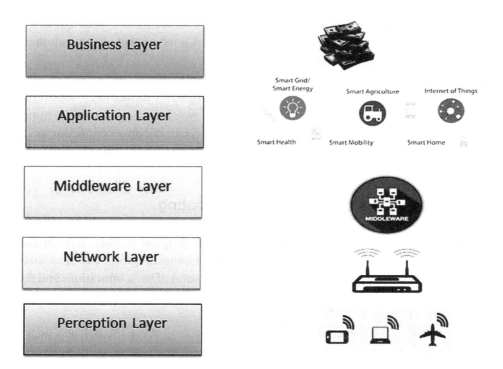

2. **Network Layer:** This layer stays on top of the Perception layer and it collects the data that was gathered from the objects in the lowermost layer and sends them to the next layer via Internet. It resembles the Network and Transport layer of the OSI model. This layer usually comprises of a gateway between the sensor networks and the internet and thus maintains a connectivity bridge between them. But in certain cases this layer may include systems for processing of information and management of network in it.

3. **Middleware Layer:** On receiving data from the Network layer it processes the data and makes automatic decisions according to the processing results and further transmits the same to the Application layer. It mainly serves the purpose of doing service management and data storage.

4. **Application Layer:** It is the final stage of data representation. Global management to any application is provided in this layer according to the related information processed in the previous layer. This layer represents the various applications that are formed according to processed data results, like smart cities, smart homes, smart healthcare, smart vehicular tracking and transportation and many others. This representation depends on devices or objects present in the Perception layer, the types of data collected from them and on the results of processing those data in the Middleware layer.

5. **Business Layer:** It is the money making layer for the service providers. Meaningful and efficient services are created according to the data received in the Application layer. Information when processed it becomes knowledge and efficiently using that knowledge makes it wisdom and such wisdom can make good money for the service provider.

IoT mainly follows Machine-to-machine (M2M) (Chowdhury, Mukherjee, & Banerjee, 2017) communication architecture which does not involve human interference. Even non-connecting real life entities can become connecting nodes by having an RFID tag or a bar code label which can be sensed via any device connected to the internet.

2.4. Integration of IoT and Cloud Computing

Cloud computing and IoT are two different technological worlds. But on their integration (Alhakbani, Hassan, &Alnuem, 2014) (Gomes, Righi, & da Costa, 2014) both these worlds can get benefited through elimination of their limitations and thus termed as CloudIoT. In Table 1 various aspects regarding cloud computation and IoT have been compared.

Figure 4 shows in what ways does cloud computing serve the IoT and depicts the CloudIoT paradigm. With increasing number of interconnected things on the

Table 1. Various aspects that are compared regarding cloud computing and IoT

Fields	Parameters					
	Reaching Range	Processing Resource	Storage Resource	Usage of Internet	Contribution to Big Data	Consisting Elements
Internet of Things	Limited	Very limited	Very limited	Convergence point	Contributes as a source for Big Data	Objects of real world
Cloud Computation	No limit	No limit (virtually)	No limit (virtually)	Medium for delivering service	Contributes in management of Big data	Virtualized physical resources

Botta, DE Donato, Persico, &Pescape, 2016.

Figure 4. The CloudIoT paradigm
Adapted from [https://blog.cloudsecurityalliance.org/].

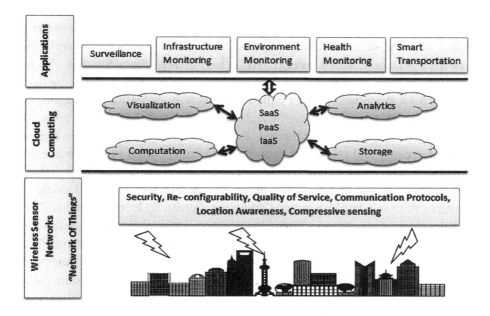

Internet, the data generated by them also increases at exponential rate and thus IoT needs unlimited storage capacities which are not possible to be made available onboard. IoT applications and services are highly complex in terms of implementation of algorithms, efficient data processing to from knowledge and then turn it to wisdom, network connectivity for efficient data sharing and transmission, and device heterogeneity. The IoT devices are cheaper and low configured and thus IoT faces three main constraints – communication constraints, storage constraints and computation constraints. IoT services features heterogeneity in terms of components, technologies and standards, and thus also lacks properties like scalability, reliability, flexibility, efficiency, interoperability, security and privacy. These properties must be maintained in IoT services to have and provide a good QoS.

Cloud infrastructure can provide IoT will all the aforementioned properties that it lacks, for achieving better QoS (Dash, Mohapatra, &Pattnaik, 2009) (Hartman, Kamburugamuve, & Fox, 2012)(Suciu et al., 2013). Cloud has all the required resources that IoT needs to eliminate its constraints and that too at low costs. To overcome communication constraints IoT can involve cloud technologies which provide a cost-effective remedy to connect, operate and follow any entity from any location on demand through featured portals and built-in applications (Rao, Saluia, Sharma, Mittal, & Sharma, 2012). Cloud technologies are capable of providing IoT with very fast network connectivity which is immensely needed for efficient monitoring of distant objects, their control, communication and coordination (Parwekar, 2011), and accessibility to processed data.

The objects in the IoT gather a lot of sensory information but this data are either non-structured or semi-structured (Aguzzi et al., 2013). IoT objects are a huge source for Big Data (Zikopoulos et al., 2011) having three characteristics – volume or data size, variety or types of data and velocity or frequency of data generation. Hence such huge amount of data calls for collection, accession, processing and visualization, archiving, sharing and searching operations of data. Cloud can provide IoT with low cost on demand unlimited storage for storing and managing the huge amount of sensory and processed data. IoT data being stored in the cloud can be dealt homogeneously by standard APIs, accessed and visualized anytime and from anywhere and can also be provided with proper level of security, and facilities for data aggregation and data integration (Zaslavsky, Perera, &Georgakopoulos, 2013).

IoT devices lack on-site processing capabilities due to limited processing resources available. Cloud can provide IoT unlimited processing power in order to facilitate data aggregation and unlimited processing, analysis of complex algorithms, better implementation of data specific decision making and prediction procedures at low cost, increase in revenue and safety, real time processing, scalable and collaborative implementation of sensor related applications, complex event management and energy-efficient task offloading (Yao, Yu, Jin, & Zhou, 2013).

CloudIoT benefited the cloud in terms of scope extension. The cloud could now deal with real world objects rather than virtualized physical resources, in a more distributed manner and with higher dynamicity. It could now create and deliver new services regarding various real life scenarios and thus gave birth to a new paradigm of "Things as a Service" as in (Christophe, Boussard, Lu, Pastor, &Toubiana, 2011), (Mitton, Papavassiliou, Puliafito, & Trivedi, 2012), (Distefano, Merlino, &Puliafito, 2012). A scenario depicting a smart city with smart services is shown in Figure 5.

Figure 5. A scenario of a smart city having smart automated services
Botta, DE Donato, Persico, &Pescape, 2016.

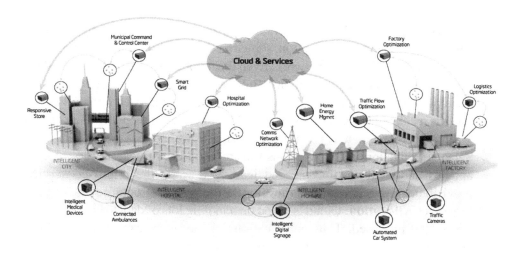

3. MAIN FOCUS OF THE CHAPTER

the integration of cloud computing in IoT is the powerful combination that has been evolved in an advanced form, creating a new era of technological growth. This integration has provided several flexibilities and advantages that have resolved many problems faced in the IoT or Cloud Computing while being implemented separately. Though the combination has brought another level of potentiality in the technology, it seeks special attention for the QoS modelling and improvement techniques for the efficient implementation of these two technologies together. IoT is the pool of self-configuring smart objects and Cloud Computing is the ubiquitous on demand service. Thus CloudIoT being the combination of both technologies lead towards the optimized QoS management which further involves credibility of applications, availability of resources and the capability of performance. Several parameters are needed to be highlighted that has great impact on modelling the QoS techniques.

3.1. Issues

3.1.1. QoS-Related Issues in Cloud Computing

Cloud computing, being the pool of resources, provides a great potential to the 'things' of Internet of Things. The huge data in Cloud computing gets the flexibility to be shared, processed, stored, and accessed on the basis of demand, irrespective of which locations they are operating from. And for proper implementation this involves several issues like -

1. **Service Monitoring:** In cloud environment, the processing of data by the nodes which may sometime be in motion, sometimes may be highly active or anytime may be excluded from the network. Even the number of nodes in cloud system is not fixed for its high dynamicity. But these nodes should be monitored by the cloud manager to excel the services. So monitoring each node for better service management is a bigger issue while integrating the advantage of this technology (Solaiman, Ranjan, Jayaraman, &Mitra, 2016).

2. **Service Provisioning:** Continuous transmission of data cause a lot of data updates and modifications needed leading towards the improved service provisioning techniques that can develop the throughput structure of the system.

3. **Resource Allocation:** Cloud is based on handling lots of data to be processed, stored and modified. Thus computations of the huge data need optimized allocation of resources. But the type of resources required by the users in cloud is totally uncertain creating a huge challenge for efficient resource allocation and management.

4. **Real Time Storage of Data and Location Identification:** Continuous data transfer may include confidential or sensitive data which needed to be stored in the nearest servers and location should be mapped for security purposes. But managing those data and storing them locally on real time creates a great problem.

5. **IP Addressing Optimization:** Larger cloud based IoT structure results in huge number of interconnected nodes. Each objects of the IoT should be assigned with an IP address but IPv4 wouldn't be the best to deploy and IPv6 would be challenging to be deployed being integrated from IPv4. Thus combination of both these IP addressing is a challenge towards the QoS improvement (Aazam, & Huh, 2013).

6. **Security and Privacy:** Connection of numerous smart moving objects, continuous data transmission and processing can cause a fatal attack on data integrity and security which can further affect the QoS of the system.

7. **Energy Consumption:** Energy consumption has always been a main issue in the distributed system. As Cloud environment features formation of numerous interconnections of nodes, data centers, servers with the IT system supports, it is obvious that Energy Consumption plays a vital role. The high performance computations, increasing workload, connection of numerous smart objects and high data transmission, multiple servers lead towards the need of efficient energy consumption models. The total energy consumption of the data centers growing exponentially every year which clearly indicates the consumption of

energy as one of the main factors that can enhance the whole system performance (Koomey, 2007).

8. **Bandwidth:** Bandwidth represents the capacity of a network in terms of data transmission or is the rate of data transmission across nodes. Cloud computing involves constant processing of huge amount of data, uploading files in servers anytime, or sharing information among the devices at the peak time. These need a higher attention on the bandwidth as it is a potential parameter for modelling QoS techniques (Mackle, 2015).

9. **Network Latency:** Latency is the delay or the time taken by a packet for a round trip i.e. the total time of receiving and sending a packet across a network. Network latency can permanently or temporarily affect the throughput of the system depending on the type of delay for data transmission thus leaves a huge impact on bandwidth as well as on QoS (Hopper, Vasserman, & Chan-TIN, 2010).

10. **Resource Management:** Cloud computing being a smart integrated technology results in processing of huge amount of data as sharing and transmitting data among objects takes place every here and there. Processing, storing or modifying this amount of data needs efficient management of resources that is a key component of QoS parameter.

11. **Service Level Agreement (SLA):** SLA is another component that is very important and plays a key role while modelling QoS architecture for a cloud based system. Cloud based IoT thus need improved SLAs for better quality management and trustworthiness.

3.1.2. QoS Related Issues in IoT

QoS is the implications to ascertain the highest level of satisfaction of customers. IoT can be thought as connection of things via Internet but not restricted only to the Internet. To maintain good QoS, the main issue arises when numerous objects or nodes in an IoT network can be connected, included or excluded, each being the active component of the whole system. For sharing and accessing data in the cloud each node or object of IoT should be uniquely identifiable. But to assign a unique identity to each of the object is really a big challenge. Moreover the increasing number of nodes in a network, architectural complexities, and communicational growth lead towards the need of several protocol deployments for the better service quality management. But formation of newer protocols is a tremendous challenge. These issues lead towards proper visualization of QoS requirements that can be relevant in terms of quality control and assurance. The tasks generated in the IoT environment can be categorized into several types like -

1. **Inquisitive Tasks:** It deals with the state of intelligent logistic items seeking the on time reliability.
2. **Control Task:** This type of tasks can take the control remotely or in place provided the timeliness.
3. **Supervising Task:** It can be periodic or aperiodic, event or environment supervising that looks for real time data. If the required data is not real time then it concerns with the reliability of that data.

The requirement of bandwidth for data transmission considering the delay in the transmission and control over the data collection tasks represent the service, user and the terminal attributes leading towards the different service level requirement that are further viewed as the service-aware QoS. These requirements of QoS should be assured in all the layers which are totally depended on the homogeneous assimilation of the requirements and effective implementation of resource allocation and scheduling accordingly.

In(Duan, Chen and Xing, 2011),a QoS architecture consisting perception, network and application layer is depicted to elaborate the QoS requirement more precisely.

In the perception layer, the data about the environment is sampled by the perception or sensing devices to be processed and provisioned for cumulative accessing. The information gained in this way is then transferred to the Network layer through wireless sensor network gateway.

In the Network layer, the received information is merged and sent to upper layer via wireless or mobile communication network or internet.

In the application layer, the received data is dealt in two stages or two sub layers. One is service layer that is reliable and trustworthy to receive, store and integrate the received data for analytics, management and decision making. The other sublayer is application layer that combines all the lower layer services and deals with intelligent logistics, precision agriculture, preservation of cultural relics, ecology environment monitoring, and intelligent transportation etc. Figure 6 shows the layers in hierarchy of QoS in IoT.

Thus, the QoS architectural viewpoint arises several aspects of QoS parameters as of below-

3.1.3. QoS Parameters in Terms of Application Layer

1. **Load Capacity:** It is the processing capability of data for specific IoT applications and concurrent quantity of users to be handled.
2. **Service Delay:** It elongates the idea of response time i.e. the time taken to receive the user's request and respond to it.

Figure 6. Layers in hierarchy of QoS in IoT
Duan, Chen and Xing, 2011.

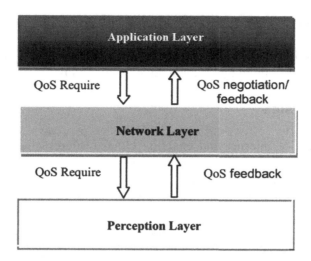

3. **Service Time:** Service Time is considered to be the life cycle of service time of IoT applications.
4. **Service Accuracy:** It the success rate of fetching the requested instructions of consumers.
5. **Service Priority:** It depicts the classification of IoT request to prioritize the service level and improve QoS.

3.1.4. QoS Parameters in Terms of Network Layer

1. **Network Latency:** It is measured by the time taken for a packet to reach from the source node to the destination node. Reduction in the network latency represents better Qos.
2. **Packet Loss Rate:** It is the number of packets that is lost per time unit which is a great concern in terms of QoS.
3. **Jitter:** Jitter is the delay that varies time to time and affects QoS of the IoT system accordingly.

3.1.5. QoS Parameters in Terms of Perception Layer

1. **Mobility:** Some IoT application like vehicle tracking, or dynamic environment monitoring needs the location information for proper implementation.

2. **Scope of Coverage:** The more the area of coverage increases the QoS also increases but it changes according to the dynamicity of the environment.
3. **Time Synchronization:** All the interconnected devices exchanging information needed to be timely synchronized else it may degrade QoS.
4. **Sampling:** The data received from the other layers should be sampled and sampling frequency to be efficient enough for QoS betterment.

3.2. Controversies

The efficient use of internet and enabling cloud resources has taken both the technology to another level of development. Thus many researchers are interested and working continuously in the domain of QoS development. Several frameworks has been proposed but each having its own problem leading towards the inefficiency of the whole system. To design the Service Oriented Architecture (SOA) the complexity of IoT and cloud forms scalability problems. The increasing number of nodes or the moving objects or the continuous data transmission creates problem for data integrity and security (Miorandi, Sicari, De Pellegrini, &Chlamtac, 2012). The deployment of heterogeneous networks forms a common problem for the abstraction of heterogeneity and lack of a common platform increases complexity. Accidental delay in data transmission or the loss of communication may affect the whole system very badly. The heterogeneity of IoT in terms of networks, protocols, devices, sensors or actuator, mode of communication increases complexity of cloud based IoT systems. Cloud and IoT applications seeks inter-cloud QoS monitoring frameworks which can provide the CSP flexibility and protection from SLA violation and dynamically handle data workload. But distributed denial of services (Paxson, 2001) can harm this model if there is no provision or consideration for that. Many frameworks are failed either to include IoT features or extends the service flexibility which can further affect the experimental results.

3.3. Problems

3.3.1. QoS Related Problems in Cloud Computing

The following points are sources of QoS related problems (Akpan, Vadhanam, 2015).

1. **Efficient QoS Provisioning:** it is a major area for various problems to occur in case of poor resource management, poor resource monitoring and improper SLA policies.
2. **QoS Metrics Monitoring:** If parameters that determine the QoS of a service are not monitored effectively then it will adversely affect the QoS of that

service. Dynamic or runtime monitoring is needed for increasing the QoS performance.

3. **Violation of SLA:** Huge penalties will be imposed on the CSP if SLA is violated. Violation of SLA needs quick reporting and fixing which further involves smart monitoring of the various QoS performance parameters related to the service.

4. **Storage and Maintenance Cost:** Efficient resource allocation in cloud is needed for minimizing storage and maintenance. Redundant data may get generated in distributed storage environment which needs to be omitted.

5. **Cost of Computational Resources:** Cost of availing computing resources depends on the time for which the resource is to be occupied, allocation policy and scheduling of tasks. Lack of proper task-to-resource mapping, service request to proper QoS specification mapping can adversely affect minimization of the cost of computation resources.

6. **Resource Allocation and Deallocation:** It is a major issue that can degrade the QoS performance if allocation and deallocation policy is inefficient and lacks dynamicity.

7. **Reliability and Accuracy:** A service can become unreliable and inaccurate due to many latencies and noise interferences in the network. This degrades the QoS performance of the service and may also make the service outputs delayed, inaccurate or tampered.

8. **Security:** A service needs to be secured and private to the CU. Service delivery must be given to authentic CUs and if resources are shared the service must maintain the privacy and integrity and mutual isolation of the CUs.

3.3.2. QoS Related Problems in IoT

The abstraction in the experimental results of various frameworks and proposed approaches bring the problems and increases the complexity at the time of implementation. The unstructured or semi structured data produced by the IoT needs real time processing which is a bigger challenge towards the integration of better QoS. System throughput improvement, delay and network latency is common problem that badly affect the high performance computing of IoT generated data. Interoperability and accountability is also a bigger part to focus. Service perform costs create an impact that has the ability to affect the QoS. Delay in perform time restricts the QoS parameters to be integrated. Reliability and load balancing is also a great issue to consider. Bandwidth allocation, allocation rate, power efficient strategies and throughput optimization with increased layer capacity is constant problem for QoS control and monitoring. Sensing precision, energy consumption, accuracy in information gathering needs deep concentration for better achievement of QoS for IoT.

3.3.3. Other Important Aspects of IoT

Human beings interact, collaborate and share their experiences with other human being by the ability to sense and communicate. For expecting objects to be able to do the same we need to integrate sensing and communicating abilities in them. The systems listed below helps objects to sense and communicate with other objects.

1. **Radio Frequency Identification (RFID) Systems:** RFID systems assign unique digital identities to objects attached to it so that they can alter digital information and services even after being integrated to any network (Kosmatos, Tselikas, &Boucouvalas, 2011). RFID comprises of two or more readers and various tags. The objects turn to be communicating nodes over the Internet after being assigned by a unique RFID tags which are used by readers to generate appropriate signal for triggering tag transmission in order to query for the presence of the objects. RFID tags usually work without any power supply available on board, unlike those needing batteries for the same (Yan, Zhang, Yang, & Ning, 2008). However RFID security is a big concern to be taken care of.

2. **Wireless Sensing Network (WSN):** These networks provide updates about the current status of things, their position, temperature, movement patterns, etc. WSNs comprises of numerous sensing nodes that communicate in a wireless multi-hop fashion. WSNs can gather useful data and information which get utilized in various fields like healthcare, governmental or environmental services, natural calamity sensing, unhygienic environmental explorations, defense, industries, etc. (Alamri et al., 2013). Bandwidth, capacity and accuracy have great impact in terms of better QoS.

3. **Unique Addressability:** IoT lead to the creation of smart environments by interconnecting real world objects within a network. IoT provided the objects with a unique digital identification and used them to uniquely address the objects needed for controlling them over the Internet. An addressing schema that is capable of distinctly identifying objects is needed to maintain certain critical features like uniqueness, reliability, persistency and scalability. Reliability and protocols standardization should be specially attended to maintain QoS.

4.   **Middleware:** It stays between the application layer and objects in the IoT environment to abstract the functioning and communication capabilities of the objects. This is needed because the interconnected objects and service applications involved are heterogeneous in nature. The processing and storage capabilities of the objects are also limited. The middleware comprises of four layers – Abstraction of object, Management of Services, Composition of Services and Applications. The trust level and monitoring should be taken care of for the improvement of QoS.

4. SOLUTIONS AND RECOMMENDATIONS

Combination of both the technologies faces several problems as discussed above. But QoS techniques are available to monitor and improve performances of the Cloud and IoT system structure.

4.1. QoS Techniques for Cloud Computing

QoS of cloud computing is understood as the level of performance, reliability, accuracy and availability that a cloud service and the host where the cloud service is hosted can provide. SLA specifies the QoS targets of a service and penalties if that SLA is violated. Violation of SLA adversely affects level of QoS and thus decreases the reputation of the Cloud Service Provider (CSP).

SLA is an agreement that is signed by Cloud User (CU) and CSP after setting the terms and conditions of the service and its violation involve huge penalties for the CSP. SLA violations can be solved by various mechanisms that involves smart monitoring of various service aspects. (Rajasekaran, Ashok &Manjula, 2014)

In (Hershey, Rao, Silio& Narayan, 2015) Hershey et al. improved the previous work of an enterprise system by enabling QoS monitoring and management system in it. Enterprise Monitoring, Management and Response Architecture in Cloud Computing Environments (EMMRA CC) created by Hershey et al. Provided a structure to the previous work through which the points at which QoS monitoring of various QoS metrics can be done, was identified.

Technical advantage obtained – This approach worked effectively to prevent cases like Distributed Denial of Service. This technique improved the QoS performance significantly.

In (Salama & Shawish, 2014) Salama et al. formulated a technique that could provision multiple CSPs to provide highly scalable and QoS assured services by having seamless cooperation with each other. The two key factors that made this QoS oriented federated framework of cloud computing possible were Cloud Coordinators (CC) and Federation Coordinators (FC).

Technical advantage obtained – Enabled CSPs to provide backup dynamically to each other during necessary situations or peak times. Protection of CSPs regarding any violation of SLA is obtained.

W.C. Chu et al. in (Chu et al., 2014) proposed a design that not only provided assistance to the ECC services but also supported dynamic analysis and monitoring of QoS metrics of the services offered by CSPs to more than one ECC consumers. Depending on the existing model the analysis and testing model was created that supported –

1. Automatic testing,
2. Monitoring at runtime.

Technical advantage obtained – Assured satisfaction to constraints in SLA.

Hasan et al. (Hassan, Song, Hossain & Alamri, 2014) worked on the workload in Big Data. They set up a simulated environment and ran a bunch of similar Big Data jobs on Amazon EC2 and accordingly compared the values of performance parameters obtained with those found in case of other approaches.

Technical advantage obtained – The approach proved to be very cost effective.

Karim et al. (Karim, Ding & Miri, 2013) worked on the mechanism of mapping required QoS of cloud services and proper QoS specifications of SaaS and their further mapping to proper IaaS service that promises optimal QoS. Analytic hierarchy process (AHP) method was incorporated in modelling the QoS specifications of cloud-based services hierarchically.

Technical advantage obtained – a new approach for end-to-end value calculation in cloud computing was obtained. The AHP incorporated model enhanced the mapping mechanism throughout the cloud layers. It also facilitated candidate cloud service rankings in favour of the CUs.

To cope with the issue of monitoring QoS requirements and SLAs in order to facilitate the process of verification and validation Lee et al. in (Lee, Tang, Chen & Chu, 2012) proposed the architecture that had an agent technology employed in it.

Technical advantage obtained – support for verification and validation was obtained. The incorporated agent technology also supported dynamic analysis of resource allocation and deployment.

In (Liao, Yu, Sun & Nian, 2012) a novel and dynamic QoS-aware data replicas deletion strategy (DRDS) was formulated by Bin et al. in order to save space and maintenance cost.

Technical advantage obtained – DRDS algorithm fulfilled QoS requirements related to performance and availability. Saved space and maintenance cost regarding distributed storage system.

To minimize the computational cost and simultaneously satisfy the QoS metrics in (Xiao, Lin, Jiang, Chu & Shen, 2010)Xiao et al. described an efficient reputation based scheme for QoS provisioning. Xiao et al. took statistical probability of response time into consideration as a practical parameter instead of focusing on a generic mean value of response time.

Technical advantage obtained – cost of computational resources was minimized with simultaneous fulfillment of QoS metrics.

Xu et al. through (Xu, Cui, Wang & Bi, 2009) brought multiple QoS constrained scheduling strategy of multi-workflows (MQMW) into existence for overcoming the issue of more than one workflows at a time with heterogeneity in QoS requirements.

Technical advantage obtained –issue of multiple workflows that can get initiated at any instant of time was resolved.

The above techniques proved to be beneficial in overcoming the issues of -

- Efficient QoS provisioning
- QoS metrics monitoring at run time
- SLA violation
- Distributed Denial of Service (DDoS) attacks
- Multiple workflows with varying QoS requirements
- Computational cost minimization
- Space and maintenance cost minimization
- Dynamic resource allocation and deployment
- Provision for seamless cooperation between CSPs
- Cost efficiency and dynamicity in VM allocation model for handling Big Data jobs

4.2. QoS Techniques for IoT

The implementation of differentiated service level was recognized by the different service levels using prioritized services. Each level had the varying requirement that was a big obstacle. But QoS need to be guaranteed in each and every layer. The architecture proposed in (Duan, Chen and Xing, 2011)contains QoS of each layer with QoS broker. A common cross layer facilities to ensemble, manage and support QoS is designed and each broker is deployed to provision and supervise the QoS requirement of each layer. Application and service layer calls the broker of network layer to pass the QoS requirement of lower layers and a least time delay of acceptance parameter is maintained. Application type and service priority is kept to translate the QoS requirement for better accuracy. Figure 7 shows the QoS architecture of IoT.

QoS monitoring automatic modules are deployed many a times. After the arrival of services it gets divided into sub parts in the application layer to send it via network layer and process it. It is then the duty of network layer to schedule the network type and sensing devices.

IoT enabled Smart Card (ISC) as proposed in (Premila, Rabara, & Jerald, 2015) is an advanced approach where access to diversified application are monitored and provisioned easily. Advancement in open web APIs allow complete development platform for the deployment of application programs. Data processing, service management subscription, co-ordination, shaping frameworks is always a better option towards increased Quality of Service. Simplified development approaches which reduce the maintenance of things and eliminate the upgradation of infrastructure are always an optimized option for the better QoS of the system. Unique device monitoring and management techniques are very important to manage and deploy the smart light weight self-configuring things.

Architectural modification and adaptation techniques like SOA (Erl, 2005) and REST for web service application are very popular where both the model signifies the interoperability among services via web. Though SOA include composite architectural blocks and complex service implementations not being ideal for creating ad-hoc applications for end (Pintus, Carboni, &Piras, 2011) it has its own advantages. REST uses HTTP-alike protocol for the proper management of resources.

Figure 7. QoS architecture of IoT
Duan, Chen and Xing, 2011.

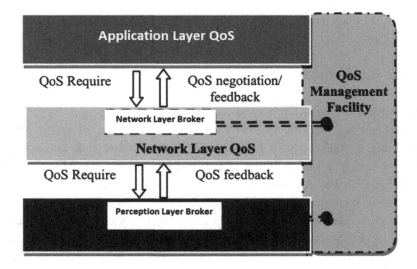

Constrained Application Protocol (CoAP) helps in interacting with 'things' by communicating in the low powered nodes in the lossy (Brandt et al., 2012) networks. This protocol is specialized for M2M communication for smart energy management and automation. An easy interface with HTTP makes it easier for discovery of services and availability of resources while fulfilling the requirement and maintaining the workload simple. So the efficient use of CoAP may improve the QoS of cloud based IoT systems.

Optimized routing path and cost efficient low powered network with higher reliability prevents network latency while the energy consumption gets controlled. The use of 6LoWPAN (Shelby, & Bormann, 2009) can bring drastic economic changes and increase the QoS of the system.

Improvement in SLA increases the reliability as well as cloud provider gets control over the agreement violation that subsequently increases the integrity and consistency of the CloudIoT systems.

5. FUTURE RESEARCH DIRECTIONS

The linking of the two technologies is a newest concept. Hence constant experimentations and implementations will lead to achieve better efficiency in terms of QoS. Advancement in existing algorithmic approaches for finding the required services and available resources will always provide the combined technology a great strength. Scheduling policy and smart object monitoring frameworks will help to reduce the cost of computation. Modification of low power networks and techniques for the reduction of energy consumption will arm the technology with newer dimensions. Innovation in the domain of SLA and security can strengthen the technology with higher accuracy. Semi structured data produced by the IoT may lead to the need of special real time processing ability and storage capacity. Optimization policies to improve the architectural upgradation and infrastructural orientation are also needed to shape the technology in stronger one.

1. **Technological Interoperability:** Interoperability is really a big issue as the concern is not limited to connecting the people but the active terms of connections between real world static or dynamic objects.
2. **Security and Privacy:** Data integrity, security, encryption and reliability is always a sensitive part in terms of maintaining QoS be it cloud computing or IoT.
3. **Flexibility:** In the emergency situation or industrial peak time fault or unavailability cannot be tolerated.

The bandwidth utilization and efficient provisioning, ultralow powered circuits, efficient resource management, fault tolerance capability, newer dimensional approaches in protocol deployment, unique address assignment, less attenuation for data transmission, new concepts and approaches for SLA and better service architecture are the areas that can re transform these two technologies shaping with higher capability and greater technological interoperability.

6. CONCLUSION

The link between cloud computing and IoT has been evolved as a great innovation which is changing the growth rate of technology constantly. Co-ordination of two new technologies signifies new advantages as well as new challenges. Proper implementation and utilization of Cloud and IoT systems seek higher attention as it has bring drastic changes in high performance computing as an on demand service highlighting the improved QoS. The challenges seek proper solution with improved QoS to continue its innovation and integration towards a great technological advancement.

REFERENCES

Aazam, M., & Huh, E. (2013). Impact of ipv4-ipv6 coexistence in cloud virtualization environment. *Annales des Télécommunications*, *69*(9-10), 485–496. doi:10.1007/s12243-013-0391-6

Aazam, M., Khan, I., Alsaffar, A., & Huh, E. (2014). Cloud of Things: Integrating Internet of Things and cloud computing and the issues involved. *Proceedings of 2014 11th International Bhurban Conference On Applied Sciences & Technology (IBCAST)*. doi:10.1109/ibcast.2014.6778179

Aguzzi, S., Bradshaw, D., Canning, M., Cansfield, M., Carter, P., & Cattaneo, G. (2013). *Definition of a Research and Innovation Policy Leveraging Cloud Computing and IoT Combination* (1st ed.). European Commission.

Akpan, H. A., & Vadhanam, B. R. (2015). A survey on Quality of service in cloud computing. *International Journal of Computer Trends and Technology*, *27*(1), 58–63. doi:10.14445/22312803/IJCTT-V27P110

Alamri, A., Ansari, W., Hassan, M., Hossain, M., Alelaiwi, A., & Hossain, M. (2013). A Survey on Sensor-Cloud: Architecture, Applications, and Approaches. *International Journal of Distributed Sensor Networks*, *9*(2), 917923. doi:10.1155/2013/917923

Alhakbani, N., Hassan, M., & Alnuem, M. (2014). A framework of adaptive interaction support in cloud-based internet of things (iot) environment. In *International Conference on Internet and Distributed Computing Systems* (pp. 136-146). Springer International Publishing.

Atzori, L., Iera, A., & Morabito, G. (2010). The Internet of Things: A survey. *Computer Networks*, *54*(15), 2787–2805. doi:10.1016/j.comnet.2010.05.010

Banerjee, S., Paul, R., & Biswas, U. (2016). Cloud Computing: A Wave in Service Supply Chain. In Handbook of Research on Managerial Strategies for Achieving Optimal Performance in Industrial Processes. doi:10.4018/978-1-5225-0130-5.ch015

Botta, A. D. E., Donato, W., Persico, V., & Pescape, A. (2016). Integration of cloud computing and internet of things: A survey. *Future Generation Computer Systems*, *56*, 684–700. doi:10.1016/j.future.2015.09.021

Brandt, A., Hui, J., Kelsey, R., Levis, P., Pister, K., Struik, R., & Alexander, R. (2012). *RPL: IPv6 Routing Protocol for Low-Power and Lossy Networks*. 10.17487/rfc6550

Chowdhury, A., Mukherjee, S., & Banerjee, S. (2017). An Approach towards Survey and Analysis of Cloud Robotics. In *Detecting and Mitigating Robotic Cyber Security Risks* (pp. 208–231). IGI Global. doi:10.4018/978-1-5225-2154-9.ch015

Christophe, B., Boussard, M., Lu, M., Pastor, A., & Toubiana, V. (2011). The web of things vision: Things as a service and interaction patterns. *Bell Labs Technical Journal*, *16*(1), 55–61. doi:10.1002/bltj.20485

Chu, W., Yang, C., Lu, C., Chang, C., Hsueh, N., Hsu, T., & Hung, S. (2014). An Approach of Quality of Service Assurance for Enterprise Cloud Computing (QoSAECC). *2014 International Conference On Trustworthy Systems And Their Applications*. doi:10.1109/TSA.2014.11

Dash, S., Mohapatra, S., &Pattnaik, P. (2009). A Survey on Applications of Wireless Sensor Network Using Cloud Computing. *International Journal of Computer Science & Emerging Technologies, 1*(4).

Distefano, S., Merlino, G., & Puliafito, A. (2012). Enabling the Cloud of Things. *2012 Sixth International Conference on Innovative Mobile And Internet Services In Ubiquitous Computing*. doi:10.1109/IMIS.2012.61

Dobre, C., & Xhafa, F. (2014). Intelligent services for Big Data science. *Future Generation Computer Systems*, *37*, 267–281. doi:10.1016/j.future.2013.07.014

Duan, R., Chen, X., & Xing, T. (2011, October). A QoS architecture for IOT. In *Internet of Things (iThings/CPSCom), 2011 International Conference on and 4th International Conference on Cyber, Physical and Social Computing* (pp. 717-720). IEEE. doi:10.1109/iThings/CPSCom.2011.125

Duce, H. (2008). *Internet of Things in 2020*. Academic Press.

Erl, T. (2005). *Service-oriented architecture* (1st ed.). Upper Saddle River, NJ: Prentice Hall.

Evangelos, A., Nikolaos, D., & Anthony, C. (2011). *Integrating RFIDs and smart objects into a Unified Internet of Things architecture*. Advances in Internet of Things.

Evolution of the Internet. (2017). Retrieved 22 March 2017, from https://www.cisco.com/cpress/cc/td/cpress/design/isp/1ispint.htm#xtocid229981

Gomes, M., Righi, R., & da Costa, C. (2014). Future directions for providing better IoT infrastructure. In *2014 ACM International Joint Conference on Pervasive and Ubiquitous Computing* (pp. 51-54). Adjunct Publication. doi:10.1145/2638728.2638752

Gubbi, J., Buyya, R., Marusic, S., & Palaniswami, M. (2013). Internet of Things (IoT): A vision, architectural elements, and future directions. *Future Generation Computer Systems*, *29*(7), 1645–1660. doi:10.1016/j.future.2013.01.010

Hartman, R., Kamburugamuve, S., & Fox, G. (2012). Architecture and measured characteristics of a cloud based internet of things. In *Collaboration Technologies and Systems (CTS), 2012 International Conference* (pp. 6-12). IEEE.

Hassan, M., Song, B., Hossain, M., & Alamri, A. (2014). QoS-aware Resource Provisioning for Big Data Processing in Cloud Computing Environment. *2014 International Conference On Computational Science And Computational Intelligence*. doi:10.1109/CSCI.2014.103

Hershey, P., Rao, S., Silio, C., & Narayan, A. (2015). System of Systems for Quality-of-Service Observation and Response in Cloud Computing Environments. *IEEE Systems Journal*, *9*(1), 212–222. doi:10.1109/JSYST.2013.2295961

Hopper, N., Vasserman, E., & Chan-TIN, E. (2010). How much anonymity does network latency leak? *ACM Transactions on Information and System Security*, *13*(2), 1–28. doi:10.1145/1698750.1698753

Karim, R., Ding, C., & Miri, A. (2013). An End-to-End QoS Mapping Approach for Cloud Service Selection. *2013 IEEE Ninth World Congress On Services*. doi:10.1109/SERVICES.2013.71

Khan, R., Ullah Khan, S., Zaheer, R., & Khan, S. (2012). Future Internet: The Internet of Things Architecture, Possible Applications and Key Challenges. In *International Conference on Frontiers of Information Technology*.

Koomey, J. (2007). *Estimating total power consumption by server in the US and the world*. Academic Press.

Kosmatos, E., Tselikas, N., & Boucouvalas, A. (2011). Integrating RFIDs and Smart Objects into a UnifiedInternet of Things Architecture. *Advances In Internet Of Things*, *01*(01), 5–12. doi:10.4236/ait.2011.11002

Lee, S., Tang, D., Chen, T., & Chu, W. (2012). A QoS Assurance Middleware Model for Enterprise Cloud Computing. *2012 IEEE 36Th Annual Computer Software And Applications Conference Workshops*. doi:10.1109/compsacw.2012.65

Liao, B., Yu, J., Sun, H., & Nian, M. (2012). A QoS-aware Dynamic Data Replica Deletion Strategy for Distributed Storage Systems under Cloud Computing Environments. *2012 Second International Conference On Cloud And Green Computing*. doi:10.1109/CGC.2012.21

Liu, Y., Dong, B., Guo, B., Yang, J., & Peng, W. (2015). Combination of Cloud Computing and Internet of Things (IOT) in Medical Monitoring Systems. *International Journal Of Hybrid Information Technology*, *8*(12), 367–376. doi:10.14257/ijhit.2015.8.12.28

Mackle, R. (2015). *Effects of Bandwidth in Cloud Computing - Latest News from Backup Technology. Latest News from Backup Technology*. Retrieved 28 March 2017, from http://blog.backup-technology.com/14845/effects-bandwidth-cloud-computing/

Mell, P., & Grance, T. (2011). *The Nist definition of Cloud Computing*. NIST Special Publications 800-145. Retrieved from http://nvlpubs.nist.gov/nistpubs/Legacy/SP/nistspecialpublication800-145.pdf

Miorandi, D., Sicari, S., De Pellegrini, F., & Chlamtac, I. (2012). Internet of things: Vision, applications and research challenges. *Ad Hoc Networks*, *10*(7), 1497–1516. doi:10.1016/j.adhoc.2012.02.016

Mitton, N., Papavassiliou, S., Puliafito, A., & Trivedi, K. (2012). Combining Cloud and sensors in a smart city environment. *EURASIP Journal on Wireless Communications and Networking*, *247*(1), ●●●. doi:10.1186/1687-1499-2012-247

Parwekar, P. (2011). From internet of things towards cloud of things. In *Computer and Communication Technology (ICCCT), 2011 2nd International Conference* (pp. 329-333). IEEE. doi:10.1109/ICCCT.2011.6075156

Paxson, V. (2001). An analysis of using reflectors for distributed denial-of-service attacks. *Computer Communication Review, 31*(3), 38. doi:10.1145/505659.505664

Pintus, A., Carboni, D., & Piras, A. (2011). The anatomy of a large scale social web for internet enabled objects. *Proceedings Of The Second International Workshop On Web Of Things - Wot '11, San Francisco.* doi:10.1145/1993966.1993975

Premila, D., Rabara, A., & Jerald, V. (2015). Quality of Service Architecture for Internet of Things and Cloud Computing. *International Journal of Computers and Applications, 128*(7), 23–28. doi:10.5120/ijca2015906605

Rajasekaran, V., Ashok, A., & Manjula, R. (2014). Novel Sensing Approach for Predicting SLA Violations. *International Journal of Computer Trends and Technology, 10*(1), 25–30. doi:10.14445/22312803/IJCTT-V10P106

Rao, B., Saluia, P., Sharma, N., Mittal, A., & Sharma, S. (2012). Cloud computing for Internet of Things & sensing based applications. In *Sensing Technology (ICST), 2012 Sixth International Conference* (pp. 374-380). IEEE. doi:10.1109/ICSensT.2012.6461705

Salama, M., & Shawish, A. (2014). A QoS-Oriented Inter-cloud Federation Framework. *2014 IEEE 38Th Annual Computer Software And Applications Conference.* doi:10.1109/compsac.2014.51

Shelby, Z., & Bormann, C. (2009). *6LoWPAN: The Wireless Embedded Internet.* John Wiley & Sons Incorporated. doi:10.1002/9780470686218

Solaiman, E., Ranjan, R., Jayaraman, P., & Mitra, K. (2016). Monitoring Internet of Things Application Ecosystems for Failure. *IT Professional, 18*(5), 8–11. doi:10.1109/MITP.2016.90

Suciu, G., Vulpe, A., Halunga, S., Fratu, O., Todoran, G., & Suciu, V. (2013). Smart cities built on resilient cloud computing and secure internet of things. In *Control Systems and Computer Science (CSCS), 2013 19th International Conference* (pp. 513-518). IEEE. doi:10.1109/CSCS.2013.58

Uckelamann, D., Harrison, M., & Michahelles, F. (2011). *Architecting the Internet of Things.* Springer-Verlag. doi:10.1007/978-3-642-19157-2

What is the Internet of Things? And why should you care? | Benson Hougland | TEDxTemecula. (2014). In *YouTube*. Retrieved 25 March 2017, from https://www.youtube.com/watchv=_AlcRoqS65E

Wu, M., Lu, T., Ling, F., Sun, J., & Du, H. (2010).Research on the architecture of Internet of things. In. *Advanced Computer Theory And Engineering (ICACTE). 3Rd International Conference, 5*.

Xiao, Y., Lin, C., Jiang, Y., Chu, X., & Shen, X. (2010). Reputation-Based QoS Provisioning in Cloud Computing via Dirichlet Multinomial Model. *2010 IEEE International Conference On Communications*. doi:10.1109/ICC.2010.5502407

Xu, M., Cui, L., Wang, H., & Bi, Y. (2009). A Multiple QoS Constrained Scheduling Strategy of Multiple Workflows for Cloud Computing. *2009 IEEE International Symposium On Parallel And Distributed Processing With Applications*. doi:10.1109/ISPA.2009.95

Yan, L., Zhang, Y., Yang, L., & Ning, H. (2008). *The Internet of Things* (1st ed.). CRC Press. doi:10.1201/9781420052824

Yao, D., Yu, C., Jin, H., & Zhou, J. (2013). Energy efficient task scheduling in mobile cloud computing. *IFIP International Conference On Network And Parallel Computing*, 344-355. doi:10.1007/978-3-642-40820-5_29

Zaslavsky, A., Perera, C., & Georgakopoulos, D. (2013). *Sensing as a service and big data*. Arxiv Preprint Arxiv:1301.0159

Zikopoulos, P., & Eaton, C. (2011). *Understanding big data: Analytics for enterprise class hadoop and streaming data*. McGraw-Hill Osborne Media.

ADDITIONAL READING

Akyildiz, I., Su, W., Sankarasubramaniam, Y., & Cayirci, E. (2002). Wireless sensor networks: A survey. *Computer Networks*, *38*(4), 393–422. doi:10.1016/S1389-1286(01)00302-4

Bellavista, P., Cardone, G., Corradi, A., & Foschini, L. (2013). Convergence of MANET and WSN in IoT Urban Scenarios. *IEEE Sensors Journal*, *13*(10), 3558–3567. doi:10.1109/JSEN.2013.2272099

Bitam, S., & Mellouk, A. (2012). ITS-cloud: Cloud computing for Intelligent transportation system. *2012 IEEE Global Communications Conference (GLOBECOM)*. doi:10.1109/GLOCOM.2012.6503418

Bonetto, R., Bui, N., Lakkundi, V., Olivereau, A., Serbanati, A., & Rossi, M. (2012). Secure communication for smart IoT objects: Protocol stacks, use cases and practical examples. *2012 IEEE International Symposium On A World Of Wireless, Mobile And Multimedia Networks (Wowmom)*. doi:10.1109/WoWMoM.2012.6263790

Bressan, N., Bazzaco, L., Bui, N., Casari, P., Vangelista, L., & Zorzi, M. (2010).The Deployment of a Smart Monitoring System Using Wireless Sensor and Actuator Networks.*2010 First IEEE International Conference On Smart Grid Communications*. doi:10.1109/SMARTGRID.2010.5622015

Casari, P., Castellani, A., Cenedese, A., Lora, C., Rossi, M., Schenato, L., & Zorzi, M. (2009). The "Wireless Sensor Networks for City-Wide Ambient Intelligence (WISE-WAI)" Project. *Sensors (Basel)*, *9*(6), 4056–4082. doi:10.3390/s90604056 PMID:22408513

Castellani, A., Bui, N., Casari, P., Rossi, M., Shelby, Z., & Zorzi, M. (2010). Architecture and protocols for the Internet of Things: A case study. *2010 8Th IEEE International Conference On Pervasive Computing And Communications Workshops (PERCOM Workshops)*. doi:10.1109/percomw.2010.5470520

Cuff, D., Hansen, M., & Kang, J. (2008). Urban sensing. *Communications of the ACM*, *51*(3), 24–33. doi:10.1145/1325555.1325562

Garroppo, R., Giordano, S., & Tavanti, L. (2010). A survey on multi-constrained optimal path computation: Exact and approximate algorithms. *Computer Networks*, *54*(17), 3081–3107. doi:10.1016/j.comnet.2010.05.017

Huang, J., Xu, C., Duan, Q., Ma, Y., & Muntean, G. (2012). Novel End-to-End Quality of Service Provisioning Algorithms for Multimedia Services in Virtualization-Based Future Internet. *IEEE Transactions on Broadcasting*, *58*(4), 569–579. doi:10.1109/TBC.2012.2198970

Kamilaris, A., Pitsillides, A., & Trifa, V. (2011). The Smart Home meets the Web of Things. *International Journal of Ad Hoc and Ubiquitous Computing*, *7*(3), 145. doi:10.1504/IJAHUC.2011.040115

Kastner, W., Neugschwandtner, G., Soucek, S., & Newman, H. (2005). Communication systems for building automation and control. *Proceedings of the IEEE*, *93*(6), 1178–1203. doi:10.1109/JPROC.2005.849726

Lazaroiu, G., & Roscia, M. (2012). Definition methodology for the smart cities model. *Energy*, *47*(1), 326–332. doi:10.1016/j.energy.2012.09.028

Tarapata, Z. (2007). Selected Multicriteria Shortest Path Problems: An Analysis of Complexity, Models and Adaptation of Standard Algorithms. *International Journal of Applied Mathematics and Computer Science, 17*(2). doi:10.2478/v10006-007-0023-2

VanMieghem, P., & Kuipers, F. (2004). Concepts of Exact QoS Routing Algorithms. *IEEE/ACM Transactions on Networking, 12*(5), 851–864. doi:10.1109/TNET.2004.836112

Walravens, N., & Ballon, P. (2013). Platform business models for smart cities: From control and value to governance and public value. *IEEE Communications Magazine, 51*(6), 72–79. doi:10.1109/MCOM.2013.6525598

Yuan, X. (2002). Heuristic algorithms for multiconstrained quality-of-service routing. *IEEE/ACM Transactions on Networking, 10*(2), 244–256. doi:10.1109/90.993305

KEY TERMS AND DEFINITIONS

Cloud: Cloud can be defined as an online on-demand computing service that features unlimited computational power and storage capacity, data sharing, virtualization, distributed computing, web services, and networking by hosting networks, processing and storage units, servers, applications, and services.

CloudIoT: The technological concept of merging cloud computing technologies with the IoT and which proved to be beneficial for both the IoT and cloud computing technology is termed as CloudIoT.

ICT: ICT stands for information and communication technology and it is a term that encapsulates all sorts of information- and communication-related devices, applications and services like radio, television, cellphones, computer network software and hardware, satellite systems, and others.

Quality of Service (QoS): Quality of service or QoS can be defined as the means to determine the capability of any network to provide better service in terms of network traffic handling, low network latency and error occurrence, maximum bandwidth enhancement, resource management, and uptime.

Radio Frequency Identification (RFID): RFID is a system by which tags attached to objects that uniquely and digitally identify them are tracked by any RFID reader through electromagnetic fields by emitting radio waves.

Service-Level Agreement (SLA): SLA is a contractual understanding between the customer and the service provider regarding the quality and type of service the customer expects from the service provider.

Service-Oriented Architecture (SOA): A type of software design or architecture in which smaller software application modules maintained and deployed separately and in distributed manner are integrated to create or provide for the functionalities of a larger software application.

Wireless Sensor Network (WSN): Wireless sensor network can be defined as a network of autonomous devices located in a distributed manner that involves incorporation of sensors in order to collect data of and track various physical and environmental conditions.

Chapter 3
Deployment and Optimization for Cloud Computing Technologies in IoT

Aditya Pratap Singh
Ajay Kumar Garg Engineering College, India

Pradeep Tomar
Gautam Buddha University, India

ABSTRACT

Cloud computing has proven itself and is accepted in industrial applications. Cloud computing is based on the co-existence and co-working of various technologies and services from different sources that together make cloud computing a success. Over the last few years, the Internet of Things (IoT) has been widely studied and being applied. The blending of these two efficient technologies may provide an intelligent perception about usage of resources on demand and efficient sharing. The adoption of these two different technologies and usage is likely to be more and more pervasive, making them important components of the future internet-based systems. This chapter focuses on the deployment models of cloud computing in relation to IoT. The implications of cloud computing in view of deployment are discussed. The issues for deployment and optimization related to the merger of IoT with cloud computing are raised.

INTRODUCTION

The cloud computing is a platform which originated from the convergence of utility computing, grid computing, and need for software as service. The cloud computing is a way of dealing with the deployment of computing resources externally like

DOI: 10.4018/978-1-5225-3445-7.ch003

processing power, storage, deployed applications as a service (Stanoevska-Slabeva &Wozniak, 2010). Platform as a Service (PaaS), Software as a Service (SaaS), and Infrastructure as a Service (IaaS) are the main three service models categorized for cloud computing. These services are made available to end-user using cloud deployment models. There are four deployment models for cloud services: public cloud, private cloud, community cloud, and hybrid cloud (Victories, 2015). These deployment models are used as shared or dedicated in the organization premises or hosted externally.

Kevin Ashton in 1999 (Ashton, 2009) coined the term Internet of Things (IoT) for supply chain management environment. The IoT paradigm includes the things (consumer electronic appliances, sensors) as a part of the internet. These intelligent and self-configuring nodes (things) are used to create a global network to fulfill one or more purposes. This way of computation opens up new possibilities for new innovations for the realization of smart cities having best infrastructure and services to enhance the quality of life for humans. The IoT is already being used for some of the very crucial services like logistics, smart cities, and health care etc. The IoT is nowadays working on cloud computing as the IoT services led to increased demands on storage space for data, processing power, and other management services. The cloud services are matured enough in current state and are capable of providing more flexible computing and data management services for IoT. The hybrid is found to be more suitable deployment model for integration of IoT with cloud services. In general, IoT can lead to the virtually unlimited capabilities and its technological constraints are compensated by the availability of resources of cloud. In this chapter, the study of these deployment models and the optimization possibilities in relation to IoT are discussed.

DEPLOYMENT MODELS

The method of providing cloud services to end users is termed as a deployment model. To exploit the full advantages of cloud services in technical and economic respect, the cloud services are to be deployed and implemented successfully. The implementation is an activity of deployment, as only by utilizing cloud services does not make an organization different from other organizations doing business in the same domain. The other same domain organizations can also implement cloud services following as model resulting IT efficiencies. The efficient deployment of cloud services indicates the realization of distinct organizational benefits to differentiate and take competitive advantage from other organizations of the same domain (Garrison, Kim, & Wakefield, 2012). The benefits with IT-oriented success can be categorized as strategic, economic and technological benefits. The strategic benefits refer here to have full focus on organizations core activities by shifting its IT functions to cloud computing provider fully or in part. An economic benefit refers to reduces IT expenses by using cloud computing vendor's expertise and technical resources. Technological benefits refer to reduced risk and cost related to having in-house technological resources by having access to state-of-the-art technology and skilled personnel. The deployment models for the cloud services play an important role for the benefits related to strategy, economic and technological. The organization utilizing cloud services has to use some of its own IT resources and capabilities to have a required control over the resources provided by the cloud vendor. This is treated as optimizing cloud benefits.

The different deployment models for cloud services are identified in the literature (Mell 2009, Zhang 2010):

Private Cloud

This deployment model is best suited for an organization with multiple consumers. In private cloud, the services are available exclusively for a particular organization as shown in Figure 1. These cloud services deployment is owned, managed and controlled by the parent organization. The private cloud deployment is based on a cloud by an organization for its in-house users only with all services under organization's control (instead of Internet). Sometimes these cloud services are deployed by the third party or in collaboration with the organization in the organization premises

Figure 1. Private cloud

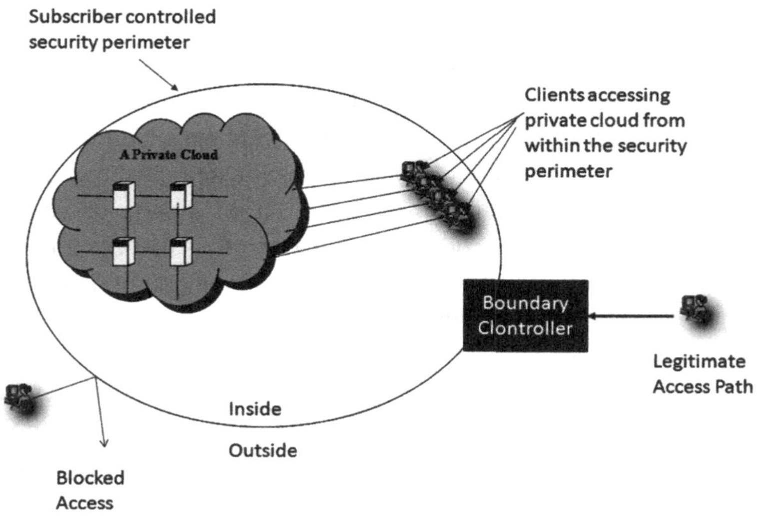

45

or off the campus. A company that already own data center and developed IT infrastructure has a good choice for private clouds with particular needs around security or performance. Private cloud deployment is not a cost efficient choice of cloud services, it seems like having own building and managing it rather renting a building without concern for managing it. But in view of security, this model has tremendous efficiency. Another name given to private cloud is "internal clouds". The multi-tenancy does not affect much in an arrangement where sharing of resources and services is minimal like in private clouds. The requirement of infrastructure in private cloud deployment may be same organization premise or sometimes at the third party location. In case of on premise infrastructure the client's firewall system address secure access concern while in case of third party location the Virtual Private Network (VPN) can be a solution for secure access to cloud services. Sometimes private cloud may also demand some customized requirements. Figure 1 shows a scenario of private cloud in an organization premises.

Not only for security issues, but also various regulatory standards such as Sarbanes-Oxley (SOX), HIPAA, or SAS 70 (Papazoglou, 2008) are to be confirmed for organization data and applications. The private cloud deployment becomes a choice in such scenarios. These regulatory standards and audits may require data privacy managed. Some SaaS service models give the privilege to have a data management on their own arrangement to ensure data privacy as per organizations requirement. Some example implementations of private clouds are Elastra, Eucalyptus, Amazon VPC (Virtual Private Cloud), and Microsoft ECI data center.

Community Cloud

This deployment model is used in a scenario where organizations with shared concern work as a community for their consumers. These concerns of organizations may include security provisions, policies, and compliance considerations. These cloud services may be managed and owned by one of the organizations, group of organizations, and the third party in or off campus as shown in Figure 2. Community clouds can also be implemented in two ways: On-Site and outsourced community cloud. In case of outsourced deployment model, a third party cloud provider is hired to host the server side. The benefit of outsourcing is that the hired third part will be an impartial unit bound by contract rules without any preferences towards participating organizations. The high-cost factor is reduced in comparison to private cloud as in community cloud the services are shared by all the member organizations which formed a community. One good example of community cloud is United States federal government. The community cloud model is a good choice for Small and Medium-sized Enterprises (SMEs) as these SMEs can hold a complex application

Figure 2. Community cloud

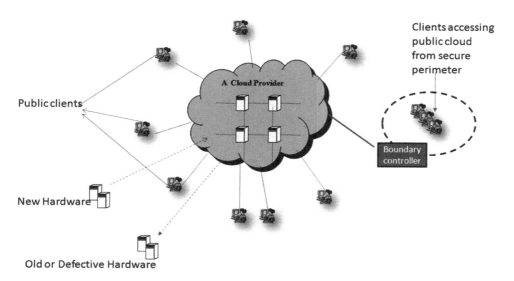

collaboratively by sharing services from each other otherwise it would not possible for a small organization to undertake a complex and large application.

The possible disadvantages may be like higher cost than public cloud and the fixed bandwidth and other resources are shared among all community member organizations.

Public Cloud

This type of deployment model provides services openly to the general public. It is in the true spirit of cloud hosting. Any valid user is allowed to access the cloud services via published interfaces using web browsers. This model is in good spirits of the cloud as the service provider renders services and infrastructure to all clients (Victories, 2015). In this deployment model, the user pays only for the time duration of usage like pay-per-use. One good example is the electric supply in our locality. In this deployment model, the users are not discriminated on any criteria as shown in Figure 3. The public cloud model is cost effective and does not require a large investment in infrastructure from businesses. The end user of public cloud needs not to be an expert on available services or having control over the supporting technology infrastructure.

This deployment model may be possessed, managed, and controlled by academic, business or government administrations. In this structure, the cost of deployment is shared by all the users. Good examples of public cloud are Google services, IBM's

Figure 3. Public cloud

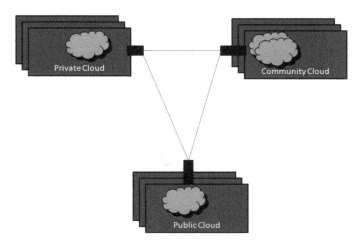

Blue Cloud, Windows Azure Services Platform. With least security provisions in public cloud model, the proper validation procedure at both cloud vendor and cloud client end can be implemented. Within the boundaries of operation, the cloud vendor and cloud client must identify their respective responsibilities.

The possible advantages of the public cloud include continuous uptime of services and data availability, training and technical help, on-demand scalability, optimum use of resources without wastage, cost reduction for the establishment of setup, Convenience, etc. The disadvantage of public cloud includes the lack of data security, Open-ended costs, Opacity, etc.

Hybrid Cloud

When private, community or public deployment models are merged with one another, this arrangement is termed as hybrid cloud. In this composition, each participating model remains individual entity but bound together using standard or copyrighted technology which permits data and application portability. With this arrangement, the user can increase the capability of cloud by aggregating, assimilation, and customization with another cloud service. This model may manage the workload as per need and demand. Using these hybrid arrangement organizations can use different deployment for different requirements like private cloud can be used for security oriented services and data storage along with less expensive public cloud for shared data and applications. As shown in Figure 4 this type of arrangement may be complex. Force.com and Microsoft Azure are two examples of this model.

Figure 4. Hybrid cloud

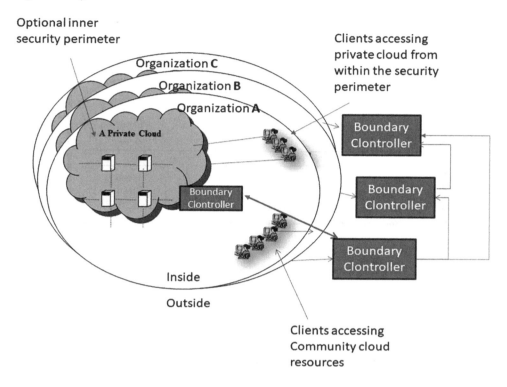

Figure 5 represents the layered architecture of cloud services with different deployment models. The deployment models are placed at the bottom as they represent the physical infrastructure for private, community, public and hybrid arrangement (Subashini & Kavitha, 2011). There may be some other nonpopular deployment models like virtual private and inter-cloud. The one layer above the bottom contains different service models which can be utilized using one of the deployment models at the bottom layer. These deployment models are at the center of cloud infrastructure establishment and are used to provide ubiquitous network, on-demand-service, multi tenancy, and measured service.

CLOUD DEPLOYMENT IMPLICATIONS

There may be some implications irrespective of chosen deployment model:

Figure 5. Layered architecture of cloud services

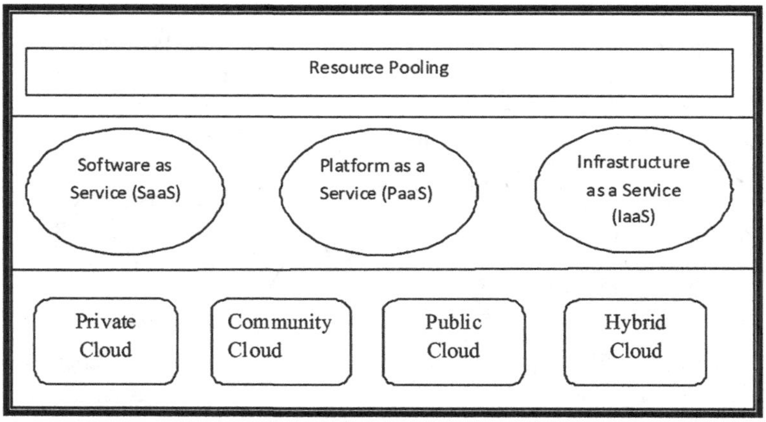

```
┌──────────────────────────────────────────────────────────┐
│  ┌────────────────────────────────────────────────────┐  │
│  │                Resource Pooling                    │  │
│  └────────────────────────────────────────────────────┘  │
│                                                          │
│   ⬭ Software as      ⬭ Platform as a    ⬭ Infrastructure │
│     Service (SaaS)     Service (PaaS)      as a Service   │
│                                            (IaaS)         │
│                                                          │
│  ┌────────┐  ┌──────────┐  ┌────────┐  ┌────────┐        │
│  │Private │  │Community │  │Public  │  │Hybrid  │        │
│  │Cloud   │  │Cloud     │  │Cloud   │  │Cloud   │        │
│  └────────┘  └──────────┘  └────────┘  └────────┘        │
└──────────────────────────────────────────────────────────┘
```

Network Dependency

For an efficient onsite or off shore cloud, a secure and reliable network is highly required. Cloud platform technologies provide technical support for the establishment of ubiquitous networking service management and its usage in the application of IoT. There is a great requirement for multi-network integration technology support in cloud services in turn to implement IoT services.

IT Skills Required by Subscribers

The cloud infrastructure will require skilled resources to manage different user devices used for accessing the cloud but in lesser number. The employees with old skills may need to update their skills as per the requirement for working in a cloud environment.

Risk From Multi-Tenancy

The risk of possible attackers is always there from a service subscriber. The "software multi-tenancy" is the term which refers to a scenario where a software instance running on a server provides access to multiple tenants (clients). This multi-tenancy risk includes security compromise and sensitive information leakage. In PaaS cloud arrangement the SaaS services are treated as tenants. Sometimes separate authorization systems are developed to handle multi-tenancy. The maximum risk of multitenancy is in public cloud and gradually reduces in the community, hybrid and Private cloud.

Data Transmission and Performance Limitations

The private cloud with on-site server deployment is always available with full bandwidth for data transmission while in other deployment models there may be limitations for bulk data requirements of client due to shared bandwidth. This kind of restrictions can be removed or reduced by provisioning high-performance and/ or high-reliability networking infrastructure.

In a cloud deployment process, the security and control must be taken care of. In deployment models like public or community clouds, the organization having onsite infrastructure has the responsibility for control and security of the cloud. This arrangement is to implement a sufficient security policy that guarantees appropriate security to ensure that risk is reduced. This is not the case in private cloud deployment as it is operated and controlled by a private organization in a premise.

CLOUD AND IOT

The proposal of MIT Auto-ID Labs for Radio Frequency Identification Devices (RFIDs) system makes a way to IoT (Tao, Cheng, Da Xu, Zhang, & Li, 2014). The RFID technique is used to acquire versatile data related to location, heat, light, and sound in real time for IoT. Various other devices and techniques are used to collect information of data related to electricity, mechanics, chemistry, biology, etc using different kinds of tools and sensors like infrared sensors, laser scanner, gas sensors, and Global Position System (GPS), etc. To establish the IoT vision, various resources are required which must be efficient, secure, market oriented, and scalable. The best answer to such requirement can be the cloud computing. The cloud computing is capable of providing such services reliably by exploiting virtualized storage technologies in next generation data centers.

With support from related researches and developments, IoT evolved itself towards the integration of information space and physical world from connecting things to things. The use of cloud computing with IoT makes it more efficient and powerful infrastructure. The sensing services from IoT stores their data on storage cloud and offers it by joining the network. The experts from a different domain can provide tools to be used in cloud computing. Like the analysts can provide data analysis software tools, data mining, and machine learning tools are provided by experts from artificial intelligence domain for creating a knowledge base, computer graphics experts can provide optimized and efficient visualization tools.

The IoT is being used in different applications background in spite of no standard and definition and uniform architecture (Miorandi, Sicari, De Pellegrini, & Chlamtac, 2012). The fast changing technology is also a constraint to set a standard for IoT architecture. These applications are smart cities, smart homes or smart buildings, smart inventory, smart business, and their implementation in environmental monitoring, product management, health-care, social security and surveillance, and so on.

A huge volume of data and communication volume is generated over cloud by IoT with very high number of devices communicating over the cloud. Such communication volume will require the deployment of competent computing devices in between IoT sensors/devices and cloud services. These computing devices mitigate the complexity and frequency of communication with the cloud. The interoperability between IoT and cloud is an issue of concern. The layered protocols and software are used to connect several nodes of IoT to cloud services. The IoT elements such as sensors, actuators, and gateways can be integrated with cloud services in data centers. There are various strategies are used to solve interoperability like the use of unique products, middleware etc. For monitoring and management of different platforms and cluster of devices, Hadoop is a choice (Díaz, Martín, & Rubio, 2016).

To enable flawless execution of various applications, exploiting full capabilities of multiple dynamic and heterogeneous resources along with the quality of service requirements of different users there is a need to improve cloud application platforms. The support of domain specific programming tools and environments is required to improve the rapid development of applications. There are some challenges related to the use of IoT and cloud in integration. These challenges are the standard for communication among IoT devices and cloud, reliability, and security.

The merger of cloud services and IoT elements would require different scheme for resource management. The resource management in this scenario would require optimization of processing scheme, resource handling for input-output, and storage management along with optimized sensor reading cycles, multi-sensor queries and shared access to expensive location-dependent IoT resources (Suciu, et al., 2013). IoT systems become complex due to the integration of cloud management techniques to manage IoT components. These cloud services play an important role as a platform for computation and data processing with management platforms for IoT.

The blending of cloud services and IoT needs a consistent software layer to be implemented between the two technologies. A cloud with IoT infrastructure must support following functions (Truong, & Dustdar, 2015):

End-to-End Engineering and Optimization

In convergence of cloud computing techniques with IoT software practitioners has to work on optimizing and developing code as per end-to-end view of the technologies involved with the due consideration of service providers for end-to-end properties. It would require creating and deploying feasible structure for IoT elements and cloud nodes as per the requirements.

Development and Production Symbiosis

There must be an arrangement in a way that reconfiguration of IoT components should not lead to interruption for running components of the application system. The system is to be configured in a manner so that it continues its develop, deploy and operation states while adding and testing IoT elements or cloud services. These systems operate critical services and should be developed in a manner so that the connection with other IoT cloud application or deployment of new element or service do not affect its live services.

Elasticity Coherence

According to Dutser et al. (Dustdar et al. 2011), the cloud's success is based on pay-per-use model. The cloud computing model supports elastic computing. As per elastic computing the required resources can be made available dynamically on demand. This process of resource management will lead to better utilization of resources. In IoT cloud environment the user is able to create and launch server instances as per their need and will be charged for only active server hours. To have such elasticity in IoT cloud system, the better coordination among cloud and IoT services to ensure coherence is required. The IoT cloud system must have well defined APIs to have runtime control on elastic competences.

CLOUD OPTIMIZATION

The main motivation for cloud computing is economic along with technological motives. The optimization of cloud computing is an activity to be followed to achieve these goals. The cloud service providers have to look forward to performing some kind of optimization of the infrastructure configuration. For optimization of a system, the following activities may be considered: monitoring, analysis, prediction, planning, and execution.

The implementation of these optimization activities to a customer by a cloud service provider is treated as local optimization. This local optimization is one of the major components of a PaaS hosting (El Kateb et al. 2014). In the current scenario, the cloud platforms focus on one-dimensional optimization like some PaaS providers provide a rule based engine to manage horizontal processing need and data storage scalability. El Kateb et al. (El Kateb et al. 2014) proposed a way to reconfigure local cloud infrastructure using a supporting tool in the form of decision-making framework. The multi-objective optimization problem can be handled using search based approaches. The authors have examined its effectiveness in the study.

The cloud with IoT also uses adaptive cloud optimization algorithms depending on the need of each deployed model. In this scenario, the cloud infrastructure is examined based on schemes for data access and storage and adapts to the service runtime with respect to cost effectiveness along with data integrity and security.

In respect to deployment of cloud services in coherence with IoT, the methods for deployment of different software components are included in cloud IoT systems at different levels of abstractions and allow continuous provisioning with procedure to configure and connect deployments. The user centric flexible and open architecture is used for IoT having cloud at its center. In such cloud centric architecture various application providers may join and share their data like wireless sensor network providers, developers, graphic designers, etc. These application providers can contribute by offering different tools related to the field of expertise. The data analyst develops compatible software tools for data analysis, data mining and machine learning tools can be contributed by artificial intelligence experts for convergence of data in to knowledge, and graphics designer can contribute by providing visualization tools.

The various applications and services contributed in cloud computing environment can be made available to users of cloud services as infrastructure, platforms or software. With the help of abstraction in cloud IoT system, the generated data by various sources with tools complexity in the background does not restrict user from exploiting the full potential of the cloud IoT system. The multiple domains of computing are integrated in cloud to build new business by provisioning scalable storage, elastic computing, and other useful tools.

CONCLUSION

In this chapter, the different models of deployment applicable for cloud computing are discussed. The private, community, public and hybrid deployment models are explained in detail. The blending of IoT with cloud computing fetches the attention hence this chapter also discussed a possible way of combining these two different technologies and the implications related to the integration of IoT with cloud services. The chapter also discusses the technical functionalities to enable both IoT and cloud services to work together with the complications involved. The scheme for cloud optimization is also discussed briefly. This blending of two heterogeneous technologies raise some research challenges like dealing with diverse quality and state of devices and technologies involved, meeting performance needs, reliability of services, privacy preservation, security, scalability, legal, and social aspects.

REFERENCES

Ashton, K. (2009). *That "Internet of Things" thing*. RFID Journal.

Díaz, M., Martín, C., & Rubio, B. (2016). State-of-the-art, challenges, and open issues in the integration of internet of things and cloud computing. *Journal of Network and Computer Applications*, *67*, 99–117. doi:10.1016/j.jnca.2016.01.010

Dustdar, S., Guo, Y., Satzger, B., & Truong, H. L. (2011). Principles of elastic processes. *IEEE Internet Computing*, *15*(5), 66–71. doi:10.1109/MIC.2011.121

El Kateb, D., Fouquet, F., Nain, G., Meira, J. A., Ackerman, M., & Le Traon, Y. (2014, March). Generic cloud platform multi-objective optimization leveraging models@ run time. *Proceedings of the 29th Annual ACM Symposium on Applied Computing*, 343-350. doi:10.1145/2554850.2555044

Garrison, G., Kim, S., & Wakefield, R. L. (2012). Success factors for deploying cloud computing. *Communications of the ACM*, *55*(9), 62–68. doi:10.1145/2330667.2330685

Mell, P., & Grance, T. (2009). The NIST definition of Cloud computing. *Natl. Inst. Stand. Technol.*, *53*(6), 50.

Miorandi, D., Sicari, S., De Pellegrini, F., & Chlamtac, I. (2012). Internet of Things: Vision, applications and research challenges. *Ad Hoc Networks*, *10*(7), 1497–1516. doi:10.1016/j.adhoc.2012.02.016

Papazoglou, M. (2008). Compliance requirements for business-process driven SOAs. *E-Government ICT Professionalism and Competences Service Science*, 183-194.

Stanoevska-Slabeva, K., & Wozniak, T. (2010). *Grid and Cloud Computing-A Business Perspective on Technology and Applications*. Berlin: Springer-Verlag. doi:10.1007/978-3-642-05193-7

Subashini, S., & Kavitha, V. (2011). A survey on security issues in service delivery models of cloud computing. *Journal of Network and Computer Applications*, *34*(1), 1–11. doi:10.1016/j.jnca.2010.07.006

Suciu, G., Vulpe, A., Halunga, S., Fratu, O., Todoran, G., & Suciu, V. (2013). Smart Cities Built on Resilient Cloud Computing and Secure Internet of Things. *Control Systems and Computer Science (CSCS), 19th International Conference on*, 513-518. doi:10.1109/CSCS.2013.58

Tao, F., Cheng, Y., Da Xu, L., Zhang, L., & Li, B. H. (2014). CCIoT-CMfg: Cloud computing and internet of things-based cloud manufacturing service system. *IEEE Transactions on Industrial Informatics*, *10*(2), 1435–1442. doi:10.1109/TII.2014.2306383

Truong, H. L., & Dustdar, S. (2015). Principles for engineering IoT cloud systems. *IEEE Cloud Computing*, *2*(2), 68–76. doi:10.1109/MCC.2015.23

Victories, V. (2015). *4 Types of Cloud Computing Deployment Model You Need to Know*. IBM developer Works. IBM.

Zhang, Q., Cheng, L., & Boutaba, R. (2010). Cloud computing: State-of-the-art and research challenges. *Journal of Internet Services and Applications*, *1*(1), 7–18. doi:10.1007/s13174-010-0007-6

Chapter 4

Examining of Data Security, Privacy, and Reliability for Cloud and Internet of Things Integration

Marcus Tanque
Independent Researcher, USA

ABSTRACT

Converging Cloud computing with Internet of Things transformed organizations' traditional technologies. This chapter examines the intersection of cloud computing and internet of things in consort with how these solutions often interact on the internet. Vendors develop CloudIoT capabilities to support organizations' day-to-day operations. IoT is a combined platform encompassing physical and virtual nodes. IoT objects comprise device-to-device data sharing, machine-to-machine provisioning, sensors, actuators, and processors. These systems may be deployed as hardware components and applications software. This chapter also emphasizes data security, reliability, resource provisioning, service-level agreement, quality of service, IoT, privacy, and device integration. This chapter also highlights operational benefits and/or security issues affecting CC and IoT technologies.

1. INTRODUCTION

This chapter evaluates benefits or challenges organizations continue to deal with. The study also calls attention to security, privacy and reliability problems affecting the integration of Cloud Computing (CC) and Internet of Things (IoT). CC and IoT have

DOI: 10.4018/978-1-5225-3445-7.ch004

altered how vendors and enterprises adopted and deployed these technologies on the global-scale. CC is a delivery platform involving services and deployment models. Such services range from Infrastructure-as-a-Service (IaaS), Platform-as-a-Service (PaaS), Software-as-a-Service (SaaS), Public Cloud (PC), Private Cloud (PC), Hybrid Cloud (HC) and Community Cloud (CC). Government senior leaders and corporate decision makers rely on these services to make organizational informed decisions. IoT is a technology, which integrates smart objects i.e.: machines, wired and wireless sensory network devices, actuators, computer processors, aggregators, e-utilities, and thermostats. These devices or systems stem from robotic solutions, decision trigger and resource sharing (Abdelwahab, Hamdaoui, Guizani, & Rayes, 2014; Qusay, 2011). Such systems deliver unlimited interoperability solutions with minimum human involvement (Aazam & Huh, 2014; Akyildiz, Su, Sankarasubramaniam, & Cayirci, 2002; Alamri, Ansari, Hassan, Hossain, Alelaiwi, Hossain, 2013). This chapter also strengthens the merging of CC and IoT capabilities, once systems are deployed (Abdelwahab, Hamdaoui, Guizani, & Rayes, 2014; Qusay, 2011). This includes building on CC and IoT technologies' multi-layered vertical barriers and opportunities, for instance Machine-to-Machine (M2M), Device-to-Device (D2D), Man-to-Man (M2M), Machine-to-Man (M2M), System-to-System, Solution-to-Solution, and Physical-to-Virtual nodes (Aazam & Huh, 2014; Akyildiz et al., 2002; Atzori et al., 2010). Additional technology trends involving CC and IoT are also discussed in this chapter (Akyildiz et al., 2002; Ballon et al., 2011; Badger et al., 2011). Merging smart objects into IoT technology networks is essential for organizations' business continuity operations. While the merger of CC, big data, robotic systems, actuators, aggregators, and sensor systems validates an organization's applied capabilities e.g., CloudIoT smart devices and/or autonomous systems (Polsonetti, 2014). CloudIoT is an infrastructure solution that delivers operational IoT architecture and framework capabilities (Alamri et al., 2013; Ballon et al., 2011). In the next decades, the adoption of IoT objects will increase significantly (Ashton, 2009). Consumers and industries are excited with such evolutions, which will influence the economies of scale (Polsonetti, 2014; Akyildiz et al., 2002; Alamri, Ansari, Hassan, Hossain, Alelaiwi, Hossain, 2013). These security solutions also expand organizational business continuity and infrastructure capabilities and/or consumers' requirements. Today, IoT devices/systems comprises a billion of interconnected smart objects. These solutions offer concerted capabilities for centralized and distributed information sharing or real-time data-provisioning (Ashton, 2009). Modern smart systems have a dual interoperability and capability functions e.g., access of deployed control devices (Polsonetti, 2014; Atzori e al., 2010; Ballon et al., 2011; Ashton, 2009; RCRWireless, 2016).

In 1985 Peter T. Lewis initially discussed the term IoT at the "U.S. Congressional Black Caucus 15th Legislative Weekend Conference". Peter defines "Internet of Things or IoT, as an integration of people, processes and technology with connectable devices and sensors to enable remote monitoring, status, manipulation, and evaluation of trends of these devices" (Lewis, 1985; Sharma, 2017; RCRWireless, 2016).

In 1999 Kevin Ashton, a British technology inventor coined the term IoT (Ashton, 2009; RCRWireless, 2016). Ashton viewed IoT solutions as interconnected smart objects. According to Ashton, these systems include sensors, actuators, and other monitoring devices (Ashton, 2009; RCRWireless, 2016). Ashton suggests that smart objects comprise hardware components and application software solutions (Ashton, 2009). The author 'Ashton' also termed Radio-frequency Identification (RFID) tagging system as a technological domain comprising intelligent devices and autonomous systems. These objects can be powered over the Internet, to support global-scale supply chain services (Polsonetti, 2014; Ashton, 2009). RFID tags delivery services for shipping merchandise. Such method involves systems designed to track all distributed automation activities with a minimum human interference (Polsonetti, 2014; Alamri et al., 2013; Atzori e al., 2010; Ashton, 2009; RCRWireless, 2016).

In 1999 IoT terminology became an echoed "catchphrase" in large-scale technology communities. Despite these resolute efforts, Lewis had made, some of the industry professionals concluded that the authors' corollaries did not provide sufficient peer review evidences. Yet Lewis is still supportive of his prior statements (Sharma, 2017; Lewis, 1985; RCRWireless, 2016). In the same year at Auto-ID Center, the term 'IoT' was reestablished under the research leadership of Ashton. Ashton is a co-founder of Auto-ID Center, a Technology Research Incubator located at Massachusetts Institute of Technology (MIT). In part, Ashton anticipated that the term 'IoT' be named 'Internet for Things (IfT).' Ashton selected the term 'IfT' as an underpinning for technological collaboration between objects and people. This concept emphasizes a synchronous integration between data exchange and transmission. Ashton also indicated that such findings will subsequently enhance the next-generation of IoT advances. This includes the connection between machines and human activities (Alamri et al., 2013; Atzori e al., 2010).

2. BACKGROUND

In the last decade, vendors have developed leading-edge CC capabilities, to strengthen smart devices' interoperability i.e., intelligent devices and autonomous systems ranging from smart grids/cities, smart e-health systems, smart farming, smart homes, and others. CloudIoT solutions consist of: CC and IoT technology integration—mind mapping capabilities often deployed on the global network environment. CC deployment and service models include: PaaS, IaaS, SaaS, PC, HC, PC, and CC solutions. These capabilities interface and scale as operational mechanisms (Abdelwahab, Hamdaoui, Guizani, & Rayes, 2014; Akyildiz et al., 2002; Ballon et al., 2011; Zhou et al., 2011; Alamri et al., 2013; Atzori et al., 2010; Badger et al., 2011). Vendors design CC and IoT technology solutions for customers and organizations (Akyildiz et al., 2002; Thierer & Castillo, 2015; Badger et al., 2011). CC and IoT solutions often are supported by an orderly response, time explicitly improved agility and platform interoperability (Akyildiz et al., 2002; Badger et al., 2011). This merger is key for the adoption/deployment of CC, IoT, and big data analytics capabilities. Such process also supports machine-to-machine, machine-to-people, machine-to-device, machine-to-cloud technology infrastructure deployment. Such technological evolutions simplify the global unified infrastructure solutions (Abdelwahab, Hamdaoui, Guizani, & Rayes, 2014; Alamri, Ansari, Hassan, Hossain, Alelaiwi, Hossain, 2013; Gubbi et al., 2013). CC and IoT services are intelligent solutions; ranging from machine-to-machine, man-to-man, man-to-mobile, real-time usability, or effective data sharing (Alamri, Ansari, Hassan, Hossain, Alelaiwi, Hossain, 2013). This concerted effort offers wide-ranging IT resource provisioning or solutions for scaling, improving productivity and growth (Gubbi, et al., 2013; Alamri et al., 2013; Atzori e al, 2010; Badger et al, 2011; Mell & Grance, 2011; Qusay, 2011).

3. MAIN FOCUS OF THE CHAPTER

This chapter amplifies on IoT analytical processes, standards and guidelines of which organizations and vendors, may conform to, when deploying IT solutions. Similarly, the chapter underlines a federation of technical elements critical to the implementation of CloudIoT capabilities. IoT is an emerging and scaling model that supports hardware components and applications software. These shared solutions span delivering products and platform services (Ballon et al., 2011; Zhou et al., 2011; Thierer & Castillo, 2015; Mell & Grance, 2011; Qusay, 2011). Industry develops IoT capabilities to support existing and the next-generation of intelligent devices and autonomous systems (Badger, Grance, Patt-Corner, & Voas, 2011; Badger, Grance, Patt-Corner, & Voas, 2011; Manyika et al, 2015, p. 7; Thierer & Castillo, 2015). CC technology is an enabling utility involving IT solutions (Abdelwahab, Hamdaoui, Guizani, & Rayes, 2014; Akyildiz et al., 2002; Alamri, Ansari, Hassan, Hossain, Alelaiwi, Hossain, 2013; Thierer & Castillo, 2015; Atzori e al., 2010; Badger et al., 2011; Chen et al., 2010; Mell & Grance, 2011; Qusay, 2011). Internet is a global-scale integrated and/or converged grid computing system, which involves distributed physical and virtual nodes (Mell & Grance, 2011; Qusay, 2011). The three IoT core pillars include: flexibility, agility, and scalability (Mell & Grance, 2011; Qusay, 2011). In the IoT infrastructure, physical and virtual nodes are geographically spread offering shared services and data-provisioning. These services are accessible via interconnected or decentralized network platforms (Akyildiz et al., 2002; Badger, Grance, Patt-Corner, & Voas, 2011; Badger, Grance, Patt-Corner, & Voas, 2011; Ballon et al., 2011; Zhou et al., 2011; Bertion et al., 2009; Manyika et al, 2015, p. 7; Thierer & Castillo, 2015; Badger et al., 2011; Chen et al., 2010; Abdelwahab, Hamdaoui, Guizani, & Rayes, 2014; Thierer & Castillo, 2015; Gubbi et al., 2013; Atzori e al, 2010; Mell & Grance, 2011). There are related technical and management areas affecting CloudIoT technologies. These domains comprise adaptive-interactive hardware-software system integration and related components. Such technical solutions may be implemented and provisioned via CloudIoT network platforms. Most of all, these methods incorporate artifacts, policies, procedures, techniques, processes, standards, encrypted security mechanisms, product/solution enhancement, and data-provisioning (Mell & Grance, 2011; Abdelwahab, Hamdaoui, Guizani, & Rayes, 2014; Akyildiz et al., 2002; Alamri, Ansari, Hassan, Hossain, Alelaiwi, Hossain, 2013; Thierer & Castillo, 2015; Gubbi, et al, 2013; Badger et al, 2011; Mell & Grance, 2011). How these IoT network solutions can be implemented or employed is crucial for organization's success. A sustainable level of collaboration between CloudIoT hardware systems and application services is a benchmark that senior leaders and decision makers should opt for while preparing, assessing, and considering IoT deployment requirements (Mell & Grance, 2011).

IoT technology was developed from shared technological solutions i.e., device-to-device data provisioning, and video surveillance. This also comprises editing and streaming, autonomous vehicle system interfaces and associated interoperability solutions. These days, vendors deploy IT solutions to support global-scale organizations and individual consumers (Abdelwahab, Hamdaoui, Guizani & Rayes, 2014; Alamri, Ansari, Hassan, Hossain, Alelaiwi, Hossain, 2013; Badger, Grance, Patt-Corner, & Voas, 2011; Ballon et al., 2011; Zhou et al., 2011; Thierer & Castillo, 2015; Mell & Grance, 2011). Figure 1 shows IoT ecosystem and how this model can communicate with other interoperable systems. This figure highlights vital IoT elements: (Gubbi et al., 2013; Badger et al., 2011; Chen et al., 2010; Mell & Grance, 2011).

3.1. CloudIoT Convergence

CloudIoT merging dates to the period, when smart devices were first deployed to the global marketplace (Gubbi, et al, 2013; Mell & Grance, 2011). In the last decade, the integration of CloudIoT changed how these systems, enterprises, and humans interacted. Increasing adoption of organizational IT capabilities has transformed the way network infrastructure solutions orthodoxly communicated (Mell & Grance, 2011; Qusay, 2011). Vendors have developed CloudIoT to support organization's

Figure 1. IoT infrastructure model

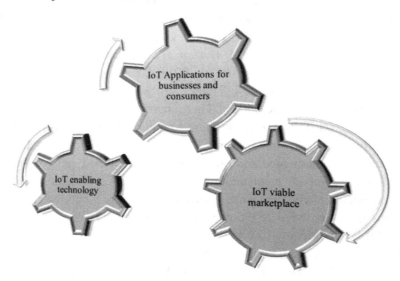

everyday business processes. These operations involve smart objects: sensors, actuators, aggregators, and clusters/processors (Gubbi, et al, 2013; Bruening et al, 2009; Mell & Grance, 2011).

In the 1970s Ashton's technical findings paved the evolution of parallel computer technologies; such as, remotely monitoring meters connected to the electrical grid system (Ashton, 2009). Ashton's historic innovations were launched as computer devices and smart machines, continued to collect, process, and exchange data in real-time (Ashton, 2009). Smart devices are designed to perform analogous activities, when powered via embedded Internet protocol (IP) consoles (Polsonetti, 2014; Akyildiz et al., 2002; Alamri, Ansari, Hassan, Hossain, Alelaiwi, Hossain, 2013). CloudIoT products and solutions comprise (Thierer & Castillo, 2015; Alamri et al., 2013; Badger et al., 2011; Bruening et al., 2009; Ashton, 2009; Mell & Grance, 2011):

- On-premise or Cloud Solutions
  - Software-as-a-Service
  - Platform-as-a-Service
- Wide Area Network Domain
- Device Domain
  - Devices, sensor systems and modules
- Service Layer Domain
  - Machine-to-Machine and IoT platforms

- Local Network Domain
  - ○ Wireless sensors, routers, hub, or aggregators
- Data and Application Domain
- Enterprise System Domain

These solutions support organizations' missions; such as, deploying these capabilities on the street, road traffic lights, smart cities, and smart grids. These solutions can be deployed as unified capabilities for environmental monitoring systems, municipal transportation signs, exhibition of street signs, and lease sensors for parking spaces in residential and commercial buildings (Alamri et al., 2013; Bruening et al., 2009).

4. INTERNET OF THINGS

IoT is a modern technology which aims to converge diverse smart objects. In contrast, IoT offer consumers and organizations the capability for sharing and provisioning data in real-time. IoT domains, trends and features comprise:

- Supply Chain
- Vertical-Market Applications
- Pervasive Positioning
- Physical-World

Democratizing CloudIoT smart objects is a significant milestone for modernizing smart devices and infrastructure components (Gubbi et al., 2013; Rao, Saluia, Sharma, Mittal, & Sharma, 2012; Danova, 2013; Manyika et al., 2015, p. 7). IoT standards are developed to support the overarching management of application framework practices; hence for inter-device integration encompassing both short and long range network connectivity (Danova, 2013; Manyika et al, 2015, p. 7; Gubbi et al., 2013). Such integrated standards comprise short and remote application protocols or frameworks. These architectures span Open Mobile Alliance's Device Management/OMA–DM 1.x (Danova, 2013; Manyika et al, 2015, p. 7; Gubbi et al., 2013), Open Mobile Alliance's Lightweight machine-to-machine or machine-to-mobile connectivity (Rao, Saluia, Sharma, Mittal, & Sharma, 2012). OMA-DM 1 protocol offers a level of integration between short-range data and client-server communication solutions (Danova, 2013; Manyika et al, 2015, p. 7; Gubbi et al., 2013). While Message Queuing Telemetry Transport (MQTT) is a technology standard supporting machine-to-machine communication protocol (Danova, 2013; Manyika et al., 2015, p. 7). IBM developed MQTT protocol to support the democratization of intelligent devices and mobile platform solutions, such as deploying Lightweight Subscribe Messaging Transport (LSMT). In the last decade, MQTT-machine-to-mobile/M2M protocol specifications are being modernized to conform with industry and regulatory compliance standards. MOTT–M2M is a fundamental resource solution for launching a long-range connectivity between smart machines and mobile devices.

The Organization for the Advancement of Structured Information Standards (OASISs) is a governing authority responsible for managing and certifying suited procedures, such as processes which can be implemented with relevant policies and guidelines (Gubbi et al., 2013). OASIS is a non-profit technology consortium found to implement, modernize, coalesce, regulate, and verify that all security solutions are in unison with the IoT standards for energy content and technology as well as emergency management practices (Danova, 2013). In contrast, AllJoyn is an available Internet and "open-source application"/framework, developed to provide standard connectivity for machine-to-mobile based solutions. While the Open Interconnect Consortium (OIC) is, a regulatory consortium established for evaluating IoT technological practices and standards for smart devices (Gubbi et al., 2013).

4.1. Evolutions and Trends

In 1998 industry introduced "ZigBee" as one of the archetypally putative IoT standards. In 2003 ZigBee was accepted as a uniformed product. Afterward, ZigBee was dubbed an industry standardized protocol for interconnecting Wide Area Networks (Rao, Saluia, Sharma, Mittal, & Sharma, 2012; Danova, 2013; Manyika et al, 2015, p. 7; WANs). In contrast, Z-Wave is a wireless connectivity protocol that was advanced to improving routine organizational operations of residential automation systems. Z-wave's operation is supported by sensors, actors/clusters, actuators smart devices (Rao, Saluia, Sharma, Mittal, & Sharma, 2012; Thierer & Castillo, 2015). Z-Wave is also a protocol that provisions automated services. Such services comprise a long-range control applications for both residential and commercial lighting (Rao et al., 2012; Danova, 2013; Manyika et al., 2015, p. 7; Gubbi, et al., 2013). When deployed to residential and commercial areas, Z-Wave generates low-powered radio frequency signals for smart electronic & computing devices, access controls e.g., commercial, and residential appliances. In contrast, bluetooth-low energy is labeled as vendor "bluetooth LE." The technology is a vendor smart version of bluetooth protocol formerly developed to interact with other hardware components and applications software. These objects are deployed in the healthcare, fitness, security, residential and entertainment areas (Rao et al., 2012; Gubbi et al., 2013). Bluetooth technology is a wireless solution that reduces power ingestion and lowers converted rates, when other IoT smart objects/ devices begin provisioning data on the network (Alamri et al., 2013). The thread was originally developed by Google-Nest, Samsung, ARM Wireless Internet Protocol as a solution for setting up direct communication between M2M smart objects. Similarly, the session starts when smart objects are deployed on the IoT global network (Manyika et al., 2015, p. 7). ARM Wireless Internet Protocol balances performance and decreases energy consumption between mobile systems and computing devices. This includes devices/machines connected to the network. Vendors advanced "Thread" architecture to support IoT protocols. These services encompass: Wi-Fi and bluetooth, which are unable to provisioning Internet Protocol Version Six/IPV6 level of communications (Rao et al., 2012; Danova, 2013; Manyika et al., 2015, p. 7; Thierer & Castillo, 2015; Tschofenig, 2015; Gubbi et al., 2013).

- *The Need for IoT Standardization.* Is it a fundamental protocol for IoT adoption? Hence, IT experts conclude that when deployed this solution may present security and implementation concerns, that might affect IoT platforms and related infrastructure adoption e.g., the functionality and resource

- *Exclusive Ecosystems, Customer, and Participant's Choice.* A process through which vendors evaluate market advantages e.g., compatible products. Such process comprises allowing stakeholders and product solutions to interact, while spawning/broadening market gains for across-the-board enterprise-focused demographics. Naturally, Market strategies and technology trends are implemented or promoted for developing client product distributions and growth margins. Thus, vendors can deal with confounding technical/market changes if acceptable market strategies are implemented

- *Technical and Cost Constrictions.* Developed as quality products to attract diverse enterprise demographics and market verticals. Conducting cost benefit and marketing analyses to decide on, how any of these offset costs can be managed; to building present-day devices to satisfy vendor's core product and marketing strategy. How vendors frame these marketing strategies may result in vendors and customers sustained business relationship

- *Schedule Risk.* A course that gives vendors' ability to process, monitor, and mitigate events. Retailers have the ability to present a right product to prospective clients. Such marketing idea encompasses the types of products available and/or sold in the marketplace. This includes developing integrated market strategies to satisfy customers' requirements. These strategies also aim to offer vendors the ability to coalesce and/or communicate on product solutions; hence measuring and finding potential market indicators; having the ability to focus on observed consumer's market technology fluctuations, to developing specific products for short/established industry benchmark or operational requirements

- *Technical Risk.* A process for measuring IoT capabilities and/or solutions—to avert technical risks and threats from affecting extensive production life-cycle, vendors study industry market solutions. This method improves IT solutions and mitigate emerging security breaches. To achieve these noticeable outcomes, vendors also develop best policies and solutions for smart devices. This includes devising better application capabilities e.g., hardware solutions & platforms to attract customers
- *Device's Performance.* IT benchmarks and CloudIoT best practices necessary for developing smart devices; lacking these industry standards may result in a production reduction, device degradation and disruptive-operational bearings. Such solutions are developed for firming up enterprises and customers' market interests. Figure 2 demonstrates CloudIoT research project matrix.

IoT smart objects are essential on how actuators, clusters, processors, and sensors often process and capture data. Cloud technology and robotic systems interface

Figure 2. CloudIoT research project matrix

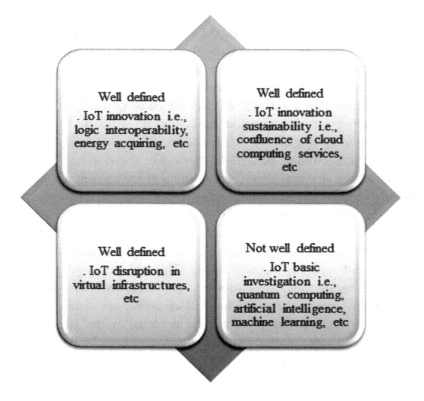

and deliver solutions to CloudIoT platforms (Gubbi et al., 2013). CloudIoT is an integrated and converged technology solution offering prime solutions for honing the next-generation of IoT smart systems/devices. CloudIoT solutions include: products/services to integrated/distributed network applications. These solutions have object-interoperability and energy-efficiency capabilities (Gubbi et al., 2013; Alamri et al, 2013; Badger et al., 2011).

4.2. Cloud Computing

CC is an enabling and scaling utility platform for delivering synchronized access and resource provisioning through configurable computing resources. These capabilities may be accessible via the Internet (Leaf, 2010, p. 2; Mell & Grance, 2010, p. 2; Mell & Grance, 2011; Bertion et al., 2009; Bruening et al., 2009). CC is "…a model for enabling ubiquitous, on-demand access to a shared pool of configurable computing resources (e.g., computer networks, servers, storage, applications and services). Such technologies may speedily be provisioned and released with minimal management effort." (Mell & Grance 2011; Qusay, 2011). Above all, CC technology is a solution that ranges from computing capabilities and relevant IT systems. These hardware components and applications software focus on the data storage and network provisioning (Gubbi et al., 2013; Bruening & Treacy, 2009; Leaf, 2010, p. 2; Mell & Grance, 2010, p. 2; Badger et al., 2011; Bruening et al., 2009). The distribution of CC platform solutions is constructed on innovative industry results. These organizational capabilities range from interconnected smart objects focusing on delivering and provisioning services (Leaf, 2010, p. 2; Mell & Grance, 2010, p. 2; Bruening & Treacy, 2009; Qusay, 2011).

The National Institute of Standards and Technology-NIST describes CC an "on-demand network access to a shared pool of configurable computing resources e.g., networks, servers, storage, applications and services provisioned and released with minimal management effort or service provider interaction" (Leaf, 2010, p. 2; Mell & Grance, 2010, p. 2; Bertion, E., Paci, F., & Ferrini, 2009; Gubbi, et al, 2013; Bruening & Treacy, 2009; Badger et al, 2011; Bruening et al., 2009; Qusay, 2011). Figure 3 illustrates cloud technology deployment and service model architecture.

- **Deployment Models**
  - *Public Cloud (PC).* An Internet standard platform for distributing shared computer-based resource pooling. These components span data and processes over physically dispersed nodes that are powered via the Internet. Internet service providers (ISPs) are responsible for implementing and supporting a pool of CC resources offered via the Internet

Figure 3. Cloud computer architectural model

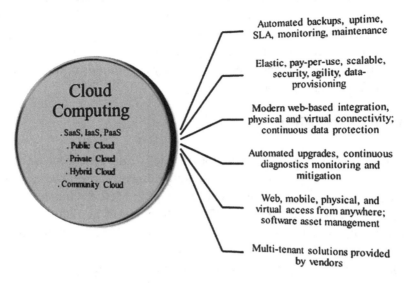

- ○ *Private Cloud (PC).* Integrated hardware components and applications software delivered through the Internet. PC offers users competitive market advantages for scaling services via Internet and/or distributed utility platform solutions. This includes the deployment of proprietary systems whose performance is monitored by an organization. In contrast, the public cloud, private cloud is serviced/owned by a single or multiple organizations
- ○ *Hybrid Cloud (HC).* A cloud utility platform or utility infrastructure with balanced on-premises and private cloud resources, coupled with third-party and public cloud delivery solutions. These solutions are delivered through resource pooling, to support real-time data provisioning processes
- ○ *Community Cloud (CC).* A collation of platforms sharing on-demand resources by means of distributed global network environment. CC resources are delivered on-premises or by third-party vendors namely ISPs. CC is administered/managed by several federal agencies and hi-tech industries or private enterprises, whose policies, procedures, and techniques can be shared through resource pooling/provisioning processes
- **Service Models**
  - ○ *Infrastructure-as-a-Service (IaaS).* A cloud delivery model offering virtualized resources to many agencies/enterprises. IaaS is one of the

three cloud service models commonly in use today. ISPs have the responsibility for promoting, launching, managing, hosting, supporting delivered computer resources via a range of an IaaS platform application capabilities/services. In the SaaS environment, all systems maintenances i.e., backups and resiliency forecasts are checked and delivered through a distributed utility IaaS platform. IaaS is a compatible, scalable, and reactive platform for managing distributed short-term workloads to a many physical/virtual network nodes. This solution is developed with embedded characteristics for offering synchronized configuration, task management and policy-focused Internal and client service offerings. IaaS services are delivered to various enterprises on hourly, quarterly, monthly, yearly, and pay-per-use basis. In the SaaS environment, users usually monitor their hardware solutions, applications software, or on-premises activities. This ensures that incurred overage charges from various ISPs services can be minimized or circumvented

o *Platform-as-a-Service (PaaS).* Cloud services can be accessible to many industries, through a variety of infrastructure solutions. PaaS gives users the ability to request, manage, and run compute applications over the cloud, without having to deal with major system degradation e.g., backing up the entire computer infrastructure as well as launching mixed applications. PaaS delivers public and private cloud services for several customers via the Internet. These capabilities are offered to both ISPs and organizations allowing for the ability to launch, manage, and support their resources: software and/or computer applications with least human participation and configuration options

o *Software-as-a-Service (SaaS).* A software licensing or a delivery model that can be distributed to various enterprises—through pay-per-use service or capability. These solutions can either be offered monthly or annually. Thus, Microsoft offers a wide range of SaaS services via centralized or federated hosting solutions. On-demand application services are provisioned, and can be made available to many customers and ISPs in real-time

5. INTERNET OF THINGS VS. CLOUD COMPUTING

Organizations continue to experience a greater degree shift of IoT products and solutions. Technology industry companies continue to develop and integrate smart solutions for the next-generation IoT infrastructure (Manyika et al., 2015, p. 7; Thierer & Castillo, 2015; Badger et al., 2011). These technological developments span Internet applications, such as smart homes, smart vehicles, smart street lights, toll roads, smart bridges, CCTV cameras, smart appliances. These smart devices and autonomous systems can be powered on the infrastructure with reduced energy ingesting, extra privacy, and enhanced security capabilities (Rao et al., 2012; Manyika et al., 2015, p. 7; Thierer & Castillo, 2015; Badger et al, 2011; Bott et al., 2016; Danova, 2013; Lee & Kyoochun, 2015; Gubbi, et al., 2013; ENISA, 2009; Intelligence, 2008; Mell & Grance, 2011; Qusay, 2011). Present-day adoption and implementation of IoT smart objects focuses on transformative solutions, e.g., human and smart objects interaction (Manyika et al., 2015, p. 7; Gubbi et al., 2013; Bruening & Treacy, 2009; Danova, 2013; Qusay, 2011). CC is a utility platform that delivers technology products and/or solutions to many customers and enterprises. This technology offers interoperable computer solutions for IoT: wireless/physical sensors, physical & virtual nodes, machines, and systems integration (Akyildiz et al., 2002; Alamri et al., 2013; Thierer & Castillo, 2015; Badger et al., 2011; Bott et al., 2016). CC technology offers a variety of application software to be provisioned over the Internet (Abdelwahab, Hamdaoui, Guizani, & Rayes, 2014; Bott et al, 2016). Figure 4 describes the Internet of Things standards and models (Aitken et

Figure 4. IoT standardized model

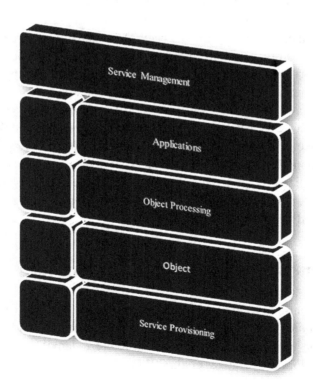

al., 2014; Alamri et al., 2013; Badger et al., 2011; Bott et al., 2016; Bruening et al., 2009; Danova, 2013; Gubbi et al., 2013; Intelligence, 2008; Lee & Kyoochun, 2015; Thierer & Castillo, 2015; Yan et al., 2008; Mell & Grance, 2011; Qusay, 2011).

Smart devices stem from computers built to process data with restricted human participation (Manyika et al., 2015, p. 7; Alamri et al., 2013). Researchers, technologists, and practitioners are committed to develop a set of core standards for CloudIoT capabilities (Manyika et al., 2015, p. 7; Alamri et al., 2013). These standards monitor and control wide-ranging organizational operations of smart objects (Rao et al., 2012; Manyika et al., 2015, p. 7; Gubbi et al., 2013; Thierer & Castillo, 2015). IoT is an emerging technology that organizations will continue to adopt/deploy many years to come (Rao et al., 2012; Gubbi et al., 2013). IoT solutions are developed to improve technology specifications/benchmark requirements. Below are integrated specifications forming the IoT paradigm (Rao et al., 2012; Manyika et al., 2015, p. 7; Thierer & Castillo, 2015; Bruening et al, 2009; Danova, 2013; Thierer & Castillo, 2015; Zhou et al., 2011):

- Pervasive Connectivity
- Prevalent Adoption of IP Networking
- Computing Economics
- Miniaturization
- Developments in Data Analytics
- Escalation of Cloud Computing
  - Device-to-Device
  - Device-to-Cloud
  - Device-to-Gateway
  - Back-end Data-Sharing
- Hyper-connected world
- Security
- Confidentiality
- Orchestration and Standardization
- Legal, Regulatory and Rights
- Emerging Economy and Growth Constraints

6. CLOUDIoT SECURITY, RELIABILITY, RESILIENCE, AND STABILITY CONCERNS

IT standards and security solutions are developed to protect technology infrastructures (Danova, 2013; Gubbi et al., 2013; Bruening & Treacy, 2009). Scientist, engineers, and IT professionals note that the lack of IoT security capabilities is a deterrent to the evolution of CloudIoT (Zhou et al., 2011; Tschofenig, 2015; Gubbi et al., 2013; Bruening & Treacy, 2009; Zhou et al., 2011; Bruening et al., 2009). Inhibited security policies, procedures, processes, techniques, and standards may expose customers to physical, cyber-attacking/hacking (Tschofenig, 2015).

IoT technology infrastructure and comparative pricing can promote vendors' security solutions, while protecting CloudIoT systems (Danova, 2013; Tschofenig, 2015; Gubbi et al., 2013). How data is provisioned, protected, and distributed is essential to organizational planning, IT strategic and business practices (Danova, 2013; Tschofenig, 2015; Danova, 2013; Gubbi et al., 2013). When exploring, or adopting new IoT security best practices leaders and decision makers should consider the following business scenarios and strategic requirements (Tschofenig, 2015; Gubbi et al., 2013; Bruening et al., 2009; Danova, 2013):

- *Good Design Security Practices.* Best practices developed for increasing IoT smart device security capabilities, such as protecting the network infrastructure from being compromised. In recent years, vendors developed security solutions to deter, repudiate, mitigate, and properly discuss existing/ emerging threats
- *Cost vs. Security Trade-offs.* Offers enterprises the ability to make informed decisions to appraise cost-benefit analyses for IoT adoption. Assessing any security risks to be decided through procedures, techniques, and processes e.g., cost-effectiveness or security trade-offs, industries ought to decide on whether these suitable resources/capabilities are apt to support IoT smart devices' day-to-day operations. CloudIoT solutions are vital to support the security specifications for the public and financial/economic growth
- *Standards and Metrics.* These provisions are germane features for IoT technical and operational standards. These standards encompass planning, implementing, and adopting attainable solutions for protecting IoT computing devices from being tampered by unsolicited users. How vendors and enterprises measure security capabilities is essential for improving IoT best practices i.e., policies, procedures/techniques, and standards
- *Data Confidentiality, Authentication, and Access Control.* Array from refining encryption mechanisms to decide on the level of IoT security for smart devices. This helps persuade against any eavesdropping or cyberattacks activities from being launched against IoT smart devices and infrastructure. Introducing robust authentication and encryption techniques are being developed or adapted to protect and prevent existing/emerging ,security threats. Improved algorithm tools and cryptologic-key e.g., products or solutions are crucial for determining best solutions. These solutions are essential for protecting IoT smart devices

- *Field-Upgradeability.* A method for ensuring IoT computing devices are built with extended product licensing and service lifetime. These provisions aim to support comprehensive CloudIoT operations. The upgradeability of solutions, such as hardware and software is essential on how these smart devices reconcile. This includes conducting infrastructure security vulnerability scans, while offering security capabilities for protecting the cloud from emerging threats. To guarantee these measures are relevantly introduced, security parameters, for example the development of avant-garde scanning tools, security applications and the centralized administration of CloudIoT resources is recommended. This includes manageable integration of security protocols as device management agent. Enterprises are evaluating current capital and operational expenditures, to decide if an infrastructure upgrading and system modernization or continuous infrastructure monitoring is required

- *Shared Responsibility.* An important model for adopting, implementing, supporting, and promoting enhanced solutions for smart devices. These advances require that vendors develop metrics/toolkit for evaluating and monitoring security vulnerabilities/gaps affecting the IT network operations. Any findings from these procedures/techniques, could shape the root cause for fast remedial solutions

- *Regulations.* Enterprises and vendors should adapt to guidelines set forth for enforcing the adoption and integration of IoT smart devices. These regulations can be underlined by organizational procedures/techniques vendors design as benchmarks to support daily infrastructure IT operations. The guidelines include, but are not restricted to negative externalities affecting everyday IoT operations (on-premise and off-premise). These procedures or techniques can be prearranged to protect enterprises' CloudIoT infrastructure resources. These measures range from various standard forms that is Internet specifications; user's privacy and data protection. Such procedures ensure for the enterprises' individual rights

- *Device Obsolescence.* A process through which enterprises and vendors use to decide on their proprietorship rights for decommissioning IoT smart devices or dealing with systems needing further upgrades. These processes, procedures, and strategies are being introduced to evaluate whether the device's life expectation or built-in features can be integrated to IoT smart devices. If a smartphone is upgraded or replaced "device obsolescence" serves as practical tool to ensure industries can trade-in their old machines for new ones. This includes the need for built-in or improved security features and interoperable capabilities. The method gives vendors the opportunity to discuss any of their immediate and/or long-term technical concerns with industry experts

7. CLOUDIoT SOLUTIONS

Connecting smart devices and autonomous systems, such as CloudIoT solutions is vital to the global marketplace. Thus, IT professionals make informed decision for the finest infrastructure analytical and security solutions. Indorsed solutions can be presented to enterprises with higher management interoperability (Gubbi et al., 2013; ENISA, 2009; Aceto et al., 2013; Abdelwahab et al, 2014; Alhakbani et al., 2014; Alhakbani et al, 2014; Bertion et al., 2009; Bruening et al., 2009; CPNI, 2010; ENISA, 2009; Kuhn, et al., 2016; Leavitt, 2009; Gubbi et al., 2013; Zhou et al., 2011; ENISA, 2009; Bruening et al., 2009; CPNI, 2010). Within the IoT environments, CloudIoT solutions are deployed to integrate an array of technologies offering IT solutions for consumers, governments, industry, and commercial companies via the Internet (Gubbi et al., 2013; Castro et al., 2014). Such distributed network services include supply chain systems, aviation, maritime, and ground infrastructures; marketing solutions, sensing networks, logistical transportation assets, actuator management, healthcare services, defense system capabilities. Often, these IoT solutions store, process, and retrieve actionable data in real-time (CPNI, 2010). Researchers, technologists, and practitioners envisage that by year 2020 thirty-billion IoT smart devices will be interconnected worldwide. This technology variability focuses on enterprises' requirements e.g., the need for promoting more collaborative environment between humans and machines (Alhakbani et al., 2014; Bertion et al., 2009; Castro et al., 2014; CPNI, 2010; Leavitt, 2009).

8. QUALITY OF SERVICE

Quality of Service (QoS) a business method offering users exclusive capabilities for supporting message delivery processes. Such processes include speeding up the signal itinerant from/to numerous device destinations on the network. Such concept stems from a set of probability solutions that devices may require to bolster their signal reception lifecycle, when connected to the Internet (Russell & Norvig, 2010; Gubbi et al., 2013; Castro et al., 2014). QoS supports the service prioritization. The traffic level decides this experienced through the network (Russell & Norvig, 2010). In QoS balanced infrastructure performance supports the IT operations on the enterprise.

According to IT experts balancing QoS with integrated/built-in block capabilities is key for supporting M2M performance. If cyberattack or power outages arise; QoS may handle the type of technical issues often occurring on the network. QoS aims to generate row data report logs to be analyzed to support any infrastructure modernizations (Russell & Norvig, 2010; Gubbi et al., 2013; Castro et al., 2014).

QoS solutions are employed to provide "forward error correction, handover, roaming, M2M reselection, automatic retransmission requests and adaptive channel coding" (Russell & Norvig, 2010; Gubbi et al., 2013; Alhakbani et al., 2014; Castro et al., 2014; Kuhn et al., 2016). In particular, QoS solutions offer decision makers the toolkit necessary to find the level of services suitable for the infrastructure performance (Russell & Norvig, 2010; Castro et al, 2014). Any obstructions on the network may be identified, evaluated, discussed, and mitigated to guarantee for better network functionality (Russell & Norvig, 2010; Castro et al., 2014). QoS toolkit is deployed on the network, to measure network performance in real-time. This output 'QoS' gives enterprises the ability to measure network connectivity and continuously deliver report outputs (Russell & Norvig, 2010; Alhakbani et al., 2014; Castro et al., 2014).

9. CIOUDIoT DEPLOYMENT AND CHALLENGES

IT professionals define intelligent and/or smarter devices as autonomous systems that will continue to dominate the overall cloud operations many years to come. Regardless of these progresses, researchers, technologists, and practitioners are still skeptical whether smart machines will ever outperform other solutions (Bertion, et al, 2009). These futurists, practitioners, and scientists also anticipate that in the upcoming years, the complexity surrounding the performance of smart devices, if not properly standardized may affect the Internet, and how humans regularly interact on a daily basis (Bertion et al., 2009; Bruening et al., 2009; Grance & Mell, 2011; Leighon, 2009; Rosenthal et al., 2010; Ross, 2010).

10. NETWORK OF THINGS

NIST defines IoT a technology instantiation of Network of Things (NoT) paradigm (Gubbi et al., 2013; Bruening & Treacy, 2009; CPNI, 2010). Comparably, NIST describes IoT as an integrated technology solution involving computing, sensing, communication, and actuation. NIST also outlines 'NoT' as a single and multiple Local Area Networks ranging from intelligence/smarter devices interconnected to the Internet (Weiss et al., 2017; Akyildiz et al., 2002; Bruening et al., 2009). Such solutions illustrate the industrial internet, social media networks and sensory networks (Weiss, et al 2017; Gubbi et al., 2013; Bruening, & Treacy, 2009; CPNI, 2010; Bruening et al., 2009; Leighon, 2009). The deference between IoT and NoT incorporates medical, financial, agricultural, safety-critical, transportation, performance-critical and high assurance areas. Both NoT workflow and dataflow have smart objects that are dispersed through multiple physical and vertical network environments. In physical space these objects often encompass vehicles, homes, computers, smart devices, road networks, office buildings and residences (Weiss et al., 2017; Gubbi et al., 2013; Bruening et al, 2009). Virtual space encompasses technologies and solutions: social media threads, software, information streaming, computer-generated machines, software, cybernetic networks (Weiss et al., 2017; Akyildiz et al., 2002; Alamri et al., 2013; Alhakbani et al., 2014; Bruening et al., 2009; Grance & Mell, 2011; Polsonetti, 2014).

11. SCALABILITY AND FLEXIBILITY

Scalability and flexibility are CloudIoT agile processes converging large-scale IoT environments. The performance of IoT objects relies on infrastructure platforms and application software capabilities to set up continued integration of "things" on global network. Smart devices are deployed, as IoT hardware components and applications software. These technological solutions are powered to share and provision data over the Internet. Despite these progresses, IT experts view scalability and flexibility as emerging platform and IT solutions built to improve the adoption of next-generation IoT intelligence devices (Alhakbani et al., 2014; Bruening et al., 2009; Leighon, 2009; Voas & Miller, 1993).

12. WIRED AND WIRELESS SENSOR NETWORKS

For many decades, filtered data was used to increase enterprises' daily operations (Akyildiz, Su, Sankarasubramaniam, & Cayirci; Ballon et al., 2011; Zhou et al., 2011; Bertion et al., 2009; Voas & Miller, 1993; Dash, Mohapatra, & Pattnaik, 2010). In the CloudIoT network environment, sensory network systems and RFIDs are combined with physical and virtual nodes that are geographically dispersed in the world (Akyildiz et al., 2002; Zaslavsky, Perera, & Georgakopoulos, 2013). Sensors, actuators, and other RFID solutions are deployed to offer load balancing, data capturing, processing, and tracking capabilities (Li & Rus, 2004; Voas & Miller, 1993; Akyildiz et al., 2002). These devices provision data for both near and continuing usability in synchronized mode (Li & Rus, 2004; Gubbi et al., 2013). There are a many types of sensory network systems deployed to physical and vertical domains. Sensory network systems entail primitive and distributed systems. When deployed on the physical or virtual network domains, primitive and distributed sensor systems may pose key security concerns aside from their outstanding level of performance. Such security risks may encompass environmental and cyber-attacks threats directed to these smart objects (Weiss et al 2017; Gubbi et al., 2013; Li

& Rus, 2004; Zaslavsky, Perera, & Georgakopoulos, 2013; Voas & Miller, 1993; Akyildiz et al., 2002; Alamri et al., 2013; Alhakbani et al., 2014; Leaf, 2010; Li & Rus, 2004; Mell & Grance, 2010).

In recent years, Wired, and Wireless Sensor Networks (W2SN) along with Radio-Frequency Identifications/RFIDs are part of continuous IoT technological growth (Li & Rus, 2004; Akyildiz et al., 2002). WSNs are a mass of network nodes sharing, processing, controlling and capturing data for a specific use. This method dates to 1980s when W2SNs were originally invented (Evangelos et al., 2011; Leaf, 2010; Li & Rus, 2004; Mell & Grance, 2010).

In 2001 these devices gained industry popularity and research drive. W2SNs are projected to give humans and computers the ability to collaborate and find any technological security constraints by setting up a protocol rules. Sensors networks are key components for RFID tagging systems, machine-to-machine, mobile devices, semantic data integration and the Internet Protocol Version Six/IPv6. Sensors have been used in aid of CloudIoT network environment (Gubbi et al, 2013; Li & Rus, 2004). These smart objects offer shared solutions, when interconnected on global network. Sensors are developed as independent intelligent solutions. Figure 5 illustrates a relationship between IoT smart objects and sensory infrastructure (Akyildiz et al., 2002; Evangelos et al., 2011; Polsonetti, 2014).

Figure 5. Sensor data networks

12.1. Primitives

Primitive systems are a collection of objects deployed to dispersed physical and vertical spaces (Weiss et al., 2017). These smart objects encompass aggregators, communication channel, external utility/e-Utility, decision trigger, actors/clusters, and sensory network systems (Gubbi et al., 2013; Weiss et al., 2017). In physical and vertical network environments, sensor network systems capture, produce, share, analyze, and transmit data to several destination nodes. IoT consists of the following five architecture layers: Application layer, middleware layer, network layer, access to gateway layer and perception layers. Each of these layers perform a vital role in the integration of IoT capabilities onto worldwide network (Weiss et al., 2017; Gubbi et al., 2013; Bruening et al., 2009).

13. ARTIFICIAL INTELLIGENCE

Artificial Intelligence (AI) is a computer science interdisciplinary concept which involves intelligence and autonomous theories or practices. The term AI was formerly devised in the 1950s by John McCarthy, a futurist from MIT. As a futurologist, McCarthy saw an imperative need to develop AI platform as an all-pervading architecture for billions of data points being processed via the Internet (Russell & Norvig, 2010). In AI, how data is sanitized, processed, provisioned, analyzed once collected is key to pattern identification and machine behavioral solutions. AI solutions are developed to guarantee that decision makers have an at once available toolkit for making informed decisions (Cooper & Mell, 2012; Russell & Norvig, 2010). This process includes detecting system weaknesses and related technical issues that may affect data normalcy or the need for corrective action as suitable (Kuhn et al., 2016; Manyika et al., 2015; Polsonetti, 2014). In particular, McCarthy defines AI as a method that includes machine learning, classic AI, simple neural networks, cognitive systems, biological neural networks, big data, and deep learning. McCarthy further designates AI as a scientific and engineering cognitive analytics concepts involving smart processes, analytical methods/procedures and mathematical/software problem solving scenarios. Smart machines and applications software display a collection of smart objects. These machines and/or applications software frequently emulate human activities. AI is a technology solution that helps organizations resolve critical issues affecting data collection, processing, analysis, and provisioning. This includes the improvement of smart automation, predictive analytics, and practical intrusion (Russell & Norvig, 2010). Vendors have developed suitable applications to balance the performance of AI analytics solutions: robust sensory systems, smart machines, and big data solutions (Russell & Norvig, 2010). Futurists and technologists are concerned that lest the following limitations: compatibility, complexity, privacy, security, protection, safety, ethical & legal issues, artificial inanity are discussed, vendors believe that organizations are skeptical in incorporating these technology solutions (Russell & Norvig, 2010; Cooper & Mell, 2012; Kuhn et al., 2016). These technological domains include natural and digital machine learning solutions built to offer interactive-integrated contemporary processes and techniques (Russell & Norvig, 2010). These proposed methods, procedures, and concepts are agents of smart machine. Such systems are equipped to perform activities ranging from analogous functions based on robotics interaction with human mind interaction, to scientific-focused learning solutions and problem solving (Russell & Norvig, 2010; Russell & Norvig, 2010).

14. RADIO-FREQUENCY IDENTIFICATION

Radio-Frequency Identification high-tech solutions are deployed to support the physical and virtual nodes (Rozados & Tjahjono, 2014). These solutions are integrated with IoT smart systems to deliver high-tech digital identification tags for data distribution (Akyildiz et al., 2002; Zhou et al., 2011; Gubbi et al., 2013; Dobre & Xhafa, 2014; Rozados & Tjahjono, 2014; Yan, Zhang, Yang & Ning, 2008; Kuhn et al., 2016; Tschofenig, 2015; Yan et al., 2008).

15. APPLICATION PROGRAMMING INTERFACES

Application programming interfaces (APIs) are key solutions for supporting application frameworks and protocols (Weiss et al., 2017; Dash et al., 2010). Back-end-data-sharing application model offer complex M2M cloud and traditional services and capabilities for system load balancing (Danova, 2013; CPS, 2014). This includes augmented cloud hosted smart devices capabilities as well as preventing a single point of failure from occurring on the infrastructure (Danova, 2013; Weiss et al., 2017; Yan et al., 2008).

16. BIG DATA ANALYTICS

Researchers and technologists predict that by year 2020 almost fifty-billion devices will be interconnected worldwide (Cooper & Mell, 2012; Dobre & Xhafa, 2014; Agrawal, Das, & Abbadji, 2011; Bertion, E., Paci, F., & Ferrini, 2009; Dobre &

Xhafa, 2014; Rozados & Tjahjono, 2014; Dobre & Xhafa, 2014; Buyya et al., 2016; Cooper & Mell, 2012; Dobre & Xhafa, 2014). Such processes and techniques involve: storage, access, transportation, and processing of massive volumes of data smart devices to process different tasks on the network (Agrawal, Das, & Abbadji, 2011; Dobre & Xhafa, 2014; Yan et al., 2008; Cooper & Mell, 2012; Buyya et al., 2016). In big data analytics, scaling computing platforms encompasses mobile computing devices i.e., sensors, aggregators, actors/clusters, and actuators is incumbent upon vendors' enhanced storage resource capabilities' implementation (Agrawal, Das, & Abbadji, 2011; Ballon et al., 2011; Zhou et al., 2011; Bertion et al, 2009; CPS, 2014; Dobre & Xhafa, 2014; Rozados & Tjahjono, 2014; Cooper & Mell, 2012; Agrawal et al., 2011; Buyya et al., 2016; Buyya et al., 2016; Cooper & Mell, 2012; Dobre & Xhafa, 2014; Lakshman & Prashant, 2010; Rozados & Tjahjono, 2014; Tschofenig, 2015; Zaslavsky et al., 2013).

17. CYBER-PHYSICAL SYSTEMS

Cyber-physical Systems (CPS) gateway solutions for delivering network solutions and capabilities to various industries (Weiss et al., 2017; CPS, 2014). Developing these smart systems/devices is essential for the interoperability of hardware components and applications software (Lakshman & Prashant, 2010). CPSs involve processors, smart vehicles, aggregators, robots, sensors, actors/clusters, smart cities, actuators. These systems have a key task to perform in the IoT-base global network environment (Weiss et al., 2017; CPS, 2014; Gubbi et al, 2013; Cooper & Mell, 2012; Cooper & Mell, 2012; Dobre & Xhafa, 2014; Lakshman & Prashant, 2010).

18. CRITICAL INFRASTRUCTURE ASSETS

In the 1960s the Supervisory Control, Data Acquisition and Automatic (SCADA) was developed. SCADA offers a controlling management method and computing capabilities. The system was developed to support large-scale functions, such as monitoring and regulating services operational on the electrical grid (Cooper & Mell, 2012; Weiss et al., 2017; Lakshman & Prashant, 2010). SCADA is a source data communications solution that supports industrial management and mission-critical. Early inventors of SCADA technology, accentuated that since the world was entering a newfangled digital marketing/technology era, the technology would be essential for mission critical programs (Cooper & Mell, 2012; Weiss et al., 2017; Rozados & Tjahjono, 2014). Continued adoption of IoT solutions has stand in for commercial and industrial computerization era, when hardware and applications software lacked highest performance, to integrate with other platforms in the world (Weiss et al., 2017; Cooper & Mell, 2012; Lakshman & Prashant, 2010). Scientists, technologists, and industrialists continue to develop both agile and highly equipped computing solutions, to scale with new IoT smart objects. IoT is a technology 'mind mapping and logical delivery infrastructure of integrated systems' devised to integrate, merge, and protect wide-ranging IT deployment of critical infrastructure resources (Weiss et al., 2017; Cooper & Mell, 2012). In non-industrialized nations, how enterprises are arranged depends on data communication solutions—these solutions may be deployed to monitor, control, and offer ubiquitous physical and vertical objects: sensory network systems, actuators, aggregators, IP network systems and wireless solutions. Critical infrastructure resources are central targets for active or future cyber-attacks (Cooper & Mell, 2012; Lakshman & Prashant, 2010; SGIP, 2014).

19. SOLUTIONS AND RECOMMENDATIONS

Lacking authentication in smart devices or autonomous systems can be detrimental to physical and vertical infrastructure networks (Weiss et al., 2017). Vendors continue to develop robust IT and security solutions to counter and/or prevent emerging attacks. Best practices are developed to protect geolocation, sensory system ownership and encryption algorithms from adversarial cyber exploitations (Weiss et al., 2017; Gubbi, et al., 2013). Researchers, inventers, and developers continue to advance hardware components and application software to allow for protecting sensor data transmission, integrity, and confidentiality measures. These solutions are key for denying, preventing, mitigating, thwarting, and degrading any adversarial physical and/or cyber-attacks launched against CloudIoT global network infrastructure. Decommissioning and replacing dated hardware with advanced smart sensory network systems is central for responsive and proactive security capabilities. This includes deciding on defense capabilities, to protect the Internet (Weiss et al., 2017; Cooper & Mell, 2012; Lakshman & Prashant, 2010).

20. FUTURE RESEARCH DIRECTIONS

CC and IoT have transformed how vendors and organizations used to do business. CloudIoT systems range from complex technology solutions powered by CC and IoT over the internet (Gubbi et al., 2013; Bruening et al, 2009). In the last decade, vendors built modern-day smart devices/platforms e.g., mobile-to-mobile, mobile-to-human, device-to-device, machine-to-machine, machine-to-cloud systems. These smart devices or platforms are embedded capabilities for powering and supporting the next-generation operations of intelligent devices and autonomous systems (Ballon et al., 2011; Weiss et al., 2017; Gubbi et al., 2013; Bruening et al., 2009; Dash et al., 2010). The adoption of CloudIoT solutions has transformed vendors' capabilities and redefine how the next-generation of smart devices will be adopted and deployed to physically dispersed/interconnected global network environments (Ballon et al., 2011; Weiss et al., 2017). In future, such evolutions and trends will decide on the path traditional solutions ought to take to interop with CloudIoT organizational technology solutions (Ballon et al., 2011; Zhou et al, 2011; Bertion et al., 2009; Gubbi et al., 2013; Bruening et al., 2009). The global scientific community of experts suggests that IoT standards, procedures/techniques and policies be upgraded to satisfy clients and stakeholders' operational requirements (Ballon et al., 2011; Zhou et al., 2011; Bruening et al., 2009; Dash et al., 2010; Stanoevska-Slabeva et al., 2009).

According to Moore's Law in the next decades, there will be vast gains on how IoT devices are powered when connected to the global network environment. This ensures that global enterprises to balance and/or regulate energy consumption by using low-power built-in sensors, to ensure that smart devices can perfectly iterate with quality of service. The process includes processes which have been made in the areas of IoT and cloud technology domains. These developments focus on converging global CloudIoT solutions, standards, protocols, architectures, and application programing interfaces/APIs. The techniques are developed to advance heterogeneous or smart devices' connectivity (Bertion et al., 2009; Weiss et al., 2017; Gubbi, Buyya, Marusic, & Palaniswami, 2013; Lakshman & Prashant, 2010).

21. CONCLUSION

IoT architectures focus on incorporating the complexity and detailed understanding of several technologies and domain options. IoT paradigm has transformed the fundamental method enterprises rely on to do business. CC solutions and IoT smart objects has transformed the way vendors and enterprises conduct business in the 21st century. IoT technologies involve sensing, computing, communication, and actuation (Weiss et al., 2017). The integration of physical, virtual, wired/wireless sensors, actors/clusters, actuators, machine-to-machine, machine-to-mobile, radio-frequency identification tagging systems, smart cities, self-driving vehicles, robotic systems is built on exclusive framework developed for reforming and integrating IT resources' pooling in support of distributed CloudIoT network environment. Such process entails streaming network resources & interoperability and deciding, how smart devices are displayed on a 'technology mind mapping' network infrastructure operations.

This chapter amplifies on various security concerns, interoperability, scalability, reliability, vulnerability, functionality, trustworthy, behavior and performance factors affecting IoT network environment and related core specifications (Weiss et al., 2017; Dash et al., 2010).

REFERENCES

Aazam, M., & Huh, E. N. (2014). Fog computing and smart gateway based communication for cloud of things. *Future Internet of Things and Cloud (FiCloud), 2014 International Conference on*, 464–470.

Abdelwahab, S., Hamdaoui, B., Guizani, M., & Rayes, A. (2014). Enabling smart cloud services through remote sensing: An internet of everything enabler. *Internet of Things Journal, IEEE, 1*(3), 276–288. doi:10.1109/JIOT.2014.2325071

Aceituno, V. (2005). *On information Security Paradigms*. ISSA Journal.

Aceto, G., Botta, A., de Donato, W., & Pescap'e, A. (2013). Cloud monitoring: A survey. *Computer Networks, 57*(9), 2093–2115. doi:10.1016/j.comnet.2013.04.001

Agrawal, D., Das, S., & Abbadji, A. (2011). *Big Data and Computing: Current State and Future Opportunities*. Retrieved from: https://www.researchgate.net/publication/221103048_Big_Data_and_Cloud_Computing_Current_State_and_Future_Opportunities

Aitken, R., Chandra, V., Myers, J., Sandhu, B., Shifren, L., & Yeric, G. (2014). Device and technology implications of the internet of things. *VLSI Technology (VLSI-Technology): Digest of Technical Papers, 1*–4. doi:10.1109/VLSIT.2014.6894339

Akyildiz, I. F., Su, W., Sankarasubramaniam, Y., & Cayirci, E. (2002). Wireless sensor networks: a survey. *Computer Networks, 38*(4), 393-422.

Alamri, A., Ansari, W. S., Hassan, M. M., Hossain, M. S., Alelaiwi, A., & Hossain, M. A. (2013). A survey on Sensor-Cloud: Architecture, applications, and approaches. *International Journal of Distributed Sensor Networks, 9*(2), 917923. doi:10.1155/2013/917923

Alhakbani, N., Hassan, M. M., Hossain, M. A., & Alnuem, M. (2014). A framework of adaptive interaction support in Cloud-based Internet of Things (IoT) environment. In *Internet and Distributed Computing Systems* (pp. 136–146). Springer. doi:10.1007/978-3-319-11692-1_12

Alter, S. (2008). Defining Information Systems as Work Systems: Implications for the IS Field. *Business Analytics and Information Systems*. Retrieved from: http://repository.usfca.edu/at/22

Ashton, K. (2009). That 'Internet of Things' things. *RFID Journal*. Retrieved from: http://www.rfidjournal.com/articles/view?4986

Atzori, A. L., Iera, A., & Morabito, G. (2010). The Internet of Things: A survey. *Computer Networks, 54*(15), 2787–2805. doi:10.1016/j.comnet.2010.05.010

Badger, L., Grance, T., Patt-Corner, R., & Voas, J. (2011). *Draft Cloud Computing Synopsis and Recommendations*. National Institute of Standards and Technology (NIST) Special Publication 800-146. US Department of Commerce. Retrieved from: http://csrc.nist.gov/publications/drafts/800-146/Draft-NIST-SP800-146.pdf

Ballon, P., Glidden, J., Kranas, P., Menychtas, A., Ruston, S., & Van Der Graaf, S. (2011). Is there a need for a cloud platform for european smart cities? *eChallenges e-2011 Conference Proceedings, IIMC International Information Management Corporation*.

Bertion, E., Paci, F., & Ferrini, R. (2009). *Privacy-Preserving Digital Identity Management for Cloud Computing*. IEEE Computer Society Data Engineering Bulletin.

Bott, A., Donato, W., Persico, V., Pescapé, A. (2016). Integration of Cloud computing and Internet of Things: A survey. *Future Generation Computer Systems*, (56), 684–700.

Bruening, P. J., & Treacy, B. C. (2009). *Cloud Computing: Privacy, Security Challenges*. Bureau of National Affairs.

Buyya, R., Ramamohanarao, K., Leckie, C., Calhieros, N., Dastjerdi, A., & Versteeg, S. (2015). *Big Data Analytics-Enhanced Cloud Computing: Challenges, Architectural Elements, and Future Directions*. Retrieved from: http://arxiv.org/abs/1510.06486

Castro, A., Víctor, V. A., Fuentes, B., & Costales, B. (2014). A Flexible Architecture for Service Management in the Cloud. *IEEE eTransactions on Network and Service Management, 11*(1), 116–125. doi:10.1109/TNSM.2014.022614.1300421

Center for the Protection of Natural Infrastructure. (2010). *Information Security Briefing on Cloud Computing, 01/2010*. Retrieved from: http://www.cpni.gov.uk/Documents/Publications/2010/2010007-ISB_cloud_computing.pdf

Chen, Y., Paxson, V., & Katz, R. H. (2010). *What is New About Cloud Computing Security? Technical Report UCB/EECS-2010-5*. Berkeley, CA: EECS Department, University of California. Retrieved from http://www.eecs.berkeley.edu/Pubs/ TechRpts/2010/EECS-2010-5.html

Chetan, S. (2017). *Correcting the IoT History*. Retrieved from: http://www. chetansharma.com

Chow, R., Golle, P., Jakobsson, M., Shi, E., Staddon, J., Masuoka, R., & Molina, J. (2009). Controlling Data in the Cloud: Outsourcing Computation without Outsourcing Control. In *Proceedings of the ACM Workshop on Cloud Computing Security (CCSW'09)* (pp. 85-90). ACM Press. doi:10.1145/1655008.1655020

Cooper, M., & Mell, P. (2012). *Tackling Big Data*. Retrieved from: http://csrc.nist. gov/groups/SMA/forum/documents/june2012presentations/f%csm_june2012_ cooper_mell.pdf

Cyber-Physical Systems Public Working Group Workshop. (2014). National Institute of Standards and Technology. Retrieved from: http://www.nist.gov/cps/cps-pwg- workshop.cfm

Danova, T. (2013). Morgan Stanley. 75 Billion Devices Will Be Connected to The Internet Of Things by 2020. *Business Insider*. Retrieved from: http:// www.businessinsider.com/75-billion-devices-will-be-connected-to-the-internet- by-2020-2013-10

Dash, S. K., Mohapatra, S., & Pattnaik, P. K. (2010). A survey on application of wireless sensor network using Cloud computing. *Int. J. Comput. Sci. Eng. Technol.*, *1*(4), 50–55.

Dobre, C., & Xhafa, F. (2014). Intelligent services for big data science. *Future Generation Computer Systems*, *37*, 267–281. doi:10.1016/j.future.2013.07.014

European Network and Information Security Agency (2009). *Cloud Computing: Cloud Computing: Benefits, Risks, and recommendations for Information Security. Report No: 2009*. Author.

Evangelos, A. K., Nikolaos, D. T., & Anthony, C. B. (2011). *Integrating RFIDs and smart objects into a Unified Internet of Things architecture*. Advances in Internet of Things.

Grance & Mell. (2011). *The NIST definition of cloud computing* (NIST Publication No. NIST SP- 800-145). Washington, DC: US Department of Commerce. Retrieved from http://csrc.nist.gov/publications/drafts/800-146/Draft-NIST-SP800-146.pdf

Gubbi, J., Buyya, R., Marusic, S., & Palaniswami, M. (2013). Internet of Things (IoT): A vision, architectural elements, and future directions. *Future Generation Computer Systems, 29*(7), 1645–1660. doi:10.1016/j.future.2013.01.010

Intelligence, S. C. B. (2008). Disruptive civil technologies. In Six Technologies with Potential Impacts on US Interests Out to 2025. Academic Press.

Kroenke, D. (2015). *MIS Essentials* (4th ed.). Boston: Pearson.

Kuhn, D. R., Hu, V., Ferraiolo, D. F., Kacker, R. N., & Lei, Y. (2016). *Pseudo-exhaustive Testing of Attribute Based Access Control Rules*. International Workshop on Combinatorial Testing at the 2016 IEEE Ninth International Conference on Software Testing, Verification, and Validation Workshops (ICSTW), Chicago, IL. doi:10.1109/ICSTW.2016.35

Lakshman, A., & Prashant, M. (2010). Cassandra: A decentralized structured storage system. *SIGOPS Oper. Syst. Rev., 44*(2), 35-40. DOI:10.1145/1773912.1773922

Layton, T. P. (2007). *Information Security: Information Security: Design, Implementation, Measurement, and Compliance*. Boca Raton, FL: Auerbach Publications.

Leaf, D. (2010). *Overview: NIST Cloud Computing Efforts, NIST Senior Executive for Cloud Computing, NIST*. Information Technology Laboratory.

Leaf, D. (2010). *Overview: NIST Cloud Computing Efforts. NIST Senior Executive for Cloud Computing, NIST* Information Technology Laboratory.

Leavitt, N. (2009). Is Cloud Computing Ready for Prime Time? *IEEE Computer, 42*(1), 15–20. doi:10.1109/MC.2009.20

Lee, I., & Kyoochun, L. (2015). The Internet of Things (IoT): Applications, investments, and challenges for enterprises. *Business Horizons, 58*(4), 431–440. doi:10.1016/j.bushor.2015.03.008

Leighon, T. (2009). *Akamai and Cloud Computing: A Perspective from the Edge of the Cloud*. White Paper. Akamai Technologies. Retrieved from http://www.essextec.com/assets/cloud/akamai/cloudcomputing- perspective-wp.pdf

Lewis, P. T. (1985). *Internet of Things*. Speech presented at the Congressional Black Caucus Foundation - 15th Annual Legislative Weekend Conference, Washington, DC.

Li, Q., & Rus, D. (2004). Global Clock Synchronization in Sensor Networks. *Twenty-third Annual Joint Conference of the IEEE Computer and Communications Societies (INFOCOM 2004)*, 564-574. doi:10.1109/INFCOM.2004.1354528

Manyika, J., Chui, M., Bisson, P., Woetzel, J., Dobbs, R., Bughin, J., & Aharon, D. (2015). *The Internet of Things: Mapping the Value Beyond the Hype.* McKinsey Global Institute.

Mell, P., & Grance, T. (2010). *Effectively and Securely Using the Cloud Computing Paradigm. NIST* Information Technology Laboratory.

Mell, P., & Grance, T. (2011). The NIST Definition of Cloud Computing (Technical report). National Institute of Standards and Technology: U.S. Department of Commerce. doi:10.6028/NIST.SP.800-145

Peltier, T. R. (2002). *Information Security Policies, Procedures, and Standards: Guidelines for effective information security management.* Boca Raton, FL: Auerbach publications.

Polsonetti, C. (2014). Know the Difference Between IoT and M2M. *Automation World.* Retrieved from: http://www.automationworld.com/cloud-computing/know-difference-between-iot-and-m2m

Prakash J. P., Mitra, K., Saguna, K., Shah, T., Georgakopoulos, D., & Ranjan, R. (2015). Orchestrating Quality of Service in the Cloud of Things Ecosystem. *Quality of Service Architecture for Internet of Things and Cloud Computing.*

Qusay, H. (2011, January). Demystifying Cloud Computing. *The Journal of Defense Software Engineering*, 16–21.

Rao, B. P., Saluia, P., Sharma, N., Mittal, A., & Sharma, S. V. (2012). Cloud computing for Internet of Things & sensing based applications. *Sensing Technology (ICST), Sixth International Conference on*, 374–380. doi:10.1109/ICSensT.2012.6461705

RCRWireless News. (2016). *Industrial IoT: Carriers Look Beyond Connectivity.* Retrieved from. https://www.5gamericas.org

Rosenthal, A., Mork, P., Li, M. H., Stanford, J., Koester, D., & Reynolds, P. (2010). Cloud Computing: A new business paradigm for biomedical information sharing. *Journal of Biomedical Informatics*, *43*(2), 342–353. doi:10.1016/j.jbi.2009.08.014 PMID:19715773

Ross, V. W. (2010). *Factors influencing the adoption of cloud computing by Decision making managers (Capella University).* ProQuest Dissertations and Theses.

Rozados, I., & Tjahjono, B. (2014). *Big Data Analytics in Supply Chain Management: Trends and Related Research*. 6th International Conference on Operations and Supply Chain Management, Bali. Retrieved from: https://www.researchgate.net/publication/270506965_Big_Data_Analytics_in_Supply_Chain_Management_Trends_and_Related_Research

Russell, S. J., & Norvig, P. (2010). *Artificial Intelligence-A Modern Approach*. Prentice-Hall, Inc.

Smart Grid Interoperability Panel. (2014). *Smart Grid Cybersecurity Committee, Guidelines for Smart Grid Cybersecurity. In NIST Interagency Report (NISTIR) 7628 Revision 1* (p. 668). Gaithersburg, MD: National Institute of Standards and Technology; doi:10.6018/NIST.IR.7628r1

Stanoevska-Slabeva, K., Wozniak, T., & Ristol, S. (2009). *Grid and Cloud Computing: A Business Perspective on Technology and Applications*. Springer Science & Business Media.

Thierer, A., & Castillo, A. (2015). *Projecting the Growth and Economic Impact of the Internet of Things*. George Mason University, Mercatus Center. Retrieved from: http://mercatus.org/sites/default/files/IoT-EP-v3.pdf

Tschofenig, H. (2015). *Architectural Considerations in Smart Object Networking*. Tech. no. RFC 7452. Internet Architecture Board. Retrieved from: https://tools.ietf.org/html/rfc7452

Voas, J. M., & Miller, K. W (1993). Semantic metrics for software testability. *Journal of Systems and Software*, *20*(3), 207-216. 10.1016/0164-1212(93)90064-5

Weiss, M., Eidson, J., Barry, C., Broman, B., Goldin, L., Iannucci, B., Lee, E. A., ...Stanton, K. (2017). Time-Aware Applications, Computers, and Communication Systems (TAACCS). NIST Technical Note (TN) 1867. National Institute of Standards and Technology. doi:10.6028/NIST.TN.1867

Yan, L., Zhang, Y., Yang, L. T., & Ning, H. (2008). *The Internet of Things: From RFID to the Next-Generation Pervasive Networked Systems*. CRC Press. doi:10.1201/9781420052824

Zaslavsky, A., Perera, C., & Georgakopoulos, D. (2013). *Sensing as a service and big data*. ArXiv Preprint arXiv:1301.0159

Zhou, J., Leppänen, T., Harjula, M. E., Ylianttila, O. T., Yu, C., Jin, H., & Tianruo, Y. L. (2011). Cloud Things: A Common Architecture for Integrating the Internet of Things with Cloud Computing. *IEEE 17th International Conference on Computer Supported Cooperative Work in Design.*

Zwass, V. (2016). *Information System.* Encyclopedia Britannica, Inc. Retrieved from: https://www.britannica.com/topic/information-system

KEY TERMS AND DEFINITIONS

Actuators: Modules offering merged controlling, monitoring machines and systems. These devices form a control signal/a basis of energy to functions. The control signal is defined as truncated energy and may be power-driven energy, inflatable, or even humanly power.

Data Privacy: A confidentiality of data for a specific entity whose information is processed in the system.

Data Security: The process for protecting computer resources such as databases and websites from unauthorized access and data protection from unauthorized users, such as actors, hackers, attackers, among others.

Internet of Things: Integrated smart systems or network solutions, such as vehicles, homes, machines, processors, sensors, actuators, and other monitoring devices. These systems integrate and distribute nodes with built-in electronic devices (i.e., software sensory systems and network solutions). These embedded capabilities give smart objects the ability to collect, exchange, and process data between physical and vertical nodes.

Network of Things: A technology equipped with distributed sensing, computing, communication, and actuation systems. This technology saves energy consumption. It also offers primitive sensory systems the ability to measure performance of all physical components running in the same network environment.

Quality of Service: Broad performance of telephony and computer network systems encompasses a broad range of system activities, users' experiences on the global network. Systematic measurement of QoS may be decided by different types of services made available via the worldwide network environment. This includes fault and bit rates, communication disruption, throughput, data availability, irregular random of activities seen in machines deployed to the global network.

Reliability of Infrastructure: A process for ensuring that infrastructure is dependable and readily available as considered necessary.

Resource Provisioning: A process for preparing and equipping network components providing new services to a variety of users.

Safeguards: Protective measures for discussing a variety of security requirements to specific information systems.

Scalability: A system, network, or solution for processing larger data amounts or related activities on the network. Reliant on the amount of data being processed, hardware or applications software should be upgraded/scaled when deployed to the global network. When there is a degradation in system performance, "scalability" can be within spread recourse allowing for scalable load balancing and system output.

Sensor Data: Offering users a direct access to capabilities. This includes data provisioned from distributed sensory network objects.

System Integration: Converging different solutions for a unique distribution of resources. In engineering the term SI refers to processing integrated subsystems into unique infrastructure unit. This includes bringing different components together (i.e., computing systems, applications software; physical or functional systems for sharing and processing information synchronously).

Chapter 5
Security Issues and Its Countermeasures in Examining the Cloud– Assisted IoT

Govind P. Gupta
National Institute of Technology, India

ABSTRACT

Internet of Things (IoT) offers the capability to connect and integrate both digital and physical objects to the internet and to enable machine-to-machine and machine-to-human communication or interactions services. The real-time adoptions and deployments of such systems for different applications such as smart cities, smart grids, smart homes, or smart environments require guaranteed security and privacy-enabled IoT services. This is due to fact that devices in the IoT generate, process, and exchange huge amounts of safety-critical data as well as privacy-sensitive information. In order to ensure secure and safe operation and to avoid cyber-attacks on such systems, it is crucial to incorporate security and privacy measures to countermeasure the different possible attacks. This chapter presents different security and privacy requirements and a taxonomy of security threats in the context of the IoT. In addition, the authors survey the most relevant defense strategies available in the literature related to IoT security with their merits and demerits.

INTRODUCTION

The Internet of Things (IoT) is characterized by a collection of heterogeneous, geographically distributed, smart devices that interact with each other on a collaborative basis to complete a particular task (Vermesan, 2011; Tsai, 2014;

DOI: 10.4018/978-1-5225-3445-7.ch005

Ning, 2012). The core objective of the IoT is to provide smart services in a variety of application domains such as Smart Homes, Smart Cities, Smart Grids and so on (Turner, 2011; Roman, 2011). In these application domains, security and privacy requirements of the IoT play a very important role which includes privacy and confidentiality of data exchanged among devices and controlling stations, access control within the IoT, and trust among connected devices and users.

Fundamental hurdles for pushing IoT and its services into the real-world applications are security, privacy and trust (Jing, 2014; Rodrigo, 2013; Sicari, 2015; Zheng, 2014). The main aim of the security services designed for the IoT is to provide secure interactions between the devices and the Internet host, and protecting the information and service provisioning of all relevant components of IoT. Generally, in a collaborative and information sharing system such as the IoT, different security and privacy services such as confidentiality, data integrity, access control, anonymity, and availability for users and smart things and trustworthiness among smart devices and users are required. These security services are very important to ensure secure communication among different entities of the IoT. Due to the heterogeneity and ad hoc nature of IoT components and the lack of computing resources such as processing power and storage, it is required to tailor existing security solutions to this new smart environment. Traditional security and privacy mechanisms cannot be directly applied to the IoT (Ning, 2012; Turner, 2011; Roman, 2011). This is due to fact that in the IoT, different communication stacks, standards and resource-constrained devices are involved. In addition, the IoT involves a high number of interconnected devices that arise the requirements of a scalable security and privacy mechanisms for this system.

This chapter presents an overview of the different security issues and threats in the context of the IoT. The author also analyzes the most relevant security strategies available in the literature related to the IoT security. The rest of this chapter is organized as follows. Section 2 provides a brief explanation on why security and privacy are required in the IoT. Following this, a brief description of the related research on privacy, authentication, data confidentiality, access control, trust and non-repudiation are discussed in Section 3. Next, a taxonomy of threats mitigation in different plane of IoT such as device plane, gateway plane and service plane are provided in Section 4. Then, Section 5 provides some security analyses of the standard IoT-related protocols. After that, research challenges and future works in the direction of IoT security are presented in Section 6. Finally, the chapter concludes.

2. SECURITY AND PRIVACY REQUIREMENTS IN THE INTERNET OF THINGS

With rapid the deployment of the IoT for different applications such as smart cities, smart home, it is expected to have innovative user experiences through strong connectivity with the smart objects spreading around the system, and also a very significant impact on human life for completing the daily activities (Vermesan, 2011). Smart objects of the IoT generate and exchange very large amounts of sensitive data which make them prone to different kinds of cyber-attacks. Cyber-attacks on IoT are very fundamental security and privacy issues since it may cause physical damage to the different components of the system as well as poses threats to human lives. In order to ensure safe and correct operation of the IoT, it is very important to assure the security and privacy requirements of the system (Roman, 2011). Figure 1 illustrates different security requirements for reliable and robust IoT.

In order to devise security and privacy solution for the IoT, there are numerous requirements such as confidentiality, data integrity, availability, anonymity, non-repudiation, freshness, authentication, authorization, and end-device functional security need to be fulfilled. These requirements can be classified into four categories such as *information security*, *access-level security* and *functional security* that are briefly described in the following sub-section.

Figure 1. Different security services required in IoT

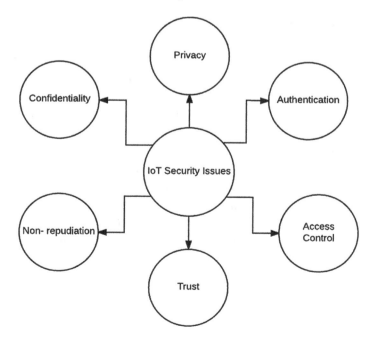

93

2.1. Information Security

To meet information security requirement, IoT needs to assure the following six security services.

1. **Confidentiality:** It assures that communicated data is not revealed to malicious or unauthorized users or devices during any interactions between them. The main goal of confidentiality is to prevent unauthorized access and allow only authorized access to the information exchanged between IoT devices. This requirement can be achieved with the application of any symmetric key cryptography. Since IoT devices have limited resources such as energy, processing power etc., light-weight ciphers and key management schemes should be adopted, taking into consideration of limited memory as well as taking care of other features of IoT architecture and communication mechanism.

2. **Data Integrity:** This service ensures that received data has not been modified on the transmission way. In the IoT, protection of the data during wireless transmission should be strictly protected against malicious attackers. In order to fulfill this security requirement, an IoT network must have security features to prevent the disclosure of the sensed data of devices to its neighbors. It assures that an unauthorized user or device cannot modify data in the transaction. This service is usually realized by computing a signature on the data under transmission, by using the asymmetric private key associated to the sender device. Data integrity signature is prepared by the sender and sent to the receiver as appended to the data packet. After successful verification of the received signature by means of the sender's public key, the receiver confirms that data was sent by the authorized user or devices in the IoT. This requirement can also be fulfilled by Message Authentication Code (MAC) computed by means of symmetric key material commonly shared between sender and receiver and appended to the sent data packet. In IoT, symmetric cryptography is employed for signature creation because it requires less computing and memory resources compared to the asymmetric cryptography.

3. **Availability:** It assures that an authorized user or device can have timely and uninterrupted information and service access to the system. The main goal of availability is to provide access to all the available services whenever it is required by users. There are various types of attacks against service availability, such as Denial-of-Service (DoS), jamming and spreading of malware in the system. Availability of the IoT services can easily be compromised by an attacker that can send a series of constant queries to a device to force it to reply. This causes the node to drain its energy untimely. Research is needed to solve these issues and counteract these attacks effectively and efficiently.

4. **Anonymity:** It assures that source of the data is hidden, by providing location privacy of the devices and data source. Data confidentiality and privacy services help in achieving anonymity requirement in the IoT. Assuring the anonymity of information sources is vital in order to more generally enforce information security. In the context of the IoT, more research is required to devise a lightweight and efficient solution for this purpose.

5. **Non-Repudiation:** The assurance that IoT devices cannot deny to have sent previously transmitted amounts of data.

6. **Freshness:** The assurance that no old information received at a recipient side has been replayed. This service guarantee the freshness of each message received at the receiving side and also prevent replay attack.

2.2. Access-Level Security

In order to ensure access level security requirement, IoT needs to fulfill following two security requirements:

1. **Authentication:** This security service ensures to verify the identity of the peer devices with which it exchanges information. This also guarantees that only legal user can get access to the devices. In most of the IoT applications, it is significant to authenticate the devices involved in device-to-device communication. For authentication of resource constrained devices, more research are required in the field of light-weight authentication protocol using contextual information such as RFID tags, NFC (near field communication) tags, and location information of device.

2. **Authorizations:** This service ensures that only authorized IoT nodes and its users are allowed to access the network services (Jing, 2014; Rodrigo, 2013). It is a very challenging service especially how to provide access permission in the IoT where not only things but also users are allowed to interact with it and also how to identify these smart devices of IoT.

2.3. End-Device Security

There are three facets of security weakness of an IoT node such as storage, software and firmware security (Jing, 2014). Data generated by the IoT nodes are placed in the memory equipped with the device as well as in the Cloud. However, security keys are generally kept within the device. Consequently, poor physical security of a device makes it susceptible to keys theft security risks. Therefore, it is very easy for the attacker to compromise the device and performing an insider-attack to the entire network. In addition, secure updates of the preinstalled software and firmware are also required in order to mitigate the device conciliation by the attackers. Software and firmware updates should be distributed and installed in a secure way, so that an attacker is not able to know the configuration settings of updated software and firmware exposed during the updating process.

2.4. Functional Security

In order to ensure functional security services, IoT needs to assure availability, self-organization, resiliency and exception handling requirements (Qazi, 2015). Availability ensures that despite DoS attacks, services of the IoT will be provided to its users (Sicari,2015; Zheng, 2014). To realize this, an automatic repairing scheme should be incorporated to bring the best possible functionality to its users.

3. OVERVIEW OF RELATED RESEARCH

As mentioned earlier, the IoT can be realized as a network of heterogeneous devices and these networks require different set of security services. In this section, a briefly discussion on the different security mechanisms for IoT and a summary of defense strategies are discussed.

3.1. Privacy

For the various application domains that are going to be offered by the IoT, privacy of the user's personal information such as their interactions with other people, movements and habits must be guaranteed. There are various solutions discussed in the literature to tackle the privacy issues in the IoT.

In (Wang, 2011), Wang *et al.* present an analysis of the privacy issues of a IoT system. The authors provide different protection schemes for the enhancement of Domain Name System (DNS) of a IoT system. The proposed mechanism is intended to authenticate legitimate users and prevent unauthorized accesses to the IoT smart devices. Yang *et al.* (Yang, 2011) have given a privacy mechanism for IoT in which they have discussed *Discretionary Access* and *Limited Access*. In (Huang, 2012), a user-controlled, context-aware k-anonymity privacy policy based access control scheme is discussed. In this scheme, a privacy protection mechanism is given for the users. In (Cao, 2011), Cao *et al.* has discussed a cluster based protocol for privacy preserving. In addition, this protocol also provides anonymity and freshness.

In order to provide privacy mechanism in the IoT, Wang *et al.* (Wang, 2014) have studied two types of encryption scheme which is based on attribute. The proposed scheme is a public key encryption scheme which provides different services such as access control, key management, and for secure data distribution. Like (Wang, 2014), Su *et al.* in (Su, 2014) also discussed an attribute-based mechanism for privacy protection in the IoT system. Ukil *et al.* (Ukil, 2014) have proposed a Privacy Preserving Data Mining (PPDM) scheme with objective to minimize data disclosure probability. This method provides a unique mechanism to a user to calculate approximately the risk of data sharing. In (Sicari, 2014), authors have discussed a layered architecture for IoT and provide a detailed discussion on quality of sensed data and its security and privacy issues. In addition, they also discussed how to integrate different data sources in the IoT system while fulfilling the privacy requirement.

3.2. Authentication and Confidentiality

In order to fulfill the demand of IoT applications, a secure interaction among different smart entities of the IoT ecosystem is required. To realize this, authentication and confidentiality play a very significant role. This section presents a concise summary of the latest research works.

Kothmayr *et al.* (Kothmayr, 2013) have discussed two-way authentication scheme for providing the authentication services in the IoT system. This scheme employed RSA algorithm and the DTLS (Modadugu, 2015) protocol for designing the authentication services for low-power IoT devises (Shelby, 2011). Proposed scheme supports different security requirements such as data integrity, confidentiality, and authenticity. In (Roman, 2012), Roman *et al.* discussed the limitation of the existing key management scheme in the context of IoT and provides different suggestions for the design of key management system for the IoT system. A similar work is also discussed in (Pranata, 2012).

Wu *et. al.* (Wu & Zhou, 2011) have proposed a signature-encryption method with aims to provide security services such as anonymity, trustworthy and attack-resistance. This method utilizes the concept of the Object Naming Service (ONS). In this method, Root-ONS is applied for the verification of Local ONS servers (L-ONS) creditability and for providing the authentication service to the devices. In order to prevent the illegal ONS, an anonymous authentication mechanism is also discussed in (Wu & Zhou, 2011). Lee et al. (Lee,Lin&Huang, 2014) have proposed an authentication scheme for low-power IoT devices in which XOR operations are used for encryption. Like (Lee, Lin & Huang, 2014), the authors in (Ye, Zhu& Wang, 2014) also used XOR manipulation based encryption method for formulating the authentication services. Similarly, an authentication and access control scheme with a goal to establish session keys through Elliptic Curve Cryptography (ECC) is proposed in (Ye, Zhu& Wang, 2014). In this scheme, an attribute-based access control policies are devised which is managed by an attribute authority. This scheme enhances mutual authentication among users and IoT units, as well as solving the resource-constrained issues such as storage and computing requirements. For IoT application, this scheme requires major medications to make it compatible to standard protocols designed for authentication.

3.3. Access Control

In the IoT, there are generally two types of role for the IoT actors: either data holders or data collectors. In order to provide secure and safe functionality of the IoT, Users and things that are used as data collectors, must be able to verify the identity of the users and things as genuine data holders, from which they receive data. In the IoT, sometimes data streams are collected and devising an adequate access control mechanism is a computational-intensive task. Several research works have addressed this issue in the literature.

Ma *et al.* (Ma, Guo & Xiong, 2013) presents a hierarchical access control scheme at the data acquisition layer. This scheme uses only a single key for both user and device and proposed a deterministic key derivation algorithm for deriving the other required keys. In this way, this scheme reduces the storage costs and also increases security, since only a limited number of keys are exchanged. An identity based system is proposed in (Papadopoulos, Yang & Papadias, 2007) for hiding personal locations in emergency situations. In this work, the proposed system verifies the identity of the user through a user authentication subsystem. Policy subsystem provides the emergency level and makes it possible to assure that only authorized users can access their location information, and only in emergency situations. In (Papadopoulos, Yang & Papadias, 2010), Papadopoulos *et al.* proposed an authentication approach on the outsourced data streaming process of a IoT system. In (Bao & Chen, 2012), the authors have discussed a continuous authentication service for data streaming generated in IoT system. In these approaches, information provided by the owner of the source data is used to verify the authenticity of the received data streams.

3.4. Trust

The concept of Trust in the IoT can be defined with respect to confidence on the integrity, reliability, ability, dependability and other characteristics of an IoT entity (Zheng, Zhang & Vasilakos, 2014). In order to formulate the level of trust of a thing in the IoT, the reputation of that thing is used as derived from the direct or indirect knowledge on the previous interactions of the smart things. To manage the trust of an entity, there should be a trust management module which helps users to overcome the perceptions of uncertainty and risk (Sicari, 2015; Zheng, 2014).

Usually, IoT environments embrace three planes: an application plane, a network plane, and a physical perception plane. In the IoT architecture, each layer is inherently connected with other layers through cyber-physical means. Each plane in the IoT has its own importance in the management of the Trust of an entity. To guarantee of the IoT architecture should be available. In other words, ensuring the trustworthiness of the network plane does not ensure the trust of the whole IoT environment. Generally, two main properties such as subjective and objective properties are used for the computation of the trust of an entity. In the literature (Roman, 2011; Qazi, 2015; Sicari, 2015; Zheng, 2014), the properties that affect the trust of an entity can be classified into two groups as follows:

- Trustor's subjective properties: trustee honesty, benevolence and goodness
- Trustee's objective properties: reputation of a IoT node regarding its earlier cooperation and behaviors.

3.4.1. Design Objective of Trust Management Systems

The main design objective of the trust management system for the IoT is to provide an efficient way to estimate trusted interaction between IoT devices and assist them in decision making for communicate and collaborate with each other. In order to provide an efficient trust management system for the IoT, the following different type of trusts (Zheng, 2014) need to be considered for adoption.

1. **Data Transmission and Communication Trust:** One of the IoT requirements is to provide secure transmission and exchanged of data packet. This trust is very useful in the context of the IoT networking and communication protocols. The main objective of this type of trust is to provide trusted path selection and key management service in the IoT infrastructure (Zheng, 2014).
2. **Data Perception Trust:** To ensure the trustworthy sensing and data gathering services in the IoT, reliable data sensing and transmission is required (Zheng, 2014). A trust management system must be focus on objective properties such as sensor reliability, sensibility, persistence, preciseness, security, and data collection efficiency in the physical perception plane of the IoT.
3. **Data Fusion and Mining Trust:** Evaluation of data fusion and mining trust is done at IoT network plane (Zheng, 2014). The requirement of the data fusion and mining trust in the IoT is motivated by the fact that a huge amount of data is collected and should be reliably handled. This trust helps when mining user's queries in trusted social computing.

4. **Identity Trust:** An IoT device's identifier need to be well managed in order to provide trustworthy services (Zheng, 2014). For this purpose, an efficient and scalable solution is required for identity management in the IoT. Identity trust belongs to the objective properties of IoT.

5. **Human–Computer Interaction Trust:** The main focus of this trust is to satisfy the subjective properties of IoT users at the application layer. By relying on this trust, a trust management system can provide a very significant support at the application layer of the IoT as well as usability in a trustworthy way (Zheng, 2014).

6. **Trust Relationship and Decision:** One of the fundamental objectives of a comprehensive trust management system is to provide a valuable approach to estimate trust associations of IoT entities (Zheng, 2014). This trust helps in making a judicious choice to communicate and collaborate with IoT entity. It belongs to all IoT planes.

7. **System Security and Robustness:** In order to provide sufficient confidence of IoT services to final users, the IoT should be enough equipped to counter multiple types of attack. The main goal of this objective is to satisfy system security and dependability, which are the objective properties of trustees (Zheng, 2014).

3.4.2. Trust Management Systems

In (Bao&Chen, 2012), Bao *et al.* proposed a distributed trust management system for the IoT. In this work, any two nodes that involved in a mutual interactions or keep in contact with each other can evaluate direct trust of each other and exchange direct trust of other nodes too. They can also evaluate indirect trust which is act as a second opinion of the peer nodes about the common peer nodes. The proposed trust management system used three main parameters for evaluation of trust, namely honesty, cooperativeness, and community-interest.

In (Nitti, Girau& Atzori, 2012), social networking concepts are utilized to design a reputation-based trust mechanism. The main motivation of this work relies on the fact that things fit in to the IoT infrastructure are competent enough to establish social bond with its owners autonomously. Mahalle *et al.* (Mahalle, Thakre & Prasad, 2013) have proposed a Fuzzy approach based Trust management system. In this scheme, trust is determined by using dynamics like suggestion, facts and experience. These trust values are mapped to authorizations and access request that are further used as a set of credentials for possibly allowing users or things to access IoT services. FTBAC framework considers three layers for the evaluation of the trust: *Access Control Layer, Device Layer, and Request Layer*. At the request layer, collection of recommendation information and evaluation of fuzzy trust was done. At access control layer, it records the fuzzy trust value with the access privilege and go-aheads in order to take decisions. This framework claims to guarantee energy efficient, flexibility and scalability.

In (Saied, 2013), a trust model is proposed in which IoT devices are able to evaluate each other's trust level according to their past behaviors. The main point of this work is to offer cooperation in a heterogeneous IoT considering the different nodes competence by utilizing a distributed approach. This scheme considers both direct and indirect information to update the final trust value. Dong *et al.* (Dong, Guan & Xue, 2012) have presented an attack-defiant trust management model. Trust relations among self-organized nodes are used for reliable routing of data packets in IoT and to avoid malicious nodes from participating in the routing process. In (Gu & Wang, 2014), a trust model is proposed for layered IoT architectures where a specific trust management mechanism is employed for providing the trustworthy services such as self-organization message exchange at each layer. The service requester takes the final decision with help of the gathered trust values as well as requester's policies. This trust model uses a novel semantics-based, fuzzy set theory for calculation of trust value. Another trust management system is proposed in (Liu, Gong & Feng, 2014) where a device behavior detection approach is employed. This system used evidence combination and Bayes algorithm for evaluation of the trust value.

3.5. Non-Repudiation Security Services

The main goal of non-repudiation is to provide a trusted audit trail. That is, a system can present a testimony of who has sent a data packet, has received a data packet.

In (Fagen, Zheng & Jin, 2016), Fagen Li *et al.* proposed a secure and efficient data transmission mechanism for providing non-repudiation security in the IoT. In particular, it considers a heterogeneous ring signcryption scheme that relies on identity-based cryptography for the encryption of data to be transmitted to server units. This method is protected against adaptive chosen cipher text attacks. In a single logical step, the proposed scheme achieves non-repudiation, confidentiality, integrity, authentication and anonymity. In (Ray, Chowdhury & Abawajy, 2016), the authors discussed a secure object tracking method for RFID based IoT devices. In order to provide non-repudiation security services, a frivolous cryptographic mechanism and Physically Unclonable Function (PUF) are employed in the tags. The main goal of this protocol is to protect RFID tags from being cloned, so ensuring accountability of the actions performed in the system.

4. SECURITY THREATS IN THE INTERNET OF THINGS

Basic necessity for the IoT is to be self-aware about security concern with help of a standard security model, due to its close association with the physical world. Security threats in the IoT can be classified in terms of target planes such as Device plane, Gateway and Network plane and Service plane [6] at which an attacker try to utilized it to perform different kinds of attacks. Figure 2 illustrates taxonomy of security threats in the IoT which will be discussed in this section with aim to classify possible vulnerabilities and their mitigation techniques.

4.1. Security Threats at Device Layer

In the IoT, different kind of heterogeneous IoT devices are involved and theses devices have limited resources due to their low cost and small size. In order to fully realize safe and secure IoT services, security mechanism must be designed and built into the devices themselves. For this purpose, each IoT device need to maintain its identity in order to prove device authentication and for signing and encryption of the observed data to maintain the data integrity and privacy. There are various kind of threats related to the device layer in the IoT such as device identity theft, unauthorized access, data leakage, device tempering, and deactivation attack that are explained in the context of the IoT as follow.

Figure 2. A taxonomy of Security threats in IoT

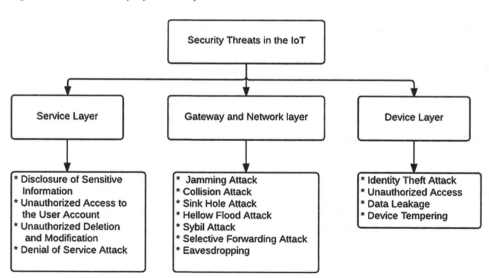

- **Identity Theft Attack:** Due to resource constrained nature and different capability and category of IoT devices, IoT device is vulnerable to this type of threat. An attacker can easily pretend to be a legitimate device and try to compromise the IoT device in order to steal its identity. In order to prevent this type of attack, physical security of the IoT device must be considered to build temper resistance devices so that it is difficult to extract confidential information such as identity, location and cryptography keys.
- **Unauthorized Access:** In this type of threat, an attacker or a legitimate user try to access the IoT devices whose access are not permitted to him. This type of threat may come under external or internal attack category. The security model for IoT devices must be firm enough to prevent unauthorized device access and also be flexible enough to support ad hoc secure interactions with people and other devices on a temporary basis.
- **Data Leakage:** Due to poor physical security, low cost, and small size of the IoT device, it is very much susceptible to intrusion, to access the both credential keys and sensor data. This type of threat can be internal or external, authorized or malicious.
- **Tampering Attack:** In this type of attack, an attacker tries to compromise the IoT devices by physically capturing it from the IoT network and collecting all information (Qazi, 2015). An attacker reprograms the compromised device and redeploys it in the field to attack the IoT network. The main goal of this type of attack is to perform an attack on confidentiality and availability of the IoT network. Tampering is belonging to the low threat category and it requires highly sophisticated techniques to be counteracted.
- **Deactivation Attack:** In this type of attack, an attacker tries to access the interface of the IoT device to shutdown or corrupt it. Its main purpose is to stop the functionality of the consistent IoT segments (Roman, 2011; Qazi, 2015). It is a highly impactful attack and cannot be detected by any software methods. The only method to protect the IoT device from outdoor manipulation is to enfold it in a protective case.

4.2. Security Threats at Gateway and Network Layer

The main role of this layer is to make available connectivity and data communication services between smart things and cloud services. Data communication in the IoT usually takes place through public or private network that are susceptible to various kind of security threats, described as follows in the context of the IoT.

- **Jamming Attack:** IoT network is highly vulnerable to the jamming based attack, as a result of the deployments of the IoT devices over an inaccessible area. This type of threat comes under a physical layer attack in which noise signals are used for creating disturbance in the transmission of legitimate signals. In order to mitigate jamming attacks, different types of mitigation methods are discussed in the literatures. One of the well-liked schemes presented by Liu *et al.* (Liu, Keranidis & Mehari, 2013) for the mitigation of jamming attacks is the monitoring of Received Signal Strength Indicator values and the analysis of the transmission range of the nodes (Liu, Keranidis & Mehari, 2013). There are some other schemes such as neutralization of the jammer signals by cancellation (Shoreh, 2014), and switching the usage of available signal spectrum (Kang, Li, Yu & Kim, 2013).

- **Collision Attack:** Collision attacks occur as results of synchronization problem during transmission (Qazi,2015). In collision attacks, an attacker overhears the channel and anticipates the message transmission time. After that, they transmit a packet when a genuine packet is sent, which causes packet collision at the communication channel (Qazi, 2015).

- **Sinkhole:** In this attack, an attacker targets a central node and compromises in order to drop packets it receives, which leads to loss of availability. This results in traffic disruption and even a kind of DoS attack. In the literature, many solutions have been proposed to mitigate it. For instance, Krontiris *et al.* (Krontiris, 2008) have discussed an intrusion detection system to detect sinkhole attacks. They incorporated the proposed mechanism in the MintRoute protocol and explained its performance in different scenario. A similar work is described by Choi *et al.* in (Choi, Cho, Kim & Hong, 2009) for the detection sinkhole attacks using link quality indicator (LQI).

- **HELLO Flood Attack:** Sometimes in an IoT network, devices are required to broadcast hello packet for neighboring discovery (Singh, Jain & Singhai, 2010). A device which received such hello packets, may presume that source of packet is in its communication range and try to use it as a relay node for forwarding of its packet towards base station. In the HELLO Flood attack, an attacker equipped with a high transmission range device could influence other IoT devices that an attacker device is located in its neighborhood. This will persuade the distant nodes to transmit its packet to the attacker node which will be vanished in the network. It is a low impact attack which aims to disrupt the availability of the IoT services. In the literature, various solutions have been proposed for mitigation of HELLO Flood attacks. In (Singh, Jain & Singhai, 2010), Singh *et al.* present an acknowledgment based solution against it. Instead, Koh *et al.* (Koh, Ming & Niyoto, 2013)[19] proposed the use of authentication and puzzle scheme for the mitigation of the HELLO Flood attacks.

- **Sybil Attack:** In Sybil attack, an attacker introduces a single device with multiple identities in the IoT network to gain an unreasonably large influence with the network. The main goal of the Sybil attack is to remove the entries of the all legitimate neighbors from the routing table of active IoT devices. Lin et al. (Lin, 2013) have discussed a Local Sybil Resistance (LSR) scheme for detecting the Sybil attacks for vehicular area networks. However, Zhou et al. (Zhou & Chao, 2011) has given a distributed, workload and passive overhearing scheme for detecting Sybil attack in the vehicular networks. In (Abbas & Merabti, 2013), Abbas et al. has proposed a lightweight scheme which detects the Sybil attack by using a set of rules for the value of RSSI for the new devices that attempt to join the IoT network.

- **Selective Forwarding Attack:** It is also called gray hole attack where a set of malicious IoT devices refuses to cooperate to forward some packets from its neighboring nodes and instead drops them. The main goal of the gray hole attack is to compromise confidentiality and availability by introducing some delay and bandwidth degradation in the IoT network. In order to detect the gray hole attack, redundancy checks, packet based detection and probing are the possible mechanisms to adopt. In (Deng, Sun,Wang & Cao, 2008), Deng et al. has proposed a scheme for detection and recovery of the network in which watermarking scheme is used for packet transmission in order to keep track of the forwarding path in the network. However, in (Shila & Anjali, 2008), Shila et al. maintains statistics of packet sequence number to detect selective forwarding attack. Kim et al. (Kim & Lee, 2008) presents an acknowledgement based detection scheme which does not require time synchronization. Instead, in (Pandarinath, 2011), Pandarinath et al. propose a novel scheme in which packets are fragmented into a large number of smaller size packets and forwarded them along the specific routing paths.

- **Eavesdropping Attack:** This type of attacks is a prerequisite for many other types of attacks and generally sender and receiver are not known the presence of this attack. In the IoT, IoT devices are extremely prone to eavesdropping due to unattended deployment. This attack is either passive or active. In passive, an attacker tries to detect traffic by overhearing the channel and take out some critical information such as pattern of communication traffic. However, in active eavesdropping, an attacker sends some query packet to initiate a particular action and observe the responses from the recipient (Qazi, 2015).

4.3. Security Threats at Service Layer

The main responsibility of this layer is to provide services such as data processing, storage and management for the individual things, data aggregation and analysis, role based access control to manage user and device identity, enforcing policies and rules services, and auditing of the users. There are various kind of threats related to this layer such as disclosure of sensitive information, unauthorized access to user account, unauthorized deletion and modification, and DoS attacks that are briefly described as follows in the context of the IoT.

1. **Disclosure of Sensitive Data:** The threat of sensitive data disclosure arises due to the multitenancy and data remanence characteristic of the cloud platform which generally provide services to cloud-enabled IoT. Protection of sensitive data such as user's account information, location of the data source, credential of keys etc. is paramount in the cloud-enabled IoT. The threat of sensitive data disclosure increases due to the increased numbers of heterogeneous devices, users and applications that causes to increase in the number of access point. This types of threat increases the risk of confidentiality and privacy breaches.

2. **Unauthorized Access to User Account:** In this type of threat, a malicious user tries to breach the user authentication and privacy to get access of user accounts. Generally, protection of the sensitive information in the cloud-enabled IoT is correlated to the user authentication process. In cloud-enabled IoT, lack of strong authentication can show the ways to unauthorized access to user account at the service layer. Through the exploitation of the weak identification or application vulnerability, an unauthorized access to the user account information may possible in the IoT.

3. **Unauthorized Deletion and Modification:** The main goal of this threat is to compromise data integrity in order to perform unauthorized deletion or modification of the data. By preventing unauthorized access to the information managed at service layer, a greater confidence in system integrity can be achieved. Through the provisioning of strong authorization and accountability mechanism, a greater level of visibility may be possible to determine who or what may have altered information managed at the service layer.

4. **DoS Attack:** This attack tries to prevent the availability of IoT services to its users. Availability refers to services offered by the IoT, being available to authorized users upon the request. A robust mechanism can be implemented at the service layer in order to prevent DoS attacks from interfering with provisioning of IoT services to legitimate users.

5. SECURITY ANALYSIS OF IOT-RELATED STANDARD PROTOCOLS

This section presents the security analysis of the IoT-related standard protocols such as 6LoWPAN (Shelby & Bormann, 2011), RPL (Wallgren & Raza, 2013) and CoAP (Rahman & Shah, 2016).

5.1. Security Analysis of 6LoWPAN

6LoWPAN (Shelby & Bormann, 2011) is a protocol stack whose main works is to provide seamless integration between Zigbee-based WSNs and Internet. Security at the 6LoWPAN extensively depends on the security provisioning mechanism of 802.15.4 sublayer. 6LoWPAN does not provide any kind of security mechanisms. Due to this reason, it suffers from different kind of attacks such as fragment repetition attack and buffer reservation attack (Hummen & Rene, 2013).

In the fragment duplication attack, a receiver IoT device is not able to validate a fragment at the 6LoWPAN layer if it receives from the same IoT device as it received previously. Since 6LoWPAN layer does not provide authentication services which causes spoofing attacks at this layer. In order to avert this attack, Hummen *et al.* (Hummen & Rene, 2013) have proposed lightweight schemes, called content chaining scheme. This scheme inserts an authentication token within each fragment which helps to verify the fragments at the receiver end. This method discards carbon copy fragments at this layer (Hummen & Rene, 2013).

In buffer reservation attack, an attacker tries to attack in the memory unit of the IoT device. Generally, an attacker exploits the verity of a fragmented packet. Due to this reason, a IoT device maintains buffer space for the packet reassembly task. If the reassembly buffer is already occupied, other received fragment are plunged at the receiver. This attack allows blocking of the reassembly buffer space of the victim node. To mitigate the packet buffer attack, split buffer approach is proposed in (Hummen & Rene, 2013).

5.2. Security Analysis of RPL

The IPv6 Routing Protocol for Low-Power and Lossy Networks (RPL) (Wallgren & Raza, 2013;Tsas, 2014; Mayzaud, 2014; Thubert, 2012) is a standard routing protocol, designed for routing of packet in the IoT network. In RPL, a destination-oriented directed acyclic graph (DODAG) between the nodes is formed. This protocol supports unidirectional traffic form 6LoWPAN devices to a DODAG root. 6LoWPAN devices can perform bidirectional communication. In (Thubert, 2012), the present specification of RPL is discussed and different control messages are presented to provide a secure version of RPL. The current version of RPL supports confidentiality, integrity, delay and replay protection for the routing messages.

In the present specification (Thubert, 2012), RPL adopts cryptographic mechanism such as AES/CCM to support security. Although the present RPL specification (Thubert, 2012) does not address how these security mechanisms may be implemented. The present version of RPL suggested mechanism to pre-configure the required key and offers security against external attacks only. The present version of RPL (Thubert, 2012) protocol does not support security mechanism for some significant functions such as secure bootstrapping, security against internal attacks, key dissemination and management.

5.3. Security Analysis of CoAP

The Constrained Application Protocol (CoAP) (Rahman & Shah, 2016) provides a set of methods to constrict metadata without conciliation of the application inter-operability. Generally, messages at the CoAP protocol are forwarded using unreliable UDP protocol. So a lightweight and reliable scheme is needed for secure transportation of the application layer packet. To provide secure transportation, CoAP uses DTLS (Modadugu & Rescorla, 2015) protocol. The present version of CoAP functions in three security modes: PreSharedKey, RawPublicKey and Certificates modes. These security modes utilize mechanism provided in DTLS and offers confidentiality, data authenticity, data integrity and non-repudiation to CoAP messages. However, it does not provide any mechanism for how to handle authentication and key negotiation.

6. RESEARCH CHALLENGES AND FUTURE WORKS

Many innovative solutions have been considered to develop the security and privacy mechanisms for the IoT. However, there are still some open research problems that require to be addressed.

1. There is an extensive research space to design privacy policies with a focus on a well-defined privacy model which can be able to handle the scalability and the dynamic environment of the heterogeneous IoT.
2. In literature, issues related to authentication and confidentiality are only partially addressed. This is due to fact that they only focus on the problem of lightweight ciphering scheme for ubiquitous environments. There is still research space for defining a standard protocol for authentication and unambiguous rules for authorities to ensure confidentiality services in the IoT.

3. There is an widespread open issue in the area of access control where a set of problems need to be solved to guarantee access control services such as: 1) How to assure permission for access control in an IoT environment where IoT devices as well as its users could be authorized to interact with the IoT ? 2) How to effectively exploit the distributed or a semi-distributed approach to effectively supervise functionalities of scalable IoT architectures?

4. There is still deficiency in the existing trust management systems that do not incorporate all available objectives. Earlier attempts only consider data transmission, perception, fusion, and mining trust. However, human–computer interaction trust, relationship and decision trust and system security and robustness trust need to be incorporated in future trust models.

5. Previous solutions for data perception trust are computationally complex and heavyweight. There is a need to define lightweight security and trust mechanisms that can run on small and resource constrained IoT devices. In addition, cross layer mechanisms must be considered for planning the trust model for heterogeneous IoT.

6. Previous research works with regard to the privacy preservation trust in the IoT are not complete. There is a need to focus on the cross-layer solutions for the developments of integrated and synchronized privacy preservation mechanisms in each layer of heterogeneous IoT. In addition, integration of data transmission and communication trust with other trust properties has not been explored in the literature. This also will be a future research challenge for realizing comprehensive Trust objectives.

7. CONCLUSION

This chapter has focused on the requirements of the security and privacy services and its various challenges for IoT ecosystem. In this book chapter, first a brief overview of security and privacy requirements for the IoT system is presented. Next, security threats at the different planes of IoT architectures are discussed. A detail discussion of the typical defense strategies proposed in the literature is discussed with their merits and demerits. Taxonomy of security threats is also explained in the context of IoT. Security analysis of the IoT-related standard protocols such as 6LoWPAN, RPL and CoAP is also discussed and presents a brief overview of the solution provided by different researchers in the literature. Finally, this chapter suggests some open research challenges in order to handle the cross plane secure integration of devices in heterogeneous IoT environments.

REFERENCES

Abbas, S., Merabti, M., Llewellyn-Jones, D., & Kifayat, K. (2013). Lightweight Sybil attack detection in MANETs. *IEEE Systems Journal, 7*(2), 236–248. doi:10.1109/JSYST.2012.2221912

Ashraf, Q. M., & Habaebi, M. H. (2015). Autonomic schemes for threat mitigation in Internet of Things. *Journal of Network and Computer Applications, 49*, 112–127. doi:10.1016/j.jnca.2014.11.011

Bao, F., & Chen, I. (2012). Dynamic trust management for internet of things applications. *Proceedings of the 2012 International Workshop on Self-Aware Internet of Things, Self-IoT '12*, 1–6.

Cao, J., Carminati, B., Ferrari, E., & Tan, K. L. (2011). CASTLE: Continuously anonymizing data streams. *IEEE Transactions on Dependable and Secure Computing, 8*(3), 337–352. doi:10.1109/TDSC.2009.47

Choi, B. G., Cho, E. J., Kim, J. H., Hong, C. S., & Kim, J. H. (2009). A sinkhole attack detection mechanism for LQI based mesh routing in WSN. In *International conference on information networking, ICOIN-2009*. Chiang Mai, Thailand: Institute of Electrical and Electronics Engineers.

Deng, H., Sun, X., Wang B, Cao Y. (2008). Selective forwarding attack detection using watermark in WSNs. *ISECS international colloquium on computing, communication, control and management, CCCM 2009.*

Dong, P., Guan, J., Xue, X., & Wang, H. (2012). Attack-resistant trust management model based on beta function for distributed routing in internet of things. *China Communications, 9*(4), 89–98.

Fagen, Zheng, & Jin. (2016). Secure and efficient data transmission in the internet of things. *Springer Journal of Telecommunication System, 62*(1), 111–122.

Gu, L., Wang, J., & Sun, B. (2014). Trust management mechanism for internet of things. *China Communications, 11*(2), 148–156. doi:10.1109/CC.2014.6821746

Huang, X., Fu, R., Chen, B., Zhang, T., & Roscoe, A. (2012). User interactive internet of things privacy preserved access control. *Proceedings of 7th International Conference for Internet Technology and Secured Transactions, ICITST 2012*, 597–602.

Hummen, R. (2013). 6LoWPAN fragmentation attacks and mitigation mechanisms. In *Proceedings of the sixth ACM conference on Security and privacy in wireless and mobile networks*. ACM.

Jing, Q., Vasilakos, A. V., Wan, J., Lu, J., & Qiu, D. (2014). Security of the Internet of Things: Perspectives and challenges. *Wireless Networks*, *20*(8), 2481–2501. doi:10.1007/s11276-014-0761-7

Kang, T., Li, X., Yu, C., & Kim, J. (2013). A survey of security mechanisms with direct sequence spread spectrum signals. *Journal of Computing Science and Engineering*, *7*(3), 187–197. doi:10.5626/JCSE.2013.7.3.187

Kim, Y. K., Lee, H., Cho, K., & Lee, D. H. (2008). CADE: Cumulative acknowledgement based detection of selective forwarding attacks in wireless sensor networks. *Proceedings of third international conference on convergence and hybrid information technology, ICCIT 2008.*

Koh, J. Y., Ming, J. T. C., & Niyato, D. (2013). Rate limiting client puzzle schemes for denial-of-service mitigation. IEEE wireless communications and networking conference, WCNC-2013.

Kothmayr, T., Schmitt, C., Hu, W., Brunig, M., & Carle, G. (2013). Dtls based security and two-way authentication for the internet of things. *Ad Hoc Networks*, *11*(8), 2710–2723. doi:10.1016/j.adhoc.2013.05.003

Krontiris, I., Dimitriou, T., Giannetsos, T., & Mpasoukos, M. (2008). *Intrusion detection of sinkhole attacks in wireless sensor networks. In Algorithmic aspects of wireless sensor networks* (pp. 150–161). Berlin: Springer. doi:10.1007/978-3-540-77871-4_14

Lee, J.-Y., Lin, W.-C., & Huang, Y.-H. (2014). A lightweight authentication protocol for internet of things. *International Symposium on Next Generation Electronics, ISNE 2014*, 1–2.

Lin, X. (2013). LSR: Mitigating zero-day Sybil vulnerability in privacy-preserving vehicular peer-to-peer networks. *IEEE Journal on Selected Areas in Communications*, *31*(9), 237–246. doi:10.1109/JSAC.2013.SUP.0513021

Liu, W., Keranidis, S., Mehari, M., Vanhie-Van Gerwen, J., Bouckaert, S., Yaron, O., & Moerman, I. (2013). *Various detection techniques and platforms for monitoring interference condition in a wireless testbed. In Measurement methodology and tools* (pp. 43–60). Berlin: Springer.

Liu, Y.-B., Gong, X.-H., & Feng, Y.-F. (2014). Trust system based on node behavior detection in internet of things. *Journal of Communication*, *35*(5), 8–15.

Ma, J., Guo, Y., Ma, J., Xiong, J., & Zhang, T. (2013). A hierarchical access control scheme for perceptual layer of IoT. *Comput. Res. Dev.*, *50*(6), 1267–1275.

Mahalle, P. N., Thakre, P. A., Prasad, N. R., & Prasad, R. (2013). A fuzzy approach to trust based access control in internet of things. *3rd International Conference on Wireless Communications, Vehicular Technology, Information Theory and Aerospace & Electronics Systems*, 1–5.

Mayzaud, A., Sehgal, A., Badonnel, R., Chrisment, I., & Schönwälder, J. (2014). A Study of RPL DODAG Version Attacks. In A. Sperotto, G. Doyen, S. Latré, M. Charalambides, & B. Stiller (Eds.), *Monitoring and Securing Virtualized Networks and Services* (Vol. 8508, pp. 92–104). Springer Berlin Heidelberg. doi:10.1007/978-3-662-43862-6_12

Modadugu, N., & Rescorla, E. (2015). *Datagram Transport Layer Security*. Available online: http://tools.ietf.org/html/rfc4347

Ning, H., & Liu, H. (2012). Cyber-physical-social based security architecture for future internet of things. *Advances in Internet of Things*, *2*(1), 1–7. doi:10.4236/ait.2012.21001

Nitti, M., Girau, R., Atzori, L., Iera, A., & Morabito, G. (2012). A subjective model for trustworthiness evaluation in the social internet of things. *IEEE 23rd International Symposium on Personal Indoor and Mobile Radio Communications*, 18–23.

Pandarinath, P. (2011). Secure localization with defense against selective forwarding attacks in wireless sensor networks. *3rd international conference on electronics computer technology, ICECT 2011*.

Papadopoulos, S., Yang, Y., & Papadias, D. (2007). Cads: continuous authentication on data streams. *33rd International Conference on Very Large Data Bases, VLDB '07*, 135–146.

Papadopoulos, S., Yang, Y., & Papadias, D. (2010). Continuous authentication on relational data streams. *The VLDB Journal*, *19*(1), 161–180. doi:10.1007/s00778-009-0145-2

Pranata, H., Athauda, R., & Skinner, G. (2012). Securing and governing access in ad-hoc networks of internet of things. *Proceedings of the IASTED International Conference on Engineering and Applied Science, EAS 2012*, 84–90. doi:10.2316/P.2012.785-070

Rahman, R. A., & Shah, B. (2016). Security analysis of IoT protocols: A focus in CoAP. *Proceeding of 3rd MEC International Conference on Big Data and Smart City (ICBDSC)*, 1-7.

Ray, Chowdhury, & Abawajy. (2016). Secure Object Tracking Protocol for the Internet of Things. *IEEE Internet of Things Journal.*

Roman, R., Alcaraz, C., Lopez, J., & Sklavos, N. (2011). Key management systems for sensor networks in the context of the internet of things. *Computers & Electrical Engineering*, *37*(2), 147–159. doi:10.1016/j.compeleceng.2011.01.009

Roman, R., Najera, P., & Lopez, J. (2011). Securing the internet of things. *IEEE Computer*, *44*(9), 51–58. doi:10.1109/MC.2011.291

Roman, R., Zhou, J., & Lopez, J. (2013). On the features and challenges of security and privacy in distributed internet of things. *Computer Networks*, *57*(10), 2266–2279. doi:10.1016/j.comnet.2012.12.018

Saied, Y., Olivereau, A., Zeghlache, D., & Laurent, M. (2013). Trust management system design for the internet of things: A context-aware and multi-service approach. *Computers & Security*, *39*, 351–365. doi:10.1016/j.cose.2013.09.001

Shelby & Bormann. (2011). *6LoWPAN: The wireless embedded Internet*. Academic Press.

Shila, D. M., & Anjali, T. (2008). Defending selective forwarding attacks in WMNs. *IEEE international conference on electro/information technology, EIT-2008.*

Shoreh, M., Hosseinianfar, H., Akhoundi, F., Yazdian, E., Farhang, M., & Salehi, J. (2014). Design and implementation of spectrally-encoded spread-time CDMA transceiver. *IEEE Communications Letters*, *18*(5), 741–744. doi:10.1109/LCOMM.2014.033114.132471

Sicari, S., Cappiello, C., Pellegrini, F. D., Miorandi, D., & Coen-Porisini, A. (2014). A security-and quality-aware system architecture for internet of things. *Information Systems Frontiers*, 1–13.

Sicari, S., Rizzardi, A., Grieco, L. A., & Coen-Porisini, A. (2015). Security, privacy and trust in Internet of Things: The road ahead. *Computer Networks*, *76*, 146–164. doi:10.1016/j.comnet.2014.11.008

Singh, V. P., Jain, S., & Singhai, J. (2010). Hello flood attack and its countermeasures in wireless sensor networks. *International Journal of Computational Science*, *7*(11), 23–27.

Su, J., Cao, D., Zhao, B., Wang, X., & You, I. (2014). ePASS: An expressive attribute-based signature scheme with privacy and an unforgeability guarantee for the internet of things. *Future Generation Computer Systems*, *33*(0), 11–18. doi:10.1016/j.future.2013.10.016

Thubert, P. (2012). *RPL: IPv6 Routing Protocol for Low-Power and Lossy Networks.* RFC 6550.

Tsai, C., Lai, C., & Vasilakos, V. (2014). Future internet of things: Open issues and challenges, ACM/ Springer. *Wireless Networks*, *20*(8), 2201–2217. doi:10.1007/s11276-014-0731-0

Tsao, T., Alexander, R., Dohler, M., Daza, V., Lozano, A., Richardson, M. (2014). *A Security Threat Analysis for the Routing Protocol for Low-Power and Lossy Networks (RPLs).* Academic Press.

Turner, S., & Polk, T. (2011). *Security Challenges For the Internet of Things.* IAB Interconnecting Smart Objects with the Internet Workshop, Prague, Czech Republic.

Ukil, A., Bandyopadhyay, S., & Pal, A. (2014). *IoT-privacy: To be private or not to be private.* Toronto: IEEE INFOCOM.

Vermesan, O., Friess, P., Guillemin, P., Gusmeroli, S., Sundmaeker, H., Bassi, A., & Doody, P. et al. (2011). *Internet of Things Strategic Research Roadmap, Cluster of European Research Projects on the Internet of Things.* CERP-IoT.

Wallgren, L., Raza, S., & Voigt, T. (2013). Routing attacks and countermeasures in the RPL-based internet of things. *International Journal of Distributed Sensor Networks*, *9*(8), 794326. doi:10.1155/2013/794326

Wang, X., Zhang, J., Schooler, E., & Ion, M. (2014). Performance evaluation of attribute-based encryption: Toward data privacy in the IoT. *Proceedings of the IEEE International Conference on Communications*, 725–730.

Wang, Y., & Wen, Q. (2011). A privacy enhanced dns scheme for the internet of things. *IET International Conference on Communication Technology and Application, ICCTA-2011*, 699–702. doi:10.1049/cp.2011.0758

Wu, Z.-Q., Zhou, Y.-W., & Ma, J.-F. (2011). A security transmission model for internet of things. *Chin. J. Comput.*, *34*(8), 1351–1364. doi:10.3724/SP.J.1016.2011.01351

Yan, Z., Zhang, P., & Vasilakos, A. V. (2014). A survey on trust management for Internet of Things. *Journal of Network and Computer Applications*, *42*, 120–134. doi:10.1016/j.jnca.2014.01.014

Yang, J., & Fang, B. (2011). Security model and key technologies for the internet of things. *Journal of China Universities of Posts and Telecommunications*, *8*(2), 109–112. doi:10.1016/S1005-8885(10)60159-8

Ye, N., Zhu, Y., Wang, R.-C., Malekian, R., & Lin, Q.-M. (2014). An efficient authentication and access control scheme for perception layer of internet of things. *Applied Mathematics & Information Sciences*, *8*(4), 1617–1624. doi:10.12785/amis/080416

Zhou, L., & Chao, H. C. (2011). Multimedia traffic security architecture for the Internet of Things. *IEEE Network*, *25*(3), 35–40. doi:10.1109/MNET.2011.5772059

Chapter 6
Examining Current Standards for Cloud Computing and IoT

Yaman Parasher
Gautam Buddha University, India

Deepak Kedia
Guru Jambheshwar University of Science and Technology, India

Prabhjot Singh
Salesforce Inc., USA

ABSTRACT

The advent of Cloud computing has acted as a catalyst for the design and deployment of scalable Internet of Things business models and applications. Therefore, IoT and Cloud are nowadays two very closely affiliated future internet technologies, which go hand in hand in non-trivial IoT deployments. Furthermore, most modern IoT ecosystems are cloud-based, as will be illustrated in the chapter. This chapter briefly introduces the main cloud computing and IoT standards.

1. INTRODUCTION

This chapter will concentrate on the standards that are designed and published by standard bodies known as Standards Defining Organizations. Such associations have a wide variety of inside procedures and membership rules, which go from totally open access to closed formal representation that can now and again require

DOI: 10.4018/978-1-5225-3445-7.ch006

the endorsement of national governments and worldwide planning bodies. The standards that are managed in this part are essentially in light of

Cloud segment here will connote gauges that is by all accounts most develop inside the Infrastructure as a Service (IaaS) and Platform as a Service (PaaS) layers. While Software as a Service (SaaS) principles additionally exist, they have a tendency to be specific to their ranges of utilization, as are not amiable to more than a short general synopsis. On the opposite side, in Internet of Things (IoT) area recent adaptations at different layer of the OSI model is talked about.

This chapter starts with the discussion of the practical definition of standards, types of communities issues, their primary cloud and IoT-related outputs, and their organizing rules for participation. The target of this part is to highlight the fundamental activities that add to the investigation of the present status and elements of the IoT along with Cloud computing standards and to discuss their findings. The main contributors of this analysis of the IoT standards landscape are the ETSI Specialist Task Force (STF), IEEE, IETF, ITU, UNIFY-IoT Coordination and Support Action (CSA), IPSO Alliance, IOTI WG03, Z-Wave Alliance etc.

The Internet of Things (IoT), as a rising innovation, can possibly support advancement in numerous mechanical parts, and in addition to help address numerous societal difficulties including energy efficiency and ageing. In any case, this potential will only materialize if IoT develops as an open platform and support a variety of applications and generate open and sustainable ecosystems. As the new applications and innovations are being done, these standards play a vital role there. There standards are used to monitor their performance. Before moving further, the ideas on customary meaning of standards, with their necessities and points of interest of association capable to place them into the mainstream.

2. EXAMINING AND ROLES OF STANDARDS AND STANDARDIZATION BODIES

Standards are made for overall compatibility of various functions of IoT and Cloud globally. It assist national and global players of research and industries with relevant global Service Setting Organizations and promoting standards around IoT and cloud technologies developed in the country. There are a number of things which needs to get standardize.

- Standardization of IoT
- Protocols standards for spectrum energy communication
- Standards within and outside the cloud for communication
- International integrity standards for data traceability and data creation.

- Energy consumption standards
- Safety and device security standards
- Data Accuracy, data privacy and security standards. The privacy law to be made congruent with the evolving IoT paradigm.

Standardization bodies are the national and international expert committee who develop and suggest to adopt globally interoperable and established IoT standards on the national or international level. The bodies should comprise of experts from the industry and research organizations in following areas:

- To develop standards for IoT architecture and their platform interoperability.
- To develop standards for an open framework of IoT.
- To develop standards for network technology to for self aware and self organizing networks, even Hybridizing of these networking technologies, storage and power networks
- To develop standards for communication technology
- To develop standards for some hardware equipment like ultra low power chipsets, on chip antennas, ultra low power single chip radios and ultra low power system on chip.
- To develop standards for software and algorithms for next generation IoT systems based social software and enterprise applications.
- To develop standards for power and energy storage technologies e.g. energy harvesting and its conversion etc.
- To certify labs by looking at their adaption of standards.
- To provide technical and financial assistance for patenting and standards creation related to IoT technologies.

2.1. Needs of Standardization

The idea behind standardization is to minimize the errors if organizations follow best practices to implement the technology for a particular level of tasks or services (because the techniques, processes and methodologies they're using have been repeatedly tested many time before). Standards debar the one from reinventing the same thing over and over again. hese are the fantastic intends to land at interoperability and consistence. Examining the time taken to make principles, they are frequently all around tried and thoroughly considered. This makes them brilliant apparatuses for acquirement and consistence inside huge partnerships, IT associations and so forth. This is driven by a standard improvement body with objective characterize as takes after

- Development, deployment and quality certification of standard
- Thrust to standardization and quality control
- Evolve a unified strategy for according recognition to standards and integrating them with growth and development of market products.

2.2. Types of Standards in the Market

There isn't just one type of standard available in the market. There are plenty in number of types and one should be acknowledged enough to know the difference between them. Figure 1 represents the types of standards those are relevance to most users in the cloud computing and IoT a market.

3. EXAMINING OF CLOUD COMPUTING STANDARDS

Cloud computing refers to accessing and sharing of information in the internet web space, rather than using our personal computers, hard drives, and local servers. The term 'Cloud' refers to an Internet web space. Cloud computing provides everything as services over the internet. It will allow us to access and manage every service over the internet from anywhere. Cloud Technology is nothing but the combination of Datacenter or multiple Data centers connected by the network with each other to share resources dynamically that comprises computation, Storage, and software. All these resources are virtualized into one big platform intelligently and automatically configured to make easy use of everything as a service. Everyone is moving to Cloud Computing to provide infrastructure as a service, making it more convenient and

Figure 1. Types of standards

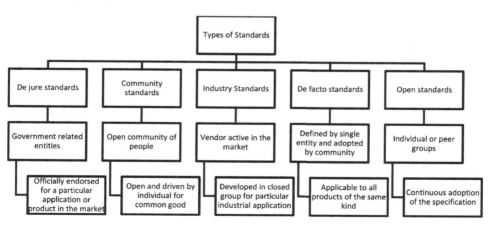

easy to maintain, automate the tasks to provide faster services to the end user. Cloud computing serves more reliable and scalable elastic services to IT Infrastructure. Cloud computing provides everything as services over the internet. It will also allow to access and manage every service over the internet from anywhere. The capabilities and breadth of cloud computing are enormous. The IT industry broke it into three categories like Software as a Service (SaaS), Infrastructure as a Service (IaaS) and Platform as a Service (PaaS) to help better define use cases.

The majority of this is a deviation from conventional on-introduce figuring which is done by means of a neighborhood server or PC. These customary strategies are progressively being abandoned. Truth be told, IDGs as of late distributed Enterprise Cloud Computing Survey (2016) found that by 2018 the run of the mill IT division will have the larger part of their applications and stages (60%) dwelling in the cloud.

3.1. Standardization Bodies in Cloud Ecosystem

There are many organizations defining standards. The organizations that oversee the standards described in this chapter are discussed in the Table 1.

3.2 Individual Standards in IoT Domain

Some of the existing Cloud computing standards and their features are explained in Table 2.

Table 1. Standardization bodies of cloud ecosystem

Standardization Body	Work
Distributed Management Task Force (DMTF)	• To design for enabling interoperable internet technology management functions. • Serves as a steering body behind both Cloud Infrastructure Management Interface and Open Virtualization Format
Organization for the Advancement of Structured Information Standards (OASIS)	• Nonprofit consortia that run the development, adoption and convergence of the open standards. • Produce standards for cloud computing, security, web services, service oriented architectures and other areas • Serves as a steering body behind Cloud Application Management for Platforms Topology (CAMPT) and Orchestration Specification for Cloud Applications (OSCA)
Open Grid Forum (OGF)	• Operates in the area of grid, cloud and other advanced distributed computing systems. • Steering body behind WS-agreement and Open Cloud Computing Interface (OCCI)
Storage Networking Industry Association (SNIA)	• Not for profit global organization responsible for promoting standards, services and technologies to empower management of information in various organizations across the globe. • Serves as a steering body behind Cloud Data Management Interface(CDMI)
Cloud Security Alliance (CSA)	Not for profit organization to provide security in the cloud infrastructure or domain

Table 2. Some existing cloud computing standards with their features

Standards in Cloud Computing	Features
Open Cloud Computing Interface (OCCI)	• A protocol and API for the management of cloud service resources, primarily for IaaS model based services. • Flexible API with a strong focus on portability, integration, innovation and interoperability.
Open Virtualization Format (OVF)	• Open standard which includes necessary virtual machine specification and configuration needed to deploy an application over any virtualization technology according to the customer's choice. • Allow automatic verification of the virtual application using public key infrastructure, enabling a safe distribution of virtual solutions from vendors to the prospective customers.
Cloud Data Management Interface (CDMI)	Standardizes data path and control path for cloud-storage products and services
Cloud Infrastructure Management Interface (CIMI)	Allows management of infrastructure as a service(IaaS),which include management of cloud resources including virtual machines, storage, and network
Cloud Application Management for Platforms (CAMP)	Make application to operate across different platform and cloud services. Its Principal component include YAML and REST API.
Topology and Orchestration Specification for Cloud Applications (TOSCA)	• Define both the service components of distributed application along with the service management interfaces. • Objective is to ensure the semiautomatic creation and management of application layer services, while guaranteeing applications' portability across various cloud implementation platforms.

4. INTERNET OF THINGS

IoT plays a vital role for developing new smart applications. IoT is an advance automatic and analytic system which can exploit the organizing, detecting, enormous information, and artificial intelligence technology to deliver advanced frameworks for an system. These frameworks permit more prominent straightforwardness, control, and execution when connected to any industry or system. IoT systems have applications transversely finished organizations through their stand-out flexibility and ability to be sensible in any condition. They update data amassing, motorization, operations, and significantly more through brilliant gadgets and viable engaging development. IoT covers a huge extent of endeavors and use endeavors that scale from a lone obliged contraption to colossal cross-arrange associations of embedded advances and cloud structures that are being related ceaselessly. Get-together it all together there are different legacy and creating correspondence traditions that allow IoT based devices and servers to banter with each other in new, more interconnected shape. With this regard, numerous unions and coalitions are creating with desires of uniting the broke and common IoT scene for a change in the present market.

4.1. Need of Standards in IoT Domain

Whenever an individual like to bring its IoT based product into the market, he/she needs to follow a set compliance that adhere to the strict regulation proposed by a body or shoould have a specific standard so as to protect their idea or business from being derailed from the mainstream process. Such standard will help them build products that have the potential to harness the vital aspects essential for its existence. But there seems to be a strict need for a set of standards that can help the manufacturers to develop actual business stuff for the IoT market. The adoption of standards will rule out the vulnerabilities in the IoT space and will eventually help us to develop novel products that can do a lot more things effectively and efficiently.

4.2 Standardization Bodies in IoT Ecosystem

With the steady high growth being seen in the IoT deployments and the hype surrounding the IoT marketplace (billions if not trillions of devices and billions of dollars in revenue) in the past few years, there has been a remarkable increase in the number of IoT development associations and standards bodies. Some of which serves as proponents of a certain technology with a primary focus on marketing while others serve as overall advocates and focus on emerging business models. Though others advocate specific standards and aim to provide a standard platform for functions such as testing and certification. While these groups are well intentioned, the initial effect of all of these groups has been to create considerable confusion in the marketplace that brings a number of challenges in the massive deployment of IoT enabled devices around the globe. Collaboration between various standards development groups and consolidation of some of the many current efforts will surely result in greater clarity for IoT technology deployment across the globe.

This section will provide an overview of some of the most influential associations and standards bodies in the area of IoT, that has been able to make a remarkable development of some phenomenal standards for the benefit of mankind as a whole. Table 3 represents the some standardization body for IoT and their work.

Table 3.

Standardization Body for IoT	Work
ITU - International Telecommunications Union	• Provides recommendations for Information and Communications Technologies (ICTs) domain. The Global Standards Initiative on the Internet of Things (IoT-GSI) has been defined in Recommendation ITU-T Y2060 report issued by them in 2012.Contains numerous study group under it. • Recently establish new study group for applications of IoT in smart cities and communities.
Allseen Alliance	• Contains approximately 140 members (as of early 2015) • Created "AllJoyn," an open source framework used in developing of various IoT projects.
IPSO Alliance	• Provides a center that seeks to provide thought leadership in establishing the Internet Protocol (IP) as a basis for connecting Smart Objects in IoT. • Use the IETF CoAP protocol between the devices running Smart Objects and connected applications.
Zigbee Alliance	• Comprises of over 400 members in its association. • Promotes the usage of Z-Wave technology for wireless control and monitoring & interoperability of IoT devices.
OIC - Open Interconnect Consortium	• Objective is to develop specification standards, set of interoperability guidelines, along with provision of certificate for devices involved in the Internet of Things. • Comprises of more than 300 member companies.
ADA - Application Developers Alliance	• Group provides information on IoT projects in the automotive industry, manufacturing, and retail, and it has also investigated the impact of wearable devices and IoT in the home. • Contains a global network of more than 75,000 members.
ISO/IEC JTC/SWG 5	Joint Technical Committee (JTC) of ISO and IEC produced a working group (SWG) that identifies market requirements and standardization gaps in deployment of IoT related activities.
IEC - International Electro technical Commission	Not for profit organization that publish and prepare International Standards for all electronic, electrical and related technologies.
IEEE - Institute of Electrical and Electronics Engineers	Perform an IoT Ecosystem Study and had developed the IEEE P2413 standard for an Internet of Things architectural framework.
Industrial Interconnect Consortium	Comprised of representatives from industry, government and academia working to develop an open framework architecture, standard specifications and security requirements for IoT technologies.
Thread Group	Dedicated to promoting the interoperability of IoT technologies and devices intended for use in the home.

Table 4. Standardization bodies in IoT ecosystem

IoT Standard	Function
IEEE 802.11ah	• A Wi-Fi version for consuming less power. • To work for frequency below 1 GHz so that it can support long range, lower power connectivity to Wi Fi certified products.
Bluetooth Smart	• A low power edition of traditional Bluetooth. • Expected to add a longer range with support for mesh networking capability
Z-Wave	• A low power technology for mesh networking • Operates at the frequency of 908.42 MHz in the US whereas 868.42 MHz in EU and empowers a single mesh network with 232 hubs
ZigBee	Designing for low power devices for home.
6LoWPAN	• Low power devices with restricted preparing capacities are expected to work and play well with IoT frameworks. • Represent IPv6 version of IEEE 802.15.4 for mesh networking.
ULE	Present itself as a low-control rendition of the Digital Enhanced Cordless Telecommunication cordless phone technology.
AllJoyn	Open-source structure in charge of coordinating network and administration layer operations for IoT devices to make interoperable items that can find, interface, and communicate specifically with other adjacent devices, frameworks, and administrations, device type etc.
ITU SG20	Responsible for designing international level standards to empower the planned improvement of IoT innovations, including machine to machine correspondences and universal sensor systems.

5. CONCLUSION

The whole chapter provides a glimpse into the most relevant standards that seems to revolutionaries the whole world in a very short span of time. From healthcare to smart home, all these standards always seems to play a vital role in our life. The chapter provides the examining of standards for Cloud and IoT systems along with their standard bodies.

REFERENCES

Chaouchi, H. (2010). *The Internet of Things – Setting the Standards*. London: Wiley.

San Murugesan & Irena Bojanova. (2005). *Cloud Integration and Standards*. London: Wiley.

Sheng, Z., & Yang, S. (2005). A survey on the IETF Protocol Suite for the Internet of Things: Standards, Challenges and Opportunities. *IEEE Wireless Communications*.

Chapter 7
Examining Different Applications of Cloud–Based IoT

Deepak Kedia
Guru Jambheshwar University of Science and Technology, India

Gurjit Kaur
Gautam Buddha University, India

ABSTRACT

The integration of Cloud computing and IoT provides the capability of omnipresent sensing services and powerful, efficient storage as well as processing of sensor data beyond the capability of distinct things or devices. The ability of Cloud platform in providing automatic and reliable decision making will boost the development of newer and innovative applications, like smart healthcare, cities, buildings, agriculture practices and buildings, etc. This chapter surveys a few key application areas where Cloud-based IoT technology can mark its impact. The Cloud-based architecture has been proposed for these applications, simultaneously examining and identifying the challenges involved. The salient points identified in this chapter will help researchers and scientists to explore newer applications based on the Cloud-IoT platform.

INTRODUCTION

With the development of wireless communication technologies, ubiquitous objects can be interactive and are connected to the Internet. These objects inter-connected through internet with in-built sensing and computing capabilities constitute the Internet of Things (IoT). It is anticipated that by 2020, there will be around 50 billion number of IoT devices while the population will reach 7.6 billion (Hou et al., 2016). A huge amount of data will be generated by these devices having different format

DOI: 10.4018/978-1-5225-3445-7.ch007

and meaning. However, due to small physical size and energy consumption, the IoT devices normally have very limited capabilities. Therefore, a cloud platform for IoT devices is must to support millions of IoT devices and provide various innovative and exciting Cloud IoT applications for the end-users.

The integration of Cloud Computing platform with IoT can enable pervasive sensing, powerful and reliable processing of sensing data and automated decision making beyond the potential of discrete IoT devices, thus motivating novelties in both areas. For an instance, cloud platforms allow the storage of sensed data and this data can be used prudently for intelligent monitoring and actuation with the help of smart things. New set of rules or techniques for data management, and artificial learning can be realized and executed centrally or in distributed manner through cloud platform in order to accomplish automatic and reliable decision making (Sivakumar et al., 2017). The efforts so made will further enhance the development of newer and interesting applications, such as cities with smart infrastructure, agriculture, smart energy distribution, healthcare and smart management of transportation. However, new challenges arise when IoT and cloud platform are integrated. There is a dire need for new and innovative network architectures and protocols that will facilitate seamless integration and big data streaming from IoT to the cloud platform.

Generally the IoT services are being offered as an isolated vertical solution in which all components of the applications are tightly linked to the specific perspective of an application. Integrating IoT services with the Cloud can ease the delivery and the deployment of these services by exploiting all the flexibility of Cloud models. In this context, the Cloud Computing framework facilitates the development of applications from an abstract viewpoint of the IoT systems.

Several solutions have been proposed or suggested to use Cloud architectures to discover sensors and actuators, to enable their connection and to create platforms capable of supporting omnipresent connectivity and various real-time applications for smart cities. Another situation in which Cloud and Internet of Things can integrate with each other to provide improved services is the smart energy management. To provide smart distribution and consumption of energy (Botta, 2016), the data collected from different sensing nodes attached to the network can be divested to a Cloud platform to exploit its computational capabilities for taking comprehensive decisions about the energy usage and distribution. These examples do not cover all aspects where there can be a cooperation between Cloud and IoT but, in these cases, IoT systems can derive many benefits from the unlimited computational capacity of cloud, thus allowing scalability and flexibility in their applications. One can face a situation in which there is peak demand of the resource usage from an IoT system or these resources can be released because the demand is poor. Finally, in each of these cases, the pay-per-use model has an important role in reducing the deployment cost of such infrastructures.

The main objective of this chapter is to explore and investigate key application areas of Cloud based IoT platform. The main applications areas examined in this chapter include smart healthcare, smart cities, smart agriculture and smart buildings. The chapter starts with introduction to hierarchical model of Cloud IoT technology. Then, the application specific Cloud IoT architectures have been discussed along with the key challenges in its implementation for each application area. Finally, the conclusion and references have been presented.

2. HIERARCHICAL ARCHITECTURE OF CLOUD IOT

To overcome the issues that arise from the convergence of IoT and Cloud Computing, a hierarchical architecture consisting of different layers exploiting multiple cloud infrastructures can be an efficient solution. Such architecture allows support to different IoT services and applications deployed on different layers so as to give the right viewpoint and knowledge of the particular domain. The computational capability of a cloud infrastructure close to IoT devices can bring many benefits to the services that have to deal with them. In this architecture as shown in Figure 1, we can identify three major components (Distefano, 2015) that include:

- **The IoT Systems:** This component includes all the physical objects, devices and machines that are capable of connecting to the Internet and produce sensing data or consume services through the network.
- **The Localized or Specialized Middleware Clouds:** The localized or specialized middleware clouds include geographically distributed cloud infrastructures which serve as a connection between the things/devices in the sub-layer and the centralized global cloud. These components can form one of several layers which can provide different aggregations and different levels of abstractions of IoT systems in the sub-layers.

Figure 1. Hierarchical architecture of cloud IoT platform

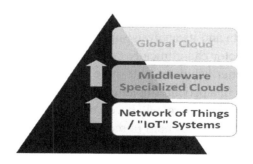

- **The Global Cloud:** This is the highest layer of hierarchical model which provides a global view of all sub-layers. This layer is not associated directly with the physical devices but it influences the middleware clouds as mediators and aggregators.

A few most important applications of Cloud IoT platform are now being investigated in detail in the subsequent sections.

3. CLOUD-BASED IOT FOR HEALTH CARE APPLICATIONS

Smart healthcare is the most attractive application areas for the integrated Cloud IoT platform. The Internet of Things has the capability to support many medical applications like remote health monitoring, knowledge dissemination, chronic diseases, general fitness, children and elderly care. Thus, various medical and imaging devices or sensors being used for diagnostic purposes will have to be intelligent and smart, thus forming a core part of the IoT network (Riazul et al., 2015). Further, the integration of cloud computing with IoT will offer the services of on-demand real time computational resources from mobile devices to supercomputers. Cloud-based IoT platform will further ease the periodic collection and broadcast of health information for guaranteed and distributed location based health services (Milovanovic & Bojkovic, 2017). The various benefits expected to be offered by Cloud IoT based healthcare services include reduced costs, better life quality, and enrichment of end-user's experience. If we look at the cloud IoT services from the viewpoint of healthcare service providers, the integrated platform is capable of monitoring the condition of health devices remotely and timely provisions or arrangements can be made for the smooth and uninterrupted operation of various devices.

The current technological trends suggest that in the near future a patient will be remotely monitored physiologically for 2 to 3 days through wearable sensors or devices prior to actual physical examination by the doctor. When that patient turns up for his actual physical examination, the doctor already has with him the patient's physiological and metabolic state, the effects of prescribed medicines and above all the statistical analysis of entire medical history of the patient under treatment. Using the available data and its analysis supported by decision support system of cloud platform, the doctor can clinically correlate all things and suggest a much better treatment for better health and life-style choices which will be effective in ensuring quality health of a patient. Implementing such a revolutionary technology in healthcare systems at global level will have a transformative impact on the society and its people. Moreover, it will help in reducing the healthcare costs drastically and thus improving the delivery and accuracy of medical diagnoses.

In the last few years, the Cloud IoT in the healthcare field has attracted a lot of attention from researchers worldwide. The researchers are working hard to address the potential of this technology by investigating practical challenges in this field. This research effort has culminated into the development of many innovative applications, services, and prototypes in the field of smart healthcare (Riazul et al., 2015). The current research trends in the health care based on Cloud IoT platform include new architectures and platforms for Cloud IoT network, new services and applications, reliability, accuracy and security of patient's data, newer and efficient wearable devices, big data, etc. Further, many countries and organizations across the globe are busy developing guidelines and policies for deploying Cloud-IoT technology in the medical field. However, it should be noted that the Cloud IoT in healthcare being in its infancy, a comprehensive understanding of its current state of research is expected to be beneficial for various aspirants interested in future research. The research and development activities in the area of smart healthcare based on the wearable devices connected through wireless sensor network (WSN) and Cloud computing platform can be regarded as initial research efforts in IoT-based healthcare. However, the latest trend is to adopt new standards and protocols for IP-based sensor networks which includes the evolving IPv6-based low power wireless personal area network, abbreviated as 6LoWPAN.

3.1 Cloud IoT System Architecture for Healthcare

Figure 2 shows the different components of a Cloud IoT architecture for a remote health monitoring system. The main components of this architecture (Hassanalieragh et al., 2015) include: Data acquisition, Data transmission, Data Concentration and Cloud Processing.

Data Acquisition is performed with the help of multiple wearable devices or sensors that monitor and measure physiological attributes, like Electrocardiogram (ECG), temperature of human body, pulse rate, muscular activities and other similar biomarkers. These sensors are connected to the network through an intermediary data

Figure 2. A remote patient monitoring system based on Cloud-IoT architecture

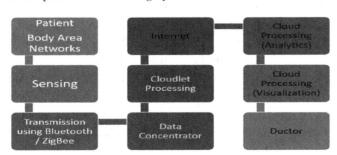

aggregator, which is most commonly a smart phone available with the patient. The Data Transmission is responsible for conveying recorded health data of the patient from his house or any other location to the healthcare service provider's data center with guaranteed security and privacy without any time delay. Normally, the data acquisition platform using sensors is armed with short range radio technologies like Zigbee or Bluetooth, which are used to transfer sensor data to the data aggregator or concentrator. The data so aggregated can further be transmitted for long lasting storage using internet connectivity on the data aggregator. Sensors in the data acquisition part are IoT enabled and therefore individual sensor's data can be retrieved through the Internet via data aggregator. Sometimes a storage-cum-processing device (referred to as a cloudlet), in proximity of a mobile client, is used to supplement its storage capability whenever there is a deficiency of mobile resources at local level. The Cloudlet can be in the form of a local processing unit (e.g. desktop computer) which is accessed directly by the data concentrator through data network (WiFi). The cloudlet can also be used for supporting time critical tasks on the patient's aggregated health data in addition to providing temporary storage. Further, in case of limitations of the mobile device which include temporary lack of connectivity or energy, the aggregated data can be sent to the cloud by the cloudlet. There are three distinct components of a Cloud Platform: (i) storage (ii) analytics and (iii) visualization (Hassanalieragh et al., 2015). The storage component is required for long duration storage of the physiological data of a patient and its use by health professionals for diagnosis and treatment. The storage of medical data on cloud platform has many challenges and it has been widely addressed by the researchers. The *Analytics* part makes use of sensory data related to health condition along with other electronic records that can help in diagnoses and prognoses for different health conditions and diseases. In order that the physicians are not burdened with the voluminous data from wearable sensors, *Visualization* is a vital prerequisite for such smart health systems. The Visualization methods present the relevant data in a readily digestible form and it will help a doctor to take a well-informed decision about patient's health.

3.2 Cloud IoT Based Services and Applications in Healthcare Sector

There are numerous applications of Cloud IoT based healthcare systems, which include care for elderly patients and children, monitoring of chronic patients, and smart monitoring and management of individual's health condition and fitness level, etc. In order to have a better understanding, this section is broadly organized in two parts: 1. Healthcare services and 2. Healthcare applications of Cloud IoT based platform. The list covered here is dynamic and additional services and numerous applications can easily be included in it. This section introduces a few important services and applications (Riazul et al., 2015).

1. **Services in Healthcare:** The Cloud based IoT platform is expected to offer a number of services in healthcare sector where each service offers certain solutions related to healthcare or well-being of an individual. The following subsection includes various types of healthcare services based on cloud IoT.

    a. **Services to Senior Citizens:** A cloud based IoT platform can meet the health care needs of ageing and differently abled persons. The aim of this service is to prolong the healthy life of elderly people in an independent, convenient and safe manner.

    b. **Drug Side Effects:** Cloud IoT based solutions can help in analysing the information regarding the health profile of a patient under medication and detect the possibility of any allergy or reaction to the administered drug through electronic record of the patient's health and allergy profile.

    c. **Community Healthcare Monitoring:** An IoT based network can be established for monitoring health condition of a local community. This network will help in sharing of health data among medical facilities and facilitate remote medical advice in the form of Virtual Hospital.

    d. **Children Health Awareness:** This service is aimed at raising awareness level of general public regarding children's mental as well as physical health, emotions and behaviour. The Cloud IoT platform can motivate youngsters to develop good eating habits under the guidance of their parents or guardians.

    e. **Wearable Device Access:** The sensors developed for Wireless Sensor Network based health services have enough capability to offer smart health services through IoT platform as well. Thus, incorporation of wearable devices into WSN based healthcare applications for Internet of Things set-up is very much desirable to extend the scope of cloud based IoT network.

    f. **Emergency Healthcare:** A range of solutions can be provided through Cloud IoT platform for indirect emergency health care, which may include availability of information, formalities during accident case, record maintenance, etc. during emergency situations.

    g. **Remote Monitoring:** This service connects the patient (user node), the internet and the monitoring medical equipment. This service allows automated and intelligent monitoring of a remotely located patient.

2. **Healthcare Applications:** A closer look at the healthcare applications of Cloud IoT is also desirable in addition to healthcare services. The users and patients directly use these applications. IoT innovations have led to various

gadgets or wearables which can provide different healthcare solutions. The various Cloud IoT based healthcare applications are described below:

a. **Blood Glucose Level Sensing:** This application involves monitoring of blood glucose level in the diabetic patients. Sensors at the patient's end transmit real time data to health service providers, who monitors and help in planning of meals, physical activities and timing of medicines.

b. **ECG Monitoring:** ECG is the record of electrical activity of human heart which provides a preliminary idea regarding the condition of heart. The application of Cloud based IoT in ECG monitoring help detect abnormal cardiac activity remotely well in advance and appropriate medical advice can be tendered to the patient.

c. **BP Monitoring:** BP must be regularly controlled and its remote monitoring based on Cloud IoT platform help in preventing further abnormalities in the body. The device for real-time BP monitoring will consist of a BP machine installed with internet enabled component. A location sensing device is then required for remote blood pressure monitoring through IoT platform.

d. **Rehabilitation of Patients:** This is one area which requires continuous, 2-way interaction between patient and health service providers. A Cloud IoT based rehabilitation system can form an effective infrastructure to support remote consultation for comprehensive rehabilitation.

e. **Effective Medication:** Patients tend to forget medication sometimes which may pose a threat to his health. IoT offers promising solution for effective medication management. An intelligent medicine box integrated with Cloud IoT platform may prove to be a boon for such patients.

f. **Smartphone-Based Healthcare Applications:** Smart phones have become indispensable part of human lives these days and various sensors and software products have made these phones a versatile tool for a lot of applications including healthcare. The smart phones have become a driver for Cloud IoT based healthcare solutions. A lot of healthcare apps have been developed by the developers for diagnostic, treatment information, drug reference, medical education, clinical communication, etc.

3.3 Challenges or Issues in Cloud IoT-Based Healthcare

There are many challenges or open issues in Cloud IoT based healthcare that need to be addressed carefully. A few important ones are elaborated below:

1. **Standardization:** A diverse range of cloud IoT based solutions are available for healthcare by many vendors. But no regulations have been followed during

the development of these solutions. As a result, there are many issues related to interfacing and interoperability. Various organizations or research groups should come forward for addressing the issue of standardization for Cloud IoT based health care.

2. **Backward Compatibility:** The transition or migration from the traditional system/devices to IoT based solutions for healthcare is a challenge. A seamless transition and backward compatibility must be ensured while introducing Cloud IoT based approaches into existing ones.

3. **Low Power Requirement:** Most of the sensors/devices integrated with Cloud IoT platform are battery powered and hence, low power consumption is a biggest challenge. Further, the communication network protocols too should consume less power. Thus, a continuous effort in this direction is required to ensure minimum possible dependency on power.

4. **Data Security:** Cloud IoT based healthcare require constant monitoring and data logging. The secured access to captured health data is very crucial as health data need to be shared with authorized user and organizations only. A few research problems that can be taken up for health data protection include: Resource efficient security, Physical security, Secure routing, Data transparency, etc.

5. **Mobility:** Access to health services anytime, anywhere is the underlying concept of Cloud IoT based healthcare solutions. Moreover, the user nodes are many a time mobile as well. The network parameters change significantly due to mobility and hence require due consideration.

4. SMART CITIES BASED ON CLOUD IOT PLATFORM

In recent years, the number of people moving towards urban or city life has seen an increasing trend. As per forecast available, by the end of 2030, more than 60% of the total population will be present in cities/urban areas. In order to face the challenges posed due to increased population in urban areas or cities, there will be a strong need for the development of smart and intelligent infrastructure in the cities. The concept of a Smart City functions in an intricate urban atmosphere, which includes many multifarious sub-systems dedicated to infrastructure, transport, modern technology, societal and political structures and hierarchy, human behavior and the economy (Gaur et al., 2015). The key components of a smart city i.e. health, transport system, homes and buildings, energy distribution, public safety, public utilities and environment etc. need to be managed intelligently and judiciously. The data obtained from these components is sensed through sensors which form a part of wireless sensor networks. Many other applications related to industry and consumer in smart cities like smart monitoring of health, intelligent homes, water, energy and environment monitoring etc. also require deployment of wireless sensor networks. Sensor nodes deployed in Smart City infrastructure generate huge amount of data that need to be used judiciously and efficiently. By the use of existing ICT infrastructure, the heterogeneous data collected from the city can be brought together. A few existing technologies for wireless communication like 3G, LTE and Wi-Fi can be used to achieve this aggregation of information. The concept of Internet of things (IoT) in a smart city involves personal computers and other surrounding electronic devices in the context of usage of embedded devices and existing internet infrastructure. The vision of Smart City is reliant on operation of billions of Cloud based IoT devices from a common place.

Currently, the applications related to a smart city are primarily deployed on premises. However, one can think of migrating existing smart city applications to the cloud platform as the Cloud computing technology has now matured up-to that point and the benefits such as dynamic resource provisioning (Vogler et al., 2016) and cost savings can be leveraged using cloud platform. Further, the concept of Internet of Cities is envisioned for future, where smart city applications will be able to operate across cities thereby creating a global and interconnected urban infrastructure. Therefore, there is an urgent need of developing such Cloud IoT based applications which could meet the requirements of unforeseen load or demand from its stakeholders. In order to realize the ubiquitous communication vision for smart cities which are globally interconnected, the integration of Cloud computing and IoT seems to be the only solution. The cloud is capable of providing long-term storage and reliable computing resources for the personalized pervasive applications delivered through the IoT as well as important backend resources (Suciu et al., 2013).

4.1 IoT Technologies for Smart Cities

In the framework of IoT, the communication between sensors should be wireless because the cost of cabling for millions of sensors will be too expensive. For interconnection between many devices, low-power standardized communication is the only viable option. It is imperative to note that cloud platform is essential in smart cities for reliable data storage and processing. The various IoT related technologies for smart cities (Talari et al., 2017) are explained below.

1. **RFID:** Radio Frequency Identification (RFID) plays an important job in the IoT based sensor network. RFID along with its readers and tags finds some applications in smart city framework such as smart grids, tracking of objects, smart healthcare, smart parking lots, etc.

2. **NFC:** Near Field Communication (NFC) is a two way communication for short distances, used particularly in smart phones and involving a centimetre range. The NFC finds application in smart cities also. One such example could be a wallet with the help of which we can use our mobile phones through NFC as our bank card, ID card, access control cards, etc.

3. **ZigBee:** ZigBee is based on the IEEE 802.15.4 standard and supports low-power and low-cost wireless communication involving sensor nodes. It is suitable for deploying wireless personal area networks (WPAN) for applications like automation of home appliances, collection of medical data, etc. Some more applications of ZigBee comprise wireless power switches, electric meters, and management of traffic and control systems. ZigBee is capable of supporting billions of devices in a city area but for limited ranges.

4. **6LoWPAN:** The 6LoWPAN standard makes use of IPv6 communication. IPv6 overcomes the problem of less number of nodes for IoT networks by providing 128-bit addresses. But it suffers from another problem that is compatibility issues with constrained nodes. This problem can be solved by using compression format for IPv6 i.e. 6LoWPAN.

5. **WSNs:** Wireless Sensor Networks (WSNs) is the backbone of IoT framework and can be used in many applications like healthcare, smart infrastructure, public utilities and environment related services. Wireless Sensor Networks integrated with RFIDs can help in acquiring data related to location and movement of people/objects, temperature, etc.

6. **LTE Networks:** LTE is a 4G standard for wireless communication for mobiles and data terminals. LTE is designed for broadband connectivity and used in Wide Area Networks requiring long distance ranges. High data cost and inability to use it for billions of devices are major problems with this service.

7. **Smart Cities Standards:** The leading standard specified for cities having smart infrastructure is IEEE 802.15 i.e. WPAN (wireless personal area network) standard. It comprises of different parts which include: Bluetooth, low rate and high rate WPAN, body area networks, visible light communication, key protocols for routing management, etc.

4.3 Smart Cities Applications in Cloud Environment

The heterogeneous infrastructure things present in a city can be merged together by using internet in the IoT platform. For providing the connectivity anytime and anywhere, all prevailing things have to be connected to the Internet. The smart cities host a large number of wireless sensor networks and linkage of intelligent nodes/devices with the internet is vital for remote monitoring such as monitoring of electricity usage, light management, parking management, transport management, etc. Figure 3 illustrates the key applications of a smart city in cloud environment (Talari et al., 2017). Though the figure is self- explanatory, a brief explanation of each of the applications in being provided below:

1. **Smart Homes:** Cloud IoT platform employs various sensors for data collection from home appliances and then appropriate decision making is done through cloud resources. Thus, this technology provides us with smart homes and appliances like smart televisions, smart metering, foolproof home security system, fire alarms, authorized entry system, temperature monitoring, etc. The sensors integrated into these appliances monitor the surroundings on real time basis and transmit the relevant data to a central controlling station located at home and the house owner can constantly monitor and control the entire home through Cloud based IoT platform and takes the best decision. Moreover, the IoT networked houses in a locality can be connected together in order to form a smart locality which can further be extended to entire city.
2. **Smart Parking Lots:** Smart parking is one of the most important features of a smart city because unorganized parking leads to many unwanted problems in a city like traffic congestion, environment pollution, revenue loss, etc. By enabling smart parking in a city, the daily life of its residents becomes simple and much organized. Smart parking requires road sensors, vehicle tracking

Figure 3. Smart Cities' Applications on Cloud IoT Platform

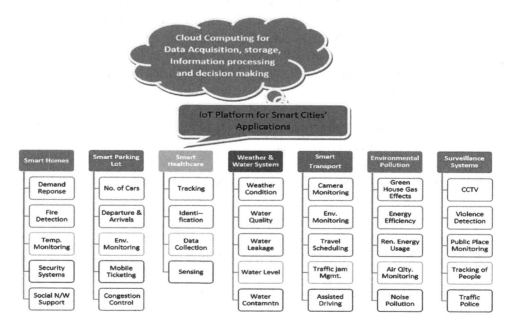

system and smart displays which enable the drivers to find nearest available parking space in the city. Smart parking further ensures safety of vehicles, cleaner environment and jam free roads.

3. **Smart Healthcare:** Smart healthcare in smart cities lead to virtual hospitals on Cloud IoT platform, which further reduces actual burden on the medical infrastructure of the city. Through sensor devices coupled with Cloud IoT, health data or status of patients can be monitored on real time basis and suitable treatment/diagnosis can be administered without physically visiting a hospital. The availability of medical literature on smart platform prevents wrong medications and incorrect diagnosis. Further, the services like location of ambulance, availability of blood, location of nearest medical facility in case of emergency, doctor's appointment, etc. can easily be delivered to the residents of a smart city.

4. **Weather and Water System:** The IoT sensors used for gathering weather data like temperature, humidity, wind speed, rainfall, etc. will help increase the efficiency of a smart city. Further, integration of smart weather module with other smart systems will introduce manifold advantage to its residents. The smart home will maintain proper ambience according to weather condition on a particular day. The smart transport system will also act accordingly. Water distribution system is also an essential component of a city. The sensors in cloud IoT environment will offer intelligent services like detection of leakage, quality, contamination of drinking water and then appropriate action by the local authorities. IoT also helps in teaching local authorities for planning and managing water distribution, sewerage system, ground water level, flood risks.

5. **Smart Transport:** Smart transport system is another important aspect of a smart city. Reducing the traffic congestion and ensuring smooth flow of traffic help in improving the quality of life of residents of a smart city. Smart transport covers both private and public domain transport. Cloud IOT platform based smart public transport system may reduce the burden on roads and other infrastructure of the city. It will lead to improved environment conditions, cost saving, time saving and overall improved city life. Tracking systems in the vehicles will ensure safety of the passengers. Further, the information dissemination through Cloud IoT platform will help authorities and citizens discipline traffic and plan the best way to reach the destination.

6. **Environmental Pollution:** A city cannot be considered smart in true sense if the air quality of that city is not fit for its residents. Therefore, real time monitoring of environmental pollution in the city is must and its residents should also be informed accordingly. The data gathered by IoT sensors help authorities take necessary action for controlling noise as well as air pollution.

A proper analysis of this data also helps the local government in formulating policy or legislation for controlling pollution in future.

7. **Surveillance Systems:** From citizen's point of view, security and peace are the most significant aspects of a city's life. Constant vigil and observation must be constantly maintained across the entire city so that no criminal activity takes place in the city. Smart Surveillance system should intelligently monitor people's activities, action and suspicious behaviour. The databases maintained with the help of Cloud IoT platform help security agencies to selectively monitor certain areas and residents should be warned in advance, if possible. In case of any emergency situation, automatic defence system of smart city should become active and security agencies must be able to control the situation well in time.

4.4 Challenges in the Implementation of Cloud IoT-Based Smart Cities

A few challenges in the implementation of Cloud IoT based smart cities are summarized in Table 1.

5. SMART AGRICULTURE USING IOT AND CLOUD COMPUTING

In order to accommodate large and increasing global population, there arise a need of increased food production by adopting modern and futuristic farming techniques. To meet this goal, new and innovative technologies and solutions need to be implemented in agriculture domain so that productivity can be enhanced by gathering and processing additional information. Added to this, the water scarcity coupled with adverse climatic conditions further demand newer and improved techniques for modern agricultural fields. As a result, there is an urgent requirement of automation and smart decision making in agriculture practices. In this regard, ubiquitous technologies like wireless adhoc networks, sensor networks, Radio

Table 1. Challenges in cloud IoT-based smart cities

S. No.	Challenges	Description
1.	Security and Privacy	Privacy and security of citizen data; smart systems resistant against cyber-attacks etc.
2.	Reliability	Reliability of networks is less due to mobility of sensor nodes
3.	Large Scale	Enormous number of distributed devices, Huge amount of data at city level for processing, storage and computation.

Frequency Identification (RFID), Internet of Things (IoT), cloud computing, remote sensing through satellite, etc. are becoming increasingly popular (Ojha et al., 2015).

Cloud based IoT platform is a potent tool to achieve the goal of smart automation in agriculture. For example, automated irrigation scheduling, optimization of plant growth, farmland monitoring, green houses gases monitoring, agricultural product and process management, crop security are a few important and potential applications.

A variety of commonly available as well as specialized sensors can be used for agricultural applications, e.g. Moisture in soil, Humidity level, Wetness in leaves, Solar Radiations, UV Radiations, Rain Gauge, Wind Fins, etc. In a typical case using IOT platform, sensors can be installed in agricultural fields, green houses, storage houses for seeds and produce, machineries and farm equipment, agriculture transportation system, and livestock; and the gathered data can be stored reliably on a cloud platform for proper monitoring and effective control (Figure 4). The cloud data can then be processed and analyzed to suggest the ways for further improvement of agricultural production through optimum use of resources, thus bridging the gap between the agricultural demand and supply. The most challenging task in any Cloud IOT system is intelligent decision making on the basis of analysis of huge amount data coming from different sensors being deployed.

Figure 4. Cloud IoT Framework for Agriculture

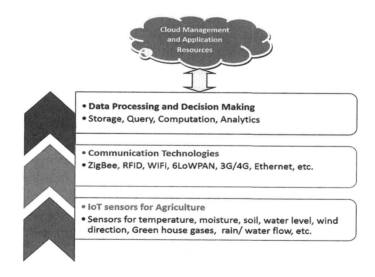

5.1 Potential Cloud IoT Applications in Agriculture

1. **Real Time Monitoring and Control of Agri Ecosystem:** Different IoT systems based on cloud computing have been suggested for real time monitoring and effective control of agriculture ecosystem, environmental conditions, green house effects, etc. Precision agriculture architecture can be put in place for sensing important parameters of soil like moisture content in soil, pH value, electrical conductivity, temperature, etc. The additional information like satellite images, aerial images, weather forecasting can further complement the decision making process for agriculture automation.

2. **Smart Irrigation Management:** Ground water is very important and crucial component of farm irrigation. The depletion of ground water level due to overuse has further made the irrigation process complex. Thus, optimized use of water resources in farming requires immediate migration to smart irrigation techniques using IoT sensors coupled with cloud framework. Though, micro-irrigation techniques are very affordable and effective but their efficiency can further be improved by gathering and processing additional information through Cloud IoT as coordinating technology.

3. **Pest and Disease Control:** In order to minimize farming cost one must monitor the possibility of manifestation of pests and other diseases in crops. The early detection of pests or diseases in fields leads to controlled and effective treatment of crops through pesticides and fertilizers. IoT sensors coupled with cloud resources can predict the occurrence of pests and diseases by sensing surrounding climate conditions like humidity, temperature, moisture, wind speed, etc and thus help in maintaining good health of crop.

4. **Monitoring of Ground Water Quality:** The presence of undesirable quantity of various salts and minerals in the ground water being used for irrigation may affect the yield as well as the quality of crop. Sensor nodes integrated with cloud resources can help in observing the quality of water and appropriate remedial action may be suggested by the experts to the farmers.

5. **Monitoring of Green-House Gases:** The presence of green-house gases in atmosphere have direct impact on the agriculture. The increased temperature of the climate affects the growth of crop adversely. An aerial system integrated with cloud IoT platform or a greenhouse monitoring system with agricultural cloud may be developed for monitoring green-house gases.

6. **Livestock Monitoring:** Livestock or cattle monitoring is an important task which consumes a lot of time of a farmer. RFID tags or other location sensing IoT devices can help in real time monitoring of cattle movement near fields. A warning system may also be integrated to intimate the presence of cattle near vegetation field so as to avoid grazing of fields.

7. **Farm Equipment and Agri-Produce Management:** Agriculture sector requires proper tracking and effective management of agricultural produce, farm machinery, etc. The Cloud IoT framework can be established for efficient real time monitoring of grain warehouse, transported grain bags and intelligent scheduling of expensive farm machinery.

8. **Knowledge Base:** Majority of the problems in agriculture and farming sector can be effectively resolved if farmers are able to get right information at right time. With the help of Cloud IoT framework, it is possible to construct a vast knowledge base to assist farmers or individuals having no prior knowledge of farming. The cloud resources are capable of storing and analysing vast structured and unstructured real time information and help farmers in proper decision making. The knowledge base may incorporate information related to crop pattern; sowing techniques; usage of fertilizers, pesticides and farm equipment; various diseases and pests; weather forecasting; storage of agricultural produce; maintenance of livestock and many more.

6. SMART BUILDING AND INFRASTRUCTURE USING CLOUD IOT

A smart building hosts a Building Management System (BMS), which is a full-fledged platform to control and monitor the electrical and mechanical parts of the building. Even the load can be managed through this system and efficiency can be improved. This system has the capability to minimize the energy requirements for heating, cooling and even for ventilation. This system can be integrated with various other hardware which can further monitor the electrical as well as mechanical systems of the building and control in real time the energy requirements according to the demand (Minoli et al., 2017). Cheaper sensors of IOT along with cloud computing infrastructure are now driving the deployment of smart buildings.

Commercial buildings require a wide range of monitoring and management where resources should be used in an optimized way. The main requirements in these buildings are to manage the light energy, proper and smart surveillance of the building, certified access management, proper monitoring, fire detection systems, burglary alarms etc. For all these requirements energy management is one of the main objective of a smart building concept. The tentative list below identifies most common elements and systems where it consumes more energy and these elements can take advantage of cloud based IoT sensing systems (Minoli et al., 2017).

- **Computer Center Room:** Racks and servers, Computers, Telecom systems, ACs of computer center, UPS.
- **Building Office Space:** Lighting systems (LED/Normal), Day and night sensors, Thermostats for temperature control.
- **HVAC Chamber:** Chiller, Modular boiler, ACs etc.
- **Cooling Systems of the Building:** Cooling towers, Roof top cooling units, Heat pumps etc.
- **Building Management System:** Management systems of various electrical, mechanical, plumbing systems, elevators and lifts systems.
- **Electrical Supply System:** Electricity distribution panel, UPS supply management, Emergency AC generators, Battery backups etc.
- **Water Supply System:** Water supply management system, Water heaters, Motors and pumps management system etc.
- **Lobby Areas:** Proper and advanced lighting systems, Different light emitting diodes sign board, Proper lighting systems for staircase area, Air circulation systems etc.
- **Commercial Building Retail Area:** LED Lighting systems, Proper cooling etc.

These smart building management system is mainly focusing on electrical energy consumption. The upcoming Cloud based IoT systems will focus on the different energy sources of a building which includes solar energy, natural gas, renewable energy, natural energy etc. Also these smart building should be able to manage the other systems like use of water and steam, etc. Cloud based IoT smart sensor technology can help the building to be smart by having controlled ventilation, dedicated outdoor air systems, energy recovery ventilators, floor air distribution, displacement ventilation, under ultraviolet germicidal irradiation and CO_2 sensors etc.

6.1 Building Blocks of a Smart Building Management System

The future smart building management systems will take data from a large number of IoT sensors which will provide the information about the energy, lightning, surveillance and process this data on the cloud based analytical tools. The building blocks of this system are briefly described below and shown in Figure 5.

- **Sensors:** The purpose of these sensors is for measuring parameters such as room occupancy, humidity, lighting levels, temperature etc. The IoT plays a role in making the sensing environment of the building smart.
- **Controllers:** The purpose of these controllers is to control the various systems but taking the inputs from the data analysis unit.

Figure 5. Cloud IoT Framework for Smart Building and Infrastructure

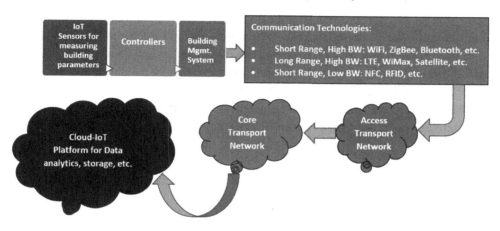

- **Communication Techniques:** Various Long and Short range communication techniques, protocols etc.
- **Cloud:** It analyzes the data, decision making, manages storage of data etc.

6.2 Points of Application in Smart Buildings

A brief summary of various points of application in Smart Buildings is given below:

1. **Access Control:** Access control to restricted and non-authorized areas and detection of unauthorized persons, if any.
2. **Indoor Climate Control:** Measurement and control of temperature, lighting, ambience, air quality, etc.
3. **Smart Thermostat:** With the help of software programming and IoT hardware support, energy consumption and saving data can be stored and analysed. The advanced scheduling and controlling through program may save time and energy.
4. **Intelligent Fire Alarm:** System with sensors measuring smoke and CO, giving both early warning and activating the fire defence system.
5. **Intrusion Detection:** Detection of breakage through door or window and prevention of intruders though smart surveillance system.
6. **Arts and Goods Preservation:** Monitoring of precious art or antique items inside the building including museums and art warehouses.

7. FUTURE RESEARCH DIRECTIONS IN CLOUD IOT SCENARIO

In this chapter, we discussed the integration of Cloud and IoT for providing various interesting applications in our day-to-day life. There are several challenges related to each of the applications which are receiving the attention of researchers worldwide. A few of the challenges have already been identified and discussed in this chapter, which include security concerns, heterogeneity, reliability, legal issues, big data, etc. Still there are open issues and future directions which require additional research efforts.

- Identification and addressing issues of large number of things and devices through IPv6 or some other futuristic protocol.
- Mobility and access network scalability requirements in large scale Cloud IoT network.
- Support for heterogeneous network and ensure network reliability and guaranteed quality of service.
- Software defined networking may be envisaged for future Cloud IoT network.
- More effective Standardized protocols, libraries and APIs for Cloud IoT based applications.
- Engineering issues related to storage of data (time stamping, predictive storage, caching of data, etc.)
- Big data analysis involving real time processing and management of big data in Cloud IoT platform.
- Algorithms and protocols for enhanced security and privacy to prevent themselves from hackers, malware, compromised gateways and security breaches to Cloud IoT system.
- Energy efficient sensor nodes along with energy efficiency in processing, transmission and management of huge data in Cloud IoT network.
- New solutions for Cloud IoT network communications particularly in context of human centric and M2M approach.

8. CONCLUSION

The amalgamation of IoT and Cloud platform will prove to be a big step ahead in the futuristic internet technologies. The Cloud based IoT platform has opened up new dimensions for advanced research and innovation. In this chapter, we discussed a few key application areas where Cloud based IoT technology can mark its impact. These application areas include smart healthcare, smart cities, smart agriculture and smart building architecture. The cloud based architecture has been proposed for these applications and the corresponding challenges involved in each have been investigated, which include security concerns, heterogeneity, reliability, legal issues, big data, etc. Lastly, certain open issues and future directions have been envisioned which require additional research efforts in providing definitive solutions.

REFERENCES

Botta, A., Donato, W., & Persico, V. (2016). Integration of cloud computing and Internet of Things: A survey. *Elsevier Journal of Future Generation Computer Systems, 56*, 684–700. doi:10.1016/j.future.2015.09.021

Distefano, M. (2015). *Cloud computing and the Internet of things: Service architectures for data analysis and management* (Doctoral dissertation). University of Pisa, Italy.

Gaur, A., Scotney, B., & Parr, G. (2015). Smart city architecture and its applications based on IoT. In *Elsevier Procedia Computer Science of 5*th *International Symposium on Internet of Ubiquitous and Pervasive Things* (vol. 52, pp. 1089-1094). London, UK: Elsevier. doi:10.1016/j.procs.2015.05.122

Hassanalieragh, M., Page, A., & Soyata, T. (2015). Health monitoring and management using Internet of things sensing with cloud based processing: Opportunities and challenges. *Proceedings of IEEE International Conference on Service Computing*, 285-292. doi:10.1109/SCC.2015.47

Hou, L., Zhao, S., Xiong, X., Zheng, K., Chatzimisios, P., Hossain, M. S., & Xiang, W. (2016). Internet of things cloud: Architecture and implementation. *IEEE Communications Magazine, 54*(12), 32–39. doi:10.1109/MCOM.2016.1600398CM

Milovanovic, D., & Bojkovic, Z. (2017). Cloud based IoT healthcare applications: Requirements and recommendations. *International Journal of Internet of Things and Web Services, 2*, 60–65.

Minoli, D., Sohraby, K., & Occhiogrosso, B. (2017). IoT considerations, requirements and architectures for smart buildings – Energy optimization and next generation building management systems. *IEEE Internet of Things Journal, 4*(1), 269–283.

Ojha, T., Misra, S., & Raghuwanshi, N. (2015). Wireless sensor networks for agriculture: The state-of-the-art in practice and future challenges. *Elsevier Journal of Computers and Electronics in Agriculture, 118*, 66–84. doi:10.1016/j.compag.2015.08.011

Riazul Islam, S. M., Kwak, D., & Kabir, M. H. (2015). The Internet of things for health care: A comprehensive survey. *IEEE Access: Practical Innovations, Open Solutions, 3*, 678–708. doi:10.1109/ACCESS.2015.2437951

Sivakumar, S., Anuratha, V., & Gunasekaran, S. (2017). Survey on Integration of Cloud Computing and Internet of Things Using Application Perspective. *International Journal of Emerging Research in Management & Technology, 6*(4), 101–108. doi:10.23956/ijermt/SV6N4/101

Suciu, G., Vulpe, A., & Halunga, S. (2013). Smart cities built on resilient cloud computing and secure Internet on things. *Proceedings of IEEE International Conference on Control Systems and Computer Science*, 513-518. doi:10.1109/CSCS.2013.58

Talari, S., Shafie-khah, M., & Siano, P. (2017). A review of smart cities based on the Internet of things concept. *MDPI Energies, 10*(4), 1–23.

Vogler, M., Schleicher, J. M., Inzinger, C., Dustdar, S., & Ranjan, R. (2016). Migrating smart city applications to the cloud. *IEEE Cloud Computing, 3*(2), 80–87. doi:10.1109/MCC.2016.44

Chapter 8
Examining IoT's Applications Using Cloud Services

Saravanan K
Anna University Regional Campus — Tirunelveli, India

P. Srinivasan
VIT University, India

ABSTRACT

Cloud IoT has evolved from the convergence of Cloud computing with Internet of Things (IoT). The networked devices in the IoT world grow exponentially in the distributed computing paradigm and thus require the power of the Cloud to access and share computing and storage for these devices. Cloud offers scalable on-demand services to the IoT devices for effective communication and knowledge sharing. It alleviates the computational load of IoT, which makes the devices smarter. This chapter explores the different IoT services offered by the Cloud as well as application domains that are benefited by the Cloud IoT. The challenges on offloading the IoT computation into the Cloud are also discussed.

1. INTRODUCTION

Cloud computing and Internet of Things (IoT) are inseparable in today's computing paradigm. Both of them complement each other by leveraging its services. The number of devices used in day-to-day life of the human as well as industries is growing rapidly since many services are automated. Cloud empowers communication among these devices seamlessly on demand basis. The characteristics of cloud such as scalability, on-demand, and pay per use will greatly help the development of IoT. The devices in

DOI: 10.4018/978-1-5225-3445-7.ch008

IoT network becomes "smarter, smaller and cheaper" by using the cloud services. In IoT, 'things' refer to any object on face of the earth, whether it is a communicating device or a non-communicating dumb object (Parwekar, 2011). Fig.1 illustrates the convergence of IoT using cloud services. Various applications and users get benefited by this merging. The three technologies such as cloud computing (Internet centric), IoT (Device centric) and Big data (Data centric) are tied together in the evolution of pervasive and ubiquitous model. Earlier in the Web 1.0 & Web 2.0 developments, Human-to-Human communication was well established in the form of web pages and social networking. Later in the Web 3.0 era, devices are communicating each other for sharing the data. Not only the data, knowledge and experience gained by the devices can also be shared to avoid duplication in learning process.

For example, cloud robotics is the emerging field which uses the cloud based IoT techniques. Here, robots act as thin-client in which the computation and storage are simply offloaded into cloud. Google car is another example for convergence of cloud and IoT, which uses the Google map services from the cloud. It receives the accurate street view images, 3D sensors and traffic patterns information on the move.

The true potential of cloud can be realized by applying IoT devices in different applications. Cost of IoT devices will be cheaper by leverage the cloud services on rental basis. As the wireless network devices are equipped with 4G/5G/GPRS/LTE technologies, service access from the cloud is not a big concern. Cloud services are provisioned primarily in the form of Software as a Service (SaaS), Platform as a Service (PaaS) and Infrastructure as a Service (IaaS). But in IoT, SAaaS (Sensing and Actuation as a Service) can also be provided by using the cloud.

Currently IoT paradigm interconnects 9 billion sensor devices and future growth is predicted to scale-up 24 billion devices in the year 2020. The data generated from

Figure 1. Convergence of cloud with Internet of Things

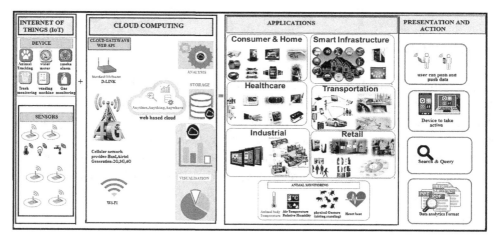

these devices will be enormous and requires cloud services for storage, processing and visualization. These devices can range from sensors, actuators, mobile devices, computers, smart home/industry/city appliances, automated vehicles and transport infrastructure components, and any network connected device that can be examined in the IoT world. Singh, D., Tripathi, G, & Jara, A. J (2014) explored the three paradigms of IoT. 1. Internet-oriented (middleware), 2. Things oriented (sensors) and 3. Semantic-oriented (knowledge). Apart from the sensors, middleware and knowledge extraction is interleaved by empowering cloud services. Resources sharing & provisioning of Cloud computing is also the key requirements for IoT platform. Riggins, F. J., & Wamba, S. F. (2015) discussed the challenges involved in implementation, practice and impact of the IoT for individual, organization, industry and society.

This chapter begins with the introduction of cloud IoT and its motivation. Drivers of cloud IoT and convergence requirement are discussed in the next section of the chapter. Followed by, the different cloud services used in IoT field are summarized. Also, the chapter elaborates the IoT applications implemented in cloud. Challenges are discussed in the last part of chapter.

1.1 Cloud IoT Drivers

Botta, A., De Donato, W., et al (2015) explored the three categories of drivers for cloud IoT - Communication, Storage and Computation.

- **Communication Driver:** Effective communication for sharing data & knowledge among the IoT devices is facilitated by cloud. Cloud offers a cost optimized solution to interconnect, trace, and manage any devices from anywhere at any time by using custom-made web portals with integrated applications. Communication capacity is not improved enough when compared to data storage density and processor power, which is increased by a factor of 10^{18} and 10^{15} respectively. Broadband capacity is improved only of 10^4, not matching the speed.
    - **Storage Driver:** IoT generates data mostly in unstructured and semi-structured format. These data are coming in huge volume (petabytes), different variety (text, audio, video, image, etc), and different velocity (speed), which leads to big data. When the devices grow in the network, storage requires unlimited capacity. Cloud offers virtually unlimited storage, which can be scaled to any level. Not only the storage services, processing, formatting, illustration, and analytics tools are also available in cloud.

○ **Computation Driver:** Offloading the computation to cloud allows the IoT devices to perform only limited on-board computation. The complex data computation not necessarily needs to be performed in the on-board IoT device. Also, computation results which are performed in the cloud can be displayed in the IoT monitor on the fly.

1.2 Need For Convergence

Convergence of Cloud and IoT will give advantages and opportunities for both the technologies. The potential of cloud & IoT can be envisaged by converging them in appropriate applications. Two types of application verticals can be evolved by merging them (Biswas, A. R., & Giaffreda, R, 2014). i) Cloud Based IoT - Applying the IoT capabilities into cloud, such as sensor data which is generated from IoT devices becomes source for cloud storage. ii) IoT-Centric Cloud, which uses the cloud services for sharing, accessing of generated data. Both of these developments are getting momentum in the present web (Gubbi, J., Buyya, R., et al, 2013).

- Anywhere, anytime access of the devices and its data can be achieved using cloud. Cloud manages the underlying IoT devices through internet and connects them using cloud infrastructure such as virtualization and multi-tenancy.
- The knowledge developed by the devices such as robots, vehicles is immediately available to the paired devices in cloud. The synergy among the devices is tackled by employing the cloud. The knowledge & experience gained from IoT device is simply shared in the cloud thus helps the similar IoT devices to utilize that knowledge. In this sense, devices can start behave as a human to avoid repetitive mistakes by analyzing the previous knowledge.
- Cloud can make IoT devices as "lighter, cheaper and smarter". When the computing task is offloaded to the high computing performance cloud systems, the computational load of IoT devices is reduced to a great extent (Saravanan, K, 2017). Cost of the IoT devices is reduced since it can access the cloud services on demand basis. It is not necessary to equip the IoT devices with all the required services running all the time. IoT cannot be said 'smart' without applying cloud.
- Readymade cloud applications can be easily configured and launched in the IoT smart devices. There are numerous cloud services already built, which can be easily customized for web and mobile platforms. It can be easily extended to IoT platform also. Cloud applications can be tailor made for IoT platform.

- The aggregation of IoT devices and its data is simply dealt using cloud. Scalability is the core characteristic of cloud and any number of IoT devices can be added into cloud. The complementary aspects of cloud and IoT are given in the Table 1.

2. IOT APPLICATIONS USING CLOUD SERVICES

Cloud offers basically three service models-Software as a Service (SaaS), Platform as a Service (PaaS) and Infrastructure as a Service (IaaS). As IoT converged with cloud service models, new type of applications such as SaaS IoT, PaaS IoT is developed. PaaS IoT refers to the cloud platform services for IoT devices. Similarly, SaaS IoT refers to the cloud applications instances launched on the IoT devices. IaaS IoT is still in infancy stage, since it needs virtualization enabled in IoT devices. Here, some of the IoT applications running in SaaS & PaaS cloud are listed.

2.1 IoT Applications Running in PaaS Platform

Carriot is one of the Paas providers for IoT devices (Mineraud, J., Mazhelis, O, 2016). It offers services in the fields of retail, banking, consumer, logistics, agriculture, energy & oil industries. It connects wide range of devices such as sensors, gateways, machines and supports the known platforms such as Arduino, Raspberry Pi, Beagle Bone and many more. Also, it offers developers the platform SDK and API's to test and deploy the IoT applications.

DeviceHub provides integrated PaaS solution platform for developing IoT projects. It articulates both hardware and web technologies along with business agility and

Table 1. IoT and cloud: complementary aspects

Aspects	IoT	Cloud
Displacement	Pervasive	Federated
Availability	Restricted	Ubiquitous
Devices	Real world devices	Virtual resources
Computation power	Bounded	Virtually scalable
Memory size	Minimal or none	Virtually scalable
Role of the web	Convergence place	Medium for launching services
Big data	Source of data	Processing and management

sagacity. It supports user friendly application interfaces to aggregate the business data with cloud intelligence and controls the multiple connected devices in off-lying mode for real time analytics. It supports remote management of IoT devices using modular PaaS platform as well as SDK for many programming languages such as python, C++, Ruby and Android.

Eurotech IoT kit targets all aspects of an IoT application from hardware interfacing, to development of on-board software, and cloud connectivity. It allows solution developers to focus on their core tasks immediately by not worrying the initial hardware/software setup. Various products ranging from M2M (Machine-to-Machine), smart devices, mobile/portable systems and embedded boards.

Exosite provides IoT PaaS platform known as Murano, which is a cloud-based solution that enables an end-to-end ecosystem to help IoT consumers to implement, deploy, and control the connected devices. It addresses the security solutions for IoT devices in unique way.

Ericsson IoT-Framework uses the REST API for IoT PaaS framework along with the Graphical User Interface. This linux based platform consolidates the generated data from different sensors in IP networks and concentrates on mash-up of different streams of data for analysis & visualization.

SensorCloud supports data format in CSV and XDR with visualization capability. It acquires, visualizes, monitors and analyzes the IoT data. With the help of MathEngine, plots and histograms can be easily presented from the sensor data. MathEngine also integrates IPython into its cloud service. It allows writing custom python scripts to process the data, all on the Cloud.

Dweet – Any IoT thing (device, mobile, gadget) which can connect to the Internet, may use dweet.io to easily publish and subscribe to data. It is established for M2M without any initial configuration. Similar to Twitter, devices can Dweet the messages to all the connected devices in the internet.

2.2 IoT Applications Running in SaaS Platform

EvryThng manages billions of intelligent IoT devices and identifies the devices uniquely in the cloud, giving each one a persistent, addressable web presence. The data profile for each device is maintained to authorize and exchange the data. It works with wide range of wireless communication technologies, starting from text messaging and smart tags (QR, bar code, NFC, BLE and RFID), to printed electronics, sensors and chips.

Another SaaS IoT, SkySpark facilitates the subject experts to confiscate their domain knowledge as rules, which can be used to validate and run against collected IoT sensor data using automated framework. It employs semantic annotation, pattern recognition, functional rules processing. Analytics engine has the ability to automatically correlate and analyze the data. It can be installed in local machine or cloud server environment.

2.3 Other IoT Cloud Service Platforms

SaaS (Sensing as a Service) is an emerging new kind of cloud service platform that provides universal access to sensor data (Perera, C., Zaslavsky, A, 2014). This service model consists of 4 levels of conceptual layers: (i) sensors and sensor owners; (ii) sensor publishers (SPs); (iii) extended service providers (ESPs); and (iv) sensor data consumers. The sensors can be categorized into three types- household, organization and commercial sensors. Sensor owner can publish the data into cloud and authorize the publishers for accessing the data by consumers. It is evident to note that there is no direct communication between sensor data consumers and sensor owners. Sensor publishers plays vital role in this communication.

Sensor cloud (presented in Fig 2) integrates the sensor networks with the consuming sensor applications to provision, monitor and control the sensors deployed in the cloud computing infrastructures. Sensor data is usually originated from various sensor networks and it is aggregated and processed using sensing/web applications. As the data is hosted in the centralized cloud, enablement of data sharing and collaborations among the sensor consumers and applications will be easier. Sensor-rich IoT devices and electronic gadgets can avail the sensor services via the cloud network.

With the aid of cloud characteristics, sensor owners can rent their IoT sensor devices to the consumers as a service, which is termed as Sensing as a Service (SaaS). It allows the consumers to avail the high-cost sensor device for their limited usage

Figure 2. Architecture of sensor cloud

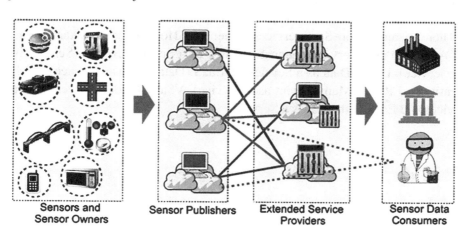

| Sensors and Sensor Owners | Sensor Publishers | Extended Service Providers | Sensor Data Consumers |

Figure 3. Service lifecycle in sensor cloud
Rao, B. P., Saluia, P, 2012.

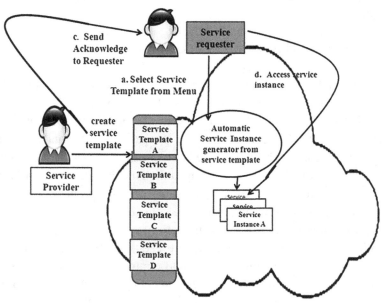

period, without bothering on maintenance and support of the devices. On the other hand, sensor owners can experience the fully utilization of the sensor devices with the rent collected from various applications by sharing the devices. Sensor cloud felicitates the consumers to easily gather, access, process, analyze & represent, store & communicate and explore hefty amounts of sensor data from different applications. Fig 3 depicts the lifecycle of sensor cloud. Service requester can select and compose the different services offered from the provider. Here, 4 service templates (A, B, C & D) launched by the provider. Upon selecting the service, service instance is launched.

There are many more SaaS services implemented for IoT such as SAaaS (Sensing and Actuation as a Service), SenaaS (Sensor as a Service),SEaaS (Sensor Event as a Service), DaaS (Data as a Service), DBaaS (DataBase as a Service), IPMaaS (Identity and Policy Management as a Service), VSaaS (Video Surveillance as a Service) and EaaS (Ethernet as a Service).

3. APPLICATIONS OF CLOUD-ENABLED IOT IN DIFFERENT DOMAINS

3.1 Health Care in Hospitals

Health monitoring is envisaged as one of the best usage of sensor clouds (Alamri, A., Ansari, W. S, 2013). Here, various wearable sensors are used to continuously monitor the health status of the patients in the hospital. Also, monitoring of animals in the livestock environment using sensor devices helps the farmers to identify the diseases earlier and maintain the good health of the cattle animals. Health monitoring can be achieved by employing the cost effective and recent wearable sensors such as accelerometer sensors, heartbeat, breath, blood pressure, physical gesture, proximity, and humidity & temperature sensors. These sensors are used to track and collect the patient's health status data such as sleep activity pattern, blood pressure, body temperature, and other respiratory conditions and pass it in the sensor cloud. Analytics is done and report is generated based on the patient health condition. In this scenario, various sensors mounted in the patient body will collect and send the data periodically to the sensor cloud via wireless technologies. Off-loading the computation to the sensor cloud makes the sensor devices thin, smarter less cost when compared with traditional sensor devices. Preprocessing of data is done in the cloud to remove the noise. The various stakeholders of the healthcare IoT such as the doctors/health employees and nurses can remotely monitor the health status. It is very helpful if the patient is affected by contagious deceases in which direct physical monitoring is difficult. Patient's data can be accessed from cloud through a web service portal with proper authentication. The IoT data flow is represented in Figure 4.

Low-cost, human-social pet robot named Pleo that successfully connects with children to supply young patients with a kind partner to enhance their stay in hospitals. Pleo robot intelligent system learns the children behavior and provides them with the best stimulus to reduce their anxiety and stress. Google Fit is a health-tracking, human gesture analytic device, that uses sensors inputs from IoT devices such as mobile placed in a human body to trace physical fitness and health status (such as walking, biking, running or cycling). It is developed in android operating system and the sensed gesture data are measured against the user's fitness levels and weight loss/gain progress over the period of times such as past 24 hours, week and month, which provide a comprehensive view of their fitness.

Figure 4. Patients monitoring using healthcare sensors

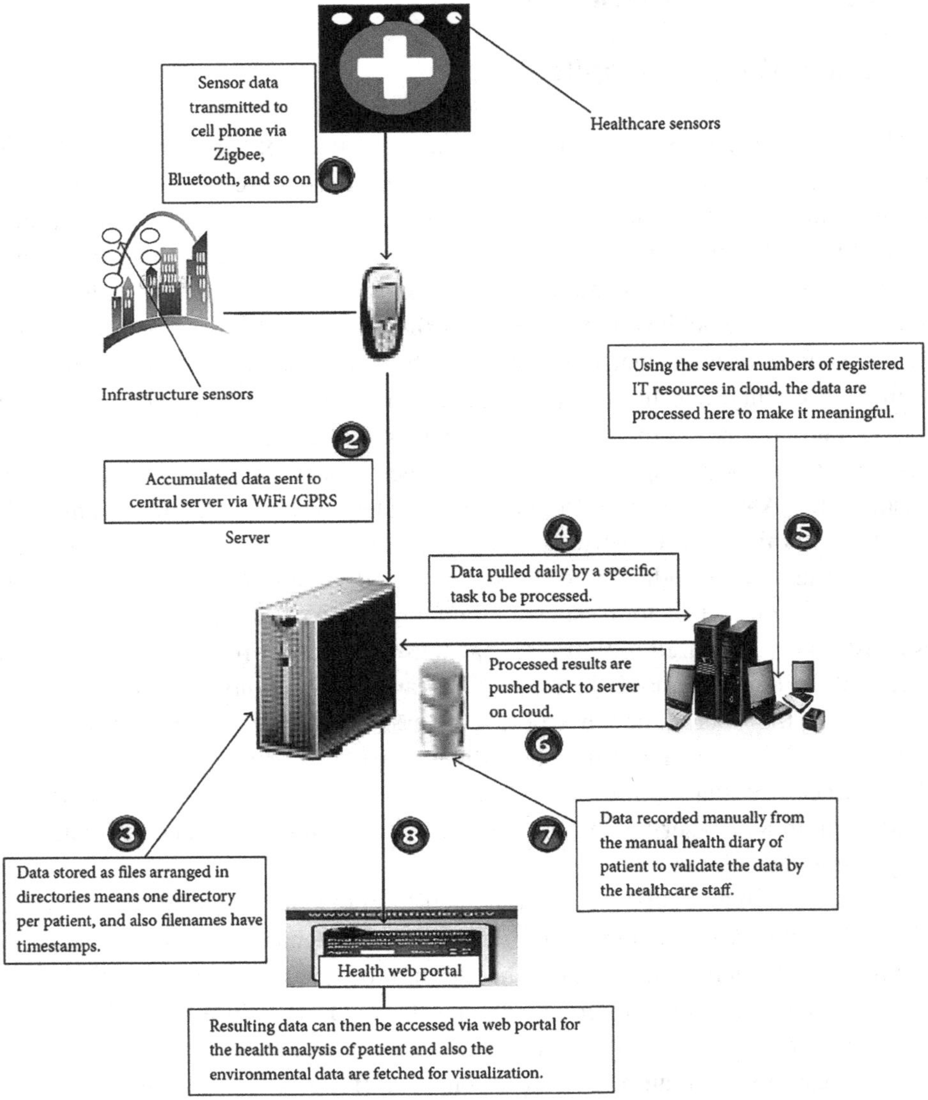

3.2 Smart City

Smart city is empowered with e-governance, citizen easy access to facilities, transport, use of ICT, power and water supply, security, etc. Administration of the city and the citizens are governed with the help of most advanced wireless sensors based IoT communication and related technologies to support value added services (Zanella, A.,

Bui, N., 2014). Smart city is a natural evolvement in the technology paced world and it is inevitable in the today service oriented community. Cloud based IoT is widely used in smart city administration to optimize the core public services, such as smart transport and vehicle parking, automated street lighting, security surveillance and maintenance of public places using CCTV cameras, protection of cultural heritage, waste management, water distribution, power supply management, networking of hospitals, and smart education.

Potential IoT applications are identified to develop smart city by different focus groups of Melbourne city, Australia. Using such a framework, IoT application developer can integrate and exploit cloud services available in the market in order to develop reliable and scalable applications. The Santander SmartCity (Hernández-Muñoz, J. M., Vercher, J. B., et al, 2011) testbed is implemented with about 3000 IEEE 802.15.4 devices, 200 GPRS modules and 2000 joint RFID tag/QR code labels deployed. These devices are placed at static locations such as streetlights, facades, bus stations as well as on- board transport vehicles such as buses and taxis. Using this smartcity testbed, multiple domain use case scenarios have been implemented in the Santander city platforms.

- **Environmental Monitoring:** Environmental parameters, such as temperature, humidity, carbon level, water level, air/water pollution, street light and car presence.
- **Outdoor Vehicle Parking Management:** 400 parking sensors installed at distant static locations to detect parking zone availability in the city.
- **Mobile Environmental Monitoring:** 150 mobile sensors are installed in movable public transport systems containing buses, taxis and police vehicles.
- **Traffic Intensity Monitoring:** Measurement of dynamic traffic parameters using sensors installed in roads. These sensors can give real time traffic volumes in peak time, road occupancy, vehicle speed or queue length.
- **Participatory Sensing:** Citizen/Traveler can also send physical sensing information through the network sensors attached in their vehicle feed into IoT SmartSantander platform. GPS coordinates, compass, environmental parameters such as air moisture, temperature, etc are captured in this way.

Cloud-based hubs contribute significantly in the implementation of an IoT centric framework for smart cities. CityHub project (Figure 5) intends to develop smart city PaaS platform by formalizing IoT framework with the data hubs. Several applications are installed in the PaaS IoT similar to Google App store. e.g., 'Bike Rack' android application gives the identified locations in the city where cyclists can safely lock their bikes in the installed bike racks freely available. This platform runs on the city bike rack data hubs. These data hubs have been implemented in UK and Canada

Figure 5. City hub smart city project
Lea, R., & Blackstock, M, 2014.

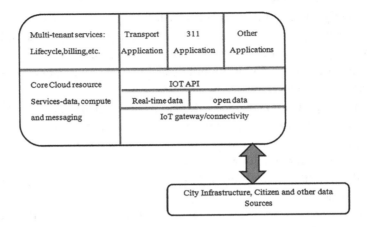

regions. It currently manages over 64,000 time-series sensor feeds and a wide range of static datasets which comprises of open data contributed by the citizens and the city datasets. It provides real time information about transportation, road and highways traffic volumes, road asset condition, planned/unplanned roadwork, air pollution, weather and flooding details. In India, smart city mission is initiated with the aim of 100 satellite based smart cities around the country to make the citizen friendly and sustainable urban development in the cities.

3.3 Smart Home

Appliances in the houses are interconnected in IoT cloud and synchronize the data. Devices will act according to the user preferences. Automatic and remote ON/OFF ability of the household devices will greatly reduce the power consumption. Monitoring the children and elderly people via the video surveillance devices connected into cloud is one of the examples for IoT cloud used in home. Smart metering by employing the appropriate sensors in the home environment gives the control over the devices and their usage.

Figure 6 represents the three use case scenarios for smart home devices. 1) Measuring home conditions - illustrating the sequence of actions performed by the user to get the temperature and humidity readings of home conditions, 2) Managing home appliances - manipulation and control of home appliances such as lights, doors, fans, washing machine and air conditioners from the remote, 3) Controlling home access - Use of RFID/Biometric tags to gain secure home access and all the activities recorded and stored in cloud IoT.

Figure 6. Smart home using cloud IoT
Soliman, M., Abiodun, T & et al, 2013.

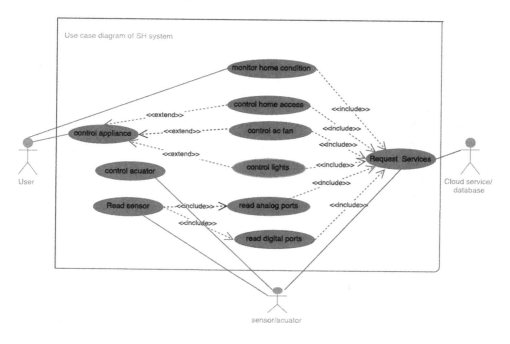

3.4 Animal Monitoring

Saravanan and Saraniya (2017) developed the animal monitoring system using IoT sensors. The system architecture is presented in Figure 7, which includes of farm and data center unit. In farm unit, wearable smart collar tag is mounted in the animal neck, which will monitor the animal health conditions such as temperature, blood pressure, and physical gesture using the different sensors and then data is accumulated and transferred into cloud gateway via wi-fi. In the data center unit, data analytics is made via the available cloud platform and visualized in real time through the user authenticated mobile IoT devices.

Cloud IoT applications require proper examination for the issues such as privacy, security, communication, data processing and analysis. Besides, virtualization and heterogeneous devices & data format also a big concern. In this chapter, these challenges are examined and narrated in the next section.

Figure 7. Animal health monitoring using IoT sensors

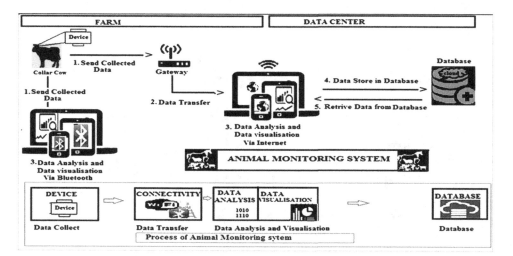

4. CHALLENGES IN CLOUD IOT

- **Cloud Security and Privacy:** The penetration threats on IoT data resides in public cloud impose primary challenge. As the public cloud gives economy of scale for sensor IoT devices by offloading of computation and memory, sensor IoT data requires secure encryption before the transferring.

- **Sensor Data Format:** Multiple data formats exist for sensors which depend upon the device vendor configuration and compatibility. Also, data streaming is done in structured, unstructured and semi-structured formats. Cloud should have the compatible drivers to preprocess the sensor data. IoT-Cloud require to provision real-time data processing and computational services for the massive sensor data. Sensor generated data varies from the human generated data as well (Chen, Y. K, 2012).

- **Virtualization of IoT:** Currently server systems can be virtualized to accommodate and launch SaaS applications & PaaS platforms, whereas IoT devices cannot be virtualized due to its computing and storage capacity. If virtualization is enabled across the IoT devices, not only generation of data, visualization and sharing of resources can also be happening at the device end.

- **Heterogeneity of Devices:** IoT interconnects more number of heterogeneous devices, each device specification is different and sensor output also varies. The communication between those devices is essential in IoT for sharing of knowledge in real time. They cannot be simply connected through wired since compatibility issues arise. Each device has its own driver to run and implement.

- **Convergence Issues:** Cloud offers services in many service models such as SaaS, PaaS and IaaS along with deployment models such as public, private, hybrid and community. Also, virtualization and resource allocation strategies have to be considered. Cloud deployment and provisioning are inherently complex. When converging the cloud with IoT, how the selection and composition of cloud services will be made is still an issue.
- **Real Time Execution:** Latency on accessing and retrieving the cloud services in real time is still a problem in IoT applications. As the cloud relies on internet, minimal downtime causes the IoT devices become stagnate.
- **Legal Regulatory and Liability Issues:** There are no standards and regulations evolved to deal the various layers of cloud IoT across the world. Also, complex accountability issues arise when comes to IoT devices connected to the cloud, since the liability and jurisdiction laws governed by whom will extend their arm will be a big concern.

5. CONCLUSION

This chapter gave insight examination on how cloud services can be integrated into IoT devices. The need for the convergence of cloud and IoT along with the advantages is detailed. Also, the different IoT application which uses cloud service platforms such as SaaS, PaaS and SAaaS are examined. Cloud IoT is already implemented in numerous domains such as smart home/city, industry automation, hospitals and transport. It is inevitable that IoT devices will grow exponentially in future and cloud makes them light-weighted smart devices.

REFERENCES

Alamri, A., Ansari, W. S., Hassan, M. M., Hossain, M. S., Alelaiwi, A., & Hossain, M. A. (2013). A survey on sensor-cloud: Architecture, applications, and approaches. *International Journal of Distributed Sensor Networks*, *9*(2), 917923. doi:10.1155/2013/917923

Biswas, A. R., & Giaffreda, R. (2014, March). IoT and cloud convergence: Opportunities and challenges. In *Internet of Things (WF-IoT), 2014 IEEE World Forum on* (pp. 375-376). IEEE.

Botta, A., De Donato, W., Persico, V., & Pescapé, A. (2014, August). On the integration of cloud computing and internet of things. In *Future Internet of Things and Cloud (FiCloud), 2014 International Conference on* (pp. 23-30). IEEE. doi:10.1109/FiCloud.2014.14

Chen, Y. K. (2012, January). Challenges and opportunities of internet of things. In *Design Automation Conference (ASP-DAC), 2012 17th Asia and South Pacific* (pp. 383-388). IEEE. doi:10.1109/ASPDAC.2012.6164978

Gubbi, J., Buyya, R., Marusic, S., & Palaniswami, M. (2013). Internet of Things (IoT): A vision, architectural elements, and future directions. *Future Generation Computer Systems*, *29*(7), 1645–1660. doi:10.1016/j.future.2013.01.010

Hernández-Muñoz, J. M., Vercher, J. B., Muñoz, L., Galache, J. A., Presser, M., Gómez, L. A. H., & Pettersson, J. (2011, May). Smart cities at the forefront of the future internet. In The Future Internet Assembly (pp. 447-462). Springer Berlin Heidelberg. doi:10.1007/978-3-642-20898-0_32

Lea, R., & Blackstock, M. (2014, December). City hub: A cloud-based iot platform for smart cities. In *Cloud Computing Technology and Science (CloudCom), 2014 IEEE 6th International Conference on* (pp. 799-804). IEEE. doi:10.1109/CloudCom.2014.65

Mineraud, J., Mazhelis, O., Su, X., & Tarkoma, S. (2016). A gap analysis of Internet-of-Things platforms. *Computer Communications*, *89*, 5–16. doi:10.1016/j.comcom.2016.03.015

Parwekar, P. (2011, September). From internet of things towards cloud of things. In *Computer and Communication Technology (ICCCT), 2011 2nd International Conference on* (pp. 329-333). IEEE. doi:10.1109/ICCCT.2011.6075156

Perera, C., Zaslavsky, A., Christen, P., & Georgakopoulos, D. (2014). Sensing as a service model for smart cities supported by internet of things. *Transactions on Emerging Telecommunications Technologies*, *25*(1), 81–93. doi:10.1002/ett.2704

Rao, B. P., Saluia, P., Sharma, N., Mittal, A., & Sharma, S. V. (2012, December). Cloud computing for Internet of Things & sensing based applications. In *Sensing Technology (ICST), 2012 Sixth International Conference on* (pp. 374-380). IEEE. doi:10.1109/ICSensT.2012.6461705

Riggins, F. J., & Wamba, S. F. (2015, January). Research directions on the adoption, usage, and impact of the internet of things through the use of big data analytics. In *System Sciences (HICSS), 2015 48th Hawaii International Conference on* (pp. 1531-1540). IEEE. doi:10.1109/HICSS.2015.186

Saravanan, K. (2017). Cloud Robotics: Robot Rides on the Cloud – Architecture, Applications, and Challenges. In *Detecting and Mitigating Robotic Cyber Security Risks* (pp. 261-274). IGI Global. doi:10.4018/978-1-5225-2154-9.ch017

Saravanan, K., & Saranya, S. (2017). An integrated animal husbandry livestock management system. *Journal of Advances in Chemistry*, *13*(6), 6259–6265.

Singh, D., Tripathi, G., & Jara, A. J. (2014, March). A survey of Internet-of-Things: Future vision, architecture, challenges and services. In Internet of things (WF-IoT), 2014 IEEE world forum on (pp. 287-292). IEEE.

Soliman, M., Abiodun, T., Hamouda, T., Zhou, J., & Lung, C. H. (2013, December). Smart home: Integrating internet of things with web services and cloud computing. In *Cloud Computing Technology and Science (CloudCom), 2013 IEEE 5th International Conference on* (Vol. 2, pp. 317-320). IEEE.

Zanella, A., Bui, N., Castellani, A., Vangelista, L., & Zorzi, M. (2014). Internet of things for smart cities. *IEEE Internet of Things Journal, 1*(1), 22-32.

Chapter 9

Examining Big Data Management Techniques for Cloud–Based IoT Systems

Jai Prakash Bhati
Noida International University, India

Dimpal Tomar
Noida International University, India

Satvik Vats
Birla Institute of Technology, India

ABSTRACT

This chapter provides an insight into big data, its technical background, and how need for it has arisen globally. The evolution of Cloud technology provides a favorable environment for IoTs to nurture and flourish, creating an exponential increase in the amount of data. The Cloud environment provides easy access to this vast data from anywhere on the globe, but this availability has given rise to some challenges for organizations in managing big data efficiently. The chapter discusses the key concepts and technical and architectural principles of big data technologies that help to curb the challenges in managing big data generated by IoTs in the Cloud environment and identifies the important research directions in this area.

1. INTRODUCTION

The world is inundated with data. In an expansive scope of various application areas, data is being gathered at an extraordinary scale. For instance, every customer transactions are being handled by Walmart and then import those transactions into databases and which are estimated to hold more than 2.5 petabytes of data. Another

DOI: 10.4018/978-1-5225-3445-7.ch009

popular social site Facebook, each day handles 250 million photos uploads and the interaction of more than 800 million users with more than 900 million objects. Around more than 5 billion people calling, tweeting, browsing and texting over mobile phones. That much explosion of data is the after effect of dramatic rise in devices situated at the outskirt if networking systems including sensors, cell phones and tablet pcs. The greatest part of this data creates new prospects to find more esteem in human genomics, social insurance, oil and gas, finance, search, surveillance and numerous different zones. As the world is entering the era of "big data". As the digital data being generated from enormous disparate sources (tweets, images and messages uploaded on social media, banking transactions, stock exchange transactions etc.) is flooding the planet. There is a buzz everywhere on the globe about none other than the "Big Data". It is emerging as new realm of Technology that is making everyone to think about it and to adopt it. What makes it so lucrative from the business point of view is its distinct approach and new techniques in dealing with the vast data frequently produced from various distinct sources. The traditional approaches that are being in use since biblical time for data analysis were based on Statistics. In these traditional statistical approaches, approximate measurement of a population is done via process of sampling. On the other hand big data solutions add up new approaches and techniques in dealing with huge data.

1.1 Big Data, "Big Thing"

The results of information technology are anything but difficulty to see a mobile phone in each pocket, a pc in bag pack and huge IT framework work places all around. In any case the less recognizable is the data itself. The evolution of data is not new. It proceeds with a pattern that began in 1970s. What has changed is the velocity and diversity of data. The results in large volume of structured and unstructured data, and the term were coined as "big data". However, there is no rigid definition of Big Data. Big Data is an analogous term portraying a circumstance dedicated to store a large volume of data that is originated very frequently from disparate sources, to process it and perform analysis of large data sets. For a data set to be viewed as big data, it must have at least one attribute that must be able to adapt a proper solution design and architecture for analysis. The traits of Big Data will help to determine the relevant data which is actually featured to be "Big" from the massive amount of data. These characteristics of Big Data are generally introduced by the five "Vs of Big Data" – volume, velocity, variety, veracity and value (Thomas Erl, et al, 2015).

- **Volume:** Big data analytics and solution process a large volume of data which is ever growing and generous. Massive data volume forces to adopt specific data storage and various processing requests. The ability to process anticipated volume of data is the main reason which draws the attention towards big data analytics, for example- Library of Congress.

- **Velocity:** In big data environments, velocity means the increasing rate at which information flows into an arguments and has taken after a comparative example to that of volume. Data velocity is put into point of view while considering that the data volume can be easily created in a moment: hundreds hours of video uploaded on YouTube, over 300 million emails, millions of photos being uploaded on Facebook, millions of transaction handled by Walmart.
- **Variety:** The next dimension of big data is variety. Big data solution support multiple formats to store structured as well as unstructured data as every unstructured form of data cannot be easily fit into relational databases. This is called data variety which leads to various challenges during data transformation, integration processing, and storage.
- **Veracity:** Veracity refers to accuracy or quality of data. As people from various domain are dealing with massive amount of data which is generated with a high velocity and in multiple forms and it is obvious that the accuracy level can never be 100% because of the presence of ambiguities, inconsistency, latency, and deception in data.
- **Value:** It is one of the most important factors of big data as it determines the potential worth of data. Higher the quality of data, the higher will be the value of data for an organization.

1.2 Technology Background of Big Data

Big Data is about voluminous data of diverse types that is streaming with a high velocity. When you move out of the world where you possess your data and have firm control over it. You have to design model that can handle the data in such a hybrid environment. The new environment needs an architecture model that comprehends both the dynamic nature of big data and the prerequisite for applying the knowledge to get profitable results. There is a need arise to design a framework that takes a holistic look/approach towards how all the things to be considered before bringing them at one place. No doubt it will take time at the beginning, but ultimately it will take time at the beginning, but ultimately and also reduce the frustration while implementing the big data solution. Good design principles have much importance while creating an environment for big data solution as technocrats have to deal with many things like storage, analytics, report generation and application. It must consider both the hardware and software. The framework must be efficient to deal with all the functional requirements like capturing the required data, data integration from various sources, organizing the data, data analysis, operation on data, decision making means you have to consider the big data as a strategy, not as a project because your architecture is prepared for the future in a broad perspective (Judith Hurwitz et al. (n.d.). The reference framework for big data is discussed in Figure 1.

Layer 0: The Physical Structure

It is the lowest level consisting of the hardware, the networking system, and a data center or data mart. The task is to find the way to utilize the available resources in efficient manner.

- **Performance:** Higher the performance, higher will be the cost.
- **Service Availability:** What per cent of availability of the service is required highly available service imposes high cost?
- **Reliability:** How much you system stands against the failures. Higher reliability increases the cost.
- **Scalability:** What size of infrastructure you require today and in future.
- **Modularity/Modifiability:** How to easily add or remove resource to/from the infrastructure.
- **Cost:** You have to keep in mind the budget you have efficient to spend on the infrastructure.

As the big data infrastructure demands high performance, high availability, reliability, the hardware resources must be efficiently capable in handling the big

Figure 1. Reference framework for big data
Source: https://www.linkedin.com/pulse/big-data-sciencesthe-technology-stack-steven-seale

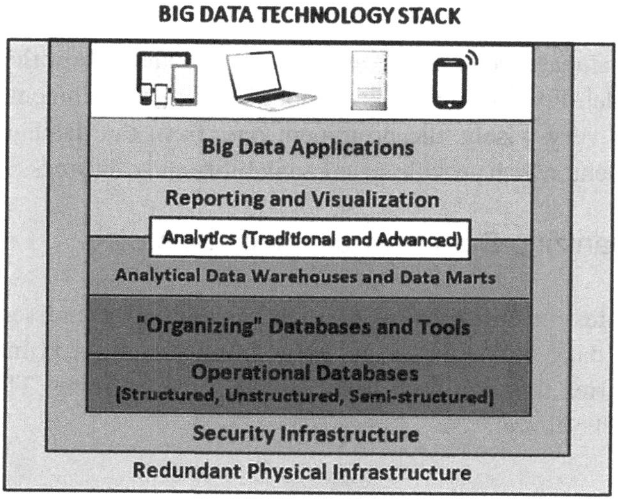

BIG DATA TECHNOLOGY STACK

data. The system must be redundant and resilience as the system redundancy ensures the resiliency to the failure. The resiliency removes the single point failure from the infrastructure.

Layer 1: Security Infrastructure

Security and confidentiality concerns are same for big data as in non-big data environment. Big data architecture should address the following challenges:

- **Data Access:** The access to data should be available only for authorized person.
- **Application Access:** Application should provide essential security from unauthorized access or usage.
- **Data Encryption:** In big data environment, data encryption and decryption will be a great challenge to deal with, as big data comes with volume, velocity and variety. Another issue, to be dealt with, is the selection of appropriate data out of the big data available.
- **Threat Detection:** A proper approach should be followed for threat detection in big data environment, because the system will be more vulnerable, to security breach as uncountable portable devices and social networks increase the risk of security threats and breaches with the generated data or information.

Security Infrastructure must fulfill compliance requirements and individual's privacy like: authorized data access, encryption- decryption, threat detection. It should log all the communication for detecting any anomaly in data or information.

Layer 2: Operational Databases

Almost all the database technologies available in the market show the characteristics like: speed, scalability and robustness in non- big data environment. Organizations have to choose very wisely, the prominent one, from the database technologies available at current, which provide speed, scalability and robustness in performance.

Layer 3: Organizing Data Services and Tools

This layer creates an environment of tools, technologies and services used for harnessing the data, validating it and assembling various data into contextually relevant categories that could be used further for processing. The technologies includes in this layer are;

- A distributed file system
- Serialization services
- ETL (Extract, Transfer and Load) services
- Work flow services for job scheduling

Layer 4: Analytical Data Warehouse and Data Marts

Typically the data warehouses and data marts were used to store the data received from disparate sources in normalized form and organized to facilitate analysis done by the strategy and planning makers in the business. But the big data brings the "action" from top-management to the entry-level employee, so that the business enables these individuals with operational roles to take care of issues in customer support, sales and services, etc.

Layer 5: Big Data Analytics

This layer provides the combination of traditional as well as advanced tools and technologies of data analytics. Traditional tools and techniques of analysis are efficient enough to handle the big data, but they need to be slightly modified to make sure that the algorithms used in these tools could cope up with voluminous data of varied structure in real-time.

Layer 6: Reporting and Visualization

Reporting Tools-This layer consists of the tools and techniques which help in providing "easy-to-understand" representation of the data or information received from different sources, with the help of various reporting formats and layouts.

Visualization Tools- these tools are advancements in reporting tools as their output is interactive and dynamic in nature because of animation techniques used in them.

Layer 7: Big Data Applications

This layer is where all the application of big data resides. Out of these available applications, you can choose any one that best suited for your business requirements.

1.3 Motivational Factors Responsible for The Big Data Adoption

New standards and technologies evolve continuously, along with that there is massive increase in frequently changing requirements, results in generation of "Big Data" which is taking the center stage in IT industry. Often they are the main drivers for data migration. Data migration process require precise planning, right tools and intensive testing to succeed which is only costly and resource intensive and can take much longer time than a couple of weeks. In the traditional way, businesses were driven almost exclusively by internal data held in their information system. But the companies are experiencing that internal data is not sufficient for executing their business in the current market scenario where the things are very dynamic in nature. They are feeling and accepting the importance of external data generated on social media sites, reviews, blogs, etc. that is of much concern for their business. And after harnessing this vast amount of data, the resulting information and/or knowledge will be a great influence in making future business strategies. And this external data is nothing but the "big data". So the organizations worldwide were experiencing the lack of a technology that could help them out in dealing with this so-called big data. And this search for the solution to this big data problem gives rise to the factors which are responsible for motivating these organizations to adopt the big data technology. Some factors which are responsible for big data adoption are discussed below.

1.3.1 Data Deluge

The size of digital information created and shared, worldwide, grew up 9 times in a span of just five years (2006-2011). At present, from overflowing inboxes to the brimming portable devices with music files, a never ending growth in digital data volume is being observed globally. The data is being received and recorded from various distinct sources: banking transactions, stock market transactions, blogs, comments on social media sites, e-commerce sites, smart cities, power grids, sensor data from IoTs, satellite data, etc. that is available in varied forms like structured, semi-structured and non-structured data. Let us consider what is happening in the realm of big data in just 60 seconds (Geoffrey Fox, 2014):

- 168 million emails sent
- 694,445 search queries posted
- 98000 + tweets posted
- 12000 + new ads posted
- 80,000 wall post on Facebook
- 510,040 comments posted on Facebook, and a lot to mention.

1.3.2 Computing Model (Emerging of Cloud Environment)

A remarkable change is noticed in the market, globally, that organizations are shifting their business applications from costly data centers to the more economical cloud services which are facilitating them in minimizing data storage and processing cost by providing pay per use option and service availability. And also this cloud environment is very attractive and favorable for Big Data Analytics (Geoffrey Fox, 2014).

1.3.3 Internet of Things (IoTs)

It is expected that there will be 24-75 billion devices on the Internet by 2020. The concept of smart cities is coming to the reality because; the machines and devices are getting smarter-and-smarter by every passing day. And this become possible because of smart sensors, that are enabling the machines and devices to communicate with each other in a smarter way and generating the big data in the form of never-ending streams of information on the cloud.

1.3.4 Understanding Customer Behavior in Dynamic Marketplace

This is the era of e-commerce where companies are expanding their reach to the customers over the globe and selling their products and services. In order to engage the existing potential customers and making new customers, they are relying on the online customer relationship management (CRM) applications which help them in gaining a better understanding of customer's behavior and preferences, by digging into the reviews, surveys, blogs posted on the Internet portals (Thomas et al. (2015).

1.3.5 Research Paradigm Shift (From Theory to Data-Driven Science)

The quest for knowledge used to, begin with grand theories. Now it begins with a huge amount of data. As the scientific research model is now shifted from first paradigm (grand theories) to fourth paradigm (data driven Sciences). The advantage of the fourth paradigm over other Paradigms is the availability of more data and fewer models, as more data usually beats the better algorithms. And ultimately this more data is actually the big data which demands Big Data Analytics for data processing and analysis (Geoffrey Fox, 2014).

1.3.6 Recommender Systems

There are a lot of cases where a person requires personalized matching of things to people or perhaps a collection of things to a group of people. Like social networking sites which bring together the people having same likes and dislikes. Another example is of matrimonial sites which suggest suitable match for a person on the basis of detailed information mention in their profile (Geoffrey Fox, 2014).

1.3.7 Data Visualization

Data visualization is another factor responsible for encouraging big data techniques adoption. Data visualization is representing the data in graphical format which enables decision makers to see analytics presented visually. It helps in understanding difficult concepts and identifying the new pattern existing in the raw data or information. Regardless of industry types or size, all types of businesses are taking benefits of data visualization techniques in making sense out of the voluminous data such as identifying the areas which need to be improved, understanding the customer behavior that helps in retaining the old customer and in making new customers, helps in predicting sales volumes in particular time period of the year. Big data have all which is required for data visualization and helps in making decision support system much reliable. The goal of the data visualization is to create graphical and pictorial representation for reporting and managing various business operations which are too complicated to understand and observe by looking at the raw data. It also helps in the comprehensiveness of the information.

1.4 Challenges in Big Data Handling

In this section, major challenges faced by the organizations in managing the big data, efficiently for the profitability of the organization has been discussed: (D. Agrawal, et al., n.d.).

1.4.1 Heterogeneity in Data

The data being generated in the real world is very heterogeneous in nature and also in unstructured form. The traditional data handling tools were designed to feed up with homogeneous and structured form of data. Consider for example the nouns and richness of natural language can provide valuable depth. The traditional data handling technologies expect data that must be homogeneous in nature. They are unable to treat the subtle difference in sound, feelings, and facial expressions to communicate in natural language. That's why data aggregation of unstructured and heterogeneous data requires much for the work as heterogeneity is a big challenge in data handling.

1.4.2 Incompleteness of Data

The raw data collected from various distinct sources may be incomplete or some data may be missing due to the ignorance of the importance of the data during collection. For example, let us consider the health record database structure in a company that sells health insurance policies. It has fields for name, DOB, blood group, occupation, conditions of living environment. If one or more piece of information related to the field is not provided by the person obviously the record is stored in the database but the corresponding attribute values will be set to NULL. Suppose a data analysis is done on the basis of occupation but there are many records in the database to where the occupation is NULL. In that case these records can be ignored in data analysis and the results of data analysis done will not be the one that are to be expected. Such kind of incompleteness in data must be managed while performing a data analysis to make out a clear picture of the data. To deal with such incompleteness of data will be a great challenge for Big Data Technology.

1.4.3 Hardware Scale

As it has been a big issue to manage voluminous data, that is increasing exponentially for a long time. In the past, this issue was diminished by making faster processors, to cope up with large volumes of data. But the data volume is getting larger and larger on a faster rate than computing resources. There is a dramatic change observed in processor Technology during last few years. Because of power constraints, clock speeds come to a halt and processors are being built with multi codes and they are increasing. Also there is a Paradigm shift in parallel processing. The parallel data processing techniques that were used in internode parallelism are not applicable directly for intra node parallel computing in a multi core processor. It also arises as a challenge in Big Data handling. As cloud computing came into existence, a new challenge that comes in the way is the sharing level of valuable resources on large clusters. For a long time people were using hard discs for data storage. They are fast enough in sequential IO performances as compared to random IO performances. So the data processing mechanism should be designed in keeping in mind about these limitations. The solid state devices are replacing hard discs in a very fast manner. So the experts have to rethink over designing of new storage systems for data processing that could overcome such kind of limitations in computing hardware.

1.4.4 Privacy and Security Issues

They are one of the major concerns in Big Data handling. There may be a possibility of data theft of confidential data. It's a great technical as well as sociological issue that must be considered on high priority basis. For example in location based services, a user needs to share his/her location with the service provider. Suppose a person ordered online for a pizza delivery at his place. The user needs to share his/her identity and the location that obviously results in privacy concern. Otherwise a potentially malicious attacker could infer the user information. Security is also a major concern in Big Data handling. If the social security data is that it could be misused that may result in various worst situations

1.4.5 Timeliness

As larger data sets take longer time for analysis. The demand of situation is designing of the data processing systems, efficient enough to process the data effectively on a faster rate. Like the analysis of Meteorological data should be quick in time in forecasting of Tsunami, Hurricane, cyclone or earthquake so that precautionary measures could be taken at right time, otherwise such information received later on will be of no use and result in havoc. So a great reduction in data analysis time will be a great challenge of much concerned in dealing with Big Data.

1.4.6 Talent Gap in Big Data Technology

Although the realm of Big Data is spreading at a faster rate and the community of technical people is growing where people are being loaded themselves with Big Data Technologies and tools like Hadoop Ecosystem. Despite the world-wide promotion of Big Data Technologies reality is that the number of skilled person is very much less. The typical experts have gained expertise with experience through tool implementation and their use in programming models. But they lack of expertise and knowledge in data management aspects. Means up to an extent they remain inexperienced in practical knowledge of Big Data Technology (D. Loshin, n.d.).

1.5 Application Areas of Big Data Technologies

Big Data is a hot buzz in today's world. Everyone is talking about Big Data, but it is also true, that Big Data is not as new thing for many companies as they are using Big Data practices for a long time. But these days, almost every organization is moving toward accepting Big Data technology and implementing it in their business for helping them to meet the business objectives of profitability. In this section, various application areas of Big Data technology have been discussed:

1.5.1 Data Analytics in Consumer Goods Sector

Big Data analytics enable an organization that is involved in consumer goods production business, to gain clear inside of consumer behavior data from public reviews, surveys conducted etc. it helps in drawing a clear picture of consumer satisfaction, demand and preferences for a particular product. It enables an organization to find new ways to maintain their existing customers as well as to grab new customers from the market place.

1.5.2 Stock Market

Big Data analytics can help in detecting any abusive trading pattern and alarm before any fraud could be performed.

1.5.3 Banking and Credit Cards Sectors

Big Data Analytics enables banks in gaining in sight of account holders data for their activity pattern. It helps to detect, if there is any strange transaction carried out at unusual locations, protecting them against any fraudulent transactions.

1.5.4 Weather Forecasting

Smart phones like Samsung Galaxy S4 comes equipped with various sensors such as barometer, thermometer, hygrometer, accelerometer to map various atmospheric readings, turning it into a weather station. Such data is collected from these handsets and feed up to weather stations where Big Data Analytics help these stations to analyses the real time data streams for updating the weather conditions and making more accurate forecasts. For example, Weather Signal App is used for accurate and improved localized weather forecasting with the help of BDA (Ben Davis, 2013).

1.5.5 In Healthcare Sector

Electronic health records stored in database could be analyzed for predicting the disease that could appear in a person's body in future by detecting the earlier age symptoms and changing pattern of health records. How valuable search information could be proved for a person from Healthcare perspective (Ben Davis, 2013).

1.5.6 Box Office Success Prediction for a New Movie Before Release

Let us take an example of a Bollywood movie "Baahubali: The Beginning" that was an Indian epic historical fiction now the sequel of this movie Baahubali: The Conclusion is going to release in the month of April 2017. BDA can process and analyze the box office collection of the first part of the movie and on the basis of it; the success rate could be predicted for the upcoming movie, in advance.

1.5.7 Access Authentication to Email Services and Net Banking Services

As Google has hundreds of millions active Google accounts worldwide and the figure is going on increasing. Google has to maintain login credentials for such a large number of users and other related data which used to gain authorized access to account services and prevent unauthorized access account hacking. BDA helps in analyzing the user access logs and identify a typical login from a different device or machine for location and send an alert to the authorized account holder to authenticate the services access through a SMS alert or e-mail sent to the account holder.

2. CLOUD-BASED INTERNET OF THINGS (IoT)

The IoT is creating a remarkable measure of data, which thus puts a colossal strain on the Internet framework. Thus, organizations are attempting to work hard and discover path to mitigate that pressure and take care of the data issues- IoT is centered on empowering automation and controlling of a broad range of real world household things with restricted storage capacity, along with significant issues like security, reliability, privacy and performance. On the other hand, cloud computing has essentially boundless capabilities in the form of storage and executing power and is a substantially more developed technology to handle most of the IoT issues to solve partially. In this matter, a novel information technology in which IoT and cloud are two integral advancement which combined together and relied upon to disorganize both present and future Internet.

2.1 Introduction to Cloud and Internet of Things (IoT)

- **Cloud:** To portray a category of cosmopolitan on-demand computing services firstly offered by various commercial vendors has been originally authored as an umbrella term for "Cloud Computing". The commercial providers are

Google, Microsoft & Amazon. It signifies a paradigm in which a computing framework is seen as a "cloud" through which an individual and businesses access application on demand from any place in the world. This model is introduced with the hidden motive that basically offer computing, software used "as a service" and storage (R. Buyya et al., Dec,2017).

The phrase "cloud" is used to represent the Internet or assorted elements of it to show its provenance in network diagrams. Cloud Computing talks about what crop up when different types of services and applications shifted into the Internet that is "cloud". The key characteristics of cloud computing with main ones being as (Introduction to Cloud Computing, 2010*): Shared Infrastructure, Dynamic provisions, Network access, Metering management.*

In short, cloud computing offers applications and services that boost up business and end-user by providing possible benefits in terms of scalability, elasticity, cost saving, reliability and pay per use feature. Despite of all these pros, cloud computing still faces some notable challenges which may originate a slow down while delivering the services on cloud such as security and privacy, continuous evolution, compliance concerns, lack of standards (Introduction to Cloud Computing, 2010).

- **Internet of Things (IoT):** The Internet has developed essentially since its origin as scholastic networks of PCs. Today it is inescapable source of information for everyone. Now, it has turn into interactive network for consumers, it includes e-tailing gateways, shopping portals and entertainment among different offering. Over the Internet, communication is no longer essentially started by human operators who are hunting down for data. Progressively smart objects such as smart phones are doing so autonomously. The IOT is not yet a substantial reality, but it appears to be likely that the idea will turn into reality, in one or other form, in the near future as the given resources and consideration being dedicated to it through different initiatives around the globe. IOT generally specifies the situation where computing capabilities and network connectivity reaches out to objects, sensors and ordinary everyday things not typically deal with PCs, permitting these devices to produce, transfer and consume the data with negligible human interference. The concept of fusing personal computer systems, sensors and networks for controlling and monitoring the devices has continued for a significant long time. Basically, it is the fusion of digital and physical world by taking various ideas and technical units' altogether. This guarantees to make an environment where smart devices would be capable to direct their transport to adjust according to the environment, self-maintain, self-configure, and self-repair and finally ever play a dynamic role in its own disposal. The concept of IoT aims to boost up the quality of human life to completely a new level (A. Becker et al., n.d). There are four communication models used by IoT implementation and each describe with its own quality and these models has been discussed by Internet Architecture board, involve: Device to Device, Device to Cloud, Device to Gateway and Back End Data Sharing. IoT brings entirely live world view for organizations and Enterprises to take the advantages. Today, how users of Internet will move into IoT, some of the sectors are illustrated; it includes smart cities, energy sector, manufacturing, aviation sector, automobile industry, Healthcare industry etc. But evolution of any technology or innovation has some impact and that remain true for IoT as well as it is still in its early phase and there are as yet many challenges to be overcome before the advantages of IoT can be fully figured it out, they are: security and privacy, connectivity, hardware, architecture, computing power and data model standards.

2.2 Role of Cloud in IoT

To increase the effectiveness in our ordinary everyday Tasks both cloud Technology and IoT serve an important role and shares a complementary relationship. A large amount of data is generated from IoTs and the pathway for these continuously generated data in order to reach its destination is being provided by the cloud Technology (A. Meola, 2016). The technical conditions likewise appear to be ready for this new revolution because the availability of Internet is getting broad day by day, so it is significantly possible to all the computing power to be packed into smaller packages, regular improvement in device power efficiency and obviously, cloud technology supports designers and providers to link everything together genuinely, personal, consistent and effective- exactly what clients need. There are many reasons according to which cloud is truly essential for the success of IoT, few of them are (A. Gupta, 2015):

- **Remote Processing Power:** It might be expected that everything will in the long run to be smart device, by bringing new requests on raw processing power. Also, miniaturization advances and 4G network availability turns out to be much more across the broad, the cloud will acts as the "Hero" by permitting developers to offload processing to cloud services.
- **Bring Down the Entry Bar for Providers Who Need the Framework:** Cloud Technology will make it accessible for those trend setters to accompany the IoT revolt, by offering an instant framework into which they can simply plug and play with their devices and services such as: Analytics and monitoring, Smoothens inter-devices and inter-services interaction, Privacy and security.

2.3 Cloud-Based IoT

The next revolution in the era of Technology is evolution of two new worlds, first IoT and the second is cloud. Nevertheless, various favored circumstances evolving from their integration have been analyzed. From one viewpoint, IoT can profit from virtually and purposely boundless resources and services of cloud to enumerate its technical constraints, for example, processing power and storage. In particular, cloud suggest a powerful solution to implement IoT service management and composition in addition to that applications that accomplish the data or the things generated by them. While on the other side, cloud can get advantage from IoT by extending its degree to manage real-world things in a dynamic and distributed way and for providing new services in a wide range of real life scenarios. The cloud and IoT shares the complementary relationship emerges from distinctive proposals and motivating the new paradigm known as cloud based IoT. Basically, the cloud behaves as a middle layer between the objects and applications, where it conceals all the functionalities and complexity important to implement. Thus, these adoptions of cloud IoT framework partially solve various IoT issues and obtained advantages (A. Botta, et al. 2014).

- **Storage Resources:** In IoT, a huge amount of structured and non-structured data typically called big data having high volume, velocity and variety produced by the broad range of information sources it means the things involved in IoT. Cloud offers virtually boundless on-demand and low cost storage to deal with the data created by IoT in a cost effective and most convenient manner. Once the data moves into the cloud, standard application interfaces are used to manage it in a homogeneous manner by ensuring it through top level security and visualized, get direct accessed from everywhere.
- **Computational Resources and Capabilities:** Because of limited computation resources, IoT devices, that never ground to do on-site processing of data. However, more powerful nodes are being used for data collection and processing but to achieve the scalability without an appropriate infrastructure is quite challenging part. The IoT requirements are fulfilled properly by the cloud because of its unlimited processing capabilities and on-demand model.
- **Communication Resources:** IoT require devices to be IP-enabled for the communication with the object which is very expensive. Cloud provide a reasonable and effective quick fix to solve this issue to connect, track and deal with anything from anywhere at whatever time with the help of built-in applications and customized portal.

- **New Competency:** IoT is portrayed by high heterogeneity of gadgets, protocols, techniques and technologies. Subsequently, adaptability, quality, interoperability, efficiency, accessibility and security can be extremely hard to achieve. The integration with cloud take care of the majority of these issues likewise providing additional characteristics in terms of ease of use, shortened deployment cost and ease of access.
- **New Scenarios:** The new cloud-based IoT model is adopted to set up new outline for smart devices and services depending upon the expansion of cloud through the objects or things.

2.4 Applications of Cloud-Based IoT

There are wide number of applications of cloud-IoT paradigm, they are discussed as (50 Sensor Applications for Smarter World, n.d.):

- **Healthcare:**
  ◦ Contribute to constant and systematic innovative change of Healthcare.
  ◦ Enabling high quality, efficient timely and effective medical services.
  ◦ Proper handling of a large amount of sensor data generated by pervasive healthcare apps, with cloud adoption, leads to elimination of expertise requirement, technical detail abstraction.
- **Smart City:**
  ◦ A common middleware for future Oriented Smart City services.
  ◦ Enable connection, discovery and integration of sensors and actuators and then platforms are created in order to support ubiquitous connectivity and real-time apps for smart cities using cloud architecture.
  ◦ The infrastructure composed of- sensor platform along with APIs for actuating and sensing and a cloud platform for automatic management, analysis and management of big data at large scale, on real world devices.
- **Smart Housing:** In order to set a smart home environment these essential requirements must be satisfied: every device should be able to connect to each other via internal network interconnection, devices should be controlled by intelligent remote from everywhere and provide automation.
- **Smart Metering:** Offer solutions for managing and monitoring of energy consumption, tank level (water, oil or gas), water flow, light and air-conditioning.
- **Smart Securities:** Provide solution by detecting people in unauthorized areas and to get access control to restricted areas.

- **Smart Agriculture:** Provide solutions to wine quality, green houses, meteorological station network for controlling and monitoring soil moisture, micro-climate conditions to maximize the quality and production of veggies and fruit and understanding weather conditions in fields to forecast rain, snow, ice formation, wind and drought changes.

3. BIG DATA MANAGEMENT IN CLOUD-BASED IOT

The term big data management is composed of two primary concerns- first big data and secondly management. In addition to that how these two work together in order to accomplish technology and business objectives.

- **Big Data:** A very large set of data which is blend of structured data extracted from RDBMS, semi-structured data extracted from RFID, XML files, non-structure data and streaming data generated from sensors, web applications, machines and social sites is usually referred as Big Data.
- **Data Management:** A broad practice that envelopes various data disciplines involving date of joining, data warehousing, data administration, data quality event processing and so on.
- **Big Data Management:** However, Big Data is entirely different in terms of content and structure with many variables within it. In order to manage the big data, big data management tools, disciplines and various frameworks are used.
- **Relationship Between Big Data and Cloud:** Cloud computing and big data are bundled together. As Big Data allow the clients by providing the capability to utilize the product to handle various user generated queries in distributed form across various data sets and returns the outcome on time. Cloud Computing provides the underlying support with the help of Hadoop. Another important reason to conjoin the Cloud and Big Data is to bring a cost effective as well as scalable platform in order to support business analytics and handling of unstructured data.

3.1 Big Data Storage Systems on Cloud

Unlike relational databases, NOSQL databases are free of any fixed schemas and joins that's why they provide efficient indexing. No SQL databases are suitable for big data handling and they follow the four database models which are discussed below (K. Grolinger, et al. Dec, 2013):

- **Key-Value Data Base Model:** This kind of database model is used where the data is vigorously changing and requires high availability, like stock market data, railways reservation data, etc. It's a simple data storage model based on key-value pairs, schema-free, efficient in distributed data storage. But this model is not suitable for the cases where relations or structures are needed. The functionality requiring relations and structures must be deployed on the client application. This type of model doesn't support data-level queries and indexing, as the values are opaque to them.

- **Column-Family Store Model:** In such type of database framework, data are stored in column-oriented form. This model provides more efficient indexing and querying as compared to the key-value store model. Here each data set is represented by a unique row-key combination which is composed of various column-families. These column-families further consist of several column-names. The structure almost resembles with key-value database model structure as here row-key is same as the key and column-functions are like values represented by the row-keys.

- **Document -Store Model:** This NOSQL database model is just similar to the key-value model of data storage. Here, a unique document-key is used to represent the location of a document stored in a database. Most of the time documents are stored in JSON format or some other derivatives of this format like CouchDB uses the JSON format; whereas MongoDB uses BSON format for data storage. The benefits of the document-store model are like; it provides a facility to store documents having various structures which provide the flexibility in data storage. It also helps in indexing of documents on the basis of the primary-key as well as document content, but they are inefficient in multiple key operations.

- **Graph Database Model:** This model is inspired by the graph theory and uses the graph as its base for data storage. They are most suitable for storing the data sets, where some kind of relationship between different data elements exists. They are efficient enough to handle the interconnectivity of data and hence much capable of searching.

3.2 Technology Used for Big Data Management in Cloud-Based IoT

At present, there are hundreds of technologies available in the market for managing big data; out of them experts can choose the best suited technology/ technologies as per the requirements. Their choice depends on what kind of problem and /or data they are dealing with. Have a look on some of them (Ruchi Agarwal, et al., 2016).

3.2.1 Hadoop

Apache Hadoop is a distributed batch processing infrastructure for parallel processing on large cluster of commodity nodes. It is an open source project of Apache which is used to implement Google's File System as Hadoop Distributed File System (HDFS) and Google's MapReduce. HDFS is required to store files in a replicated manner across different nodes to provide fault tolerance and high availability during execution of any program in parallel fashion and also capable to manages large volume of data either in terabytes or petabytes scale. Hadoop has followings features which make it capable to handle big data challenges:

- **Scalability:** Hadoop framework provides the scalability feature by automatically redistributing of data and computation jobs to accommodate hardware changes. There is no need to change the data format, if the size of data grow, add the new computational node to manage it.
- **Flexibility:** Hadoop does not require the input data in relational form to analyze; it supports both structured as well unstructured data equally. Hadoop is free of schema and capable to work on any type of data from any number of nodes.
- **Cost Efficiency:** Hadoop framework use the commodity hardware to store and compute large size of datasets usually in tera-bytes and penta-bytes. This commodity hardware is cheap in price and makes big data computation affordable in parallel fashion on number of nodes.
- **Fault Tolerance:** This feature of Hadoop makes it able to recover the data and computational failures caused by any node failure or network congestion. It is very important part of Hadoop framework because computational failure is very common in big data analytics. Hadoop ensures the fault tolerance by making replicas of the same file and storing them on different nodes and by re-initializing the job at respective node which had failed earlier to compute the required task.

Core: Architecture of Hadoop

Hadoop architecture describes the Hadoop software library which consists of HDFS, Hadoop MapReduce, HBase, Pig, HIVE and others integrated modules. The layered architecture of Hadoop software framework is shown in Figure 2.

In Hadoop framework Flume is a distributed system which is responsible to collects, aggregates and transmit log data from disparate source to centralize store. Sqoop is responsible to import and export of data in between structured data stores and Hadoop. HBase and HDFS (Hadoop distributed file system) are mainly

Figure 2. Core- architecture of Hadoop framework

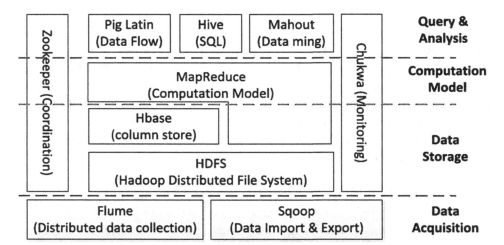

responsible for storage of big data. HDFS is the main unit of Hadoop framework consists of sigble Name node that is responsible for handling the file system metadata and Data nodes that are responsible for storing actual data. In actual scenario, a large size input data file is divided into blocks and these blocks are stored in a set of Data nodes. To guarantee the fault tolerance, each block has many replications which are distributed in different Data nodes in Hadoop environment and prevent the data missing during computation of data. MapReduce is also the important part of Hadoop system architecture which is basically a programming module. The MapReduce framework has a single master Job Tracer and one slave Task Tracker per cluster node. Here Job Tracker is responsible for assigning the task or jobs to Task Tracker which performs the computational job on data and send feedback to Job Tracker about the status of job. Job Tracker is also responsible for re-initialization of jobs to Task Trackers, in case of any fault occurred in data transmission.

Pig and Hive module support SQL-like high level declarative languages. Pig is more suitable for performing the task where data flow is considered while Hive supports ad hoc queries and data summarization. On the other hand, Mahout is a data mining library which support graphical user interface as well. Mahout consists of many core algorithms to perform data mining tasks such as classification, clustering, frequent item sets mining. To monitor and manage the distributed applications which execute on Hadoop, Zookeeper and Chukwa are used. More specifically, Zookeeper is responsible for maintain configuration, naming, providing group services and distributed synchronization. Chukwa is responsible for analyzing the system status.

3.2.2 MapReduce

It is the kind of programming model that expressing the distributed computation for large amount of the data. It also provides the execution frame work for large amount of the data processing on clusters for group of servers. In other sense, it has been concluded that, map reduce present a fame work which runs on the computational cluster. MapReduce expressed into the form of two functions, Map and Reduce. Map function usually applied on data set and provides the list of the result. And Reduce function selects and resolves the results from many mapping operation which is executed in parallel. Map reduce model divides the input dataset into independent subsets that are processed by Map and Reduce function. Compute nodes and storage nodes, usually both are same. According to the map reduce model, program, which is written into functional fashion are parallelized without any external interference and executed on large cluster for group of hardware. Runtime system records the information with respect to broken data, schedule program execution on every machine which helps to handle the machine failure and provide management control to inter machine communication.

- **Map Reduce Design:** In map reduce model, user define the map function which process the (key, value) that generate a set of intermediate (key, value) pairs and reduce function merge that all values which is associated with the key values. According to map reduce design every Map() operation is completely independent from others, So that Map() operation works in parallel. In same manner Reduce() operation also work independently. By the Map() function, it takes the one pair of the data from the data domain and gives a list of pair either from same domain or from other domain which may be different from the initial one. In every (k1, v1) pair in parallel gives the list of (k2, v2) pair in execution of each Map() operation. When the (k2, v2) pair is produced, then map reduce frame work collects all pairs of (k2, v2) with their same keys from all list and it into a group. Then sort that group by keys.

Map (k1, v1) → list (k2, v2)

After the Map() operation, Reduce() function is applied on to these groups in parallel. And provide set of values of the same domain that accepts key K2 and list (v2) for K2. This operation merges all the possible values to form the smaller list which may call v3.

Reduce (k2, list (v2)) → list (v3)

So, MapReduce model transform a list of (key, value) into another list of values.

Figure 3 shows how the input data first split out into pieces of data, commonly known as block or chunk of data at various nodes where map function work on block-data. Reduce function uses the shuffled block-data of various nodes and aggregate them to generate final output. This output finally stored in HDFS.

- **HDFS:** HDFS is stands for Hadoop distributed file system, which is design for to store large amount of the data set with strong reliability, and provide stream to data set which having high bandwidth. If talk about the large cluster, thousands or more than thousands of servers either it will host or client are attached to storage and their execution with respect to the user application. HDFS architecture as shown in Figure 4 is a part of the Hadoop framework.
- **HDFS Client:** By the HDFS client, user application task provide access of the file system, which is as same as the conventional file system. HDFS has authority of reading, writing and deleting the files and create and delete the directories according to operation provided.
- **HDFS Name Node (Master):** It maintain the name space of the file system, it maintain the cluster and their related information which is formed earlier

Figure 3. MapReduce key-value pair's generation
Source: Verification and validation of mapreduce program model for parallel k-means algorithm on hadoop cluster (Kumar et al., 2013).

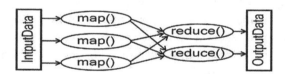

Figure 4. The architecture of HDFS
Source: Verification and validation of mapreduce program model for parallel k-means algorithm on hadoop cluster (Kumar et al., 2013)

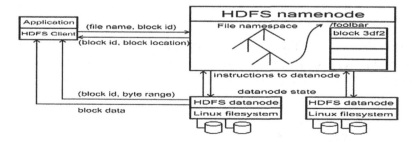

and previously also. It also supports the replication of the data blocks and maintains its track which is evenly distributed. It maintains the files and block list consist into the each file. It also maintains the Meta data concept. It maintains the track of directory creation and deletion into an activity log.

- **Data Nodes (Slaves):** It maintains the storage of the local file system, that local file system consist of the blocks of data and Meta data for every blocks. These data and Meta data provide service to the task that they going to execute, it maintain and send the status of the periodic report to the name node. And it also provides the data block to different nodes required by the name node.

3.3 Big Data Management of Cloud-Based IoTs

The IoTs generate big data in continuous manner at high pace that need to be managed, processed and analysed for decision making. And this data can't be handled by traditional conjunction of hardware and software, which is running out of storage capacity and data processing capabilities. Here the cloud- environment comes into existence as a "Life Saver" for organizations that were facing challenges of big data. Let us take a scenario to understand, how the entire process goes on from generation of big data by a wide range of information sources to management & processing of data on Hadoop Framework via cloud. The Figure 5 describes a 3-tier architecture for big data management.

Figure 5. Three-tier architecture for big data management

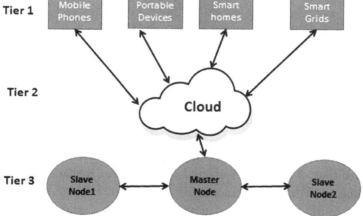

Tier 1: This tier comprise of wide range of IP-enabled information sources (IoTs) viz. mobile phones, portable devices, smart homes, smart grids, sensor networks, etc. that are continuously pumping out big data in unstructured, structured and incomplete form, onto the cloud platform.

Tier 2: This tier consists of cloud environment, composed of various powerful nodes capable of big data collection and processing, since IoTs have limited computational resources due to which these are unable to perform out site processing of big data. And these requirements of IoTs can only be fulfilled properly by cloud as it avails unlimited computing power and on-demand model of services.

Tier 3: This tier consists of Hadoop Framework and Mapreduce programming model where various nodes are created, out of which one acts as master node(name node) and rest of all behaves as slaves(data nodes) and proved services for data processing. Each node avails the underlying support for the distributed storage and processing by Hadoop Distributed File System (HDFS). The master node fetches the big data, need to be processed, from cloud environment by firing a valid query. Once the master node receives the data, it creates various slave nodes based on the data size available for processing and distribute it among slave nodes. Slave nodes receive the data from master node based on a particular attribute and create a schema for that data and store it in structured format. Then process and analyze the data and submit the results back to the master node which in turn proved the results onto the cloud. Once the processed data move on to the cloud, standard application programming interfaces (APIs) are used to manage it in a homogeneous manner by ensuring it, through top level security and visualization techniques and get direct access from anywhere for decision makers.

3.4 Future Trends of Big Data Management in Cloud Environment

How big data technologies play important role in handling the big data in cloud environment and what will be the trends to be follow in future? The following segment will provide the solution to this problem.

- **Potential Growth in Big Data Management Technology Implementation and Its Use:** A survey conducted in the global market for predicting the potential growth in implementation and use of BDM technologies reveals exciting results. According to survey report 60% of participants, who took part in survey, shows their interest in BDM Technologies (Hadoop tools comma

MapReduce, HDFS, NOSQL Database Management Systems, Streaming data, Private cloud, In-memory database, etc.) and committed them to accept these technologies in their business within a span of 3 years. The results indicate a dramatic increase in usage of BDM Technologies (Philip Russom, 2013).

- **Migration From Data Centers to the Cloud:** Almost all size of organizations: whether they are a small mid-size for even large companies for planning to migrate on to the cloud from the costly data centers. They want to minimize the expenditure on traditional data centers and taking their business applications to the ultimate Cloud, that provides them greater flexibility in processing and business operations (Mary Shacklett, 2016).

- **Aggregation of Digital Data (Unstructured Form):** Every organization is planning to make a critical shift in their data aggregation approaches, means to bring the heterogeneous and unstructured stream of data generating out of distinct data coming in the form of tweets, social media comments, blogs and machine data from IoTs (Mary Shacklett, 2016).

- **Harnessing the Hidden Opportunities Out of the Dark Data:** Gartner Inc., a consulting and market research company defines the dark data as the data collected, processed and stored by a company during their regular business practices, but never be used to gain insight of it. The opportunity is under the dark data the information on knowledge buried within the dark data, if exposed and included in data aggregation process could results in providing the company a much comprehensive picture of past performances that could prove to be a great help in making future Strategies for business (Mary Shacklett, 2016).

4. CONCLUSION

In today's scenario, big data is generating exponentially with high velocity and in a diverse form, obtained from IoTs like sensory data from smart grids, smart homes & smart cities, etc. approximately at the rate of one peta bytes data per day and it requires a reliable distributed platform for the management and analysis of big data which is being provided by Hadoop Framework and MapReduce Programming Model. This open source project contains individual modules (Pig, Hive, Hbase, Zookeeper, Mahout, Flume, Sqoop, Chukwa) in itself which can be integrated to core module such as MapReduce and HDFS for desired computational and data management purposes.

REFERENCES

Agarwal, R. (2016). *Knowledge Discovery Using Big Data Analytics with practical Approach on Hadoop*. LAMBERT Academic Publishing.

Agrawal, D. (n.d.). *Challenges and Opportunities with Big Data: A community white paper*. Retrieved from https://www.purdue.edu/discoverypark/cyber/assets/pdfs/BigDataWhitePaper.pdf

Almoqren, N., & Altayar, M. (2016). The Motivations for Big Data Mining Technologies Adoption in Saudi Banks. *International Conference on Information Technology (Big Data Analysis) (KACSTIT)*. doi:10.1109/KACSTIT.2016.7756075

Becker, A. (n.d.). *Internet of Things*. Retrieved from https://atos.net/content/dam/global/documents/your-business/atos-white-paper-internet-of-things.pdf

Botta, A. (2014). On the Integration of Cloud Computing and Internet of Things. *International Conference on Future Internet of Things and Cloud*. doi:10.1109/FiCloud.2014.14

Buyya, R. (2017). *Cloud Computing: Principles and Paradigms*. John Wiley & Sons.

Erl, T. (2015). *Big Data Fundamentals Concepts, Drivers & Techniques*. Prentice Hall.

Fox, G. (2014, January). *Big Data Applications & Analytics Motivation: Big Data and the Cloud; Centerpieces of the Future Economy*. Retrieved from https://www.slideshare.net/Foxsden/big-data-applications-analytics-motivation-big-data-and-the-cloud-centerpieces-of-the-future-economy

Grolinger, K. (2013, December). Data Management in Cloud Environments: NoSQL and NewSQL Data Stores. *Journal of Cloud Computing: Advances, Systems and Applications*. Retrieved from https://journalofcloudcomputing.springeropen.com/articles/10.1186/2192-113X-2-22

Gupta, A. (2015). *The Role of Cloud Tech in the Internet of Things*. Retrieved from https://www.knowlarity.com/blog/the-role-of-cloud-tech-in-the-internet-of-things/

Hurwitz, J. (n.d.). *Big Data for Dummies*. John Wiley & Sons .

IBM Cloud. (n.d.). *What is Cloud?* Retrieved from https://www.ibm.com/cloud-computing/learn-more/what-is-cloud-computing/

Introduction to Cloud Computing. (2010). Retrieved from https://www.dialogic.com/~/media/products/docs/whitepapers/12023-cloud-computing-wp.pdf

Kumar. (2013). Verification and validation of mapreduce program model for parallel k-means algorithm on hadoop cluster. *International Journal of Computer Applications, 72*(8).

Loshin, D. (n.d.). *Addressing Five Emerging Challenges of Big Data.* Retrieved from https://www.progress.com/docs/default-source/default-document-library/Progress/Documents/Papers/Addressing-Five-Emerging-Challenges-of-Big-Data.pdf

Meola, A. (2016). *The roles of cloud computing and fog computing in the Internet of Things revolution.* Retrieved from http://www.businessinsider.com/internet-of-things-cloud-computing-2016-10?IR=T

Rose, K. (2015). *The Internet of Things: An Overview.* Retrieved from https://www.internetsociety.org/sites/default/files/ISOC-IoT-Overview-20151221-en.pdf

Rouse, M. (2012). *Cloud Computing.* Retrieved from http://searchcloudcomputing.techtarget.com/definition/cloud-computing

Russom, P. (2013). *Managing Big Data.* Retrieved from https://www.sas.com/content/dam/SAS/en_us/doc/whitepaper2/tdwi-managing-big-data-106702.pdf

50 . Sensor Applications for Smarter World. (n.d.). Retrieved from http://www.libelium.com/resources/top_50_iot_sensor_applications_ranking/

Shacklett, M. (2016). *6 Big Data Trends to Watch in 2017.* Retrieved from http://www.techrepublic.com/article/6-big-data-trends-to-watch-in-2017/

Solution Approaches for Big Data. (n.d.). Retrieved from https://sp.ts.fujitsu.com/dmsp/publications/public/wp-bigdata-solution-approaches.pdf

Chapter 10
Examining Software–Defined Networking for Cloud–Based IoT Systems

Garima Singh
Indira Gandhi Delhi Technical University for Women, India

ABSTRACT

The Internet of Things (IoT) represents the current and future state of the internet. The large number of things (objects) connected to the internet produces a huge amount of data that needs a lot of effort and processing operations to transfer it to useful information. Maximizing the utilization of this paradigm requires fine-grained QoS support for differentiated application requirements, context-aware semantic information retrieval, and quick and easy deployment of resources, among many other objectives. These objectives can only be achieved if components of the IoT can be dynamically managed end-to-end across heterogeneous objects, transmission technologies, and networking architectures. In this chapter, Software Defined Systems (SDS) is described as a new paradigm to hide all complexity in traditional system architecture by abstracting all the controls and management operations from the underling devices (things in the IoT) and setting them inside a middleware layer, a software layer, using a software-based control plane.

1. INTRODUCTION

After a couple of years, world is going to witness a technology transformation because Internet will interface billions of "things" which will be communicating with each other (Perera et al., 2014a). Devices associated to this IoT will be highly

DOI: 10.4018/978-1-5225-3445-7.ch010

assorted in nature and will provide functions such as processing, sensing, storing capabilities. All the communicating objects will collaborate with themselves in a machine-to-machine pattern and with the users as well, upheld by their undeniably smartphones and other mobile devices, prompting a more unavoidable and deeply engaging Internet. This will encourage an extensive variety of utilizations in fields such as industrial automation and home, optimization of public services, real-time healthcare monitoring, energy management, etc.

The stretch of the IoT has constraint of complex necessities to both frameworks organization and internetworking plans in present and future frameworks.. To make it honest to goodness, networks have to welcome heterogeneity in devices as well as in networking behavior and underlying protocols. The IoT components are sorted out in 4 layers, as shown in Figure 1. The principal layer is the sensing layer, consist all RFIDs, Wireless Sensor Networks (WSN) and sensors. Data delivered through this layer is gathered with the help of aggregation layer (Layer 2). Distinctive sorts of aggregators are conceivable relying upon the sensing devices of the first layer. Aggregators either handle the information specifically or transfer that information to the other processing nodes of Layer 3. After information is handled, it can be transferred to the Cloud by means of an Internet connection (Layer 4), where it will be available to get used by countless.

In this way, unmistakably the IoT gives an amazing networking atmosphere in form of applications and devices both. In any case, IoT has most difficult issue of heterogeneity, which is required to exist with an exceptional extension. For instance, the sensing layer is relied upon to use diverse technologies like ZigBee and Bluetooth Low Energy (BLE) (Perera et al., 2014b). Diverse transmission technologies might be utilized, such as 3G/4G and WiFi, to guarantee the connectivity of diligent level at Layers 2 and 3. To bolster these transmission technologies, network operators use segments from various sellers, confounding their management and diminishing their interoperability. Besides, operators and service providers are progressively actualizing system and server virtualization arrangements for the end goal to amplify the use of their assets, which presents huge administration issues. Rapid and proficient deployment of services improvement of information delivery and boosting up the use of the Big Data generated by the IoT are the challenges at Layer 4 to maintain a fine-grained end-to-end Quality. The initial move in direction of this colossal enterprise is the description of general schemes to segregate data and control planes in routing and switching elements. This has gone well with the improvement of intermediate network elements, which now end up with mere packet forwarders, and the meaning of a all-purpose control protocol that is utilized to set them with the essential forwarding rules to achieve with the goal of the network. In addition, this scheme likewise proposes a conceptually centralized *brain* which has the knowledge of topology and condition of the network to take decisions about packet forwarding, represents them with forwarding rules, and correspond them to the forwarding entities. Thinking about the qualities of SDN from the IoT viewpoint gives the motivation to think how SDN can be utilized to maintain the heterogeneity in systems and objects while designing a greater cooperation scheme by simply integrating into the network another higher layer control arrangement that connects with the SDN controllers. In addition, Cloud computing designs are relied upon to assume a noteworthy part in utilizing a portion of the applications, services, and network of the IoT (Palattella et al., 2013). To put it plainly, the programmable elements which are the primary drivers behind the theory of SDN, presents a noteworthy prospective for the heterogeneity and interoperability in the few layers of the IoT.

Two key advantages of SDN are the capacity to disentangle the network by abstracting its abilities and conveying applications all the more rapidly, and also the capacity to dispense with provisioning blunders and increment security and consistence through policy-based automation. Automation includes reconsidering how organize administrations are enacted. One should move from a setup driven approach with related layers of operational complexity to a policy based auto-instantiation demonstrate where network services are sent utilizing characterized business and network layouts. For Cloud services to flourish, the network framework must progress toward becoming as unique, as virtualized, and as consumable as the compute infrastructure. Progressively organizations will appreciate the more noteworthy business deftness and operational disentanglement of a virtualized network, utilizing SDN, to empower Cloud environments that are responsive, strategy driven and exceedingly computerized.

2. SDN AND CLOUD-BASED IOT RELATIONSHIP

Software defined networking (SDN) have one essential features of the purported "IT-zation or softwarization" of telecom infrastructures. SDN doesn't simply influence of Layer two and layer three services like networking and switching but additionally impacts layer four to layer seven (Arbiza et al., 2015).

Be that as it may, SDN and IoT are not reliant on each other, but rather they are positively commonly useful. Software-Defined Radio (SDR) can improve the interoperability and set up the infrastructure for future devices with the goal that they aren't confined by bandwidth or frequency. A portion of the present issues confronted by the industry can be settled by giving a end-to-end wireless platform for IoT. This, thus, can empower optimized communication from a sensor network to a wider area via a radio network. Integrating an IT-based SDR into IoT devices can deal with all base band processing via multi-cores processors on a customary

IT platform. This can be fixing to speeding up technologies like vector processors, parallel processors, and SIMD.

In other words, SDR can act as the central hub or router where several users can connect to the device via Wi-Fi, cellular, or Bluetooth to control or get data from any wireless device. One of the best things about SDR is the fact that you can essentially enhance signal processing with low latency. Further, you can also use some wireless optimization technologies like:

- Energy efficiency design
- Dynamic spectrum allocation
- Interference mitigation IT-based SDR systems like Crimson TNG will be highly adaptable to handle various needs of deployment.

Further, wireless optimization like 4G can efficiently enhance the spectrum to enable long distance coverage while being highly resistant to interference. With SDR, various large-scale auto optimization technologies can be built on a Self-Organize Network (SON). As everything can be handled from one platform, it will be much easier to support and add value to each IoT device. This is what makes SDR special; it can essentially bridge communication and data transfer of many wireless devices including ones that may be thought to be impossible (e.g. baby monitor through Wi-Fi or control your Bluetooth device through a cellular connection). SDR has been around for decades, so it's a tried and tested solution that offers high stability, flexibility, and reliability. It's a platform that is ideal to put up a communications infrastructure for IoT applications. IoT will Enable SDR to Finally Realize its True Potential It's all about machine-to-machine communication and this makes SDR best suited for this type of new technology. So far, SDR was primarily used by defense, public and emergency service, and for research and development. With IoT, the potential is limitless as data analytics, social media, and internet of services can all be enhanced by this technology. With everything working effortlessly together, it has a real potential of being something revolutionary. Without wireless communication, there won't be an IoT to talk about. As a result, design teams are forced to build a device capable of seamless connectivity, enhanced control, and efficiency. These heterogeneous systems will need to incorporate distributed networks, FPGA computation, and real-time elements. As wireless systems become more complex, algorithms need to be designed to deal with issues surrounding security, coexistence, bandwidth, and power efficiency. As a result, prototypes need to be built with real world signals and not just theoretical paradigms. Currently, the prototyping methods have been inefficient, so SDR innovation has been derailed by inefficient software that has been indirect and disjointed. There needs to be a platform designed to bridge the gap and create a unified design to transfer the algorithm to hardware. That is essentially the next step to build a better IoT solution. New products like Crimson TNG is the right choice as it offers extensive flexibility that can aid rapid prototyping to compute elements that control behaviors in the generic wide bandwidth RF front end, user-programmable FPGAs, and multicore processors. At the moment, the tools to enable rapid seamless transition of algorithms on a processor are non-existent. FPGAs offer this capability using specialization tools, which if used effectively, combine with the flexible radio front end and offer a complete solution. The demand for the end product is insatiable, so as we approach 5G, communication system design standards will be improved significantly.

Yet, now there are the conditions for a leap forward: indeed, the telecom industry is thinking about this conceivably impactful because of the development of low-latency, ultra-broadband connections and elite processing power. Technology today has all the earmarks of being prepared for a practical organization of SDN.

This is a possibly huge change of the telecom infrastructure. In the long haul, the refinement between the network and the Cloud is probably going to vanish, as an ever increasing number of capacities will be performed either in the network or in the Cloud contingent upon the execution prerequisites and costs advancements. The control and coordination capacities will be the key in calculation for achievement restraining the complexity of an infrastructure executing millions of software transactions. The most vital necessity will be guaranteeing ultra-low application latency.

Indeed, even still, these patterns are making network and Cloud computing advancement available to all ventures in any piece of the world on an equivalent premise. This advancement will decrease the limits for new players to enter the telecom and Information Communication Technology (ICT) markets: rivalry is being moved to the domain of programming.

Actually, even today information and data are promptly achieving practically every edge of the world through ultra-broadband, low- latency systems, where an enormous amount of computing via the Cloud is accessible to change it into knowledge. Be that as it may, this is the meaning of "intelligence": the capacity of preparing and exchanging information to comprehend what's occurring in the environment, to adjust to changes and to learn. Accessibility of tremendous measure of Cloud processing and capacity, interconnected by adaptable and quick network will be make an unavoidable "machine intelligence" ready to transform the space-time physical measurements of life, as the physical direct presence of human will be less and less required to play out specific occupations or assignments.

When all is said in done, we can contend that these patterns are quickening the move towards the Digital Society and the Digital Economy, where the network frameworks, more unavoidable and embedding processing and storage capabilities, will turn into the "nervous system" of our general public. This will empower new administration situations. This empowers the working of IoT. In the book *The Second Machine Age*, the writers Brynjolfsson and McAfee contend the exponential development in the computing power of machines, the measure of advanced data and the quantity of moderately cheap interconnected devices will bring soon the "machines" to do things that we, people, are normally doing today. This is again another feature of a similar IT-zation slant: the formation of another and inescapable "machine knowledge", bolstered by an exceedingly adaptable system, having ability to change the economy.

3. ARCHITECTURES OF SDN FOR CLOUD BASED IOT

IoT is going to scale upto 50 billion devices by the year 2020, it will have a need of an agile and flexible infrastructure with SDN that only a mature virtualized Cloud-based architecture can deliver.

The drive for virtualization began with Cloud technologies and has evolved to include technologies like SDN and NFV. The lynchpin that holds the key to success for all of these Cloud-enabled, virtualized architectures is the need for a unified and holistic management and orchestration system. This system must be able to understand the disparate components within the architecture through analytics, have the heuristics intelligence to analyze the data from a broad ecosystem perspective and orchestrate the environment through policies, as well as have the ability to enact changes automatically to adjust for shifting conditions.

Meanwhile, IoT must find a way for devices with diverse functions and a myriad of connectivity models to function within the networks and Internet of today. WiFi, Bluetooth, and cellular wireless are just a few of the access technologies IoT devices will use to connect to the Internet. SDN for Cloud based IoT presents the biggest challenge to network design that network architects have seen in a long time. To properly manage the number of devices, their harmonic connections, and bandwidth consumption, a massive network infrastructure must be put in place to manage the peak loads. Network resources can be allocated and de-allocated as needed by the network-aware, ecosystem-aware management and orchestration system.

3.1 The Main Characteristics of the Architecture

3.1.1 Analytics

The system must be able to collect information from unrelated technologies and multiple vendors. Data from network components, application health metrics, DNS information, routing topologies, and many other elements must be collected. The management and orchestration system must understand the inter-relationships between these different data points relative to the specific architecture and configuration of the virtualized infrastructure.

3.1.2 Heuristics

Once the data is collected, an intelligence needs to exist that understands the inter-relationships between these data points and how it relates to the delivery of the business applications and, in turn, understand how the application is impacted by the real-time analytical data. Individual customer and application-based policies have to be programmed into the system to provide a functional understanding that the heuristics engine can leverage to present meaningful and holistic information.

3.1.3 Orchestration

Once the intelligent management and orchestration system understands the architecture and behavior of the application delivery infrastructure, it can make recommendations and provide insight to enact changes to the current environment to adjust the Cloud ecosystem to optimize the application delivery based on different application service level assurance (SLA) levels. Not all applications and functions are created equal. The HVAC automation system has different resilience and performance requirements than the assembly line automation infrastructure, which, in turn, has different requirements than the personal health and monitoring devices.

3.1.4 Automation

Ultimately, it is essential to automate the processes of the management and orchestration system. Removing the human element removes the chance for human error and reduces the operational needs to support the infrastructure that may have thousands of devices and applications on it, if not billions.

3.2 Ideal Architectures

The Open Networking Foundation (ONF) have obtained leading role in SDN standardization. The SDN architecture model is shown in the Figure 1 [Mashal et al, 2015] In the SDN architecture model, there are Control layer, Application Layer and Infrastructure Layer. Here the Application Layer consists the end-user business applications. The Control Layer consists of SDN controllers which belong to the control plane. It offers the control functionality which is logically centralized and used to manage the network forwarding behavior all the way through an open

Figure 1. Layered IoT structure

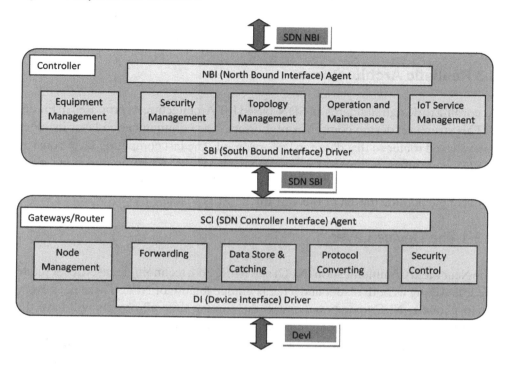

interface. The Infrastructure Layer consist of devices such as switches and routers which belong to the data plane. It provides packet switching and forwarding.

To understand IoT, it is important to have the IoT architecture model in mind. Several interesting IoT architecture models have been proposed (e.g., IEEE, 2014; Atzori & Iera, 2010; Minerva et al., 2015). These exiting IoT architecture models focus on different application aspects related to IoT. In this book chapter, the role of SDN on the IoT architecture will be studied. Layering the IoT architecture into Service Layer, Network Layer, and Sensing Layer based on Marshal et al. (2015) and Koponen (2010). The Service Layer provides information services according to the user. The Network Layer includes the gateway and the routes for the data transmission from gateways to different application users. The Sensing Layer includes sensing devices such as sensors, actuators, and RFID (Radio Frequency Identifier). These devices are usually not expensive but smart enough for sensing. They sense and collect data from different physical, human, and natural worlds in an intelligent and collaborative way, and temporarily store the collected data in the devices with small amount of memory. The collected data are then transmitted to the gateway which is done usually by wireless transmission using MQTT (Message Queue Telemetry

Transport) protocol or HPTT (Hypertext Transfer) protocol. Since the quantity of sensed and collected data may be large, the data compression and the aggregation methods may be used for the adequate data transmission.

3.3 Realistic Architectures

According to design standards an SDN-based IoT Architecture, is proposed in Figure 2. This structural design comprises of 4 layers. The communication layer includes gateway and router so that data can be forwarded. The last computing layer consists of SDN controllers, billing and accounting mechanisms. A new architecture for IoT is described by looking into the today's networking models where Cloud will help to make the administration of the vast IoT network viable.

3.3.1 The Device Layer

The Near Field Communication (NFC) and RFID both technologies used to facilitate the IoT. Acting as both reader and a tag is unique feature of NFC. These days every smart phone is NFC operational and in the coming time all objects will have the RFID tag. This RFID can examine several tags at once but NFC used to examine single tag at a time. These sensors are the great tools of IoT for incorporating RFID tages along with sensors (Mashal et al., 2015). Low energy Bluetooth is also one of the leading tool for tagging these types of devices.

Quick response (QR) code is one more competitor of low-cost tagging. The achievement of the QR code standard straightforwardly depends on pervasiveness of its reader. As it is a utilization of the high-resolution camera available in each and every smart phone.

These are technologies which we have to use at Device layer to make SDR enable IoT applications.

3.3.2 Network Layer

Heterogeneity ends at this layer. The primary motive of this layer is to interface vertical silos networks with the data received from the device layer. Subsequently, the most important part is software defined gateways on this layer. The communication in between the heterogeneous network islands is the responsibility of this gateway. It will do the translation of address etc., able to route the access control etc. The layer of gateways will virtualized the underlying objects and they will get unique addresses (IPv6). A considerable measure of work has been done with regards to applying SDN in various spaces, for example: Telecom (Hampel et al., 2013), Cellular Network

(Jin et al., 2013), Ad-hoc Network, Wireless Network (Alcaraz et al., 2010). The most general thing among these proposed arrangements is the utilization of an OF switches controlled by a SDN controller rather than specific gateways.

One more organizing problem is how to place the computing power (i.e. data servers). Placing them on the edge gateways will bring a number of power consumption problems and keep out heavy processing. Then again, putting them on a central server would be hurtful in respects of system inaccessibility and it will expand latency inquiries for progressing applications, for example, keen industrial facility. Thus a hybrid model is required, designating the processing power between the Cloud and the fog hubs. The fog hubs arranged in the edge passages could be required to improve overall proficiency Along these lines, applying smart algorithms figuring out which information must be assembled locally and which information must be send to the Cloud and which must be overlooked is basically required for the information administration designs.

3.3.3 Control Layer

The arrangement of network for all calculations are dealt with at this layer. Collecting the topology data, preparing the sending rules by sorting out the steering calculations, applying booking calculations and portraying security rules are the real elements of this layer. Fundamentally, the southbound interface is utilized for the association with the passages; an enlargement of Open Flow will be required and the design of the SD-entryways ought to be conceivable through specific administration conventions. The northbound interface (e.g. REST) is the method of correspondence amongst controller and application layer. Regardless, the centralization of the control may act adaptability hindrances. Accordingly, one have to realize some conveyed framework (East/West-bound interfaces) to deal with this issue; Thus, Onix (Koponen et al., 2010), ONOS (Berde et al., 2014), and OpenDaylight (Medved et al., 2014) are the instances of controllers demonstrating dispersed plan capacities. Besides, a virtualization layer is incorporated (e.g. FlowVisor, Open Virtex, and so forth.) to ensure fine-grained stream administrations. On a very basic level, the centralization of the control will influence the security change of this design. The controller needs to control the portals and furthermore need to control the central systems which have SDN hubs by affect.

3.3.4 Application Layer

The softwarization uncovers its handiness at this layer. Through the data given by the control layer many capacities are executed and are progressively included here. One more favorable position of owing focal control is the limit of passing on comparable applications on different SD-Gateways. Regardless, the security controls on the application layer ought to be particularly expected for ensuring dependable data use by the unmistakable applications. Thusly, the QoS administration application is fundamental in the IoT case. Fundamentally, some IoT application zones like e-Health, Industrial control are extremely pivotal and have a need of high QoS parameter; subsequently, scanning for a pleasant QoS administration calculation will be a basic enabling operator of some IoT applications. Each other application that can be streamlined and overhauled using the joined control perspective is Billing administration. In this way, pushed security structure (e.g. Shiro, SecKit) will be used at the product layer to give some versatility and dependability to the security and assurance administration.

IoT administrations at the administration layer are work through administration engineers and administrators by the programming of the SDN controllers. As per the current situation and necessity of the system, one focal SDN controller or a few controllers are utilized to control the capacities agreeably. As per the SDN theory, the controllers are conveyed in a physically dispersed way however sensibly they are brought together.

The functions of the major components in the architecture are the following:

3.3.5 SDN Controllers

The controllers control the information sending as well as. As appeared in Figure 3, SDN controllers have the accompanying capacities:

1. Hardware administration, for example, virtual system assets, arranging passages/ switches, tenets and approaches for managing the information in the ensuing gadgets and so forth.
2. IoT benefit administration, for example, refreshing calculations for Data Processing and Storage focus, putting away and reserving strategies and furthermore adjusting and erasing administrations bolstered by portals.
3. Topology administration, for instance refreshing topology and directing estimation.
4. Operation and upkeep (O&M): observing UIs, keeping up working logs, overseeing practical modules goes under this.
5. Security administration for instance verifying administration access and identifying clashes.
6. Actualizing SDN south bound (SB) and north bound (NB) interfaces.

3.3.6 Gateways/Routers

As appeared in Figure 3, the duty of passages/switches is information sending in the systems. Alongside sending information, Gateways can store nearby information, or process the information through the SDN controller's guidelines. Different elements of passages/switches are administration of hub, security control and convention changing over. Information will be prepared as per the chosen strategy.

When all is said in done, the accompanying capacities for handling information are required:

1. Capacities for speaking with adjacent IoT gadgets to gather information at that point sending the information to information handling focuses or remote portals for facilitate investigation and might be for perpetual capacity.
2. Capacities for speaking with IoT gadgets at remote side.
3. Capacities for application specific information investigation and handling.

3.3.7 Data Processing and Storage Center

The information gathered from IoT gadgets and sinks in the systems will be particularly put away here as coordinated by the controller. Likewise, system and calculations for getting ready information for instance mining of information and changing over information design are performed in this with the assistance of controller. Like doors, the principle work of this part is to give the required information in the required organization for clients. Along these lines, this segment is related with the correspondence layer.

3.3.8 Sinks

They are in charge of collecting and storing the data acquired from IoT devices. Not at all like gateways, can't they be programmed by SDN controllers. Be that as it may, contingent upon their capacities, they can perform basic preparing, for example, disposing of some repetitive data acquired from the sensors.

4. ACCOUNTING AND BILLING CENTER

Novel in connection to the standard systems administration administrations, which use for the most part the system data transmission, yet IoT administrations exhaust both capacity and figuring assets. In like manner, new administrations will be given on ask for, which may have need of help from benefit engineers. Thus, new frameworks for bookkeeping and charging should be considered. For the most part, bookkeeping and charging depend on measure of information, devoured time and the administrations used by applications. Regardless, the fundamental is that passages/switches and controllers give exact frameworks to measuring the usage of different sorts of advantages. SDN North Bound Interface (SDN NBI) is utilized to pass the guidelines to controllers to control the passages/switches. For the most part, the accompanying data ought to be brought through SDN NBI:

1.   IoT operations and its administration rationale, for example, calculations, projects and guidelines for information preparing and new administrations ; erasing, adjusting and questioning about the administration operation, and so forth.
2.   Methodology and approaches for information reserving and capacity. For instance, where and what kind of data should be held or secured; what data should be secured in the Data Processing and Storage Center, et cetera.
3.   Methodologies related with security, interoperability, bookkeeping, and charging, and so on.
4.   Information related with the operation and upkeep of the systems administration organization, including controllers, for instance cautions, logs and diverse limits described by ONF (Aguado et al., 2015). The south headed interface generally comprehends the dynamic request and response courses between the controller and the switches/doors. In addition, it is used to outline the switches. Thus, standard traditions, for instance, OpenFlow can be used. In any case, a portion of the gadgets store and hold data, and may need to reinforce various data outlines for interoperability, the OpenFlow conventions ought to be widened.

5. TECHNOLOGIES FOR ENABLING SDR IN CLOUD BASED IOT

The intention of SDN framework is to give a consistent quality in the measure of brought together control as a result of the nearness of a particular SDN controller and decentralized operations through stream based steering and rescheduling inside the system segments; this unfaltering quality is perceived through associations amongst controllers and controlled gadgets. While, the present acknowledgment of SDN advances is still far from tending to the dynamic and heterogeneous needs of IoT. DCNs (Curtis et al., 2011; Al-Fares et al., 2010) is well known utilization of SDN advances today, where the primary point is to gather the system particular measurements (e.g., transmission capacity utilization) from hubs arranged through quick interconnections inside the datacenter.

Right now, SDN techniques are executed on remote systems. OpenRadio (Bansal et al., 2012) gives decoupling the control plane from the information plane to help effortlessness of migration of clients starting with one kind of system then onto the next effectively, in PHY and MAC layers. CellSDN (Li et al., 2012) demonstrates the procedures for cell applications that are overseen by supporter need, set up of physical areas - giving better control of system streams than beforehand conceivable. The remote SDN plan gives the major building obstructs for administering IoT, be that as it may they are insufficient. The south-bound application to IoT must help components that conceptual out the system heterogeneity, despite simply holding its motivation on connecting to a particular lower-level access arrange. In addition, the structure must help north-bound, higher layer cooperations, i.e., to the heterogeneous applications and their prerequisites.

As appeared in Figure 2, the information is gathered from arrange/gadget through information accumulation segment from the IoT condition and keeps it spared in databases. The layered parts given in left side uses this data. Administrator/Analyst APIs are uncovered by the controller, which makes the administration of control

Figure 2. SDN based Layered IoT structure

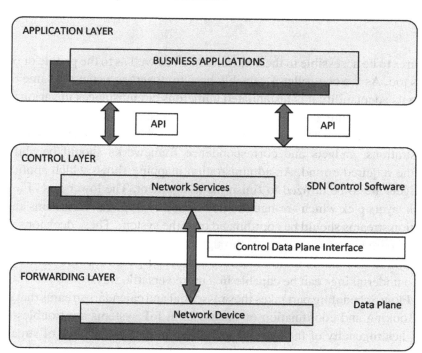

Figure 3. SDN based controllers and gateways structure for IoT

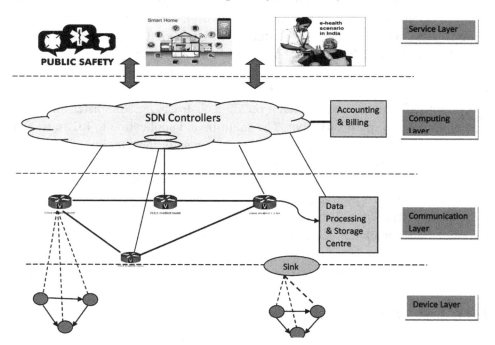

procedures to be accessible to the controller itself as well as to the people or outside projects too. As the controller is sensibly brought together, yet at the same time to enhance its adaptability it is instantiated numerous circumstances in various areas. As appeared in Figure 2, undertakings are the largest amount of reflections in IoT systems that portray what is required; this leaves open the choice of what applications/ administrations, gadgets and correspondence frameworks should be abused to satisfy the required errand. An administration mapping shows which applications and gadgets are to be utilized to finish the assignment. The lower level Flow and Network layers pick which arrange should be used for application streams and how application streams should be coordinated over the system. These decisions will be passed on to the comparing gadgets through the correspondence and control layer. Such a layered view has benefits since it covers the purposes of enthusiasm of lower layers so undertakings can be capable in a more versatile way.

The Flow Scheduling part takes these essential and calendars streams that satisfy them. Booking and coordination of the assets in IoT systems are troublesome in view of heterogeneity of the systems and different QoS necessities of streams. A legitimately brought together administration and coordination part is proposed to utilize.

At last the controller triggers the important correspondences in the IoT, e.g., an order like "steering the video information sent from Camera 001 by means of Ethernet" will be sent to the gadgets along the way.

6. SERVICES ENABLING THROUGH SDN FOR CLOUD-BASED IOT NETWORKS

6.1 Software Tunable Analog Radio Components for IoT

IoT engine needs an adaptable and tunable simple front-end which will be capable react to irregular undertakings. programming tunable simple radio is be considered as a stage to satisfy every such prerequisite which comprise of bland programming tunable segments, for example, programming tunable-channels, programming tunable information converters, programming tunable-intensifiers, programming tunable-various reception apparatus frameworks and programming tunable-duplexing gadgets. Here, the nonexclusive parts are enhanced to achieve any self-assertive undertakings given by IoT motor through reconfigurable computerized radio. Programming Tunable-ADC (ST-ADC) and Software Tunable-DAC (ST-DAC) should be a component of reconfigurable advanced radio stage while the Software Tunable-Multiple Antenna Systems (ST-MAS) should be segment of programming tunable simple radio stage. However, contingent upon the usage decision they are considered as independent pieces from the two stages.

6.2 Software Tunable-Filters for IoT

SDR needs IF and RF channels that can be updated for given channel particulars for instance subjective focus recurrence and data transfer capacity without trading off the execution. The required execution parameter of such channels in SDR is magnificent out-of-band dismissal, low inclusion misfortune, and high influence dealing with. Planning of such channels with the present advancements for IoT is a testing undertaking. Be that as it may, there are some successful approaches towards this target, for instance, electronically tunable channel outline (Zhao et al., 2005). This channel depends on Low Temperature Co-let go Ceramic innovation having dielectric capacitors which is voltage-controlled as tuning components called as Parascan varactors (Balakrishnan et al., 1997). Another venturing stone towards achieving the above goal is a tunable UWB Band Pass Filter (BPF; Stevens, 1997), which is a ring resonator based structure having the pass band of 3.8 GHz to 9.2 GHz and shunt capacitor to the ground at the stub end is utilized as tuning unit.

6.3 Software Tunable Antenna Systems for IoT

Antennas are essential and vital components of each radio framework. Pick up of radio wire and its radiation design (half power shaft width) are the two key highlights that impact the framework execution and its scope. An expansive number of current receiving wires are expected to work for a particular recurrence range and transfer speed. While in SDR, receiving wire ought to have uniform qualities over an extensive variety of frequencies. In a manner of speaking, a perfect SDR for IoT needs programming tunable reception apparatus with the goal that streamlining for execution will be improved the situation a self-assertive data transfer capacity and focus recurrence given by subjective motor. Likewise, the necessity for UWB and multi-band reception apparatuses is expanding. Various Input and Multiple-Output radio wire (MIMO) frameworks, reconfigurable reception apparatuses and brilliant receiving wires are currently turning into a fundamental piece of remote interchanges frameworks and they will absolutely assume an essential part in SDR for IoT. Due to minimal effort, little size and omni-directional examples shorted fix radio wire is the most favored approach for the usage of SDR in IoT. In Standish (2004), shorted fix reception apparatus based electronically tunable receiving wire for SDR is proposed.

6.4 Software Tunable Data Converters for IoT

The most imperative nature of SDR is that the operation and abilities of radio can be reconfigured capability broadcasting live, in spite of arranging at the time of design. Blocks f SDR which are reconfigurable recommends basic changes to radio attributes, for example, regulation sorts, channel coding/unraveling techniques, working transporter frequencies, recurrence spreading/despreading calculations, different access plans and transfer speeds when contrasted with the equipment radio which will change its equipment to make in these qualities. This adaptability of SDR is required and imperative for IoT. Information converters (ADC and DAC) is an interface between the simple and computerized world. Along these lines, coordinating a more noteworthy measure of preparing carefully requires moving information converters towards reception apparatus.

An ADC contains a sampler taken after by a quantizer. As examining rate is one of the basic part of ADCs on opposite side it is a likewise impediments towards perfect SDR as the as indicated by the Nyquist hypothesis the required transmission capacity of the flag for ADC ought to be not as much as half of the inspecting rate. Crafted by quantizer is to change over the discrete examples of persistent plentifulness into bits of a word length. This word length is utilized to decide the determination and quantization mistake of ADC. Alongside the quantization clamor, the execution of ADC is influenced by powerful and static nonlinearity highlights of ADCs itself. The proportion of the mean estimation of the root-entirety square of all other unearthly parts, including sounds, however barring DC to the root-mean-square (rms) flag plentifulness is called as Signal-to-Noise-and-Distortion (SINAD). SINAD involves all segments in charge of clamor and bending in this way gives great proposals about the general dynamic execution of an ADC. The execution of Effective Number Of Bits (ENOB) which stipulate the dynamic execution of an ADC for particular abundancy, recurrence and examining rate will turns out to be diverse in view of the mutilations from a perfect ADC that lone incorporates the quantization clamor. While intellectual radio needs extraordinary waveforms with recognized transfer speed and working focus recurrence, the SDR just needs the competency of progressively reconfigurable ADC. In order to keep up such testing rate, determination, capacity, SINAD of the ADC is required to be reconfigured and advanced by reconfigurable computerized radio i.e SDR which influences it to best for IoT. To streamline the execution of ADC, observing of above parameters by reconfigurable computerized radio is required. Reconfiguring the clock circuit administration square will change the inspecting rate, through which any sort of clock flag is produced and provided to reconfigurable pieces. The base stage clamor level is should have been cleaned and fulfilled by progressively created clock flag showed by reconfigurable computerized radio as stage commotion of clock flag is a vital parameter of SDR execution.

DACs have qualities like most extreme inspecting rate, determination, dynamic range, monotonicity, and stage contortion which are very like ADCs. DAC execution is upgraded through reconfigurable computerized radio in view of its criticism data. A summed up DAC structure has resistor string, DAC enlist and took after by yield cradle speaker pieces is given in (Nanda et al., 2000). One can allude to Kallel (1990) for the fundamental operation of DAC.

7. IOT SECURITY AND PRIVACY THROUGH SDN

7.1 Privacy Risk Management and Accountability

Privacy Guidelines have a new provision i.e. Accountability. To be accountable, An organization has to demonstrate about their present work and future plans with personal data and have to explain why to fulfill the accountability column.

The revised Privacy Guidelines of OECD states risk management as a main approach in developing programmes for privacy management for accountability. In order to justify the risks of misuse, the analysis process of data can be analyzed by the assessment; this will help in identifying the errors or mistakes of the analytical process.

To be viable, the extent of any privacy risk evaluation must be adequately expansive to consider the extensive variety of damages and advantages, yet adequately easy to be connected routinely and reliably. The IoT conditions can make the assessment of risk as challenging task, because of various stakeholders, such as device manufacturers, third-party applications, social platforms and others. For example the data broadcasted by the smart meter in this case one has to determine who is responsible for risk weather it is the homeowner who is get benefitted through the device, or the manufacturers or power company who provided it, or it may be the third-party company who stores the data processor who does the math, the greater part of the above. Therefore, the degree to which a complete risk management approach can reinforce use of the OECD Privacy Guidelines' standards is a theme for additionally work that could likewise consider angles that might be particular to the IoT.

7.2 Security and Privacy

Public trust and acceptability are the main aspects in the implementation of the IoT. One has to define access rights and different levels of policies for IoT because data flow into network which will be shared and utilized by numerous applications (specialist organizations).

Keeping privacy matter in mind it is the user who has the authority to decide that who can use the data. Though the concerning security, methods of encryption used in energy constraint devices and developing new security mechanisms are essential. Furthermore, the high scale network will need some more restrictions related to the authorization methods and authentication. New management paradigms for username/password pairs and public/private keys have to be considered.

Therefore, because of the high significance of this point a cross-disciplinary research exertion between software engineering and electrical building workforce at Stanford University, UC Berkeley, and the University of Michigan, has been propelled (Balakrishnan et al., 1997). Moreover, numerous different organizations, mainstream researchers and administrative offices have applied endeavors towards finding an entire answer for the security and protection concerns.

7.3 Advantages of SDR in Cloud-Based IoT

- **Dynamic Load Management:** This empowers administrators to screen and coordinate programmed changes in data transfer capacity given general system stack. Perfect for worldwide IoT suppliers preparing for exponential increments in gadgets and information.

- **Administration Chaining:** This empowers administrators to arrangement virtual security highlights like VPNs, firewalls and validation and fix approach resistances for execution in accordance with given supporter's qualifications. Likewise, circulation feasible for NAT, DPI, Access control and so on.
- **Data Transmission Calendaring:** This enables administrators to plan when and how much activity a client or application will require at particular time. Relevant to IoT benefits the same number of gadgets send information intermittently as it were.

8. CHALLENGES OF SDR IN CLOUD-BASED IOT

8.1 Heterogeneous and Common Identification Method

Objects can make use of distinguished recognition methods, mostly associated with the underlying network protocol they are having. So as to allow them to interoperate one have to review the distinguished recognition methods utilized by the protocols and are supported by the IoT network.

8.2 Representation of IoT Agents

Even though the IoT agents have small work to do, that is reason they are lightweight, every object is not capable of doing representation of an agent by itself. Yet, there are many other places where their instantiation can be done on behalf of those objects, for example the SDN forwarder (switch), their connected network gateway, or even collectively with the IoT controller but as a different module. Evaluation of these alternatives is done through different perspectives in order to choose the best for the design or even presuming that more than one must be considered.

8.3 Algorithm for Routing

Locating the path between two objects can be done through many routing algorithms but they have limitation of working only on one topology. But a routing algorithm having two separate but overlapped topologies is the demand of architecture, the overlay IoT topology and the underlying SDN topology. Different aspects for example bandwidths or policies should be considered by algorithm. To fit with objective a proper algorithm is required so that it can deal with requirements of the task.

8.5 Formulation of Forwarding Rule

After the calculation of path, it has to be reflected in different rules by the IoT controller which will be sent to different forwarders (switches). Even though it is not an easy task, as there is no direct formulation. So, different adaptations, underlying protocols, matching fields, mappings are considered. A general actions necessary to properly forward a packet towards its destination is required.

8.6 Stabilization of Northbound API

Present models of SDN have northbound API which is used by external modules like IoT controller for the communication of control operations to the SDN controller. Though, this API is not stabilized nor well defined so the stabilization of such interface is required.

8.7 Modularity of IoT Controller

The main functions of the IoT controller are described in the chapter but it should be open for future enhancements. This requires an intensive investigation of the most broad and strong module frameworks and how they have advanced on time so the selected alternative guarantees the development capacity of the proposed approach.

8.8 Procedure for Deployment

An initial deployment procedure is needed to be analyzed and designed in accordance with the currently available infrastructures of SDN for IoT. This is the key aspect required to be fulfilled for the implementation of the SDR in IoT.

8.9 Scalability

The IoT is utilized as a part of exceptionally various fields like savvy agribusiness, industry, brilliant coordination's, keen matrix, clever transportation, shrewd natural assurance, shrewd security, savvy home, human services, and so forth. Therefore, the information anticipated by cisco (Evans, 2011) says that the quantity of associated gadgets will reach around 50 billion by 2020. Thus, the wide sending of IoT is led by the IP convention which is a web empowering agent convention. Then again, IPv4 has experienced the diminishment in its delivers so it critical to move to IPv6 with the expansive number of the items which are tended to particularly (Jara et al., 2013). This is not by any methods the simply ramifications of the high versatility, another building arrangements is required remembering the reasonability issue.

8.10 Big Data

There are different models of data generation at different rate having different volume is stored and analyzed so that it can used by IoT applications. i.e. SQL and NonSQL languages, Machine learning and data mining many other analytic tools are to be exploited. As a result, the connection with the Cloud and other storage techniques must be considered.

9. CONCLUSION

Software defined networking plays a vital role in Cloud based IoT systems. It works as centralized brain which has the knowledge of topology and condition of the network to take decisions about packet forwarding, represents them with forwarding rules, and correspond them to the forwarding entities. In this chapter the introduction about SDN, its relationship between with Cloud based IoT systems is explained briefly. Then different architectures, main characteristics of each architecture, realistic architecture of SDN for Cloud based IoT systems are discussed. An exhaustive discussion is done for SDN based layered IoT structure. Different technologies for enabling SDR in Cloud based IoT, security and privacy through SDN, challenges of SDR in Cloud based IoT are also described.

REFERENCES

Aguado, A., López, V., Marhuenda, J., de Dios, Ó. G., & Fernández-Palacios, J. P. (2015). ABNO: A feasible SDN approach for multivendor IP and optical networks. *Journal of Optical Communications and Networking*, 7(2), A356–A362. doi:10.1364/JOCN.7.00A356

Al-Fares, M., Radhakrishnan, S., Raghavan, B., Huang, N., & Vahdat, A. (2010, April). Hedera: Dynamic Flow Scheduling for Data Center Networks. In NSDI (Vol. 10, pp. 19-19). Academic Press.

Alcaraz, C., Najera, P., Lopez, J., & Roman, R. (2010). Wireless sensor networks and the internet of things: Do we need a complete integration? *1st International Workshop on the Security of the Internet of Things (SecIoT'10).*

Arbiza, L. M., Bertholdo, L. M., dos Santos, C. R. P., Granville, L. Z., & Tarouco, L. M. (2015, April). Refactoring internet of things middleware through software-defined network. In *Proceedings of the 30th Annual ACM Symposium on Applied Computing* (pp. 640-645). ACM. doi:10.1145/2695664.2695861

Atzori, L., Iera, A., & Morabito, G. (2010). The internet of things: A survey. *Computer Networks, 54*(15), 2787–2805. doi:10.1016/j.comnet.2010.05.010

Balakrishnan, H., Padmanabhan, V. N., Seshan, S., & Katz, R. H. (1997). A comparison of mechanisms for improving TCP performance over wireless links. *IEEE/ACM Transactions on Networking, 5*(6), 756–769. doi:10.1109/90.650137

Bansal, M., Mehlman, J., Katti, S., & Levis, P. (2012, August). Openradio: a programmable wireless dataplane. In *Proceedings of the first workshop on Hot topics in software defined networks* (pp. 109-114). ACM. doi:10.1145/2342441.2342464

Berde, P., Gerola, M., Hart, J., Higuchi, Y., Kobayashi, M., Koide, T., & Parulkar, G. et al. (2014, August). ONOS: towards an open, distributed SDN OS. In *Proceedings of the third workshop on Hot topics in software defined networking* (pp. 1-6). ACM. doi:10.1145/2620728.2620744

Curtis, A. R., Mogul, J. C., Tourrilhes, J., Yalagandula, P., Sharma, P., & Banerjee, S. (2011). DevoFlow: Scaling flow management for high-performance networks. *Computer Communication Review, 41*(4), 254–265. doi:10.1145/2043164.2018466

Evans, D. (2011). The internet of things: How the next evolution of the internet is changing everything. *CISCO White Paper, 1*(2011), 1-11.

Hampel, G., Steiner, M., & Bu, T. (2013, April). Applying software-defined networking to the telecom domain. In INFOCOM, 2013 Proceedings IEEE (pp. 3339-3344). IEEE.

IEEE. (2014). *Special Report: The Internet of Things*. Available: http://theinstitute. ieee. org/static/specialreport- the-internet-of-things

Jara, A. J., Ladid, L., & Gómez-Skarmeta, A. F. (2013). The Internet of Everything through IPv6: An Analysis of Challenges, Solutions and Opportunities. *JoWua, 4*(3), 97–118.

Jin, X., Li, L. E., Vanbever, L., & Rexford, J. (2013, December). Softcell: Scalable and flexible cellular core network architecture. In *Proceedings of the ninth ACM conference on Emerging networking experiments and technologies* (pp. 163-174). ACM. doi:10.1145/2535372.2535377

Koponen, T., Casado, M., Gude, N., Stribling, J., Poutievski, L., Zhu, M., . . . Shenker, S. (2010, October). Onix: A distributed control platform for large-scale production networks. In OSDI (Vol. 10, pp. 1-6). Academic Press.

Li, L. E., Mao, Z. M., & Rexford, J. (2012, October). Toward software-defined cellular networks. In *Software Defined Networking (EWSDN), 2012 European Workshop on* (pp. 7-12). IEEE. doi:10.1109/EWSDN.2012.28

Mashal, I., Alsaryrah, O., Chung, T. Y., Yang, C. Z., Kuo, W. H., & Agrawal, D. P. (2015). Choices for interaction with things on Internet and underlying issues. *Ad Hoc Networks*, *28*, 68–90. doi:10.1016/j.adhoc.2014.12.006

Medved, J., Varga, R., Tkacik, A., & Gray, K. (2014, June). Opendaylight: Towards a model-driven sdn controller architecture. In *World of Wireless, Mobile and Multimedia Networks (WoWMoM), 2014 IEEE 15th International Symposium on a* (pp. 1-6). IEEE.

Minerva, Biru, & Rotondi. (2015, May). Towards a definition of the Internet of Things (IoT). *IEEE Internet Initiative*.

Palattella, M. R., Accettura, N., Vilajosana, X., Watteyne, T., Grieco, L. A., Boggia, G., & Dohler, M. (2013). Standardized protocol stack for the internet of (important) things. *IEEE Communications Surveys and Tutorials*, *15*(3), 1389–1406. doi:10.1109/ SURV.2012.111412.00158

Perera, C., Zaslavsky, A., Christen, P., & Georgakopoulos, D. (2014). Context aware computing for the internet of things: A survey. *IEEE Communications Surveys and Tutorials*, *16*(1), 414–454. doi:10.1109/SURV.2013.042313.00197

Perera, C., Zaslavsky, A., Liu, C. H., Compton, M., Christen, P., & Georgakopoulos, D. (2014). Sensor search techniques for sensing as a service architecture for the internet of things. *IEEE Sensors Journal*, *14*(2), 406–420. doi:10.1109/JSEN.2013.2282292

Standish, R. K. (2004). Why Occam's razor. *Foundations of Physics Letters*, *17*(3), 255–266. doi:10.1023/B:FOPL.0000032475.18334.0e

Stevens, W. R. (1997). *TCP slow start, congestion avoidance, fast retransmit, and fast recovery algorithms*. Academic Press.

Zhao, B., & Valenti, M. C. (2005). Practical relay networks: A generalization of hybrid-ARQ. *IEEE Journal on Selected Areas in Communications*, *23*(1), 7–18. doi:10.1109/JSAC.2004.837352

Chapter 11
Extending IoTs Into the Cloud-Based Platform for Examining Amazon Web Services

Jagdeep Kaur
The NorthCap University, India

Meghna Sharma
The NorthCap University, India

ABSTRACT

The public cloud Amazon Web Service (AWS) provides a wide range of services like computation, networking, analytics, development and management tools, application services, mobile services, and management of Internet-of-Things (IoT) devices. The Amazon Web Services (AWS) IoT is an excellent IoT cloud platform and is exclusively responsible for connecting devices into various fields like healthcare, biology, municipal setup, smart homes, marketing, industrial, agriculture, education, automotive, etc. This chapter highlights many other initiatives promoted by AWS IoT. The main motive of this chapter is to present how AWS IoT works. The chapter starts with the design principles of AWS IoT services. Further, the authors present a detailed description of the AWS IoT components (e.g., Device SDK, Message Broker, Rule Engine, Security and Identity Service, Thing Registry, Thing Shadow, and Thing Shadow Service). The chapter concludes with a description of various challenges faced by AWS IoT and future research directions.

DOI: 10.4018/978-1-5225-3445-7.ch011

INTRODUCTION

Internet-of-things (IoT) consists of internetworking of physical devices, objects embedded with sensors, actuators, software, electronics, network connectivity that allow these objects to collect and exchange data. This term was first used by (Ashton, 2011) to connect RFID and supply-chain through internet. Over the past few years due to various factors like cheap sensors, cheap bandwidth, cheap processing, smartphones, ubiquitous wireless computing, big data etc. IoT has emerged as the most promising technology to connect the different devices. It is helping to achieve the goal of smart homes and smart cities. Few examples of IoT based applications are:

- **Hydroponic System:** It is used for automated watering the plants and taking care of all the needs of plants for optimal growth.
- **Smart Waste Management System:** It takes care of full garbage bins and unattended garbage. It sets up the right route and timely schedule.
- **Smart Sprinkler Control:** With the help of smartphone the sprinkler can be controlled from anywhere.
- **Blood Pressure Monitor:** With a wearable cuff and health mate app one can hassle free monitor his/her blood pressure.
- **Fitness Tracker Devices:** Many wearable devices like FitBit, Jawbone allows to monitor physical activities, sleep pattern etc.
- **Smart Homes:** With the help of devices like Nest Thermostat to regulate temperature according to surroundings and Amazon echo to control light, music and other house hold appliances with the voice control.

This tremendous increase in the IoT devices is draining the computing resources required to maintain the connectivity and data collection required by these devices. The data generated by these devices is putting strain on internet infrastructure. The industry is working in different ways to solve this data problem. The cloud computing provides a right solution to this problem. The IoT and Cloud computing are two complementary technologies. The large amount of data generated by IoT can be easily managed by Cloud computing.

Since 2005, when the cloud computing has emerged it has changed our life style and work style (Armbrust, 2010). Cloud computing is supported by various processing engines like Apache spark(Zaharia, 2010), Apache Hadoop (Shvachko, 2010), Google File System (Ghemawat, 2003)etc.The cloud computing can be categorized into different types like public cloud, private cloud, hybrid cloud, Software as Service (SasS), Infrastructure as Service (IasS) and Platform as Service (PasS). The public cloud are owned by companies and they provide access to users over public network. The private cloud is like the public cloud except that there is a single access by user/organization/company etc. The hybrid cloud is a mix of two. In SaaS, the user/organizations run the applications in the cloud which connect to the other users through web browsers. Whereas, PaaS is used to build and deliver cloud based application. It eliminates the need to buy and maintain hardware, software, hosting etc. The cloud IoT is a type of PaaS which helps to interconnect the devices. Some of the popular cloud IoT are Amazon Web Services AWS Cloud, GE Predix, Google Cloud IoT, Microsoft Azure IoT Suite, IBM Watson, and Salesforce IoT Cloud. Each of the cloud offers a different range of services.

The main purpose of this chapter is to present an insight into how AWS IoT works. In order to achieve this following objectives are formulated:

- The state-of-art of Cloud IoT.
- To study the design principles of AWS.
- How the various AWS IoT components AWS IoT Components viz. Device Gateway, Message Broker, Rule Engine, Security and Identity Service, Thing Registry, Thing Shadow and Thing Shadow Service interact?
- The challenges faced by AWS IoT.

These objectives are explained in the subsequent sections.

STATE-OF-ART OF CLOUD IOT

With the emergence of cloud computing and Internet-of-Things making contributions for creating the smart world many researchers have made studies in these areas (Mohammad, 2009). According to (Josyula, 2016) an interoperable platform for IoT devices and cloud services is proposed. It has been demonstrated that without using a separate application server how an android application can be used to save efforts and cost. Another work by (Weisong, 2016) introduced the concept of edge computing and addressed the various issues like response time requirement, battery life constraint, bandwidth cost saving etc. at the edge of the network. Suciu et al. (George, 2013) proposed a generic platform for IoT and cloud computing interoperability study. They worked on the interoperability of RFID, NFC, M2M, sensor, actuators, context aware services etc.

AWS IOT

The AWS IoT can be further studied in terms of the design principles its components.

Design Principles

AWS platform is popular among the consumer, commercial and industrial ends. The design principles are responsible for the success of IoT platform. The core principles are: Standard protocols, security, scalability, Quality of Service, usability and cost reduction. These are explained as follows:

1. **Standard Protocols:** There is a flexibility to integrate variety of devices and machines to internet using standard protocols. Even the different data sources and enterprise systems are connected through standard protocol. The protocols work effectively for all the operating systems. Moreover, the customer can easily make transition to some other competitor technology if he/she is not satisfied.

2. **Security:** As the devices are generating large amount of data and the users can directly control a device hence security is prime concern. AWS IoT provides a secure duplex translation between device protocols.

3. **Scalability:** IoT applications require the ability to scale across different location in order to maintain data consistency and lower latency for better response from devices.'

4. **Quality of Service:** High performance of the IoT applications is expected due to guaranteed message delivery. Before the cloud technology came into picture, the organizations used to hire extra hardware to handle immense amount of data generated by the devices. But now it can be easily handled with cloud and IoT devices.

5. **Usability:** For the developers using modern technology it should be easy to develop the cloud based IoT solutions.

6. **Cost Reduction:** The AWS platform offers consumption based pricing model. Hence the total cost can be directly estimated from the infrastructure required and efforts required to process, store and analyze the sensor data received from IoT solutions.

AWS IOT COMPONENTS

AWS IoT delivers a duplex and highly secure communication between the IoT applications and its associated devices and the AWS cloud. It helps to collect, store and analyze data from these devices. Moreover, mobile applications are also made to control these devices through mobiles or tablets. The main components are: Device Gateway, Message Broker, Rule Engine, Security and Identity Service, Thing Registry, Thing Shadow and Thing Shadow Service. These are described briefly here:

1. **Device SDK:** It facilitates secure and efficient communication of devices with the cloud IoT.
2. **Message Broker:** It delivers a way for publishing and receiving messages between devices and IoT applications. It uses Message Queue Telemetry Transport (MQTT) protocol. With MQTT over Web socket every browser becomes MQTT device. It also make use of HTTP REST to publish, subscribe and receive messages
3. **Rule Engine:** It associates AWS IoT to peripheral devices and and other AWS services like AWS Lambda, Amazon S3 and Amazon DynamoDB.
4. **Security and Identity Service:** It is responsible for keeping the credentials safe for secure communication between the devices and message broker & rule engine.
5. **Thing Registry:** The devices are allocated resources like certificates, MQTT client ids etc. for easy management and troubleshooting of the devices.
6. **Thing Shadow:** The existing state information of a device or app is stored in the form of a JSON (Java Script Object Notation) document. It gives consistent information of the devices connected to the AWS cloud.

WORKING OF AWS IOT

The AWS IoT connects the devices to the cloud and the applications in the cloud interact with the devices. Most of the IoT applications allow users to control the devices remotely through the mobile apps or collect and analyze the sensor data produced by it (Guide, 2017). The connected devices report their states by publishing messages in MQTT topics. When a message is published it is sent to the MQTT message broker that forwards messages to all the clients subscribed for that topic. The Thing registry maintains the entries of all the connected devices of AWS IoT, describing the certificates used by the devices for secure communication. The rules can be formulated based on the data in the message received. The thing registry also maintain information consisting of last reported state and the desired state requested by an application. The thing shadow respond to the application by providing the JSON document and then it can control the thing by requesting the change in state. The messages can be delivered to various AWS services such as Lambda, DynamoDB, Firehose, Kinesis, S3, Simple Queue Service (SQS), and Simple Notification Service (SNS) without any extra fees.

The working of AWS IoT components can be understood better by viewing the interaction between the components as schematically presented as in Figure 1.

Each of the components is explained in detail in this section.

Figure 1. AWS IoT components

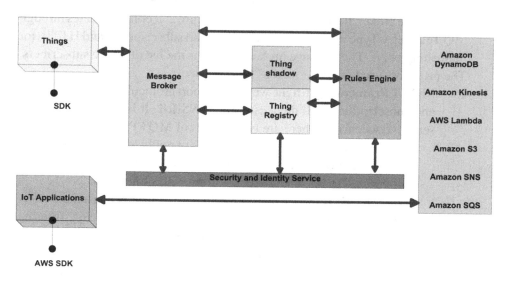

1. **Device SDK:** This component helps to quickly connect the device and the applications to AWS IoT. The Software Development Kit consists of open-source libraries, developer manuals with examples to develop innovative IoT product based on different hardware platform. This component provides SDK for connecting the hardware platform like Raspberry Pi to AWS IoT. The different SDKs provided are:
   a. AWS SDK for Mobile (Android and IoS)
   b. AWS SDK for Arduino Library (Arduino Yun)
   c. AWS IoT SDK for embedded OS (C SDK)
   d. AWS IoT SDK for Java
   e. AWS IoT SDK for embedded Linux Platform(Java Script SDK)
   f. AWS IoT SDK for Python
2. **Message Broker:** With the increase in the number of connected devices in IoT and the number messages generated by them a robust messaging service is required. In a computer network, a message broker is an intermediate program that translates the formally-defined messages from the sender to the formally-defined messages for the receiver. It is the core of the AWS IoT Components. It works on the basis of publish-subscribe model. The connected devices, say the sensors send the measurement values to the message broker. The message broker in turn sends this information to all the subscribers, say apps or tablets, who have listed to receive messages for this topic. Hence, the publishing consists of process of sending messages to the message broker and

subscribing is the process of receiving messages from the publishers through the message broker. It can be represented by Figure 2. It communicates through MQ Telemetry Type protocol (for publishing and subscription) and HTTP (for publishing only). The message broker maintains the list of all the subscribers. The protocols used are described as follows:

a. **MQTT Protocol:** It is a light-weight transport protocol used for publishing and subscription of all devices in the AWS IoT. It is used in resource–sensitive scenarios. There are two aspects of MQTT:

    i. **CLIENT:** The MQTT client consists of publishers and subscribers. It can be any device where the MQTT library is running and is connected to MQTT broker over any kind of network.

    ii. **BROKER:** As described above the MQTT broker can handle many connected clients. It is responsible for message receiving, filtering and sending the messages to subscribed clients. It also take cares of authentication and authorization of clients.

b. **HTTP:** It is a TCP/IP based protocol for delivering data on the World Wide Web. The HTTP specification specifies how clients request data will be constructed and sent to the server and how the server respond to these requests. The REST API is used to link clients using HTTP protocol with the message broker. The MQTT protocol is better than the HTTP protocol in the following ways:

    i. It is having 93 times faster throughput.

    ii. It requires 11.89 times less battery power to send the data.

    iii. It requires 170.9 times less battery to receive data.

    iv. It needs 50% less power to keep connected.

    v. It is using eight times less network overhead.

Figure 2. The message broker

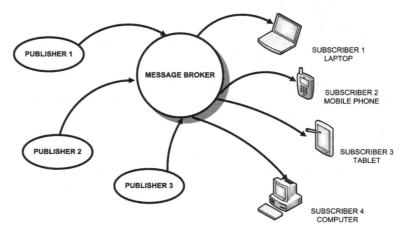

3. **Rule Engine:** The rule engine evaluates the messages received form the publishers (Guide,2017). It further deliver the messages to the AWS service based on certain business rules. It is shown in the Figure 3. The rule engine performs the following tasks:
   a. It filters the data received from a connected device.
   b. It writes data received from a device to an Amazon DynamoDB database.
   c. It publishes data to an Amazon SQS queue.
   d. It also sends the data from an MQTT message to Amazon Machine learning to make predictions based on an Amazon ML model.

4. **Security and Identity Service:** The Transport Layer Service (TLS) encrypts the data to and from AWS IoT to the connected devices, as depicted in Figure 4. The data is protected in AWS IoT using strong security features. Moreover, the identity principals of authentication are used with mobile apps, web-based applications and desktop applications. For example, X.509 certificates are

Figure 3. The rule engine

Figure 4. Security and identification in AWS IoT

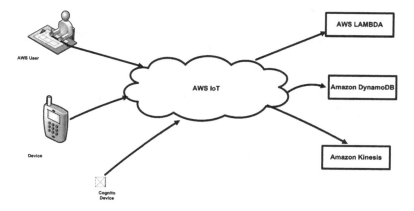

used by AWS IoT devices, IAM users, groups and roles are used by desktop applications and web applications, Amazon cognito identities are used by mobile applications.

5. **Thing Registry:** A thing is a representation of a device on the AWS cloud. In the Thing registry all the connected devices in the AWS IoT are represented by things. It is shown in Figure 5. It maintains records of the associated devices to the AWS IoT account. The mobile apps provided alongside, will create the required AWS IoT resources. The functions like emails generation, text messages or deployment of other services can be easily started.

6. **Thing Shadow:** Its main task is to store and recover present state of the thing or device. The thing shadow can be used to get and set the state of the device over HTTP or MQTT irrespective of its connection with the internet. The thing report the present state to other shadows and get the preferred result from the shadow. The shadow reports the difference, if any, between the desired and the reported state along with the version number and meta-data. The last reported state of the device can be retrieved in the mobile app. The JSON document service has the following property: state, metadata, timestamp, client token and version.

The three main driving factors for the success of the AWS IoT are: firstly anyone can connect a device, secondly any device can connect securely and thirdly it is easy to start. Apart from these the consumption based model allows for the payment to be based on the usage. There is no minimum amount charged per device. These

Figure 5. Thing registry

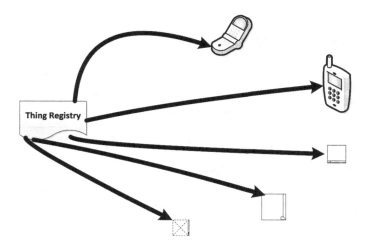

Figure 6. Thing shadow

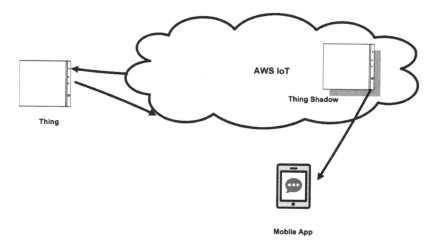

features make it quite popular among many organizations. The most attractive feature of AWS IoT is its pricing. Usage based payment is done and there is no minimum charges to be paid.

CHALLENGES

Although AWS IoT is gaining popularity all over but there are some challenges that need to be addressed. The authors identified the following challenges:

- **Availability of Variety of SDKs and Tools:** Due to availability of large number of SDKs for different hardware platforms, it becomes difficult to make a choice.
- **Variety of Communication and Application Protocols:** Considering the large variety of protocols available for communication, it becomes difficult for the developer to choose an appropriate protocol.
- **Scalability:** It is a major challenge to scale the applications for large number of devices.
- **Security and Management:** With the explosion of large number of devices and associated data on the IoT cloud it becomes cumbersome to maintain the security.
- **Integration of Cloud and Mobile Applications:** The connection between the two becomes difficult and may vary case to case.

- **Cultural Differences:** Due to the cultural differences existing among different parts of the world it is not possible to use the same set of solution for the same problem across the world.

CONCLUSION

The internet is used today for information processing, social networking and for availing different services. There are some devices that can be readily connected to the internet like the ATMs and the mobile phones. According to an estimate, by 2025 there will be approximately 80 billion devices connected to the internet. The cloud computing paradigm offers ubiquitous access to configurable resources like servers, storage, application and services. The IoT and cloud computing together offers various advantages. They together can be used as Software as Service, Platform as a Service or Infrastructure as a Service. Here, in this chapter the authors will explore the Platform as a Service aspect of this combination. The term Internet-of-things consists of network of connected components where the world wide web is the network and the components are all the devices that can be connected to it. Initially, RFID was the main technology later on with the advent of wireless sensor networks and Bluetooth enabled device the current trend has now shifted towards the Internet-of-Things. The public cloud AWS provides a wide range of services like computation, networking, analytics, development and management tools, application services, mobile services and management of IoT devices. This chapter presents the detailed study of AWS IoT platform. It starts with the introduction of cloud computing and IoT. It covers the various applications of this technology. It presented a detailed description of the AWS IoT components and how they work together. It also highlighted the various challenges and the research directions in this area.

REFERENCES

Armbrust, M., Fox, A., Griffith, R., Joseph, A. D., Katz, R., Konwinski, A., & Zaharia, M. (2010). A view of cloud computing. *Communications of the ACM*, *53*(4), 50–58. doi:10.1145/1721654.1721672

ASD Guide. (n.d.). Available online: http://docs. aws. amazon. com/AutoScaling/ latest. DeveloperGuide/as-dg. pdf

Ashton, K. (2011). That 'internet of things' thing. *RFiD Journal, 22*(7).

Ghemawat, S., Gobioff, H., & Leung, S. T. (2003, October). The Google file system. *Operating Systems Review*, *37*(5), 29–43. doi:10.1145/1165389.945450

Josyula, S. K., & Gupta, D. (2016, October). Internet of things and cloud interoperability application based on Android. In *Advances in Computer Applications (ICACA), IEEE International Conference on* (pp. 76-81). IEEE. doi:10.1109/ICACA.2016.7887927

Mohamed, A. (2009). A history of cloud computing. *Computer Weekly*, 27.

Shi, W., Cao, J., Zhang, Q., Li, Y., & Xu, L. (2016). Edge computing: Vision and challenges. *IEEE Internet of Things Journal*, *3*(5), 637–646. doi:10.1109/JIOT.2016.2579198

Shvachko, K., Kuang, H., Radia, S., & Chansler, R. (2010, May). The hadoop distributed file system. In *Mass storage systems and technologies (MSST), 2010 IEEE 26th symposium on* (pp. 1-10). IEEE. doi:10.1109/MSST.2010.5496972

Suciu, G., Halunga, S., Vulpe, A., & Suciu, V. (2013, July). Generic platform for IoT and cloud computing interoperability study. In *Signals, Circuits and Systems (ISSCS), 2013 International Symposium on* (pp. 1-4). IEEE. doi:10.1109/ISSCS.2013.6651222

Zaharia, M., Chowdhury, M., Franklin, M. J., Shenker, S., & Stoica, I. (2010). Spark: Cluster computing with working sets. *HotCloud, 10*(10-10), 95.

Chapter 12
Examining Data Lake Design Principle for Cloud Computing Technology and IoT

Deepak Saini
Publicis Sapient, India

Jasmine Saini
Jaypee Institute of Information Technology, India

ABSTRACT

In the Cloud-based IoT systems, the major issue is handling the data because IoT will deliver an abundance of data to the Cloud for computing. In this situation, the cloud servers will compute the big data and try to identify the relevant data and give decisions accordingly. In the world of big data, it is a herculean task to manage inflow, storage, and exploration of millions of data files and the volume of information coming from multiple systems. The growth of this information calls for good design principles so that it can leverage the different big data tools available in the market today. From the information consumption standpoint, business users are exploring new insights from the big data that can uncover potential business value. Data lake is a technology framework that helps to solve this big data challenge.

1. HISTORY AND EVOLUTION

In this section, the foundational concepts about Data Lake are covered. This section will start with why and how the necessity of Data Lake arose, the various data lake related terminologies prevalent in industry, justify the need of Data Lake. Some design principles for Data Lake will also be discussed.

DOI: 10.4018/978-1-5225-3445-7.ch012

In order to efficiently store, organize, process, and present data, architects came up with a number of design approaches. These data management approaches are good for IT, however, these are not agile and easily understandable by business. Also its turnaround time and cost is higher than what business expected. This created a barrier between IT and business.

Data architecture and data governance created by IT was rigid, as they constrained by high cost of storage, slow processing power of compute, whereas business needed agility and interactive insights fast. The time to change or implement a new request for a business insight was too slow. There was burning need to overcome this mismatch between IT and business, and increase the agility in data management solutions. Hence, it became necessity that both business and IT collaborate to manage the data. Figure 1 represents the traditional design approach for processing data for reporting.

In new era of data management, the traditional concepts of Online Transactional Processing (OLTP) systems, Online Analytical Processing (OLAP) systems, Data warehouse (DWH), Relational Database Management (RDBMS), Business Intelligence (BI) is augmented, but not replaced, by new concepts like Big Data Processing, Data Lake, No SQL, Predictive and Prescriptive Analytics, Data Science.

These new disciplines introduced whole new approach for data management. The approaches promote agility through flexible schema design, store all and discard none philosophy, massive parallel processing, distributed computation, etc. These new approaches are now possible because –

- Storage cost has become cheaper
- Computation of data is distributed in multiple machines.

Figure 1. Traditional design approach for processing data for reporting

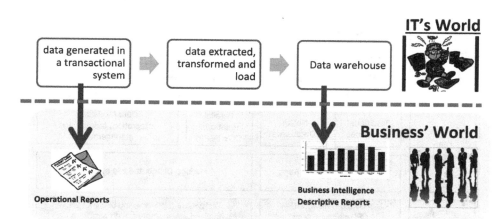

- A technology – Hadoop – was invented that harnesses the power of grid computing using numerous of community hardware in parallel (Author, Tom, 2015)
- Scalability of hardware resources using cloud computing has become easy.
- Capacity of RAM and cache has increased, enabling in-memory storage and computing

It is noteworthy to mention that the nature of data production has also changed. Take for example, logistics and postal service companies like United Postal Service or FedEx. In earlier days their transactions were mostly manually recorded, which was slowly and in limited. Today, most of their operations are automated. Not only the volume and speed of data has increased, but also the nature of data is highly varied. Consider the sensor data sending binary data-streams, machine logs, and data from social media, from mobile devices, RFIDs - there are many data sources and data types available now. Some of these data can be structured in rows and columns of a table, but most of these are semi-structured (for example machine logs) and even unstructured (e.g. image files).

To deal with such data variety, volume and velocity, Data Lake, a data management approach is in focus recently. Figure 2 represents the Data management landscape. Data Lake approach encourages not creating information maps upfront; rather

Figure 2. Data management landscape

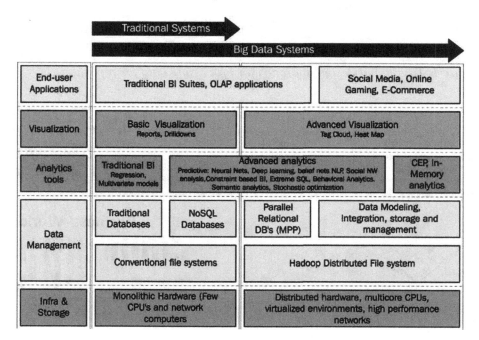

delay the understanding of ingested raw data till there is a need of such information (Pradeep 2015). In other words, all the produced data need not be inferred at the start of a program. All data produced can just be stored in Raw Zone of Data Lake for future potential use. Technologies are available to enrich metadata (information to describe raw data) while storing them in its native format. Technologies are also available that can later explore these metadata and churn analytics from these data. Data Lake becomes an information hub not only for IT, but also for the business to explore & discover data and create insights in future.

2. DATA LAKE

Definition: "A Data Lake is a storage repository that stores vast amount of raw data in its native format, including structured, semi-structured and unstructured data. The data structure and requirements are not defined until the data is needed." (Tamara Dull). The term "Data Lake" was coined by James Dixon in 2010. The data lake originally envisioned in 2010, was meant to capture all enterprise data in a centralized a location. Gradually the scope of the lake increased, and it started storing relevant external data, from sources like Twitter, and enriched the metadata by adding tags like – lineage, visibility, context, timestamp etc. In recent advancement, a need for curate data store on top of raw data, is realized, and lakeshore marts (data marts) are added to cater to the analytics from Data Lake. Here's an analogy -

Former Definition: Raw Data Zone Only

A Data Lake has flexible definitions – in fact the definition has evolved over time. Initially the definition of Data Lake is just about organizing the data in raw storage. "Store all, discard nothing" was the philosophy. However this raw data was organized with help of metadata. Meta data is the information that describes the raw data. For example, if a weather sensor sent some temperature, humidity, etc, these data can be enriched with the location of recording, the weather station that sent the data, etc. Note such enrichment with metadata does not change the raw data (temperature or humidity) but adds more information to the raw data. This Raw Storage Data Hub sufficed the definition for Data Lake initially (Alex., 2017)

Current Definition: Raw and Curated Data Zones

While keeping all the raw data for future use, there is immediate need to curate a part of this raw data hub. Such curation required change in the raw data, for example schema change (e.g. grouping related attributes together), format change (e.g. binary to text), applying standardization and apply cleanup and consistency rules using master data management. The Data Lake thus now also houses a curated zone along with raw zone. The Definition of Data Lake evolved to include curated data as well as raw data.

But at its core, a Data Lake is data storage and processing repository in which all of the data in an organization can be placed so that every internal and external systems', partners', and collaborators' data flows into it and insights spring out. The Table 1 highlights few key differences between traditional data warehouse and the new data lake

3. PROPERTIES OF DATA LAKE

- Data Lake is a huge repository that holds every kind of data in its raw format until it is needed by anyone in the organization to analyze.
- Data Lake is not Hadoop. Data Lake is an approach to build data repository which needs use of different tools. Hadoop only implements a subset of functionalities.
- Data Lake is not a database in the traditional sense of the word. A typical implementation of Data Lake uses various file stores,NoSQL and In-Memory databases that could co-exist with its relational counterparts.
- A Data Lake cannot be implemented in isolation. It has to be implemented alongside a data warehouse as it complements various functionalities of a DW.

Table 1. Differences between traditional data warehouse and Data Lake

	Data Warehouse	**Data Lake**
Data	Structured, Processed	Structured, Semi-structured, Unstructured, Raw
Processing	Schema On Write	Schema on Read
Storage	Expensive for large volume	Designed for low cost storage
Security	Mature	Maturing
Integration	Tightly Coupled	Loosely Coupled
Exploration & Query Experience	Prepared, Defined	Exploratory, On Demand
Search	Limited	Wide & Deep
Governance	Matured	Maturing
Provisioning	Easy	Difficult

- It stores large volumes of both unstructured and structured data. It also stores fast-moving streamed data from machine sensors and logs.
- It advocates a Store-All approach to huge volumes of data.
- It is optimized for data crunching with a high-latency batch mode and it is not geared for transaction processing.
- It helps in creating data models that are flexible and could be revised without database redesign.
- It can quickly perform data enrichment that helps in achieving data enhancement, augmentation, classification, and standardization of the data.
- All of the data stored in the Data Lake can be utilized to get an all-inclusive view. This enables near-real-time, more precise predictive models that go beyond sampling and aid in generating multi-dimensional models too.
- It is a data scientist's favorite hunting ground. He gets to access the data stored in its raw glory at its most granular level, so that he can perform any ad-hoc queries, and build an advanced model at any time—iteratively. The classic data warehouse approach does not support this ability to condense the time between data intake and insight generation.

Data Dump/Data Swamp/Dry Lake

Lack of governance on data being stored in Data Lake makes it a data dump. In short, that dump of data is unusable for analytics. While data lake approach warrants any change to the data, it encourages enriching the data with metadata. Properties of data element like lineage and timestamp if not captured at the time of storing, cannot be generated later. A data without having its history of origination makes little sense during the analysis. Data Dump/Data Swamp/Dry Lake all refers to the fact of ungoverned data storage, where the quality of data is severely compromised and the data storage turns into useless information occupying terabytes of disk.

Data Puddle

Data puddles are isolated data stores which misses the enterprise view. When each department in the business extracts data from Raw storage and starts interpreting the data with blinders, gradually the data marts becomes isolated. The extent of such isolation may result in forming islands of data, which misses enterprise context. Same entity is inferred differently by different department. Master Data Management loses its value in such scenario, and there is no single version of truth. For example, a product catalog is built in house by each department – and the product names differ from department to department. There is no way enterprise analytics can happen in such a scenario. A common reason for forming data puddles is because business finds it difficult to consume the data from lake. They seek the short cut to achieve business interest. It's the responsibility of data lake architecture to provide an easy way of consuming the data from Data Lake or create the lake shore marts which do not cast off the enterprise context of the data.

Data River

Some interpret Data Lake as stagnant and still reservoir of data. The interpretation is - data gets dumped over and over again, without being used much. While, the correctness of this interpretation can be debated, it is important that the adaptation of Data Lake should be monitored. The success of a data lake interpretation depends whether more and more people in the organization gets benefitted from the information stored in lake or the lakeshore data marts. In scenarios the data flow is streaming in nature (fast flowing data in small packets) and the analytics generation is real time – there is high amount of fluidity involved. Technologies like Kafka, Kinesis, Spark Stream and more exist for handle such demands. Not only the velocity of the data is high, but also the variety of data quite different. While some data may be binary in nature, other may be machine logs and sensor data that need real time analysis. Information Lifecycle Management of such influx of data inflow becomes very important. In such scenarios the term prevalent in the industry is Data River to show the dynamic nature of the data; however, the foundational concept is the same as Data Lake.

Data Reservoir

To make things more confusing, some people use the term data reservoir to describe this process of going from raw data, to Hadoop, and then out to structured stores. In this approach, the idea is that you slowly refine the data over time to get to what is made available. To this extent, the phrase data reservoir is emerging to describe a Hadoop centric platform that is still built with the idea of structure, as opposed to the data lake, which lacks structure or control.

All queries can run against the entire data pool, along with the information from multiple outside data sources.

4. BENEFITS OF DATA LAKE SERVICES

While the concept of Data Lake is very appealing, the real question is - what are benefits of Data Lake to an organization. Here are some listed below:

- **Break Organization Silos:** Data Lake brings the organization data in a single platform. So did traditional EDW. The property that makes it different from EDWs, is that the lake does not need its architectural authorization by IT. The data landing in lake do not need to shape it to fit a predefined schema or a data model made by IT. The Lake can be consumed by anyone and everyone in the business as long as the person understands how to read data from distributed storage. All in the organization are sourcing their information from a single point and hence the analytics has better enterprise meaning.

- **Gain Agility (Timely Business Insights):** Because the Lake is schema-less, business does not have to wait months to reflect a change in data to its analytics. In short, the time to market reduces from months to days. The qualities of insights are better, because analytics is not limited by a subset of data defined in IT created data model. Lake stores all, and it depends on the consumer what information will be used for analytics, it is no longer limited by a rigid schema of EDW which only captured a subset of data generated in origin.

- **Mine Value From Unknown Data:** The biggest value of Data Lake is probably the new insights that can get discovered from unknown data sets. Take for example – how does a social media impacts the sales. Such analysis which may be hidden deep inside the lake can be unveiled using Data Science techniques. This was not possible using traditional DWH approaches. The fact that data remains unchanged in Lake makes such data exploration and discovery "pure", compared to any such analytics on transformed and aggregated data.

- **Harness the Power of big Data in a Cost Effective Manner:** The barrier of high cost for advanced analytics is now going away with emergence of distributed storage and compute technologies. Cloud platform providers also play a big role in reducing the cost. Distributed storage and computing – running of multiple machines, and harnessing their power in parallel – is inherent to all the Big Data technologies e.g. Map Reduce and Spark. Traditional approach emphasized on horizontal scaling which is not only costly, but also has architectural limitation. The big data technologies are capable or working on hundreds of community hardware at very low price. The bottom line is Big Data technologies are far cheaper, smarter and efficient to work on high data volumes.

- **Enable a Data Driven Mindset in Organization:** The Data Lake approach, at the end of the day, blurs the difference between IT and other organizations in business. Its garners a mindset of the entire organization towards a data driven and analytics approach. Such organizational change is expected to benefit an organization as a whole.

5. CHALLENGES OF IMPLEMENTING DATA LAKE

ROI of Unknown Data Discovery

Concept of Data Lake is still new, its technologies are maturing. It's remains burning question in the mind of CXOs what is the ROI and when the break-even of the investment will be achieved.

A Data Lake has two zones of data storage –

- Raw Zone
- Curated Zone(s)

While business can immediately benefit from curated zones (data marts on lake shore), exploration and discovering value from unknown and semi/unstructured data from Raw Zone is technically challenging. It needs special skill of Data Science which is costly. A Data Scientist needs to be incubated typically one to two years in an organization to understand the business context. Moreover, the raw data may need some treatment/filtering before they can be used in data science tools. These data preparation takes time. And lastly outcomes of Data Science and unveiling insights is just a probabilistic approach, there is no absolute guarantee that it will make recommendation that will make quick turnaround in business. While these questions, can only be answered with time; the other option of not adapting to the change makes an organization a late runner in the competition. This is particularly true to some industries like retail, where the adoption of Data Lake and Big Data is faster. There is no one fit all road map of Data Lake for all organizations. In financial organizations, typically nibble the new technology stage by stage, evaluating the benefits in each stage.

6. DESIGN PRINCIPLES OF DATA LAKE

Data Ingestion Principles

- Data Lake ingest Raw Data, in whatever form (e.g. binary, image, audio, text, xml, etc.) the source provides. There is no assumption about the schema of the data, each data source can use whatever schema it likes. Furthermore the source systems are free to change their inflow data schemas at will, and downstream consumers and ingestion mechanisms, will have to cope with that change. However, such disruptive changes are desired to be as minimal as possible.

Data Storage Principles

- The Data once put inside the lake is immutable, and observations once stated cannot be removed, (although it may be refuted later)
- Data Lake advocates "Store All" philosophy. Data Lake actually encourages organizations to add new data sources, and not fear about what might be useless information. In essence there is no useless information in Data Lake.
- Though it's said lake is immutable, Data LifecycleManagement is required for cost optimization and data security. LCM defines the rules to classify the data into hot, warm or cold tiers and is explored in more details in the architecture section of this document.

Data Consumption Principles

- It's up to the consumer of the data to make sense of the data for their own purpose.
- Since Data Lake typically deals with large data which is not readily consumable, the Data Lake architecture is also responsible for curating the data into consumable schema. This brings two distinct consumption patterns:
  - **Raw Data Consumption:** For Data Exploration and Data Science to dig unknown insights.
  - **Curated Data Consumption:** For Data Analysis of known KPIs and analytics.
- Data organization and schema/folder structures needs to be built in a self-describing manner, so that it's easy for non-technical users to consume the data. Keep in mind, just like IT, non-technical business users have an equal if not greater interest in browsing information stored Data Lake.

Data Governance Principles

- **Governance Around Raw Zone:** Strong Governance principles around meta data tagging can prevent the raw zone from becoming data swamp. While Data Lake encourages on the flexibility for retaining their data in its native format in Raw Zone, there needs to be strict guidelines about the meta data schema and the mandates that needs to be attached with each data element as they are being ingested. Delaying metadata tagging only complicates the exercise. For example the origin information of the data (lineage) is best captured right at the time of the ingestion.
- **Data Security:** Data Security is of paramount importance for Raw Data. There can be confidential information (for example – personally identifiable

information that can help build customer profiles) but such data needs to be encrypted so that it does not land in wrong hand. For this reason, access to Raw is highly restricted only to handful data scientist. Sensitive data leaving raw zone needs to anonymize. Some highly sensitive data (for example credit card, social security numbers) cannot even be persisted even in raw zone and needs to be anonymized during the data ingestion process.

- **Governance Around Data Provisioning:** The Raw zone of the lake is restricted to handful of stakeholders – namely the data scientist. Special data science and data engineering skills are required to make sense from the raw data. Hence the Raw zone of the lake should not be accessed by mass consumers directly. Relatively few people work on this Raw Zone of Data Lake, and they uncover very useful view of the lake. In fact such data exploration and discovery exercises, brings out interesting insights, which pave way to a number of curated data marts. A large number of downstream users (the mass consumers), can treat these curated marts, also known as lakeshore data marts, as an authorities source of their context.

7. DATA LAKE ARCHITECTURE

Data Governance and Security Layer

The responsibility of Data Governance and Security Tier is to control the access for defining and modifying data in the lake – right up to the lowest data granularity level i.e. each data value.

The foundational practices, that influence data security is true for Data Lake as they were for traditional data stores. For example, data classification provides a way to categorize organizational data based on levels of sensitivity; least privilege limits access to the lowest level possible while still allowing normal functions; and encryption protects data by way of rendering it unintelligible to unauthorized access. These tools and techniques are important because they support objectives such as preventing financial loss or complying with regulatory obligations.

Privilege Management- who has access to which data - it ensures that only authorized and authenticated users are able to access data from Data Lake, and only in a manner that is intended.

Such governance is deep till the data element level, which is a huge advantage over traditional way of implement security which is on schema level, or row level or column level. Attribute Level Access Control (ABAC), governed by visibility metadata tags on each data element, can help in data provisioning to users. Tools like

Figure 3. Data lake architecture

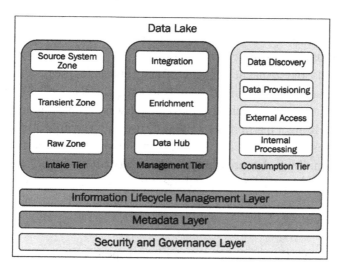

DataGuise can discover sensitive data from Data Lake by using advanced search and recognition patterns and can mask or change the Personally Identifiable Information.

Data Provisioning–how data is accessed– is very important both for raw and curated stores. From the stand point of separation of duty, it's recommended to separate the raw zone and the curated zone in HDFS. The Raw Zone may be accessed by handful of Data Scientist, whereas curated zone, which has tighter security, may be accessed by business mass. For security and compliance reason, you may even mask data during ingestion to Data Lake.

- For raw zone, the general principal is to have restricted access, typically to handful of data scientists. Huge population of raw data that can help in building a good sample set is important for data science. Since raw zone is most native form of data, security concern is highest here. That is the reason raw zone access is given to a very handful people in the organization.

Sometimes, some sections of raw data may be opened to business users, but care should be taken to anonymize the sensitive data.

- For curated zone, however, managing data security and provisioning is easier since data is better organized in schema. Managing entity, row or attribute level security can be achieved easily using tools like Apache Knox, Data Guise, etc.

Data encryption at rest can be done using various key management systems including AES 256. Data encryption in transit is also required and SSL/TLS are popular methods for that. Having secured end points (sFTP, https) is recommended for all point of data ingestion/consumption/

Hadoop tools like Apache Ranger offers centralized security framework to manage fine grain access control over Hadoop data access components. Using Ranger admin can set up policies for individual users and groups and enforce them within Hadoop. Ranger has ability to integrate users and groups from organization's active directories with Data Lake. Apache Ranger currently supports authorization, authentication, auditing, data encryption and security administration for the following HDP components like HDFS, Hive, Hbase, Storm, Knox, Solr, Kafka, and YARN.

Metadata Layer

The metadata layer is the heart of Data Lake. The responsibility of metadata layer are –

- **Build Lineage:** Capture vital information about the data as it enters the data lake. Examples – lineage (source of data), timestamp, transformation if any, context – to provide the background and the significance of the data stored in the Data Lake.

Figure 4. Metadata layer

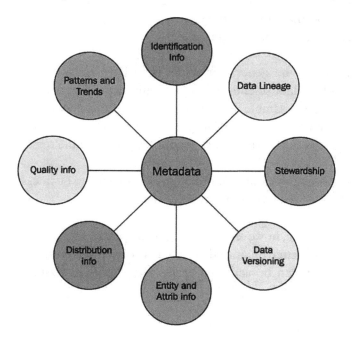

- Index the metadata so that user can search before they access the data value itself.
- Carry out intelligent auto tagging by discovering the raw data with auto detection techniques like Regular Expressions, Machine Learning, Ontology, crowdsourcing.
- Build a business data catalog that can be leveraged by business users for self-service BI
- Metadata process does not only tag Raw Data but also tags curated data.
- Metadata tagging is crucial for flagging the data quality in lake shore data marts. Data quality makes sense in data marts since these are subject area based.
- Data enrichment in curated data zone.
- Provision the data securely to data engineers and data scientists so that they can wrangle and visualize the data inventory, create hive tables or open the prepared files directly in analytics BI tool.

Data discovery tools like Waterline Data ease "data wrangling". Please see the appendix for more information on Waterline Data.

Meta Data Tagging Approach

An approach to organize data inside the lake raw zone is using key/value pair store. This is a schema-on-read approach, making all the relevant information associated with every piece of data stored in the form of metadata tag. Data lakes require advanced metadata management methods, including machine-assisted scans, characterizations of the data files, and lineage tracking for each transformation.

Key/Value Store: A Key-Value store can be used for storing entire data of an organizations data repository. The Key uniquely identifies the value or attributes to describe the raw files in the data lake. However there are other associated fields – known as metadata that describes the value. There are four types of tags that serve as pointer to the data within a cell. These are - primary tag, the tag group, the time stamp, and the Row ID.In addition, the cell contains information on visibility, presented in a logical expression that governs who has access to the data in the cell and under what circumstances. The cell also contains information on data lineage – where the data originated, and what changes it has undergone since origination.

- **Primary Tag:** Is the attribute that describes the value. For example, the name of a person, the address of a person, the stock name which is traded, etc.

- **Timestamp Tag:** The most important being the timestamp tag. Storing value with time stamp enables time scale analysis. For example, the date and the time of the various stock transaction is stored in the Timestamp tag.
- **Visibility Tag:** Helps in data provisioning – and can help who can view the data element. Such data element level visibility tag brings most granular security control on data lake elements – Attribute Based Access Control (ABAC) system. Compare this with access control traditional data warehouses – which is merely table based, or at the most row or column based, which is quite expensive to implement.
- **Row Id:** The entire group of rows (or data elements) – usually all relating to a single element of entity or person – are given the same Row ID number. This designate that they are directly connected to one another. This also allows the closely related data to be shared or horizontally partitioned in the close disk location in the underlying storage. In the example, the birth date, account number and stock transactions are all associated with John Doe because they all have the same Row ID. In the Data Lake, there can be hundreds and even thousands of rows with the same Row ID.
- **Lineage Tag:** Provides the history of the data element – its origin and transformation information.

Self-Describing Folder Structure

A simple way to store data into Data Lake is to follow a self-describing folder structure that will make best sense to business. This is relevant for Raw Data Storage. For example Customer Data is stored under "Customer" Folder. If the customer information is extracted from ERP system like Siebel and SAP, can have subfolders by source. The subfolders can then be horizontally partitioned by date/time. The same data can be stored in another hierarchy based on customer demographic classification. True there is data duplication in the lake area, but again storage is cheap. The decision of when and how the duplicity of data is needed – depends on the needs of organizational units. The marketing unit of your organization may want to see data organized by customers, while the engineering other unit may like to see the data by products. To cater to both the departments – the data hub in Data Lake may need redundant data to be stored in both the places, but organized in two different hierarchies. The self-describing hierarchies make the Data Lake acceptable to business, so that they can explore the data files for more business insights.

There is no need to worry about syncing data across various hierarchical structures (folder paths) because no data ever gets updated and deleted. Data is always appended with timestamp values. The data intake process needs ensure that every hierarchy stores the required data (if necessary redundantly), in way that makes navigation easy. This simple approach of storing data relies more on easy self-descriptive navigation rather than meta data tagging. Between the two approaches - most of the companies now rely on strong metadata tagging approach.

Information Lifecycle Management Layer

Data Lake advocates Store All approach - No deletes, no updates only append all the incoming data. With storage cost reducing every day, this sound quite exciting. However, it may not make practical sense to keep data for infinite time. To put into perspective – financial institutes is generally practices 7 years data retention. Add 5 years buffer to that – does it make sense to retain every transactional data which are more than 12 years old? Storing such old record means meta data of each value is indexed and potentially gets scanned for search on Data Lake.

Information Lifecycle Management ensures that there are governing rules to classify are hot data, warm data and cold data. This layer primarily defines the strategy and policies for classifying which data is valuable and how long we should store a particular dataset in the Data Lake. These policies are implemented by tools that automatically purge, archive, or down tier data based on the classified policy.

For example, Amazon offers four categories of distributed object storage system – S3, S3 Redundant Storage, S3 Infrequent Access and Glacier. Lifecycle Management Rules can be defined for each object stored in S3.

Figure 5. Information lifecycle of management layer

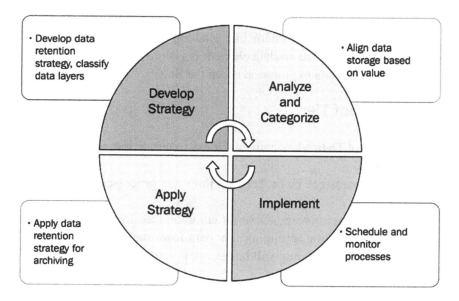

Data Intake Tier

The Data Intake Tier is responsible for connecting to the data sources for acquiring data in its native form in consumable increments.

The intake layer has three zones:

- **Source System Zone:** Responsible for connectivity to various internal and external source systems. The timelines of data acquisition can be real time streams, micro batches or batches. Data are generally "pulled" from ODS, DWH, OLTP, NoSQL systems, Mainframes whereas "pushed" from clickstreams, machine logs, social media like Twitter, sensor data, etc.
- **Transient Zone:** It's a temporary staging zone to ensure correctness of data being acquired. This zone is responsible for checking the file or the data has really arrived. Such validation and integrity check can be made by noting the file size, record count, MD5 checks. Sometimes high level cleansing (for example duplicate files, out of sync records, bad and incomplete record sets) happens in transient zone. Once the data moves to Raw Zone they are purged from the Transient Zone. Transient Zone needs to handle the data validation failures viz. corrupt or incomplete data files. It does not check the content for duplicity, data sanity, etc. Generally a handshake mechanism to acknowledge data transfer is in place, but this is not a hard and fast rule, it also depends on the capability the source system. In short, the ingestion layer can be stateless or Stateful depending on the source systems.
- **Raw Zone**: This is the most important data storage area of Data Lake. Raw Zone forms the essence of Data Lake and is typically implemented using a distributed file based system like Hadoop HDFS. As pointed in earlier sections – till Raw Zone no data element is altered, but data elements may be tagged for easier data exploration down the line.

Data Management Tier

The responsibility of Data Management Tier is to curate the raw data and persist it in curated zone(s).

The curation process can be broken into three sub processes

- **Integration Zone:** Is responsible for common transformation, aggregations, etc by joining, sorting, grouping raw data from multiple sources/hierarchy/ folders/metadata and doing validation, quality and integration checks.

Figure 6. Transient zone

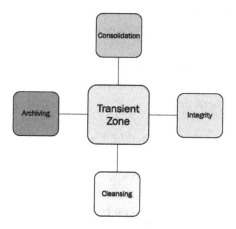

Figure 7. Data management tier

Lake shore data marts

There are references to the master data in the integration zone. Such referential data (or their lookups) may be stored in memory for fast and frequent access. There can be reference miss scenarios where integration rule (cleansing, validation, enrichment) fails. In such cases, three approaches can be considered –

- **Dead Letter Queue:** Push the data in a zone for delayed integration(cleansing, validation, enrichment)
- **Approximation:** Particularly for stream ingestion, algorithms for approximation like HyperLog may be applied and let the integration queue proceed. Such approximation may later be exacted, when data is re-processed through batch integration at the end of the day. This technique is advised by Lambda architecture.
- **Discard the Data**: Depending on the data volume and significance – data that fails validation rules may be discarded all together. Since raw data is

anyway saved, discarding small amount of data from curated zone may not affect analytics. But this completely depends on the significance of data and the say analytics will be carried out on this data.

Under no circumstances, flow in integration zone can get stuck because of some error in validation. Building strong logic for handling different error scenarios is crucial in data management tier.

- **Enrichment Zone:** Is responsible for data enhancement, augmentation, classification, standardization. Example – adding location attributes information to incomplete addresses.
- **Data Hub Zone:** Are the repository where curated data is stored for consumption by business. There can be more than one repository. The type of data store can be No SQL database, or relational atabase, a columnar database, a distributed file store or combination of these. The data consumption tier will dictate the type of data store in data hub. The consumption pattern largely depends on the kind of data being handled. For example in retail industry where the data attributes are varied, consumption tier will have applications for search which calls for building a No SQL database. For the same retail industry there may be BI reports that needs dimensional analysis of figures across millions of rows. In such situation relational columnar database may be required in Data Hub. The retail company may like to go with Data Mart approach for its business in different continents. Now if advanced analytics needs to be carried out on the huge data sets generated from each geography, distributed file system can work better. In short, the consumption methods will determine the type of the data store you are going to design in Data Hub Zone.

These are like lake shore data marts designed for data consumption by each LoB and for each subject area. They are like data marts (in traditional DW implementations), but they are flexible in structure and have a unique property of being schema-less. This means – the Data Hub is has attributes which can differ between one record to other. The hierarchy can also change between records. Agility is the key to the data model of Data Hub and hence NoSQL databases are typically used to store the curated data.

The Data Hub is governed by a discovery process that is internally implemented as search, locate, and retrieve functionality through tools such as Elasticsearch or Solr/Lucene. A discovery is made possible by the extensive metadata that has been collected in the previous zones.

The data hub stores relational data in common relational databases such as Oracle and MS SQL server. It stores non-relational data in related technologies (for example, Hbase, Cassandra, MongoDB, Neo4J, and so on.)

Figure 8 depicts the capabilities of the Data Hub Zone.

Data Consumption Tier

The responsibility of the data consumption tier is to provision the raw data from raw zone and curated data from data hub to the right consumers of Data Lake. The provisioning process needs to treat security and governance as its most critical responsibility by reading the visibility metadata and the context of the information being purveyed.

There are two distinct consumers of Data Lake –

- **Data Scientists:** Who explore and mine raw data and discover new insights,
- Business analysts and other external and internal users – who explore the curated data and create dashboards and reports to analyze and monitor a known KPI or search for more information in already, discovered data.

While there handful of Data Scientist applying sophisticated and advanced data science techniques on raw data, there are higher number of consumers for curated data. Irrespective of who the consumer is – security and governance needs to be tailored based on the data consumer group. The sensitivity and visibility metadata plays an important role in order to apply the security and governance policies. As explained earlier tools like DataGuise can automatically discover the sensitivity in the data. For example – SSN, Phone Numbers and other Personally Identifiable Information can be discovered using advanced search, and the sensitivity flag can be attached with each data element. Hence data provisioning can happen for each data element and the user and group access can be controlled with governance tools like Ranger.

Figure 8. Data hub zone

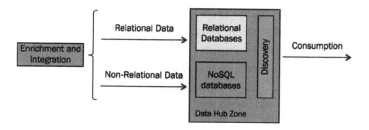

8. DATA LAKE FOR CLOUD TECHNOLOGIES AND IoT

Data lake is also implemented using the Internet of Things. IoT harnesses the capabilities of the cloud and interconnects machines that are embedded with sophisticated software and sensors . here data lake can provide industrial enterprise solutions. It will perform some basic design review, explorat it and do its testing. It will result in production and storage of real time data which ultimately provides a new context and decision making directions. Thus, the scalable data lake and IoT, along with predictive analytics, are increasing sustainability of devices and optimizing resources, thereby transforming the façade of our technological innovations. There are some important aspects of Data lake:

- **Endless Storage Without a Strategy Is Hopeless:** Store All without an objective and strategy is not a sustaining approach – They key philosophy of storing everything in Data Lake without being judgmental at the time of ingestion is contradicted with this consideration. Inflection point in the rate of data creation is reached. Unless we are willing to start throwing away all huge quantities of it anyway, it cannot continue to use the same technologies and the tools to store and analyze it. Unless valuable insights are generated from the business data lake, it will be perceived by business just a useless expense to store endless amount of data Lifecycle management of Data Lake will become a matter of high importance in future.

- **Importance of Reliability:** The reliability of data is a result from many dimensions. The data has to be correct, contextual and same value of reference needs to be there across the data in Data Lake. While most of the systems seem reliable on the surface, as the volume approaches larger scale the loss in reliably starts creeping. Erasure coding is often used in such cases, but with the velocity of the data increasing to near real time ingestion, storage and analysis, reliability checks in streaming data also becomes important. In short data governance to ensure reliability needs to happen faster, and in more efficient way.

- **Metadata Support Needs to be Richer and Smarter:** Technologies available today for metadata support of petabyte scale data are very nascent. There is huge opportunity to mature the metadata support technology particularly for unstructured data. There are only handful commercial tools available today for the limited metadata support. Hierarchy of metadata is also not supported fully. Indexing and Search on metadata also has lots of scope to mature. The success of business Data Lake like to the fact how easily data is accessible to data consumers – and easy and right search of metadata is the key to that success. Ontology, better taxonomy, richer lineage and advanced searching techniques will evolve to make data consumption easier from Data Lake.

- **Compatibility:** Technological compatibility of big data platforms with traditional and evolving tools is important. There needs to be seamless integration and easy migration path to and from the traditional technology and big data technologies. For example most the access to Data Lake today is often designed for http Rest API, which is not fully compatible with all the applications for moving data in and out of business Data Lake. It's important that the data lake technology has good compatibility story, and a cost effective means of integrating with standard protocols and applications like NFS, CIFS, S3, etc.

- **Make Compliance a Priority:** One of the assurances to reliability is adhering to compliance. For example, the foundational principle of Raw Zone of data lake – data remains unchanged – can be fortified further if SEC rule 17a-4(f), Dodd-Frank is followed. Such simple patent defenses are examples where data owners must be able to first certify that their data has not been modified, deleted or tampered with. Also such reliability needs to be established in reasonable amount of time, generally 24 hours. This can be a huge challenge when the similar data comes of multiple sources, the sources are not compliance certified and the reliability through compliance certification needs to be established on streaming data.

- **Velocity of Ingest and Consumption Will Grow Faster:** The speed of data ingress and egress is only going to grow with time. Not only the integration technologies, but also governance, discovery, storage, cache and processing technologies also need to keep pace with the speed. Map Reduce is falling short to address this is already seen, Spark is replacing compute algorithms, and there will be hybrid architecture like Lambda evolving further that can cater to batch and real time computes in future.

- **Multi-Tenancy and Resource Balancing Will Become a Norm:** Multiple departments and even multiple organizations using data pools from Data Lake will become norm in future. The storage layer will be isolated further from compute and the resources will be tailored for multi-tenancy consumption of data from Data Lake. This means highly elastic infrastructure that can horizontally scale out and scale in as per the demand. Data Lake will be like a market place for provisioning raw data for insights for big organization. Take for example Twitter and Facebook. Their feeds are provisioned as market place commodity to different data consumers round the globe who analyze and use them as per their need. Twitter and Facebook feeds are perfect example of multi-tenancy provisioning model. Data Lake of large organization will grow towards the multi-tenancy model in future.

9. CONCLUSION

Business Data Lake is itself a new concept. The adoption rate is very impressing, however, like any fast growing technology, if the objective is not clear and design fundamentals are not strong, Data Lake will not be able to stand the test of change and time. When IoT will be combined with the well governed data lakes it actually shines. This integration is has the ability to model complex systems, simulate scenarios and predict operational outcomes efficiently.

REFERENCES

Dull, T. (2015).Data Lake vs Data Warehouse: Key Differences. Retrieved from http://www.kdnuggets.com/2015/09/data-lake-vs-data-warehouse-key-differences.html

Gorelik, A. (2017). The Enterprise Big Data Lake. O'Reilly Media.

Misra, P. P., & John, T. (2017). *Data Lake for Enterprises*. Packt.

Pasupuleti, P., & Purra, B. S. (2015). *Data Lake Development with Big Data*. Packt.

White. (2015). Hadoop: The Definitive Guide work. O'Reilly Media/Yahoo Press.

Chapter 13
COT:
Evaluation and Analysis of Various Applications With Security for Cloud and IoT

Swati Jaiswal
SKN Sinhgad Institute of Technology and Science, India

Supriya Sarkar
SKN Sinhgad Institute of Technology and Science, India

Chandra Mohan B
VIT University, India

ABSTRACT

The Cloud of Things (CoT) is the multi-domain, emerging, and dynamic technology in today's era. Cloud of Things can perform security services and virtualization with different sensor devices for a powerful and scalable high-performance computing. The author emphasizes the evaluation of various applications used in Cloud of Things. The chapter has been this chapter is divided into two parts which cover the significance of the Cloud and Internet of Things. The chapter focuses on introduction of the Cloud, IoT, and CoT and shows the security and challenges occurring in CoT. It also covers the security issues in IoT with different applications. The chapter will help the academician, researchers, and industry professional to further investigate the associated area of Cloud IoT, and it also helps them find solutions from different perspectives.

DOI: 10.4018/978-1-5225-3445-7.ch013

INTRODUCTION

The term "Cloud computing" involves performing computer tasks utilizing administrations and conveyed totally through the Internet. Cloud computing (D.Miorandi, 2012) is an improvement a long way from applications and holding up to be presented on a person's computing systems towards the applications being encouraged on the web. (The "cloud" implies the Internet and was more appealing by specific stream blueprints and diagrams, which have a tendency to use a cloud picture to address the Internet.). In simple terms, the cloud computing means storing and accessing of data and programs through internet in place of any physical media like hard drive or any external memory (like flash memory, CD etc). The cloud is not about having personal or devoted network or server at residence it is about storing data over the mass database with the help of internet. Storing data at home network or office network also doesn't means that people are utilizing cloud concept. The "cloud" is considered as integration of various types of hardware devices and software programs that work collectively to convey many aspects of computing to the consumer as an online service. As per the analysis given by Lenovo.com, 95% of people these days are using cloud as storage for many purposes like storing mobile pictures, social networking updates and also for online banking etc. From cloud computing a user can manage various data files and related applications using digital device which works with internet (Burak Kantarci, 2014).

As per IEEE (S Kumar, 2012):

Cloud computing is a combination of grid, distributed and parallel computing which is used to achieve virtualization for enabling convenient, on-demand network access to a shared pool of computing resources. It is composed of five essential characteristics (on-demand self-service, ubiquitous network access, location-independent resource pooling, rapid elasticity, and measured service), three delivery models (SaaS, Paas, and Iaas), and four deployment models (public, private, hybrid and community).

Cloud computing cultivates flexibility and consistent adaptability of IT resources that are offered to clients through the Internet. It enables endeavors to enhance the modelling and distribution of IT services by providing them access of services with minimum cost (R. Buyya, 2013). This is the reason why the usage of cloud computing growing day by day.

There are many applications which are emerging in cloud with IoT like smart city, health monitoring, transportation and infrastructure. In this perspective smart cities like advance communication infrastructure, advance traffic monitoring are used for avoiding congestion. It also provides the optimized use of physical city infrastructure. This solution provides easily while data present over cloud and provide security for each services. On the other hand patient can take medical treatment easily by monitoring parameter like blood pressure, breathing and body temperature that can be accessed easily from patient database if it is available on cloud.

Today, IoT technologies are applied for monitoring purpose like environmental monitoring. It is used for monitoring animal's life, temperature, wind, rainfall, river height, water pollution etc. In the field of security surveillance IoT play vital role. According to security in IoT privacy preserving for personal identification, infringement, changes the policy due to renovation work going on. So, it enhanced the flexibility and reduces operational cost.

CLOUD OF THINGS

The Internet of Things (IoT) has been the subject of a several reviews due its extensive variety of applications. The IoT comprises of devices with processing and communicating capability that are interconnected utilizing the Internet, called smart devices. The growth of the number of smart devices or objects are used on the day-to- day gives a substantial amount of information that require an infrastructure for storing and processing them. The cloud computing can give satisfactory models and infrastructure for storing and accessing the large volume of data for high versatility. The author (M Moriera,2015) defines an approach to data management and IoT services using Software Defined Network (SDN) in a cloud computing infrastructure. The SDN is another paradigm that demonstrates in the local centralization of the system control plan. The SDN permits administrators to develop and execute different administrations at the core of the system rapidly. It additionally empowers arrangement with the cloud design, giving automatic dissemination and application portability on a large scale. The Table 1 illustrates the related algorithms which combines the use of IoT, cloud computing and SDN.

The author (V. Radhakishan,2011) exhibited a review concentrated on comprehension an approach that is effective for grouping and working of sensor hubs utilizing SDN. The author utilized system virtualization and Open Flow

Table 1. Comparison of technology

Author's	Cloud Computing	IoT	SDN
Gonzalez et al. (2016)	No	Yes	Yes
Bull et al. (2016)	No	Yes	Yes
Aazam et al. (2016)	Yes	Yes	No
MINER	Yes	Yes	Yes

advancements to create virtual hubs and mimicked a framework with 500 devices controlled by SDN. The author (Takashi Kimata, 2014), proposed the utilization of a SDN gateways as a dispersed medium to monitor information coordinated to IoT based devices. With this, it was conceivable to recognize odd conduct and react suitably, for example, blocking, sending or QoS. Aazam explains (David O Manz, 2017) the expansion of IOT with cloud computing to provide better services to the user.

The two worlds combined i.e. Cloud and Internet of Things has seen an independent evolution. Due to the result of their integration large number of data can be accessed and manipulated by the user. It provides large storage space, efficient use of resource and anytime accessing of data.

MINER (Management of IoT Elements in a Cloud Using Software Defined Networks)

The MINER (M Moriera, 2015) engineering is made out of three substantial modules. The first module speaks to the distributed computing stage and the all segments of this first module are conveyed as an administration in a cloud supplier that utilizations multi-inhabitant virtual machine techniques. The second module is spoken to by the expansion of a part that is sent in each keen question that makes up that is utilized by the application. At last, the third module is spoken to by the customer application that uses the smart objects.

Various types of services has been defined in MINER (Luigi Atzori, 2010) they are as follows:

- The Persistence Service is represented as a database to endure data that is collected about the computational condition of the smart objects. This unites the data expected to convey the workload over the different brilliant smart objects accessible in the earth.
- The Scheduling Service utilizes SDN technology to give services and actions for the proper management of network resources for the smart object.
- The Monitoring Service part is an administration layer for questioning and storing in the Persistent Service. All data about smart objects, their computational characteristics and organize utilization status are conveyed to the Monitoring Service to be stored.
- The Controller Service manages effective communication between smart objects scheduled by scheduling services.

The thought is to use the capacities and infrastructure of the cloud united to the control plan of the SDN to lessen the infrastructure and computational expenses.

It is not very easy to connect all the devices to IoT and store the data in cloud. There are many issues arises these days in IoT with cloud computing. Other than data storage and remote connectivity CoT is also gaining popularity in business work. Due to the usage of CoT in population business, making it a bigger threat from attackers. In CoT heterogeneous networks may involve, that uses different types of data and services.

CHALLENGES IN COT

IoT and Cloud are the recent trends in engineering field. CoT provides the use of distributed and heterogeneous objects over the internet. It also provides the mechanism to improve reliability and scalability with reduced cost. Table 2 depicts different areas of confidentiality required in CoT. Though CoT poses many challenges like:

1. Consistency and accessibility of CoT services
2. Security execution for CoT environment
3. Difficult to implement cryptography, data security and portability
4. Manage power consumption and storage
5. Reduction in use of redundant data.

In the past years, organizations collected data from various sources, which was stored in databases and examined as reports. But in recent times Internet of things made the things easier with the use of internet and various sensing devices together.

Table 2. Area of confidentiality in CoT

Confidentiality Have Relation With Areas	Area Consist of / Accomplished by	Description
Intellectual property rights	Inventions designs artistic, musical and literacy work	Intellectual Property (IP) should be protected legally.
Covert channel	Timing of messages or inappropriate use of storage mechanism	Attack responsible to transfer information objects between processes that are not supposed to be allowed to communicate by the computer security policy.
Traffic analysis	concentrate on rate and volume of traffic.	for restricting this there should be constant rate of message traffic.
Encryption	converting messages from readable format to unreadable format	Process of Encoding messages.
Inference	Database security	Ability to use and relate information protected at higher security leage.

Hancke, 2013.

Since the IoT has a constraint of limited storage, privacy and security issues, it is considered as small things. To improve the efficiency of IoT, the physical world of IoT is mapped with the virtual domain of internet. The cloud of things poses various security risks to its users. In order to overcome these issues, appropriate mechanisms are required against attacks. Apart from security CoT poses many issues like resource allocation, unnecessary communication of data, protocol support and energy efficiency and many more. Some of them are discussed here(K.Uma, 2017). Table 3 illustrates various issues and their solutions for CoT applications in brief.

1. **Security and Privacy Issue:** In CoT, the cloud manager is responsible for providing services to user for IoT. An IoT is a collection of smart devices, which can be connect or disconnect to internet at any time. Discovering new services and updates for users can become a problem in CoT. Managing each and every device, nodes and their security is a crucial task in CoT. The devices, nodes in IoT are highly susceptible to security attacks. Also Cloud computing and IoT are having data security issues. The solution to the above problem is to prevent the sensitive data from being damaged.

2. **Protocol Support:** Internet is a collection of homogeneous objects and devices, which works on different protocols and requires different things to connect over the network. As the IoT sensors works on different protocols like ZigBee, wireless HART etc. use of different protocols poses a big issue in CoT because many standards are not approved.

3. **Resource Allocation:** Allocating resources to IoT objects is one of the important issues in CoT. It is very difficult to identify which resources of clouds will assign to which IoT objects. The mapping of resources to IoT objects are solely dependent on the type of sensor used, frequency of generated data, and their type.

Table 3. Issues and solution of CoT

S. No.	Issue	Description of Issue	Solution
1	Security and privacy issue	Not having sufficient security issues	Prevent sensitive data against attacks
2	Protocol support	Use of different protocols	Associate different protocols with IoT and cloud computing
3	Resource allocation	Difficulty in mapping of resources in cloud with IoT objects	Use of different parameters like frequency, size and type of data
4	Unnecessary communication of data	Consumption of bandwidth, storage and power	Communicate or distribute the essential data over the internet using smart devices

4. **Unnecessary Communication of Data:** Due to the integration of cloud and IoT, a bulk of data is communicated over the internet. On the cloud side the data is communicated with the help of application and used by the user as per their requirement. So there is a possibility of communication of redundant data, due to that there is a waste of bandwidth, energy, resources and storage space. If user will communicate or distribute the essential data over the internet using smart devices then the above problem can easily overcome.

EVALUATION AND ANALYSIS OF APPLICATIONS WITH SECURITY

According to Gartner Incorporation (Rob van der Meulen, 2015), by 2020 it is estimated that the 20.8 billions of connected devices is expected to grow exponentially with the use of IoT. The player for this development is not only human population but the fact is the devices which are used in every day like refrigerators, cars, AC, lights and operational technologies are becoming connected entities with the globe. This world of interconnected smart things communicates with human-to-machine, machine to machine (M2M) and it uses sensor to sense the data, from physically environment.

Nowadays, autonomous car like manufactured by many companies like Google, Tesla, BMW, and Volvo. Through 5G network the driverless car move from one point to another point. Through this, a smart device reduces traffic, accidents, congestion and cost of parking. Internet of things is used everywhere, it works as ubiquitous computing. So it can be used in smart cities, agriculture, Manufacture companies, energy management, Military surveillance, etc.

Each device communicates with each other through internet via Wifi, Bluetooth, 4G, 5G. IoT gives a platform which makes life smart and better. IoT works with heterogeneous network, distributed environment make scalable and more robust. Nowadays, huge amount of data from trillion devices sense and stored into cloud through gateway using 6LowPAN, Zigbee protocols.

Now a days the industries and personals are getting more and more involved and dependent on IoT based services for smooth, efficient and economical operations. The relation and dependency between technology and industry is depicted in Figure 1.

The most of the fundamental issues of elements in securing an IoT infrastructure are around Device identity and mechanisms to authenticate it. Authentication is the process of conforming or verifying. In cryptography digital signature of the user is used for authentication. As IoT devices may not required computation of power, memory or storage to support the authentication protocols for encryption or decryption which mentioned earlier.

Figure 1. IoT in industry
S. Jaiswal, 2017.

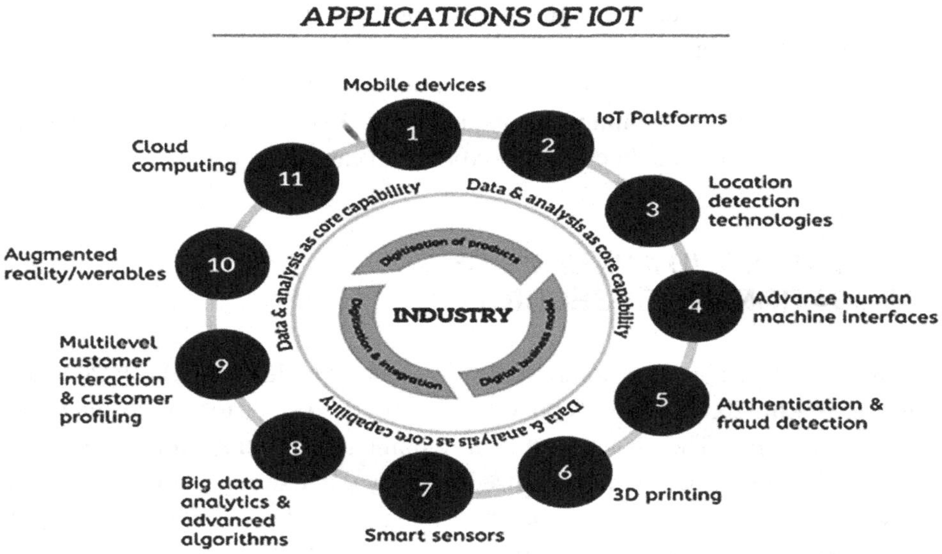

IoT *(*S. Jaiswal, 2017*)*, could be bargained by various arrangements of attacks. Numerous dangers could be happened amid the assembling Procedure.

1. **Eavesdropping Attack:** Compromise the authenticity, integrity and confidentiality of Users data. In addition, due to this attack, privacy of individual in the IoT is truly menaced, particularly if the information acquired by the aggressor is vital and contains individual data.
2. **DOS:** Things are helpless against asset weariness assault such as Denial-of-Service (DoS) attacks in which aggressors send a mass immersion of unending solicitations to particular things all together to drain their assets. In this way, arrange accessibility can be disturbed by flooding the system with countless bundles.
3. **Identity Theft:** Things must be verified before joining the system. Notwithstanding, not at all like conventional systems, the thing's character is not the same as the character of its hidden components that have diverse distinguishing proof codes as indicated by the article and their administrations.
4. **Need Resilience Against Replication Attack:** There is a possibility that the attacker can replay old messages that have been sent in previous communication.
5. **Man-In-Middle Attack:** When the data retrieval and storage operations are carried out there is a possibility of third party will attack on data.

So for achieving security, a system needs to achieve Confidentiality, Authentication, Integrity, Authorization, Non-repudiation and Availability.

There are various applications in with cloud have been challenging issues for security such as in vehicle to vehicle communication, Machine to machine communication, smart city. Basically all the application based on security parameters like data confidentiality, integrity, authentication control and many more. Some of the applications like M2M and smart city are discussed in brief.

M2M Communication

Machine to machine communication include many application like smart building, home, military and weather forecasting etc Whereas, different devices interact with each other via heterogeneous network.

If each device connected heterogeneous then large number of data is stored into cloud and processes it. For managing V2V, V2I communication M2M is needed. M2M communication is used to communicate application with a group of devices.

Many users have referred to Machine-to-Machine (M2M) communications and interchange and consider one or the same. In M2M, an attacker is likely to use MITM attack. To avoid the man in middle attack, digital certificates can be used in which server authenticates a client request by presenting validating certificate. Still M2M requires some difficult security algorithms which work against attacks and improves efficiency.

- **Smart City:** In today's world automation plays a vital role. With the adoption of smart city, the world entered into new era of technology. Smart city not only improves the life of industry but also it embraces their impact on business, and residents. A smart building that equipped with smart devices or electrical devices, communicated with each other in the presence of internet. As per the survey given by Poul Nielson, with the rise of new technologies there is a chance of malicious attacks and vulnerability to the devices. In smart cities, everything will be connected to government, financial, transportation and a transactional service makes it easier for an attacker to unused the data. To overcome security issues, requires a proper IT infrastructure security which avoids the malfunctioning and hacking against smart devices.

Today's strong encryption and highly secure network with authentication that based on cryptographic suites such as Advanced Encryption Suite (AES) for confidential data process, Rivest Shamir Adleman (RSA) for digital signatures for IoT elliptic curve protocol used as security purpose and key transport and for key negotiations and management used Diffie Hellman. If the protocols are robust then it required high compute platform a resource.

There are some components to secure the IoT environment as depicted in Figure 2.

Authentication, access control, confidentiality, scalable, computation time and privacy

For achieving above parameters multiple cryptography techniques are designed to provide security to networks.

Table 4 contains traditional algorithms which work with wired networks, WSN, M2M but these algorithms are not feasible with IoT. Current scenario requires strong algorithms for providing security to devices which works with internet. Table 5 enlists multiple security algorithms and security issues for achieving IoT security.

Figure 2. Security issues in IoT

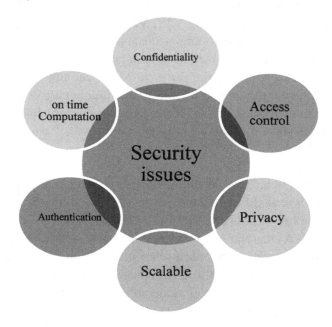

Table 4. Security algorithms

S. No.	Algorithm	Purpose
1	AES (Symmetric algorithm)	Confidentiality
2	RSA (Asymmetric key)	Digital Signature key based
3	Diffie Hellman	Key agreement
4	Elliptic curve cryptography	Digital Signature key
5	SHA-I (Hash algorithms)	Integrity

S. Jaiswal, 2017.

Table 5. Comparison table based on IoT security

IOT Network Technology for MITM Attack	Methods Used (Key)	Security Issues						Computation Time
		Authentication	Access Control	Confidentiality	Privacy	Scalable	
MRP(Message Recognition Protocol) (M.S. Stout,2016)	No public key	yes	No	No	Yes	No	Not Defined
DTLS(Datagram Transport Layer Security) (Thomas K, 2013)	Public key Cryptography	Yes	No	Yes	Yes	No	
ICAC(Identity Driven Capability based Access control) (P. N. Mahalle, 2013)	Public Key Cryptography	Yes	Yes		Limited	Yes	
IECAC(Identity Establishment and capability based Access control)((P. N. Mahalle, 2012)	Secret key based on (ECC)	Yes	Yes	No	Yes	Yes	
AUPS(Open source authenticated published /subscribe system) (Alessandra Rizzardi 2016)	Key Management	Yes	No		limited	No	
LCKES(Lightweight collaborative key establishment scheme)(Yosra Ben Saied 2014)	Asymmetric key	Yes	No		No	Yes	
TCGA(Threshold Cryptography based Group Authentication scheme)((P. N. Mahalle, 2015)	Symmetric key Encryption	yes	yes		No	Yes	O(n2)

CONCLUSION

In the last few years, IoT covered most of the market with latest technology and applications. Day-by-day a new IoT based application launched in the market which helps for the smooth execution of task. But due to the involvement of internet, IoT suffers lots of new troubles and security issues. Due to the advancement of high-tech applications and devices, traditional security algorithms for IoT devices and CoT are not feasible for providing security. In this chapter, various algorithms and security parameters are evaluated. So for achieving security in CoT, a system needs to achieve Confidentiality, Authentication, Integrity, Authorization, Non-repudiation and Availability. Devices require smart and complex algorithms against attacks and vulnerabilities.

REFERENCES

Atzori, Iera, & Morabito. (2010). *The Internet of Things: A survey*. Elsevier.

Ben Saied, O. Zeghlache, & Laurent. (2014). Lightweight collaborative key establishment scheme for the Internet of Things. Elsevier.

Benin, Toledo, & Tromer. (2015). Secure Association for the Internet of Things. *International Workshop on Secure Internet of Things*.

Buyya. (2013). Introduction to the IEEE Transactions on Cloud Computing. *IEEE Transactions on Cloud Computing, 1*(1).

Hancke, G. P., & Silva, B. C. E. (2013). The role of advanced sensing in smart cities. *Sensors (Basel), 13*, 1. PMID:23271603

Jaiswal, S., & Chandra, M. B. (2017). A Survey: Privacy and Security to Internet of Things with Cloud Computing. *International Journal of Control Theory and Applications, 10*(1).

Kantarci, B., & Mouftah, H. T. (2014). Sensing Services in Cloud-Centric Internet of Things: A Survey, Taxonomy and Challenges. *IEEE Conference*.

Kothmayr, T., Schmitt, C., Hu, W., Brünig, M., & Carle, G. (2013). *DTLS based security and two-way authentication for the Internet of Things*. Elsevier.

Kumar & Goudar. (2012). Cloud Computing–Research Issues, Challenges, Architecture, Platforms and Applications: A Survey. *International Journal of Future Computer and Communication, 1*(4).

Mahalle, A. Prasad & Prasad. (2012). Identity Establishment and Capability Based Access Control (IECAC) Scheme for Internet of Things. *IEEE Conference*.

Mahalle, A., Prasad, & Prasad. (2013). Identity driven Capability based Access Control (ICAC) Scheme for the Internet of Things. *IEEE International Conference on Advanced Networks and Telecommunications Systems (ANTS)*.

Mahalle, P., & Prasad. (2015). Threshold Cryptography-based Group Authentication (TCGA) Scheme for the Internet of Things (IoT). *IEEE Conference*.

Manz & Edgar. (2017). Cyber security research book. In *Protecting IoT Against Man-in-the-Middle Attacks*. Syngress.

Miorandi, Sicari, De Pellegrini, & Chlamtac. (2012). Internet of things: Vision, applications and research challenges. *Ad-Hoc Networks, 10*(7), 1497-1516.

Nazir, M. (2012). Cloud Computing: Overview & Current Research Challenges. *IOSR Journal of Computer Engineering, 8*(1), 14–22.

Neto, de Souza, da Rocha, Coutinho, & Moreira. (2015). MINER: An approach for Management of IoT elements in a cloud using software de_ned networks. *5th International Workshop on Advances in ICT Infrastructures and Services (ADVANCE 2015)*.

Petrolo, Loscrì, & Mitton. (2014). *Towards a Smart City based on Cloud of Things.* Academic Press.

Radhakishan, V., & Selvakumar, S. (2011). Prevention of Man-in-the-Middle Attacks using ID Based Signatures. *2011 Second International Conference on Networking and Distributed Computing.*

Rizzardi, S. Miorandi, & Coen-Porisini. (2016). AUPS: An Open Source Authenticated Publish/Subscribe system for the Internet of Things. Elsevier.

Sowe, S. K., Kimata, T., Dong, M., & Zettsu, K. (2014). Managing Heterogeneous Sensor Data on a Big Data Platform: IoT Services for Data-intensive Science. *IEEE 38th Annual International Computers, Software and Applications Conference Workshops*, 295-300.

Stout, W. M. S., & Urias, V. E. (2016). *Challenges to Securing the Internet of Things.* IEEE. doi:10.1109/CCST.2016.7815675

Uma, Parvin, & Poorani. (2017). Analysis of various issues in cloud of things (COT). *Journal of Chemical and Pharmaceutical Sciences, 10*(1).

Zhang, Cheng, & Boutaba. (n.d.). Cloud computing: state-of-the-art and research challenges. *Journal of Internet Service and Application, 1*(1), 7-18.

Chapter 14
Examining Communication Technologies of IoT for Best QoS

Jayashree K
Rajalakshmi Engineering College, India

Babu R
Rajalakshmi Engineering College, India

Chithambaramani R
Rajalakshmi Engineering College, India

ABSTRACT

The Internet of Things (IoT) architecture has gained an increased amount of attention from academia as well as the industry sector as a significant methodology for the development of innovative applications and systems. Currently, the merging of this architecture with that of Cloud computing has been largely motivated by the need for various applications and infrastructures in IoT. In addition to this, the Cloud ascends as an eminent solution that would help solve various challenges that are faced by the IoT standard when varied physical devices. There are an excessive number of Cloud service providers the web along with many other services. Thus, it becomes critical to choose the provider who can be efficient, consistent, and suitable, and who can deliver the best Quality of Service (QoS). Thus, this chapter discusses QoS for cloud computing and IoT.

DOI: 10.4018/978-1-5225-3445-7.ch014

INTRODUCTION

A network that connects several physical "things" also called objects, with electronics, required software and adequate sensors, enabling these to exchange information and data with servers and other devices using various means of communication framework is referred to as Internet of Things (IoT) (Bertino 2016). IoT is branded by real world and consists of little things that have limitations in storage as well as the processing ability. There are many issues associated with dependability, performance, privacy as well as security. There are enormous capabilities when it comes to storage of data and processing ability, virtually when it comes to cloud computing. It is highly developed and many IoT issues are solved to some extent.

Introducing IoT into the internet results in lot of smart objects gets connected to the internet and these objects generate large amount of data that cannot be handled by normal databases. If the objects have very simple interface then they cannot even perform small amount of computation that might be necessary. Hence cloud concepts are integrated with IoT so that storing and computation is done in the cloud. Managing huge amount of data can be easily done by combining IoT with cloud (Suchetha & Guruprasad, 2015). Hence, a fresh IT standard with cloud and IoT as the two balancing technologies that are merged together will surely disrupt the current as well as the future Internet (Zhou et al, 2013 & Chao et al, 2011). Hence, when the complementary technologies such as Cloud and IoT are integrated as one module into a novel IT paradigm, it will disturb both present as well as forthcoming Internet.

Smart towns and societies, smart home and metering, Healthcare, Video observance, automatic and smart transport, smart grid and smart energy, smart logistics and monitoring of environmental conditions are some of the primary applications that are developed using Cloud and IoT. Increase in the amount of data, their types and unpredictability leads to the issue of QoS.

Section 2 introduces the background of cloud computing. Section 3 discusses the related work based on QoS of IoT, cloud computing and Cloud of Things (CoT). Section 4 explains the communication technologies involved in IoT. Section 5 explains the solutions. The conclusion of the chapter is described in Section 6.

BACKGROUND

Cloud Computing Platforms

The computing services that are being delivered through internet is cloud computing. With these cloud provisions, software and hardware that are managed by third parties are allowed to be accessed by individuals and businesses (Lovesum, et al., 2014).

Infrastructure as a Service (IaaS), Platform as a Service (PaaS) and Software as a Service (SaaS) are some of those services.

Software as a Service (SaaS)

A model for software distribution in which the retailers or service providers provide applications and these are made accessible to internet users through a browser is referred to as SaaS. Cloud providers manage the setup and platforms that run these applications. Instead of purchasing a license for every computer SaaS provides a cost-effective way for business organizations to use software when highly required (Helen et al, 2015).

Platform as a Service (PaaS)

PaaS delivers ready to use atmosphere for users to support entire lifecycle of custom application. Applications are written by the developers as per the specifications of a particular platform. PaaS provides platform that basically includes resources like operating system, database, web server, programming language, libraries which automatically scales to meet the demands. Consumer do not need to manage resources but can configure settings for application hosting environment. Google App Engine, Red Hat OpenShift, Engine Yard are PaaS providers (Makwana 2014).

Infrastructure as a Service (IaaS)

The primary constituents of the Cloud IT are contained in IaaS and it also provides admission to computers, features of networking such as practical and devoted hardware as well as space for data storage. Access to hardware such as server, storage and network are provided by this. Also related software such as operating systems, technology for virtualization and file system, can also be accessed as a provision (Bhardwaj et al, 2010).

The foremost features that are offered by cloud computing are self-service on-demand, broad access to network, resource amalgamation, rapid elasticity and unhurried Service (Ghasemzadeh, 2014).

RELATED WORK

There are certain relationships between cloud computing and IoT and the connections between them, how they benefit from each other are shown in some surveys. (Botta et al, 2016) have discussed that virtually unlimited capabilities are of a great benefit to IoT and also that properties of cloud can reimburse for its technological limitations namely, storage, processing and communication. Cloud will also be of a great benefit to IoT in order to handle the real-world objects in a more dispersed and lively manner. Provision of new services in many cases of real life situations is another application.

The connections can be made between smart objects and applications using cloud as an intermediate layer has been suggested by Cavalcante et al, 2016. Efficient usage of information and the resources given by the objects is the main goal.

(Ren et al. 2011) show cases an architecture of QoS for IoT resultant from the investigation of the existing QoS methodology. This is in relation to the features of IoT in a layered basis, such as application layer, network layer and insight layer each of which insist the need for the dependable QoS paradigm. The authors have designed a control mechanism from enumeration of QoS requirements. A cross – layer QoS management facility has also been designed with agents present in the lower layers to support the switch mechanism.

The need for QoS aware scheduling systems for the IoT service oriented systems has been presented by (Saima & Kun, 2013). There is a top down decision-making process across the layers of the three-layer QoS scheduling model, making use of different optimization steps that are based upon service necessities and applications. This framework is inclusive of the QoS monitoring done across layers through decomposition of tasks into executable ones for QoS attributes to monitor. A three-layer provision related IoT framework is the foundation for QoS monitoring. Markovian decision process is used for maximizing service quality at the application layer. When it comes to the network layer, the connection cost is minimized with the use of decision making algorithms. These methods may include QoS features used in traditional QoS methodologies. At the layer of sensing, decision making is used based on the sensing ability and the QoS necessities of application user for efficient sensing expenses and optimal usage of edge nodes, usage of energy and information precision. Defining and measuring the QoS metrics in this model is defined using QoS monitoring component at each of the layer in the paradigm of IoT.

The authors highlight some of the intelligent sensor applications used for the analysis of various QoS applications in IoT environment (Tingxun SHI et al, 2013). Also shows supplies that QoS can be improved by mapping QoS parameters such as accessibility, dependability, energy productivity, accuracy with the real time and behavioural designs to obtain across-layer solution impacting the behaviour designs of particle applications. There is interdependency amongst QoS execution across layers and flexibility and dynamic behavioural patterns.

The QoS provision is implemented for facility oriented as well as wide-ranging IoT systems with the concept of general publish/subscribe (Medha & Kulkarni, 2014). These use the procedures of 'smart dispatch' and 'goal aware system' for

QoS methodology in the IoT systems. This was not available in the previous ones. The message broker is modified in order to meet QoS in IoT systems, which also leads to minimisation of faults and results in improved resource allocation.

The QoS metrics such as throughput, dependability and availability is presented by (Ming & Yan 2011) with the use of directed graph, when the QoS is based upon computational modelling for WSN/IoT by routing protocols. Mathematical representations and four varied service compositions such as series, parallel, branch and circulation approach is used for the implementation. Computation of QoS with the use of different formulae for all the composite modes is also done.

Consensus protocol with distributed optimization has been presented in this paper (Giuseppe et al, 2014). To better the network period and QoS maximisation in resource controlled and active IoT environment, where the IoT modules join and depart from the network, in an IoT scenario this protocol is proposed. The implementation of this algorithm is done on the distributed service nodes, based on the distributed optimization protocol, of an IoT scenario. This coordinates each other into task clusters in addition to providing a unified service to the applications requiring it.

Cloud can be considered to be a leeway to the IoT systems. This is for the requirement and integration of cloud services. It is a great challenge to arrive at Service Level Agreements (SLAs) amongst providers of cloud service and the consumers, due to their conflicting likings. Hence these negotiations between the SLAs and QoS in the cloud based IoT paradigm using a negotiation protocol in order to achieve great quality of service (Xianrong et al, 2014).

A data storage agenda for cloud platform that renders storage of huge IoT data efficiently and also integrates unstructured and structured data (Jiang et al, 2014). This framework also combines multiple databases and manages diverse data generated and collected by sensors. The devices involved in IoT generate massive data that would rapidly increase and therefore the IoT storage solutions must also be efficient to handle and manage this huge data. The proposed framework has four main modules such as file repository, database module, service module and resource configuration module.

The authors focus on message scheduling which points to service provisioning (Abdullah &Yang 2014). Here, messages are grouped as, either superior priority or best effort messages and then the suitable QoS scheduling algorithm is suggested. The different sensor lumps are categorized into IoT subgroups, each of which has an agent delivering for all lumps and handles separate lines for best effort and high priority messages. For message scheduling, network layer routing methodologies are also considered in this architecture.

A dynamic resource allocation scheme for cloud environment, that has considered both task and machine diversity has been proposed (Zhang et al, 2014). Workloads are grouped into different classes having same characteristics using K-means clustering. Then the algorithm dynamically sets the number of lively servers in order to save energy.

The author discusses a perspective of the CloudIoT applications where network communication is an important but a small component (Khodkari & Maghrebi 2016). Certain parameters related to cloud have to be used in conjunction with network parameters such as bandwidth, jitter and delay. These parameters are I/O operations and CPU throughput, devices, network type, and application. This is to determine the overall QoS of the cloud IoT applications. The larger vision of the CloudIoT, like the sensing-as-a-service paradigm can be realized by understanding and carefully developing the QoS metrics and also the corresponding SLAs. These take into consideration the complexity introduced by each layer.

A framework for Intelligent Urban Traffic Management System has been discussed by Yu et al, 2012. It is an application of cloud computing and IoT. Intelligent monitoring and management of traffic in cities is done by cloud computing. Smart Urban Traffic Management framework has three different layers such as perception layer is nothing but sensors and sensor gateways and its main function is to collect information along with object identification. Network layer receives the information from perception layer, processes it and transmits to application layer. It is constituted of network, network management system etc.

IOT SERVICES

The key enabling technology that have been discussed by Xu et al (2014) is Radio Frequency IDentification (RFID). RFID is the introductory technology for IoT and this enables microchips to transfer the identification material to a reader through wireless communication. IoT involves various tracking technologies such as RFID systems, barcode, and intelligent sensors. RFID tags and RFID readers are the constituents of a simple RFID system. The RFID framework is increasingly being used in industries, such as logistics as well as monitoring of healthcare services, because of its ability to track and identify physical objects as well as devices. This system includes various other benefits such as giving the exact real-time information about the devices involved, also reduces labour expenses, simplifies business flow, increases the accuracy of catalogue information and also improves the business proficiency. Numerous manufacturers, suppliers and vendors in many industries use the RFID system.

Promoting the RFID system further, RFID can be combined with WSNs in order to more efficiently track the objects in real time. Electromagnetic sensors, biosensors, off-board sensors, sensor tags, independent tag, are some of the upcoming wireless smart sensor technologies. Execution and distribution of industrial amenities and applications are further facilitated using the sensor devices. Integration of data gathered by the sensors with that of the data from RFID helps in development of highly influential IoT applications that are suitable to the manufacturing environments.

EXAMINING COMMUNICATION TECHNOLOGIES IN IOT

IoT generally contains various electronic and mobile devices along with some equipment from industries. These devices have varied capacities when it comes to communicating with other devices, networking, processing of the data and storing it. Nowadays smart phones have highly improved communication, networking and data processing capacities. On the other hand, devices like heart rate monitors have limited capabilities when it comes to communication and computation. With the use of networking technologies and communication these things can be connected. WSNs, WLAN, wireless mesh networks are some of the heterogenous networks involved in IoT. In addition to facilitating interaction amongst several devices using the internet, a Gateway can also influence its knowledge about network through local execution of some optimization algorithms. It thus handles several complicated features involved in communication. Protocols and standards for communication include

ZigBee

This is dependent on small rate Wireless Personal Area Network (LR-WPAN). Zigbee is the IEEE 802.15.4 standard for less power and limited range.

Bluetooth

Bluetooth is used to enable many point-to-point as well as point-multipoint configurations that are based on Wireless Personal Area Network. This device is an IEEE 802.15.1 standard for lesspower small distance radio frequency which is cheap and the Bluetooth Low Energy technology significantly reduces power consumption.

Light Fidelity

Light Fidelity is a Visible Light Communication (VLC) scheme which uses light rather than radio waves and hence it is optical. Rapid pulses of visible light in the range of 400THz to 800THz are used for data transmission. Data transmission takes place through LED and is acknowledged by photoreceptors. The gathered ones are transformed to digital data.

Wi-Fi

The operation of Wi-Fi is based upon three interoperable technologies namely, Direct Sequence Spread Spectrum, Frequency Hopping Spread Spectrum (FHSS), and Infrared (IR). Wi-Fi supports both point-to-point as well as point-multipoint arrangements.

Long Term Evolution (LTE)

LTE is based on WWAN and this is a 4G wireless broadband standard which was established by the Third Generation Partnership Project (3GPP). An uplink data rate up to 75 Mbps and a downlink up to 300Mbps is provided by Long Term Evolution. This is a cost-effective solution for the M2M services in IoT.

Networks Involved in IoT

Information exchange and data communication are supported by the IoT network using internet. Internet is not necessary to be involved for communication in case of Wireless Sensor and Actuator Networks (WSANs) or Ad Hoc Networks.

Service Management in IoT

Execution and administration of high quality IoT applications that meet the needs of users is referred to as service management in IoT. The architecture of IoT is service related and is aware of framework in which all objects such as physical or virtual is allowed to communicate with each other. This feature enables every component to offer its services in the form of standard services. These increase the productivity of the objects as well as networks that are part of the IoT.

Smart Phones

Significant amount of private data about the owner is gathered through smart phones.

Cloud Computing

Cloud computing can at as an enabling platform to support IoT (Ziegeldorf et al. 2014). Having flourished over the last ten years, cloud computing paradigm provides ways to handle any predictable explosion of information in IoT. The area of focus are protection of data and prevention of information leakage, reviewing and derivation, and processing of private information in the private research in cloud computing. Basically, back ends for storage, processing and accessing the data in IoT applications are largely implemented by cloud platforms.

Integration of Cloud and Internet of Things

Typically, the IoT facilities are provided as isolated vertical solution were all components of the applications are tightly coupled to a precise setting of application. Bringing services of IoT in the cloud can provide comfort in the delivery and the deployment of them by enabling all the plasticity of cloud models (Distefano, 2015).

Quality of Service in Integration of cloud and Internet of Things

The non-functional features of the services of cloud are presented by QoS. Price for execution, execution length, dependability, availability, and reputation are the five generic QoS properties present in cloud services. The flexible processes, includes adaptive service such as execution time, availability, cost, repute, and quality of data. (Gupta et al, 2015). With increase in the amount of data and their types, unpredictability also increases which is when QoS becomes a problem. Any kind of data and any quantity of data can be instigated at any moment (Gubbi et al, 2012). QoS is mostly measured in terms of bandwidth, delay, jitter, and packet loss ratio. Reliant upon the type of information and its emergency to be sent to the sync node, QoS must be maintained or reinforced. In CoT, varied types of networks will be involved, which supports several types of data and facilities. The network should have the plasticity to back all types of data, as per their necessities along with QoS support (Jayavardhana et al, 2012).

FUTURE RESEARCH DIRECTIONS

The advantages of using a cloud based IoT architecture prototype have been discussed in all of the recent research activities. But there are certain issues associated with the cloud of objects. These are, protocol sustenance, energy efficient, Resource allocation, management of identity, IPv6 deployment, discovery of service, Quality of Service provisioning, place of data storage, Security and privacy, and Unwanted communication of information (Lakshmi 2013).

CONCLUSION

There are practically unlimited proficiencies and the possessions of cloud from which IoT benefits largely and can compensate for the technological constraints such as storage, processing, energy. Implementation of IoT amenity management and composition as well as provisions that use the things or the data produced by them can be offered effective solutions from the cloud infrastructure. Cloud also benefits from IoT through extension of its scope in order to deal with real world objects in a more elaborated and dynamic way, also for providing new services in a varied number of real life cases. It is very much evident that the integration of IoT and cloud computing enables resource sharing more efficiently. But the research demands the necessity of QoS requirements. These must be capable enough to deliver real time provisions and applications with ensured quality. The basis of cloud computing, IoT and the survey that was done in QoS of cloud computing and IoT is discussed in this chapter.

REFERENCES

Aazam, M., Hung, P. P., & Huh, E. (2014). Cloud of Things: Integrating Internet of Things with Cloud Computing and the Issues Involved. *Proceedings of International Bhurban Conference on Applied Sciences & Technology.* doi:10.1109/IBCAST.2014.6778179

Bertino, E. (2016). Data Security and Privacy in the IoT. *Proc. 19th International Conference on Extending Database Technology (EDBT).*

Bhardwaj, S., Jain, L., & Jain, S. (2010). Cloud computing: A study of infrastructure as a service (IaaS). *International Journal of Engineering and Information Technology,* *2*(1), 60–63.

Botta, A., de Donato, W., Persico, V., & Pescapé, A. (2016). Integration of cloud computing and internet of things: A survey. *Future Generation Computer Systems,* *56*, 684–700. doi:10.1016/j.future.2015.09.021

Cavalcante, E., Pereira, J., Alves, M. P., Maia, P., Moura, R., Batista, T., & Pires, P. F. et al. (2016). On the interplay of Internet of Things and Cloud Computing: A systematic mapping study. *Computer Communications, 89–90,* 17–33. doi:10.1016/j.comcom.2016.03.012

Chao, H. C. (2011). Internet of things and cloud computing for future internet . *Lecture Notes in Computer Science.*

Garg, S. K., Versteeg, S., & Buyya, R. (2011). SMICloud: A Framework for Comparing and Ranking Cloud Services. *Proc of Fourth IEEE*. doi:10.1109/UCC.2011.36

Giuseppe, C. (2014). Objects that Agree on Task Frequency in the IoT: a Lifetime-Oriented Consensus Based Approach. *IEEE World Forum on Internet of Things (WF-IoT)*, 383-387.

Gubbi, J., Buyya, R., Marusic, R., & Palaniswami, R. (2012). *Internet of Things (IoT): A Vision, Architectural Elements, and Future Directions*. Technical Report CLOUDS-TR-2012-2.

Gupta & Singh. (2015). Quality of Services in Cloud Computing: Issues, Challenges and Analysis. *International Journal of New Innovations in Engineering and Technology, 3*(3), 76-82.

Jeya. (2015). A Survey on Quality of Service in Cloud Computing. *International Journal of Computer Trends and Technology, 27*(1).

Jiang, Xu, & Cai, Jiang, Bu, & Xu. (2014). An IoT-Oriented Data Storage Framework in Cloud Computing Platform. *IEEE Transactions on Industrial Informatics, 10*(2).

Khan, I., & Sawant, D. D. (2016, April). A Review on Integration of Cloud Computing and Internet of Things. *International Journal of Advanced Research in Computer and Communication Engineering, 5*(4), 1046–1050.

Khodkari, H., & Magjrebi, S. G. (2016). Necessity of the integration Internet of Things and cloud services with quality of service assurance approach. *Bulletin de la Société Royale des Sciences de Liège, 85*, 434–445.

Lakshmi, Girija, & Pers. (2013). Integration of Cloud Computing for IoTya. *International Journal of Emerging Research in Management & Technology, 4*(5).

Liu, D. B., & Guo, B. (2015). Combination of Cloud Computing and Internet of Things (IOT) in Medical Monitoring Systems. *International Journal of Hybrid Information Technology, 8*(12), 367–376. doi:10.14257/ijhit.2015.8.12.28

Lovesum & Krishnamoorthy. (2014). QOS Based Cost Efficient Resource Allocation in Cloud. *Journal of Theoretical and Applied Information Technology*.

Makwana. (2014). A Survey on QoS in IaaS. *International Journal of Science and Research*.

Medha, S., & Kulkarni, D. B. (2014). Enabling QoS Support for Multi-Core Message Broker in Publish/Subscribe System. *Advance Computing Conference (IACC) IEEE International*, 774-778.

Ming, Z., & Yan, M. (2012). A Modeling and Computational Method for QoS in lOT, Software Engineering and Service Science (ICSESS). *IEEE 3rd International Conference*.

Ren, D., Chen, X., & Xing, T. (2011). A QoS Architecture for IoT. In *International Conferences on Internet of Things, and Cyber, Physical and Social Computing.* IEEE.

Saima, A., & Kun, Y. A. (2013). QoS Aware Message Scheduling Algorithm in Internet of Things Environment. *IEEE Online Conference on Green Communications (OnlineGreenComm)*, 175-180.

Suchetha, & Guruprasad. (2015). Integration of IoT, Cloud and big data. *Global Journal of Engineering Science and Reserarches, 2*(7), 251-258.

Tingxun, S. H. I. (2013). Quality Driven Design of Program Frameworks for Intelligent Sensor Applications. *20th Asia-Pacific Software Engineering Conference*, 442-449.

Vecchiola, C., Pandey, S., & Buyya, R. (2009). High-performance cloud computing: A view of scientific applications. *Proc. 10thInt. Symp. Pervasive Systems, Algorithms, and Networks (ISPAN)*, 4–16. doi:10.1109/I-SPAN.2009.150

Wang, H.-I. (2014, March). Constructing the green campus within the internet of things architecture. *International Journal of Distributed Sensor Networks*.

Xianrong, Z. (2014). Cloud Service Negotiation in Internet of Things Environment A Mixed Approach. *IEEE Transactions on Industrial Informatics, 10*(2), 1506–1515. doi:10.1109/TII.2014.2305641

Xu, L. D., He, W., & Li, S. (2014). Internet of Things in Industries: A Survey. *IEEE Transactions on Industrial Informatics, 10*(4), 2233–2243. doi:10.1109/TII.2014.2300753

Yu, X., Sun, F., & Cheng, X. (2012). Intelligent Urban Traffic Management System Based on Cloud Computing and Internet of Things. *International Conference on Computer Science and Service System*, 2169-2172. doi:10.1109/CSSS.2012.539

Zhang, Q. (2014). Dynamic Heterogeneity-Aware Resource Provisioning in the Cloud. *IEEE Transactions on Industrial Informatics, 2*(1).

Zhou, J., Leppanen, T., Harjula, E., Ylianttila, M., Ojala, T., Yu, C., & Jin, H. (2013). Cloudthings: A common architecture for integrating the internet of things with cloud computing. In CSCWD. IEEE. doi:10.1109/CSCWD.2013.6581037

KEY TERMS AND DEFINITIONS

Cloud of Things: The integration of IoT and cloud computing.

Cloud Service: A cloud service is any service made accessible to users on demand through the internet from a cloud computing provider server.

Infrastructure as a Service: It denotes the primary hardware resources such as network, storage, and compute resources, typically with virtualization technology.

IoT Device: A typical computing device that joins wirelessly to a network and has the capability to communicate data.

Software as a Service: It is a software distribution technique that delivers access to software and its functions remotely as a web-based service.

Compilation of References

50 Sensor Applications for Smarter World. (n.d.). Retrieved from http://www.libelium.com/resources/top_50_iot_sensor_applications_ranking/

Aazam, M., & Huh, E. N. (2014). Fog computing and smart gateway based communication for cloud of things. *Future Internet of Things and Cloud (FiCloud), 2014 International Conference on*, 464–470.

Aazam, M., Khan, I., Alsaffar, A., & Huh, E. (2014). Cloud of Things: Integrating Internet of Things and cloud computing and the issues involved. *Proceedings of 2014 11th International Bhurban Conference On Applied Sciences & Technology (IBCAST)*. doi:10.1109/ibcast.2014.6778179

Aazam, M., & Huh, E. (2013). Impact of ipv4-ipv6 coexistence in cloud virtualization environment. *Annales des Télécommunications, 69*(9-10), 485–496. doi:10.1007/s12243-013-0391-6

Aazam, M., Hung, P. P., & Huh, E. (2014). Cloud of Things: Integrating Internet of Things with Cloud Computing and the Issues Involved. *Proceedings of International Bhurban Conference on Applied Sciences & Technology*. doi:10.1109/IBCAST.2014.6778179

Abbas, S., Merabti, M., Llewellyn-Jones, D., & Kifayat, K. (2013). Lightweight Sybil attack detection in MANETs. *IEEE Systems Journal, 7*(2), 236–248. doi:10.1109/JSYST.2012.2221912

Abdelwahab, S., Hamdaoui, B., Guizani, M., & Rayes, A. (2014). Enabling smart cloud services through remote sensing: An internet of everything enabler. *Internet of Things Journal, IEEE, 1*(3), 276–288. doi:10.1109/JIOT.2014.2325071

Aceituno, V. (2005). *On information Security Paradigms*. ISSA Journal.

Aceto, G., Botta, A., de Donato, W., & Pescap'e, A. (2013). Cloud monitoring: A survey. *Computer Networks, 57*(9), 2093–2115. doi:10.1016/j.comnet.2013.04.001

Agarwal, R. (2016). *Knowledge Discovery Using Big Data Analytics with practical Approach on Hadoop*. LAMBERT Academic Publishing.

Agrawal, D. (n.d.). *Challenges and Opportunities with Big Data: A community white paper*. Retrieved from https://www.purdue.edu/discoverypark/cyber/assets/pdfs/BigDataWhitePaper.pdf

Agrawal, D., Das, S., & Abbadji, A. (2011). *Big Data and Computing: Current State and Future Opportunities*. Retrieved from: https://www.researchgate.net/publication/221103048_Big_Data_and_Cloud_Computing_Current_State_and_Future_Opportunities

Aguado, A., López, V., Marhuenda, J., de Dios, Ó. G., & Fernández-Palacios, J. P. (2015). ABNO: A feasible SDN approach for multivendor IP and optical networks. *Journal of Optical Communications and Networking, 7*(2), A356–A362. doi:10.1364/JOCN.7.00A356

Aguzzi, S., Bradshaw, D., Canning, M., Cansfield, M., Carter, P., & Cattaneo, G. (2013). *Definition of a Research and Innovation Policy Leveraging Cloud Computing and IoT Combination* (1st ed.). European Commission.

Aitken, R., Chandra, V., Myers, J., Sandhu, B., Shifren, L., & Yeric, G. (2014). Device and technology implications of the internet of things. *VLSI Technology (VLSI-Technology): Digest of Technical Papers,* 1–4. doi:10.1109/VLSIT.2014.6894339

Akpan, H. A., & Vadhanam, B. R. (2015). A survey on Quality of service in cloud computing. *International Journal of Computer Trends and Technology, 27*(1), 58–63. doi:10.14445/22312803/IJCTT-V27P110

Akyildiz, I. F., Su, W., Sankarasubramaniam, Y., & Cayirci, E. (2002). Wireless sensor networks: a survey. *Computer Networks, 38*(4), 393-422.

Alamri, A., Ansari, W., Hassan, M., Hossain, M., Alelaiwi, A., & Hossain, M. (2013). A Survey on Sensor-Cloud: Architecture, Applications, and Approaches. *International Journal of Distributed Sensor Networks, 9*(2), 917923. doi:10.1155/2013/917923

Alcaraz, C., Najera, P., Lopez, J., & Roman, R. (2010). Wireless sensor networks and the internet of things: Do we need a complete integration? *1st International Workshop on the Security of the Internet of Things (SecIoT'10).*

Al-Fares, M., Radhakrishnan, S., Raghavan, B., Huang, N., & Vahdat, A. (2010, April). Hedera: Dynamic Flow Scheduling for Data Center Networks. In NSDI (Vol. 10, pp. 19-19). Academic Press.

Alhakbani, N., Hassan, M. M., Hossain, M. A., & Alnuem, M. (2014). A framework of adaptive interaction support in Cloud-based Internet of Things (IoT) environment. In *Internet and Distributed Computing Systems* (pp. 136–146). Springer. doi:10.1007/978-3-319-11692-1_12

Alhakbani, N., Hassan, M., & Alnuem, M. (2014).A framework of adaptive interaction support in cloud-based internet of things (iot) environment. In *International Conference on Internet and Distributed Computing Systems* (pp. 136-146). Springer International Publishing.

Almoqren, N., & Altayar, M. (2016). The Motivations for Big Data Mining Technologies Adoption in Saudi Banks. *International Conference on Information Technology (Big Data Analysis) (KACSTIT).* doi:10.1109/KACSTIT.2016.7756075

Alter, S. (2008). Defining Information Systems as Work Systems: Implications for the IS Field. *Business Analytics and Information Systems.* Retrieved from: http://repository.usfca.edu/at/22

Arbiza, L. M., Bertholdo, L. M., dos Santos, C. R. P., Granville, L. Z., & Tarouco, L. M. (2015, April). Refactoring internet of things middleware through software-defined network. In *Proceedings of the 30th Annual ACM Symposium on Applied Computing* (pp. 640-645). ACM. doi:10.1145/2695664.2695861

Armbrust, M., Fox, A., Griffith, R., Joseph, A. D., Katz, R., Konwinski, A., & Zaharia, M. (2010). A view of cloud computing. *Communications of the ACM, 53*(4), 50–58. doi:10.1145/1721654.1721672

ASD Guide. (n.d.). Available online: http://docs. aws. amazon. com/AutoScaling/latest. DeveloperGuide/as-dg. pdf

Ashraf, Q. M., & Habaebi, M. H. (2015). Autonomic schemes for threat mitigation in Internet of Things. *Journal of Network and Computer Applications, 49*, 112–127. doi:10.1016/j. jnca.2014.11.011

Ashton, K. (2009). That 'Internet of Things' things. *RFID Journal*. Retrieved from: http://www. rfidjournal.com/articles/view?4986

Ashton, K. (2011). That 'internet of things' thing. *RFiD Journal, 22*(7).

Ashton, K. (2009). *That "Internet of Things" thing*. RFID Journal.

Atzori, Iera, & Morabito. (2010). *The Internet of Things: A survey*. Elsevier.

Atzori, L., Iera, A., & Morabito, G. (2010). The Internet of Things: A survey. *Computer Networks, 54*(15), 2787–2805. doi:10.1016/j.comnet.2010.05.010

Badger, L., Grance, T., Patt-Corner, R., & Voas, J. (2011). *Draft Cloud Computing Synopsis and Recommendations*. National Institute of Standards and Technology (NIST) Special Publication 800-146. US Department of Commerce. Retrieved from: http://csrc.nist.gov/publications/ drafts/800-146/Draft-NIST-SP800-146.pdf

Balakrishnan, H., Padmanabhan, V. N., Seshan, S., & Katz, R. H. (1997). A comparison of mechanisms for improving TCP performance over wireless links. *IEEE/ACM Transactions on Networking, 5*(6), 756–769. doi:10.1109/90.650137

Ballon, P., Glidden, J., Kranas, P., Menychtas, A., Ruston, S., & Van Der Graaf, S. (2011). Is there a need for a cloud platform for european smart cities? *eChallenges e-2011 Conference Proceedings, IIMC International Information Management Corporation*.

Banerjee, S., Paul, R., & Biswas, U. (2016). Cloud Computing: A Wave in Service Supply Chain. In Handbook of Research on Managerial Strategies for Achieving Optimal Performance in Industrial Processes. doi:10.4018/978-1-5225-0130-5.ch015

Bansal, M., Mehlman, J., Katti, S., & Levis, P. (2012, August). Openradio: a programmable wireless dataplane. In *Proceedings of the first workshop on Hot topics in software defined networks* (pp. 109-114). ACM. doi:10.1145/2342441.2342464

Bao, F., & Chen, I. (2012). Dynamic trust management for internet of things applications. *Proceedings of the 2012 International Workshop on Self-Aware Internet of Things, Self-IoT '12*, 1–6.

Becker, A. (n.d.). *Internet of Things*. Retrieved from https://atos.net/content/dam/global/documents/your-business/atos-white-paper-internet-of-things.pdf

Ben Saied, O. Zeghlache, & Laurent. (2014). Lightweight collaborative key establishment scheme for the Internet of Things. Elsevier.

Benin, Toledo, & Tromer. (2015). Secure Association for the Internet of Things. *International Workshop on Secure Internet of Things*.

Berde, P., Gerola, M., Hart, J., Higuchi, Y., Kobayashi, M., Koide, T., & Parulkar, G. et al. (2014, August). ONOS: towards an open, distributed SDN OS. In *Proceedings of the third workshop on Hot topics in software defined networking* (pp. 1-6). ACM. doi:10.1145/2620728.2620744

Bertino, E. (2016). Data Security and Privacy in the IoT. *Proc. 19th International Conference on Extending Database Technology (EDBT)*.

Bertion, E., Paci, F., & Ferrini, R. (2009). *Privacy-Preserving Digital Identity Management for Cloud Computing*. IEEE Computer Society Data Engineering Bulletin.

Bhardwaj, S., Jain, L., & Jain, S. (2010). Cloud computing: A study of infrastructure as a service (IaaS). *International Journal of Engineering and Information Technology*, 2(1), 60–63.

Biswas, A. R., & Giaffreda, R. (2014, March). IoT and cloud convergence: Opportunities and challenges. In *Internet of Things (WF-IoT), 2014 IEEE World Forum on* (pp. 375-376). IEEE.

Bott, A., Donato, W., Persico, V., Pescapé, A. (2016). Integration of Cloud computing and Internet of Things: A survey. *Future Generation Computer Systems*, (56), 684–700.

Botta, A., De Donato, W., Persico, V., & Pescapé, A. (2014, August). On the integration of cloud computing and internet of things. In *Future Internet of Things and Cloud (FiCloud), 2014 International Conference on* (pp. 23-30). IEEE. doi:10.1109/FiCloud.2014.14

Botta, A., Donato, W., Persico, V., & Pescape, A. (2016). Integration of Cloud computing and Internet of Things: A survey. *Future Generation Computer Systems*, 56, 684–700. doi:10.1016/j.future.2015.09.021

Brandt, A., Hui, J., Kelsey, R., Levis, P., Pister, K., Struik, R., & Alexander, R. (2012). *RPL: IPv6 Routing Protocol for Low-Power and Lossy Networks*. 10.17487/rfc6550

Bruening, P. J., & Treacy, B. C. (2009). *Cloud Computing: Privacy, Security Challenges*. Bureau of National Affairs.

Buyya, R. (2017). *Cloud Computing: Principles and Paradigms*. John Wiley & Sons.

Buyya, R., Ramamohanarao, K., Leckie, C., Calhieros, N., Dastjerdi, A., & Versteeg, S. (2015). *Big Data Analytics-Enhanced Cloud Computing: Challenges, Architectural Elements, and Future Directions*. Retrieved from: http://arxiv.org/abs/1510.06486

Buyya. (2013). Introduction to the IEEE Transactions on Cloud Computing. *IEEE Transactions on Cloud Computing, 1*(1).

Cao, J., Carminati, B., Ferrari, E., & Tan, K. L. (2011). CASTLE: Continuously anonymizing data streams. *IEEE Transactions on Dependable and Secure Computing, 8*(3), 337–352. doi:10.1109/TDSC.2009.47

Castro, A., Víctor, V. A., Fuentes, B., & Costales, B. (2014). A Flexible Architecture for Service Management in the Cloud. *IEEE eTransactions on Network and Service Management, 11*(1), 116–125. doi:10.1109/TNSM.2014.022614.1300421

Cavalcante, E., Pereira, J., Alves, M. P., Maia, P., Moura, R., Batista, T., & Pires, P. F. et al. (2016). On the interplay of Internet of Things and Cloud Computing: A systematic mapping study. *Computer Communications, 89–90*, 17–33. doi:10.1016/j.comcom.2016.03.012

Center for the Protection of Natural Infrastructure. (2010). *Information Security Briefing on Cloud Computing, 01/2010*. Retrieved from: http://www.cpni.gov.uk/Documents/Publications/2010/2010007-ISB_cloud_computing.pdf

Chao, H. C. (2011). Internet of things and cloud computing for future internet . *Lecture Notes in Computer Science*.

Chaouchi, H. (2010). *The Internet of Things – Setting the Standards*. London: Wiley.

Chen, Y. K. (2012, January). Challenges and opportunities of internet of things. In *Design Automation Conference (ASP-DAC), 2012 17th Asia and South Pacific* (pp. 383-388). IEEE. doi:10.1109/ASPDAC.2012.6164978

Chen, Y., Paxson, V., & Katz, R. H. (2010). *What is New About Cloud Computing Security? Technical Report UCB/EECS-2010-5*. Berkeley, CA: EECS Department, University of California. Retrieved from http://www.eecs.berkeley.edu/Pubs/TechRpts/2010/EECS-2010-5.html

Chetan, S. (2017). *Correcting the IoT History*. Retrieved from: http://www.chetansharma.com

Choi, B. G., Cho, E. J., Kim, J. H., Hong, C. S., & Kim, J. H. (2009). A sinkhole attack detection mechanism for LQI based mesh routing in WSN. In *International conference on information networking, ICOIN-2009*. Chiang Mai, Thailand: Institute of Electrical and Electronics Engineers.

Chowdhury, A., Mukherjee, S., & Banerjee, S. (2017). An Approach towards Survey and Analysis of Cloud Robotics. In *Detecting and Mitigating Robotic Cyber Security Risks* (pp. 208–231). IGI Global. doi:10.4018/978-1-5225-2154-9.ch015

Chow, R., Golle, P., Jakobsson, M., Shi, E., Staddon, J., Masuoka, R., & Molina, J. (2009). Controlling Data in the Cloud: Outsourcing Computation without Outsourcing Control. In *Proceedings of the ACM Workshop on Cloud Computing Security (CCSW'09)* (pp. 85-90). ACM Press. doi:10.1145/1655008.1655020

Christophe, B., Boussard, M., Lu, M., Pastor, A., & Toubiana, V. (2011). The web of things vision: Things as a service and interaction patterns. *Bell Labs Technical Journal, 16*(1), 55–61. doi:10.1002/bltj.20485

Chu, W., Yang, C., Lu, C., Chang, C., Hsueh, N., Hsu, T., & Hung, S. (2014). An Approach of Quality of Service Assurance for Enterprise Cloud Computing (QoSAECC). *2014 International Conference On Trustworthy Systems And Their Applications.* doi:10.1109/TSA.2014.11

Cooper, M., & Mell, P. (2012). *Tackling Big Data.* Retrieved from: http://csrc.nist.gov/groups/SMA/forum/documents/june2012presentations/f%csm_june2012_cooper_mell.pdf

Curtis, A. R., Mogul, J. C., Tourrilhes, J., Yalagandula, P., Sharma, P., & Banerjee, S. (2011). DevoFlow: Scaling flow management for high-performance networks. *Computer Communication Review, 41*(4), 254–265. doi:10.1145/2043164.2018466

Cyber-Physical Systems Public Working Group Workshop. (2014). National Institute of Standards and Technology. Retrieved from: http://www.nist.gov/cps/cps-pwg-workshop.cfm

Danova, T. (2013). Morgan Stanley. 75 Billion Devices Will Be Connected to The Internet Of Things by 2020. *Business Insider.* Retrieved from: http://www.businessinsider.com/75-billion-devices-will-be-connected-to-the-internet-by-2020-2013-10

Dash, S., Mohapatra, S., &Pattnaik, P. (2009). A Survey on Applications of Wireless Sensor Network Using Cloud Computing. *International Journal of Computer Science & Emerging Technologies, 1*(4).

Dash, S. K., Mohapatra, S., & Pattnaik, P. K. (2010). A survey on application of wireless sensor network using Cloud computing. *Int. J. Comput. Sci. Eng. Technol., 1*(4), 50–55.

Deng, H., Sun, X., Wang B, Cao Y. (2008). Selective forwarding attack detection using watermark in WSNs. *ISECS international colloquium on computing, communication, control and management, CCCM 2009.*

Díaz, M., Martín, C., & Rubio, B. (2016). State-of-the-art, challenges, and open issues in the integration of internet of things and cloud computing. *Journal of Network and Computer Applications, 67*, 99–117. doi:10.1016/j.jnca.2016.01.010

Distefano, M. (2015). *Cloud computing and the Internet of things: Service architectures for data analysis and management* (Doctoral dissertation). University of Pisa, Italy.

Distefano, S., Merlino, G., & Puliafito, A. (2012). Enabling the Cloud of Things. *2012 Sixth International Conference on Innovative Mobile And Internet Services In Ubiquitous Computing.* doi:10.1109/IMIS.2012.61

Dobre, C., & Xhafa, F. (2014). Intelligent services for Big Data science. *Future Generation Computer Systems, 37*, 267–281. doi:10.1016/j.future.2013.07.014

Dong, P., Guan, J., Xue, X., & Wang, H. (2012). Attack-resistant trust management model based on beta function for distributed routing in internet of things. *China Communications, 9*(4), 89–98.

Duan, R., Chen, X., & Xing, T. (2011, October). A QoS architecture for IOT. In *Internet of Things (iThings/CPSCom), 2011 International Conference on and 4th International Conference on Cyber, Physical and Social Computing* (pp. 717-720). IEEE. doi:10.1109/iThings/CPSCom.2011.125

Duce, H. (2008). *Internet of Things in 2020*. Academic Press.

Dull, T. (2015).Data Lake vs Data Warehouse: Key Differences. Retrieved from http://www.kdnuggets.com/2015/09/data-lake-vs-data-warehouse-key-differences.html

Dustdar, S., Guo, Y., Satzger, B., & Truong, H. L. (2011). Principles of elastic processes. *IEEE Internet Computing, 15*(5), 66–71. doi:10.1109/MIC.2011.121

El Kateb, D., Fouquet, F., Nain, G., Meira, J. A., Ackerman, M., & Le Traon, Y. (2014, March). Generic cloud platform multi-objective optimization leveraging models@ run time. *Proceedings of the 29th Annual ACM Symposium on Applied Computing*, 343-350. doi:10.1145/2554850.2555044

Erl, T. (2005). *Service-oriented architecture* (1st ed.). Upper Saddle River, NJ: Prentice Hall.

Erl, T. (2015). *Big Data Fundamentals Concepts, Drivers & Techniques*. Prentice Hall.

European Network and Information Security Agency (2009). *Cloud Computing: Cloud Computing: Benefits, Risks, and recommendations for Information Security. Report No: 2009*. Author.

Evangelos, A., Nikolaos, D., & Anthony, C. (2011). *Integrating RFIDs and smart objects into a Unified Internet of Things architecture*. Advances in Internet of Things.

Evans, D. (2011). The internet of things: How the next evolution of the internet is changing everything. *CISCO White Paper, 1*(2011), 1-11.

Evolution of the Internet. (2017). Retrieved 22 March 2017, from https://www.cisco.com/cpress/cc/td/cpress/design/isp/1ispint.htm#xtocid229981

Fagen, Zheng, & Jin. (2016). Secure and efficient data transmission in the internet of things. *Springer Journal of Telecommunication System, 62*(1), 111–122.

Fox, G. (2014, January). *Big Data Applications & Analytics Motivation: Big Data and the Cloud; Centerpieces of the Future Economy*. Retrieved from https://www.slideshare.net/Foxsden/big-data-applications-analytics-motivation-big-data-and-the-cloud-centerpieces-of-the-future-economy

Garg, S. K., Versteeg, S., & Buyya, R. (2011). SMICloud: A Framework for Comparing and Ranking Cloud Services. *Proc of Fourth IEEE*. doi:10.1109/UCC.2011.36

Garrison, G., Kim, S., & Wakefield, R. L. (2012). Success factors for deploying cloud computing. *Communications of the ACM, 55*(9), 62–68. doi:10.1145/2330667.2330685

Gaur, A., Scotney, B., & Parr, G. (2015). Smart city architecture and its applications based on IoT. In *Elsevier Procedia Computer Science of 5th International Symposium on Internet of Ubiquitous and Pervasive Things* (vol. 52, pp. 1089-1094). London, UK: Elsevier. doi:10.1016/j.procs.2015.05.122

Ghemawat, S., Gobioff, H., & Leung, S. T. (2003, October). The Google file system. *Operating Systems Review*, *37*(5), 29–43. doi:10.1145/1165389.945450

Gil, D., Ferrandez, A., Mora, H., & Peral, J. (2016). Internet of Things: A Review of Surveys Based on Context Aware Intelligent Services. *Sensors (Basel)*.

Giuseppe, C. (2014). Objects that Agree on Task Frequency in the IoT: a Lifetime-Oriented Consensus Based Approach. *IEEE World Forum on Internet of Things (WF-IoT)*, 383-387.

Gomes, M., Righi, R., & da Costa, C. (2014). Future directions for providing better IoT infrastructure. In *2014 ACM International Joint Conference on Pervasive and Ubiquitous Computing* (pp. 51-54). Adjunct Publication. doi:10.1145/2638728.2638752

Gorelik, A. (2017). The Enterprise Big Data Lake. O'Reilly Media.

Grance & Mell. (2011). *The NIST definition of cloud computing* (NIST Publication No. NIST SP- 800-145). Washington, DC: US Department of Commerce. Retrieved from http://csrc.nist.gov/publications/drafts/800-146/Draft-NIST-SP800-146.pdf

Grolinger, K. (2013, December). Data Management in Cloud Environments: NoSQL and NewSQL Data Stores. *Journal of Cloud Computing: Advances, Systems and Applications*. Retrieved from https://journalofcloudcomputing.springeropen.com/articles/10.1186/2192-113X-2-22

Gubbi, J., Buyya, R., Marusic, R., & Palaniswami, R. (2012). *Internet of Things (IoT): A Vision, Architectural Elements, and Future Directions*. Technical Report CLOUDS-TR-2012-2.

Gubbi, J., Buyya, R., Marusic, S., & Palaniswami, M. (2013). Internet of Things (IoT): A vision, architectural elements, and future directions. *Future Generation Computer Systems*, *29*(7), 1645–1660. doi:10.1016/j.future.2013.01.010

Gu, L., Wang, J., & Sun, B. (2014). Trust management mechanism for internet of things. *China Communications*, *11*(2), 148–156. doi:10.1109/CC.2014.6821746

Gupta & Singh. (2015). Quality of Services in Cloud Computing: Issues, Challenges and Analysis. *International Journal of New Innovations in Engineering and Technology, 3*(3), 76-82.

Gupta, A. (2015). *The Role of Cloud Tech in the Internet of Things*. Retrieved from https://www.knowlarity.com/blog/the-role-of-cloud-tech-in-the-internet-of-things/

Hampel, G., Steiner, M., & Bu, T. (2013, April). Applying software-defined networking to the telecom domain. In INFOCOM, 2013 Proceedings IEEE (pp. 3339-3344). IEEE.

Hancke, G. P., & Silva, B. C. E. (2013). The role of advanced sensing in smart cities. *Sensors (Basel)*, *13*, 1. PMID:23271603

Hartman, R., Kamburugamuve, S., & Fox, G. (2012). Architecture and measured characteristics of a cloud based internet of things. In *Collaboration Technologies and Systems (CTS), 2012 International Conference* (pp. 6-12). IEEE.

Hassanalieragh, M., Page, A., & Soyata, T. (2015). Health monitoring and management using Internet of things sensing with cloud based processing: Opportunities and challenges. *Proceedings of IEEE International Conference on Service Computing*, 285-292. doi:10.1109/SCC.2015.47

Hassan, M., Song, B., Hossain, M., & Alamri, A. (2014). QoS-aware Resource Provisioning for Big Data Processing in Cloud Computing Environment. *2014 International Conference On Computational Science And Computational Intelligence*. doi:10.1109/CSCI.2014.103

Hernández-Muñoz, J. M., Vercher, J. B., Muñoz, L., Galache, J. A., Presser, M., Gómez, L. A. H., & Pettersson, J. (2011, May). Smart cities at the forefront of the future internet. In The Future Internet Assembly (pp. 447-462). Springer Berlin Heidelberg. doi:10.1007/978-3-642-20898-0_32

Hershey, P., Rao, S., Silio, C., & Narayan, A. (2015). System of Systems for Quality-of-Service Observation and Response in Cloud Computing Environments. *IEEE Systems Journal*, *9*(1), 212–222. doi:10.1109/JSYST.2013.2295961

Hopper, N., Vasserman, E., & Chan-TIN, E. (2010). How much anonymity does network latency leak? *ACM Transactions on Information and System Security*, *13*(2), 1–28. doi:10.1145/1698750.1698753

Hou, L., Zhao, S., Xiong, X., Zheng, K., Chatzimisios, P., Hossain, M. S., & Xiang, W. (2016). Internet of things cloud: Architecture and implementation. *IEEE Communications Magazine*, *54*(12), 32–39. doi:10.1109/MCOM.2016.1600398CM

Huang, X., Fu, R., Chen, B., Zhang, T., & Roscoe, A. (2012). User interactive internet of things privacy preserved access control. *Proceedings of 7th International Conference for Internet Technology and Secured Transactions, ICITST 2012*, 597–602.

Hummen, R. (2013). 6LoWPAN fragmentation attacks and mitigation mechanisms. In *Proceedings of the sixth ACM conference on Security and privacy in wireless and mobile networks*. ACM.

Hurwitz, J. (n.d.). *Big Data for Dummies*. John Wiley & Sons .

IBM Cloud. (n.d.). *What is Cloud?* Retrieved from https://www.ibm.com/cloud-computing/learn-more/what-is-cloud-computing/

IEEE. (2014). *Special Report: The Internet of Things*. Available: http://theinstitute. ieee. org/static/specialreport- the-internet-of-things

Intelligence, S. C. B. (2008). Disruptive civil technologies. In Six Technologies with Potential Impacts on US Interests Out to 2025. Academic Press.

Introduction to Cloud Computing. (2010). Retrieved from https://www.dialogic.com/~/media/products/docs/whitepapers/12023-cloud-computing-wp.pdf

Jadhav, P. A., & Hammadi, J. (2015). Applications and Architecture of Cloud-Based Internet of Things (IOT). *International Journal of Advanced Research in Computer Science and Software Engineering*, *5*(5).

Jaiswal, S., & Chandra, M. B. (2017). A Survey: Privacy and Security to Internet of Things with Cloud Computing. *International Journal of Control Theory and Applications*, *10*(1).

Jara, A. J., Ladid, L., & Gómez-Skarmeta, A. F. (2013). The Internet of Everything through IPv6: An Analysis of Challenges, Solutions and Opportunities. *JoWua*, *4*(3), 97–118.

Jeya. (2015). A Survey on Quality of Service in Cloud Computing. *International Journal of Computer Trends and Technology, 27*(1).

Jiang, Xu, & Cai, Jiang, Bu, & Xu. (2014). An IoT-Oriented Data Storage Framework in Cloud Computing Platform. *IEEE Transactions on Industrial Informatics*, *10*(2).

Jing, Q., Vasilakos, A. V., Wan, J., Lu, J., & Qiu, D. (2014). Security of the Internet of Things: Perspectives and challenges. *Wireless Networks*, *20*(8), 2481–2501. doi:10.1007/s11276-014-0761-7

Jin, X., Li, L. E., Vanbever, L., & Rexford, J. (2013, December). Softcell: Scalable and flexible cellular core network architecture. In *Proceedings of the ninth ACM conference on Emerging networking experiments and technologies* (pp. 163-174). ACM. doi:10.1145/2535372.2535377

Josyula, S. K., & Gupta, D. (2016, October). Internet of things and cloud interoperability application based on Android. In *Advances in Computer Applications (ICACA), IEEE International Conference on* (pp. 76-81). IEEE. doi:10.1109/ICACA.2016.7887927

Kang, T., Li, X., Yu, C., & Kim, J. (2013). A survey of security mechanisms with direct sequence spread spectrum signals. *Journal of Computing Science and Engineering*, *7*(3), 187–197. doi:10.5626/JCSE.2013.7.3.187

Kantarci, B., & Mouftah, H. T. (2014). Sensing Services in Cloud-Centric Internet of Things: A Survey, Taxonomy and Challenges. *IEEE Conference*.

Karim, R., Ding, C., & Miri, A. (2013). An End-to-End QoS Mapping Approach for Cloud Service Selection. *2013 IEEE Ninth World Congress On Services*. doi:10.1109/SERVICES.2013.71

Khan, R., Ullah Khan, S., Zaheer, R., & Khan, S. (2012). Future Internet: The Internet of Things Architecture, Possible Applications and Key Challenges. In *International Conference on Frontiers of Information Technology*.

Khan, I., & Sawant, D. D. (2016, April). A Review on Integration of Cloud Computing and Internet of Things. *International Journal of Advanced Research in Computer and Communication Engineering*, *5*(4), 1046–1050.

Khodkari, H., & Majjrebi, S. G. (2016). Necessity of the integration Internet of Things and cloud services with quality of service assurance approach. *Bulletin de la Société Royale des Sciences de Liège*, *85*, 434–445.

Kim, Y. K., Lee, H., Cho, K., & Lee, D. H. (2008). CADE: Cumulative acknowledgement based detection of selective forwarding attacks in wireless sensor networks. *Proceedings of third international conference on convergence and hybrid information technology, ICCIT 2008*.

Koh, J. Y., Ming, J. T. C., & Niyato, D. (2013). Rate limiting client puzzle schemes for denial-of-service mitigation. IEEE wireless communications and networking conference, WCNC-2013.

Koomey, J. (2007). *Estimating total power consumption by server in the US and the world.* Academic Press.

Koponen, T., Casado, M., Gude, N., Stribling, J., Poutievski, L., Zhu, M., . . . Shenker, S. (2010, October). Onix: A distributed control platform for large-scale production networks. In OSDI (Vol. 10, pp. 1-6). Academic Press.

Kosmatos, E., Tselikas, N., & Boucouvalas, A. (2011). Integrating RFIDs and Smart Objects into a UnifiedInternet of Things Architecture. *Advances In Internet Of Things, 01*(01), 5–12. doi:10.4236/ait.2011.11002

Kothmayr, T., Schmitt, C., Hu, W., Brunig, M., & Carle, G. (2013). Dtls based security and two-way authentication for the internet of things. *Ad Hoc Networks, 11*(8), 2710–2723. doi:10.1016/j.adhoc.2013.05.003

Kothmayr, T., Schmitt, C., Hu, W., Brünig, M., & Carle, G. (2013). *DTLS based security and two-way authentication for the Internet of Things.* Elsevier.

Kroenke, D. (2015). *MIS Essentials* (4th ed.). Boston: Pearson.

Krontiris, I., Dimitriou, T., Giannetsos, T., & Mpasoukos, M. (2008). *Intrusion detection of sinkhole attacks in wireless sensor networks. In Algorithmic aspects of wireless sensor networks* (pp. 150–161). Berlin: Springer. doi:10.1007/978-3-540-77871-4_14

Kuhn, D. R., Hu, V., Ferraiolo, D. F., Kacker, R. N., & Lei, Y. (2016). *Pseudo-exhaustive Testing of Attribute Based Access Control Rules.* International Workshop on Combinatorial Testing at the 2016 IEEE Ninth International Conference on Software Testing, Verification, and Validation Workshops (ICSTW), Chicago, IL. doi:10.1109/ICSTW.2016.35

Kumar & Goudar. (2012). Cloud Computing–Research Issues, Challenges, Architecture, Platforms and Applications: A Survey. *International Journal of Future Computer and Communication, 1*(4).

Kumar. (2013). Verification and validation of mapreduce program model for parallel k-means algorithm on hadoop cluster. *International Journal of Computer Applications, 72*(8).

Lakshman, A., & Prashant, M. (2010). Cassandra: A decentralized structured storage system. *SIGOPS Oper. Syst. Rev., 44*(2), 35-40. DOI:10.1145/1773912.1773922

Lakshmi, Girija, & Pers. (2013). Integration of Cloud Computing for IoTya. *International Journal of Emerging Research in Management & Technology, 4*(5).

Layton, T. P. (2007). *Information Security: Information Security: Design, Implementation, Measurement, and Compliance.* Boca Raton, FL: Auerbach Publications.

Lea, R., & Blackstock, M. (2014, December). City hub: A cloud-based iot platform for smart cities. In *Cloud Computing Technology and Science (CloudCom), 2014 IEEE 6th International Conference on* (pp. 799-804). IEEE. doi:10.1109/CloudCom.2014.65

Leaf, D. (2010). *Overview: NIST Cloud Computing Efforts, NIST Senior Executive for Cloud Computing, NIST.* Information Technology Laboratory.

Leaf, D. (2010). *Overview: NIST Cloud Computing Efforts. NIST Senior Executive for Cloud Computing, NIST* Information Technology Laboratory.

Leavitt, N. (2009). Is Cloud Computing Ready for Prime Time? *IEEE Computer, 42*(1), 15–20. doi:10.1109/MC.2009.20

Lee, J.-Y., Lin, W.-C., & Huang, Y.-H. (2014). A lightweight authentication protocol for internet of things. *International Symposium on Next Generation Electronics, ISNE 2014*, 1–2.

Lee, S., Tang, D., Chen, T., & Chu, W. (2012). A QoS Assurance Middleware Model for Enterprise Cloud Computing. *2012 IEEE 36Th Annual Computer Software And Applications Conference Workshops.* doi:10.1109/compsacw.2012.65

Lee, I., & Kyoochun, L. (2015). The Internet of Things (IoT): Applications, investments, and challenges for enterprises. *Business Horizons, 58*(4), 431–440. doi:10.1016/j.bushor.2015.03.008

Leighon, T. (2009). *Akamai and Cloud Computing: A Perspective from the Edge of the Cloud.* White Paper. Akamai Technologies. Retrieved from http://www.essextec.com/assets/cloud/akamai/cloudcomputing- perspective-wp.pdf

Lewis, P. T. (1985). *Internet of Things.* Speech presented at the Congressional Black Caucus Foundation - 15th Annual Legislative Weekend Conference, Washington, DC.

Li, L. E., Mao, Z. M., & Rexford, J. (2012, October). Toward software-defined cellular networks. In *Software Defined Networking (EWSDN), 2012 European Workshop on* (pp. 7-12). IEEE. doi:10.1109/EWSDN.2012.28

Liao, B., Yu, J., Sun, H., & Nian, M. (2012). A QoS-aware Dynamic Data Replica Deletion Strategy for Distributed Storage Systems under Cloud Computing Environments. *2012 Second International Conference On Cloud And Green Computing.* doi:10.1109/CGC.2012.21

Lin, X. (2013). LSR: Mitigating zero-day Sybil vulnerability in privacy-preserving vehicular peer-to-peer networks. *IEEE Journal on Selected Areas in Communications, 31*(9), 237–246. doi:10.1109/JSAC.2013.SUP.0513021

Li, Q., & Rus, D. (2004). Global Clock Synchronization in Sensor Networks. *Twenty-third Annual Joint Conference of the IEEE Computer and Communications Societies (INFOCOM 2004)*, 564-574. doi:10.1109/INFCOM.2004.1354528

Liu, W., Keranidis, S., Mehari, M., Vanhie-Van Gerwen, J., Bouckaert, S., Yaron, O., & Moerman, I. (2013). *Various detection techniques and platforms for monitoring interference condition in a wireless testbed. In Measurement methodology and tools* (pp. 43–60). Berlin: Springer.

Liu, Y.-B., Gong, X.-H., & Feng, Y.-F. (2014). Trust system based on node behavior detection in internet of things. *Journal of Communication, 35*(5), 8–15.

Liu, Y., Dong, B., Guo, B., Yang, J., & Peng, W. (2015). Combination of Cloud Computing and Internet of Things (IOT) in Medical Monitoring Systems. *International Journal Of Hybrid Information Technology, 8*(12), 367–376. doi:10.14257/ijhit.2015.8.12.28

Loshin, D. (n.d.). *Addressing Five Emerging Challenges of Big Data*. Retrieved from https://www.progress.com/docs/default-source/default-document-library/Progress/Documents/Papers/Addressing-Five-Emerging-Challenges-of-Big-Data.pdf

Lovesum & Krishnamoorthy. (2014). QOS Based Cost Efficient Resource Allocation in Cloud. *Journal of Theoretical and Applied Information Technology*.

Mackle, R. (2015). *Effects of Bandwidth in Cloud Computing - Latest News from Backup Technology. Latest News from Backup Technology*. Retrieved 28 March 2017, from http://blog.backup-technology.com/14845/effects-bandwidth-cloud-computing/

Mahalle, A. Prasad & Prasad. (2012). Identity Establishment and Capability Based Access Control (IECAC) Scheme for Internet of Things. *IEEE Conference*.

Mahalle, P. N., Thakre, P. A., Prasad, N. R., & Prasad, R. (2013). A fuzzy approach to trust based access control in internet of things. *3ʳᵈ International Conference on Wireless Communications, Vehicular Technology, Information Theory and Aerospace & Electronics Systems*, 1–5.

Mahalle, A., Prasad, & Prasad. (2013). Identity driven Capability based Access Control (ICAC) Scheme for the Internet of Things. *IEEE International Conference on Advanced Networks and Telecommunications Systems (ANTS)*.

Mahalle, P., & Prasad. (2015). Threshold Cryptography-based Group Authentication (TCGA) Scheme for the Internet of Things (IoT). *IEEE Conference*.

Ma, J., Guo, Y., Ma, J., Xiong, J., & Zhang, T. (2013). A hierarchical access control scheme for perceptual layer of IoT. *Comput. Res. Dev., 50*(6), 1267–1275.

Makwana. (2014). A Survey on QoS in IaaS. *International Journal of Science and Research*.

Manyika, J., Chui, M., Bisson, P., Woetzel, J., Dobbs, R., Bughin, J., & Aharon, D. (2015). *The Internet of Things: Mapping the Value Beyond the Hype*. McKinsey Global Institute.

Manz & Edgar. (2017). Cyber security research book. In *Protecting IoT Against Man-in-the-Middle Attacks*. Syngress.

Mashal, I., Alsaryrah, O., Chung, T. Y., Yang, C. Z., Kuo, W. H., & Agrawal, D. P. (2015). Choices for interaction with things on Internet and underlying issues. *Ad Hoc Networks, 28*, 68–90. doi:10.1016/j.adhoc.2014.12.006

Mayzaud, A., Sehgal, A., Badonnel, R., Chrisment, I., & Schönwälder, J. (2014). A Study of RPL DODAG Version Attacks. In A. Sperotto, G. Doyen, S. Latré, M. Charalambides, & B. Stiller (Eds.), *Monitoring and Securing Virtualized Networks and Services* (Vol. 8508, pp. 92–104). Springer Berlin Heidelberg. doi:10.1007/978-3-662-43862-6_12

Medha, S., & Kulkarni, D. B. (2014). Enabling QoS Support for Multi-Core Message Broker in Publish/Subscribe System. *Advance Computing Conference (IACC) IEEE International*, 774-778.

Medved, J., Varga, R., Tkacik, A., & Gray, K. (2014, June). Opendaylight: Towards a model-driven sdn controller architecture. In *World of Wireless, Mobile and Multimedia Networks (WoWMoM), 2014 IEEE 15th International Symposium on a* (pp. 1-6). IEEE.

Mell, P., & Grance, T. (2011). The NIST Definition of Cloud Computing (Technical report). National Institute of Standards and Technology: U.S. Department of Commerce. doi:10.6028/NIST.SP.800-145

Mell, P., & Grance, T. (2011). *The Nist definition of Cloud Computing.* NIST Special Publications 800-145. Retrieved from http://nvlpubs.nist.gov/nistpubs/Legacy/SP/nistspecialpublication800-145.pdf

Mell, P., & Grance, T. (2009). The NIST definition of Cloud computing. *Natl. Inst. Stand. Technol.*, *53*(6), 50.

Mell, P., & Grance, T. (2010). *Effectively and Securely Using the Cloud Computing Paradigm. NIST* Information Technology Laboratory.

Meola, A. (2016). *The roles of cloud computing and fog computing in the Internet of Things revolution.* Retrieved from http://www.businessinsider.com/internet-of-things-cloud-computing-2016-10?IR=T

Milovanovic, D., & Bojkovic, Z. (2017). Cloud based IoT healthcare applications: Requirements and recommendations. *International Journal of Internet of Things and Web Services*, *2*, 60–65.

Mineraud, J., Mazhelis, O., Su, X., & Tarkoma, S. (2016). A gap analysis of Internet-of-Things platforms. *Computer Communications*, *89*, 5–16. doi:10.1016/j.comcom.2016.03.015

Minerva, Biru, & Rotondi. (2015, May). Towards a definition of the Internet of Things (IoT). *IEEE Internet Initiative.*

Ming, Z., & Yan, M. (2012). A Modeling and Computational Method for QoS in IOT, Software Engineering and Service Science (ICSESS). *IEEE 3rd International Conference.*

Minoli, D., Sohraby, K., & Occhiogrosso, B. (2017). IoT considerations, requirements and architectures for smart buildings – Energy optimization and next generation building management systems. *IEEE Internet of Things Journal*, *4*(1), 269–283.

Miorandi, Sicari, De Pellegrini, & Chlamtac. (2012). Internet of things: Vision, applications and research challenges. *Ad-Hoc Networks*, *10*(7), 1497-1516.

Miorandi, D., Sicari, S., De Pellegrini, F., & Chlamtac, I. (2012). Internet of things: Vision, applications and research challenges. *Ad Hoc Networks*, *10*(7), 1497–1516. doi:10.1016/j.adhoc.2012.02.016

Misra, P. P., & John, T. (2017). *Data Lake for Enterprises*. Packt.

Mitton, N., Papavassiliou, S., Puliafito, A., & Trivedi, K. (2012). Combining Cloud and sensors in a smart city environment. *EURASIP Journal on Wireless Communications and Networking*, *247*(1), ●●●. doi:10.1186/1687-1499-2012-247

Modadugu, N., & Rescorla, E. (2015). *Datagram Transport Layer Security*. Available online: http://tools.ietf.org/html/rfc4347

Mohamed, A. (2009). A history of cloud computing. *Computer Weekly*, 27.

Nazir, M. (2012). Cloud Computing: Overview & Current Research Challenges. *IOSR Journal of Computer Engineering*, *8*(1), 14–22.

Neto, de Souza, da Rocha, Coutinho, & Moreira. (2015). MINER: An approach for Management of IoT elements in a cloud using software de_ned networks. *5th International Workshop on Advances in ICT Infrastructures and Services (ADVANCE 2015)*.

Ning, H., & Liu, H. (2012). Cyber-physical-social based security architecture for future internet of things. *Advances in Internet of Things*, *2*(1), 1–7. doi:10.4236/ait.2012.21001

Nitti, M., Girau, R., Atzori, L., Iera, A., & Morabito, G. (2012). A subjective model for trustworthiness evaluation in the social internet of things. *IEEE 23rd International Symposium on Personal Indoor and Mobile Radio Communications*, 18–23.

Ojha, T., Misra, S., & Raghuwanshi, N. (2015). Wireless sensor networks for agriculture: The state-of-the-art in practice and future challenges. *Elsevier Journal of Computers and Electronics in Agriculture*, *118*, 66–84. doi:10.1016/j.compag.2015.08.011

Palattella, M. R., Accettura, N., Vilajosana, X., Watteyne, T., Grieco, L. A., Boggia, G., & Dohler, M. (2013). Standardized protocol stack for the internet of (important) things. *IEEE Communications Surveys and Tutorials*, *15*(3), 1389–1406. doi:10.1109/SURV.2012.111412.00158

Pandarinath, P. (2011). Secure localization with defense against selective forwarding attacks in wireless sensor networks. *3rd international conference on electronics computer technology, ICECT 2011*.

Papadopoulos, S., Yang, Y., & Papadias, D. (2007). Cads: continuous authentication on data streams. *33rd International Conference on Very Large Data Bases, VLDB '07*, 135–146.

Papadopoulos, S., Yang, Y., & Papadias, D. (2010). Continuous authentication on relational data streams. *The VLDB Journal*, *19*(1), 161–180. doi:10.1007/s00778-009-0145-2

Papazoglou, M. (2008). Compliance requirements for business-process driven SOAs. *E-Government ICT Professionalism and Competences Service Science*, 183-194.

Parwekar, P. (2011). From internet of things towards cloud of things. In *Computer and Communication Technology (ICCCT), 2011 2nd International Conference* (pp. 329-333). IEEE. doi:10.1109/ICCCT.2011.6075156

Pasupuleti, P., & Purra, B. S. (2015). *Data Lake Development with Big Data*. Packt.

Paxson, V. (2001). An analysis of using reflectors for distributed denial-of-service attacks. *Computer Communication Review*, *31*(3), 38. doi:10.1145/505659.505664

Peltier, T. R. (2002). *Information Security Policies, Procedures, and Standards: Guidelines for effective information security management*. Boca Raton, FL: Auerbach publications.

Perera, C., Zaslavsky, A., Christen, P., & Georgakopoulos, D. (2014). Context aware computing for the internet of things: A survey. *IEEE Communications Surveys and Tutorials*, *16*(1), 414–454. doi:10.1109/SURV.2013.042313.00197

Perera, C., Zaslavsky, A., Christen, P., & Georgakopoulos, D. (2014). Sensing as a service model for smart cities supported by internet of things. *Transactions on Emerging Telecommunications Technologies*, *25*(1), 81–93. doi:10.1002/ett.2704

Perera, C., Zaslavsky, A., Liu, C. H., Compton, M., Christen, P., & Georgakopoulos, D. (2014). Sensor search techniques for sensing as a service architecture for the internet of things. *IEEE Sensors Journal*, *14*(2), 406–420. doi:10.1109/JSEN.2013.2282292

Petrolo, Loscrì, & Mitton. (2014). *Towards a Smart City based on Cloud of Things*. Academic Press.

Pintus, A., Carboni, D., & Piras, A. (2011). The anatomy of a large scale social web for internet enabled objects. *Proceedings Of The Second International Workshop On Web Of Things - Wot '11, San Francisco*. doi:10.1145/1993966.1993975

Polsonetti, C. (2014). Know the Difference Between IoT and M2M. *Automation World*. Retrieved from: http://www.automationworld.com/cloud-computing/know-difference-between-iot-and-m2m

Prakash J. P., Mitra, K., Saguna, K., Shah, T., Georgakopoulos, D., & Ranjan, R. (2015). Orchestrating Quality of Service in the Cloud of Things Ecosystem. *Quality of Service Architecture for Internet of Things and Cloud Computing*.

Pranata, H., Athauda, R., & Skinner, G. (2012). Securing and governing access in ad-hoc networks of internet of things. *Proceedings of the IASTED International Conference on Engineering and Applied Science, EAS 2012*, 84–90. doi:10.2316/P.2012.785-070

Premila, D., Rabara, A., & Jerald, V. (2015). Quality of Service Architecture for Internet of Things and Cloud Computing. *International Journal of Computers and Applications*, *128*(7), 23–28. doi:10.5120/ijca2015906605

Qusay, H. (2011, January). Demystifying Cloud Computing. *The Journal of Defense Software Engineering*, 16–21.

Radhakishan, V., & Selvakumar, S. (2011). Prevention of Man-in-the-Middle Attacks using ID Based Signatures. *2011 Second International Conference on Networking and Distributed Computing*.

Rahman, R. A., & Shah, B. (2016). Security analysis of IoT protocols: A focus in CoAP. *Proceeding of 3rd MEC International Conference on Big Data and Smart City (ICBDSC)*, 1-7.

Rajasekaran, V., Ashok, A., & Manjula, R. (2014). Novel Sensing Approach for Predicting SLA Violations. *International Journal of Computer Trends and Technology*, *10*(1), 25–30. doi:10.14445/22312803/IJCTT-V10P106

Rao, B., Saluia, P., Sharma, N., Mittal, A., & Sharma, S. (2012). Cloud computing for Internet of Things & sensing based applications. In *Sensing Technology (ICST), 2012 Sixth International Conference* (pp. 374-380). IEEE. doi:10.1109/ICSensT.2012.6461705

Ray, Chowdhury, & Abawajy. (2016). Secure Object Tracking Protocol for the Internet of Things. *IEEE Internet of Things Journal*.

RCRWireless News. (2016). *Industrial IoT: Carriers Look Beyond Connectivity*. Retrieved from https://www.5gamericas.org

Ren, D., Chen, X., & Xing, T. (2011). A QoS Architecture for IoT. In *International Conferences on Internet of Things, and Cyber, Physical and Social Computing*. IEEE.

Riazul Islam, S. M., Kwak, D., & Kabir, M. H. (2015). The Internet of things for health care: A comprehensive survey. *IEEE Access: Practical Innovations, Open Solutions*, *3*, 678–708. doi:10.1109/ACCESS.2015.2437951

Riggins, F. J., & Wamba, S. F. (2015, January). Research directions on the adoption, usage, and impact of the internet of things through the use of big data analytics. In *System Sciences (HICSS), 2015 48th Hawaii International Conference on* (pp. 1531-1540). IEEE. doi:10.1109/HICSS.2015.186

Rizzardi, S. Miorandi, & Coen-Porisini. (2016). AUPS: An Open Source Authenticated Publish/Subscribe system for the Internet of Things. Elsevier.

Roman, R., Alcaraz, C., Lopez, J., & Sklavos, N. (2011). Key management systems for sensor networks in the context of the internet of things. *Computers & Electrical Engineering*, *37*(2), 147–159. doi:10.1016/j.compeleceng.2011.01.009

Roman, R., Najera, P., & Lopez, J. (2011). Securing the internet of things. *IEEE Computer*, *44*(9), 51–58. doi:10.1109/MC.2011.291

Roman, R., Zhou, J., & Lopez, J. (2013). On the features and challenges of security and privacy in distributed internet of things. *Computer Networks*, *57*(10), 2266–2279. doi:10.1016/j.comnet.2012.12.018

Rose, K. (2015). *The Internet of Things: An Overview*. Retrieved from https://www.internetsociety. org/sites/default/files/ISOC-IoT-Overview-20151221-en.pdf

Rosenthal, A., Mork, P., Li, M. H., Stanford, J., Koester, D., & Reynolds, P. (2010). Cloud Computing: A new business paradigm for biomedical information sharing. *Journal of Biomedical Informatics*, *43*(2), 342–353. doi:10.1016/j.jbi.2009.08.014 PMID:19715773

Ross, V. W. (2010). *Factors influencing the adoption of cloud computing by Decision making managers (Capella University)*. ProQuest Dissertations and Theses.

Rouse, M. (2012). *Cloud Computing*. Retrieved from http://searchcloudcomputing.techtarget. com/definition/cloud-computing

Rozados, I., & Tjahjono, B. (2014). *Big Data Analytics in Supply Chain Management: Trends and Related Research*. 6th International Conference on Operations and Supply Chain Management, Bali. Retrieved from: https://www.researchgate.net/publication/270506965_Big_Data_Analytics_in_Supply_Chain_Management_Trends_and_Related_Research

Russell, S. J., & Norvig, P. (2010). *Artificial Intelligence-A Modern Approach*. Prentice-Hall, Inc.

Russom, P. (2013). *Managing Big Data*. Retrieved from https://www.sas.com/content/dam/SAS/ en_us/doc/whitepaper2/tdwi-managing-big-data-106702.pdf

Saied, Y., Olivereau, A., Zeghlache, D., & Laurent, M. (2013). Trust management system design for the internet of things: A context-aware and multi-service approach. *Computers & Security*, *39*, 351–365. doi:10.1016/j.cose.2013.09.001

Saima, A., & Kun, Y. A. (2013). QoS Aware Message Scheduling Algorithm in Internet of Things Environment. *IEEE Online Conference on Green Communications (OnlineGreenComm)*, 175-180.

Salama, M., & Shawish, A. (2014). A QoS-Oriented Inter-cloud Federation Framework. *2014 IEEE 38Th Annual Computer Software And Applications Conference*. doi:10.1109/compsac.2014.51

San Murugesan & Irena Bojanova. (2005). *Cloud Integration and Standards*. London: Wiley.

Saravanan, K. (2017). Cloud Robotics: Robot Rides on the Cloud – Architecture, Applications, and Challenges. In *Detecting and Mitigating Robotic Cyber Security Risks* (pp. 261-274). IGI Global. doi:10.4018/978-1-5225-2154-9.ch017

Saravanan, K., & Saranya, S. (2017). An integrated animal husbandry livestock management system. *Journal of Advances in Chemistry*, *13*(6), 6259–6265.

Shacklett, M. (2016). *6 Big Data Trends to Watch in 2017*. Retrieved from http://www.techrepublic. com/article/6-big-data-trends-to-watch-in-2017/

Shelby & Bormann. (2011). *6LoWPAN: The wireless embedded Internet*. Academic Press.

Shelby, Z., & Bormann, C. (2009). *6LoWPAN: The Wireless Embedded Internet*. John Wiley & Sons Incorporated. doi:10.1002/9780470686218

Sheng, Z., & Yang, S. (2005). A survey on the IETF Protocol Suite for the Internet of Things: Standards, Challenges and Opportunities. *IEEE Wireless Communications.*

Shila, D. M., & Anjali, T. (2008). Defending selective forwarding attacks in WMNs. *IEEE international conference on electro/information technology, EIT-2008.*

Shi, W., Cao, J., Zhang, Q., Li, Y., & Xu, L. (2016). Edge computing: Vision and challenges. *IEEE Internet of Things Journal, 3*(5), 637–646. doi:10.1109/JIOT.2016.2579198

Shoreh, M., Hosseinianfar, H., Akhoundi, F., Yazdian, E., Farhang, M., & Salehi, J. (2014). Design and implementation of spectrally-encoded spread-time CDMA transceiver. *IEEE Communications Letters, 18*(5), 741–744. doi:10.1109/LCOMM.2014.033114.132471

Shvachko, K., Kuang, H., Radia, S., & Chansler, R. (2010, May). The hadoop distributed file system. In *Mass storage systems and technologies (MSST), 2010 IEEE 26th symposium on* (pp. 1-10). IEEE. doi:10.1109/MSST.2010.5496972

Sicari, S., Cappiello, C., Pellegrini, F. D., Miorandi, D., & Coen-Porisini, A. (2014). A security- and quality-aware system architecture for internet of things. *Information Systems Frontiers*, 1–13.

Sicari, S., Rizzardi, A., Grieco, L. A., & Coen-Porisini, A. (2015). Security, privacy and trust in Internet of Things: The road ahead. *Computer Networks, 76*, 146–164. doi:10.1016/j.comnet.2014.11.008

Singh, D., Tripathi, G., & Jara, A. J. (2014, March). A survey of Internet-of-Things: Future vision, architecture, challenges and services. In Internet of things (WF-IoT), 2014 IEEE world forum on (pp. 287-292). IEEE.

Singh, V. P., Jain, S., & Singhai, J. (2010). Hello flood attack and its countermeasures in wireless sensor networks. *International Journal of Computational Science, 7*(11), 23–27.

Sivakumar, S., Anuratha, V., & Gunasekaran, S. (2017). Survey on Integration of Cloud Computing and Internet of Things Using Application Perspective. *International Journal of Emerging Research in Management & Technology, 6*(4), 101–108. doi:10.23956/ijermt/SV6N4/101

Smart Grid Interoperability Panel. (2014). *Smart Grid Cybersecurity Committee, Guidelines for Smart Grid Cybersecurity. In NIST Interagency Report (NISTIR) 7628 Revision 1* (p. 668). Gaithersburg, MD: National Institute of Standards and Technology; doi:10.6018/NIST.IR.7628r1

Solaiman, E., Ranjan, R., Jayaraman, P., & Mitra, K. (2016). Monitoring Internet of Things Application Ecosystems for Failure. *IT Professional, 18*(5), 8–11. doi:10.1109/MITP.2016.90

Soliman, M., Abiodun, T., Hamouda, T., Zhou, J., & Lung, C. H. (2013, December). Smart home: Integrating internet of things with web services and cloud computing. In *Cloud Computing Technology and Science (CloudCom), 2013 IEEE 5th International Conference on* (Vol. 2, pp. 317-320). IEEE.

Solution Approaches for Big Data. (n.d.). Retrieved from https://sp.ts.fujitsu.com/dmsp/ publications/public/wp-bigdata-solution-approaches.pdf

Sowe, S. K., Kimata, T., Dong, M., & Zettsu, K. (2014). Managing Heterogeneous Sensor Data on a Big Data Platform: IoT Services for Data-intensive Science. *IEEE 38th Annual International Computers, Software and Applications Conference Workshops*, 295-300.

Standish, R. K. (2004). Why Occam's razor. *Foundations of Physics Letters, 17*(3), 255–266. doi:10.1023/B:FOPL.0000032475.18334.0e

Stanoevska-Slabeva, K., & Wozniak, T. (2010). *Grid and Cloud Computing-A Business Perspective on Technology and Applications*. Berlin: Springer-Verlag. doi:10.1007/978-3-642-05193-7

Stanoevska-Slabeva, K., Wozniak, T., & Ristol, S. (2009). *Grid and Cloud Computing: A Business Perspective on Technology and Applications*. Springer Science & Business Media.

Stevens, W. R. (1997). *TCP slow start, congestion avoidance, fast retransmit, and fast recovery algorithms*. Academic Press.

Stout, W. M. S., & Urias, V. E. (2016). *Challenges to Securing the Internet of Things*. IEEE. doi:10.1109/CCST.2016.7815675

Subashini, S., & Kavitha, V. (2011). A survey on security issues in service delivery models of cloud computing. *Journal of Network and Computer Applications, 34*(1), 1–11. doi:10.1016/j. jnca.2010.07.006

Suchetha, & Guruprasad. (2015). Integration of IoT, Cloud and big data. *Global Journal of Engineering Science and Reserarches, 2*(7), 251-258.

Suciu, G., Halunga, S., Vulpe, A., & Suciu, V. (2013, July). Generic platform for IoT and cloud computing interoperability study. In *Signals, Circuits and Systems (ISSCS), 2013 International Symposium on* (pp. 1-4). IEEE. doi:10.1109/ISSCS.2013.6651222

Suciu, G., Vulpe, A., Halunga, S., Fratu, O., Todoran, G., & Suciu, V. (2013). Smart cities built on resilient cloud computing and secure internet of things. In *Control Systems and Computer Science (CSCS), 2013 19th International Conference* (pp. 513-518). IEEE. doi:10.1109/CSCS.2013.58

Su, J., Cao, D., Zhao, B., Wang, X., & You, I. (2014). ePASS: An expressive attribute-based signature scheme with privacy and an unforgeability guarantee for the internet of things. *Future Generation Computer Systems, 33*(0), 11–18. doi:10.1016/j.future.2013.10.016

Talari, S., Shafie-khah, M., & Siano, P. (2017). A review of smart cities based on the Internet of things concept. *MDPI Energies, 10*(4), 1–23.

Tao, F., Cheng, Y., Da Xu, L., Zhang, L., & Li, B. H. (2014). CCIoT-CMfg: Cloud computing and internet of things-based cloud manufacturing service system. *IEEE Transactions on Industrial Informatics, 10*(2), 1435–1442. doi:10.1109/TII.2014.2306383

Thierer, A., & Castillo, A. (2015). *Projecting the Growth and Economic Impact of the Internet of Things*. George Mason University, Mercatus Center. Retrieved from: http://mercatus.org/sites/default/files/IoT-EP-v3.pdf

Thubert, P. (2012). *RPL: IPv6 Routing Protocol for Low-Power and Lossy Networks*. RFC 6550.

Tingxun, S. H. I. (2013). Quality Driven Design of Program Frameworks for Intelligent Sensor Applications. *20th Asia-Pacific Software Engineering Conference*, 442-449.

Truong, H. L., & Dustdar, S. (2015). Principles for engineering IoT cloud systems. *IEEE Cloud Computing*, *2*(2), 68–76. doi:10.1109/MCC.2015.23

Tsai, C., Lai, C., & Vasilakos, V. (2014). Future internet of things: Open issues and challenges, ACM/ Springer. *Wireless Networks*, *20*(8), 2201–2217. doi:10.1007/s11276-014-0731-0

Tsao, T., Alexander, R., Dohler, M., Daza, V., Lozano, A., Richardson, M. (2014). *A Security Threat Analysis for the Routing Protocol for Low-Power and Lossy Networks (RPLs)*. Academic Press.

Tschofenig, H. (2015). *Architectural Considerations in Smart Object Networking*. Tech. no. RFC 7452. Internet Architecture Board. Retrieved from: https://tools.ietf.org/html/rfc7452

Turner, S., & Polk, T. (2011). *Security Challenges For the Internet of Things*. IAB Interconnecting Smart Objects with the Internet Workshop, Prague, Czech Republic.

Uckelamann, D., Harrison, M., & Michahelles, F. (2011). *Architecting the Internet of Things*. Springer-Verlag. doi:10.1007/978-3-642-19157-2

Ukil, A., Bandyopadhyay, S., & Pal, A. (2014). *IoT-privacy: To be private or not to be private*. Toronto: IEEE INFOCOM.

Uma, Parvin, & Poorani. (2017). Analysis of various issues in cloud of things (COT). *Journal of Chemical and Pharmaceutical Sciences*, *10*(1).

Vecchiola, C., Pandey, S., & Buyya, R. (2009). High-performance cloud computing: A view of scientific applications. *Proc. 10thInt. Symp. Pervasive Systems, Algorithms, and Networks (ISPAN)*, 4–16. doi:10.1109/I-SPAN.2009.150

Vermesan, O., Friess, P., Guillemin, P., Gusmeroli, S., Sundmaeker, H., Bassi, A., & Doody, P. et al. (2011). *Internet of Things Strategic Research Roadmap, Cluster of European Research Projects on the Internet of Things*. CERP-IoT.

Victories, V. (2015). *4 Types of Cloud Computing Deployment Model You Need to Know*. IBM developer Works. IBM.

Voas, J. M., & Miller, K. W (1993). Semantic metrics for software testability. *Journal of Systems and Software*, *20*(3), 207-216. 10.1016/0164-1212(93)90064-5

Vogler, M., Schleicher, J. M., Inzinger, C., Dustdar, S., & Ranjan, R. (2016). Migrating smart city applications to the cloud. *IEEE Cloud Computing*, *3*(2), 80–87. doi:10.1109/MCC.2016.44

Wallgren, L., Raza, S., & Voigt, T. (2013). Routing attacks and countermeasures in the RPL-based internet of things. *International Journal of Distributed Sensor Networks*, *9*(8), 794326. doi:10.1155/2013/794326

Wang, X., Zhang, J., Schooler, E., & Ion, M. (2014). Performance evaluation of attribute-based encryption: Toward data privacy in the IoT. *Proceedings of the IEEE International Conference on Communications*, 725–730.

Wang, H.-I. (2014, March). Constructing the green campus within the internet of things architecture. *International Journal of Distributed Sensor Networks*.

Wang, Y., & Wen, Q. (2011). A privacy enhanced dns scheme for the internet of things. *IET International Conference on Communication Technology and Application, ICCTA-2011*, 699–702. doi:10.1049/cp.2011.0758

Weiss, M., Eidson, J., Barry, C., Broman, B., Goldin, L., Iannucci, B., Lee, E. A., ...Stanton, K. (2017). Time-Aware Applications, Computers, and Communication Systems (TAACCS). NIST Technical Note (TN) 1867. National Institute of Standards and Technology. doi:10.6028/NIST.TN.1867

What is the Internet of Things? And why should you care? I Benson Hougland I TEDxTemecula. (2014). In *YouTube*. Retrieved 25 March 2017, from https://www.youtube.com/watchv=_AlcRoqS65E

White. (2015). Hadoop: The Definitive Guide work. O'Reilly Media/Yahoo Press.

Wu, M., Lu, T., Ling, F., Sun, J., & Du, H. (2010).Research on the architecture of Internet of things. In. *Advanced Computer Theory And Engineering (ICACTE). 3Rd International Conference, 5*.

Wu, Z.-Q., Zhou, Y.-W., & Ma, J.-F. (2011). A security transmission model for internet of things. *Chin. J. Comput.*, *34*(8), 1351–1364. doi:10.3724/SP.J.1016.2011.01351

Xianrong, Z. (2014). Cloud Service Negotiation in Internet of Things Environment A Mixed Approach. *IEEE Transactions on Industrial Informatics*, *10*(2), 1506–1515. doi:10.1109/TII.2014.2305641

Xiao, Y., Lin, C., Jiang, Y., Chu, X., & Shen, X. (2010). Reputation-Based QoS Provisioning in Cloud Computing via Dirichlet Multinomial Model. *2010 IEEE International Conference On Communications*. doi:10.1109/ICC.2010.5502407

Xu, L. D., He, W., & Li, S. (2014). Internet of Things in Industries: A Survey. *IEEE Transactions on Industrial Informatics*, *10*(4), 2233–2243. doi:10.1109/TII.2014.2300753

Xu, M., Cui, L., Wang, H., & Bi, Y. (2009). A Multiple QoS Constrained Scheduling Strategy of Multiple Workflows for Cloud Computing. *2009 IEEE International Symposium On Parallel And Distributed Processing With Applications*. doi:10.1109/ISPA.2009.95

Yang, J., & Fang, B. (2011). Security model and key technologies for the internet of things. *Journal of China Universities of Posts and Telecommunications, 8*(2), 109–112. doi:10.1016/S1005-8885(10)60159-8

Yan, L., Zhang, Y., Yang, L., & Ning, H. (2008). *The Internet of Things* (1st ed.). CRC Press. doi:10.1201/9781420052824

Yan, Z., Zhang, P., & Vasilakos, A. V. (2014). A survey on trust management for Internet of Things. *Journal of Network and Computer Applications, 42*, 120–134. doi:10.1016/j.jnca.2014.01.014

Yao, D., Yu, C., Jin, H., & Zhou, J. (2013). Energy efficient task scheduling in mobile cloud computing. *IFIP International Conference On Network And Parallel Computing*, 344-355. doi:10.1007/978-3-642-40820-5_29

Ye, N., Zhu, Y., Wang, R.-C., Malekian, R., & Lin, Q.-M. (2014). An efficient authentication and access control scheme for perception layer of internet of things. *Applied Mathematics & Information Sciences, 8*(4), 1617–1624. doi:10.12785/amis/080416

Yu, X., Sun, F., & Cheng, X. (2012). Intelligent Urban Traffic Management System Based on Cloud Computing and Internet of Things. *International Conference on Computer Science and Service System*, 2169-2172. doi:10.1109/CSSS.2012.539

Zaharia, M., Chowdhury, M., Franklin, M. J., Shenker, S., & Stoica, I. (2010). Spark: Cluster computing with working sets. *HotCloud, 10*(10-10), 95.

Zanella, A., Bui, N., Castellani, A., Vangelista, L., & Zorzi, M. (2014). Internet of things for smart cities. *IEEE Internet of Things Journal, 1*(1), 22-32.

Zaslavsky, A., Perera, C., & Georgakopoulos, D. (2013). *Sensing as a service and big data.* Arxiv Preprint Arxiv:1301.0159

Zaslavsky, A., Perera, C., & Georgakopoulos, D. (2013). *Sensing as a service and big data.* ArXiv Preprint arXiv:1301.0159

Zhang, Cheng, & Boutaba. (n.d.). Cloud computing: state-of-the-art and research challenges. *Journal of Internet Service and Application, 1*(1), 7-18.

Zhang, Q. (2014). Dynamic Heterogeneity-Aware Resource Provisioning in the Cloud. *IEEE Transactions on Industrial Informatics, 2*(1).

Zhang, Q., Cheng, L., & Boutaba, R. (2010). Cloud computing: State-of-the-art and research challenges. *Journal of Internet Services and Applications, 1*(1), 7–18. doi:10.1007/s13174-010-0007-6

Zhao, B., & Valenti, M. C. (2005). Practical relay networks: A generalization of hybrid-ARQ. *IEEE Journal on Selected Areas in Communications, 23*(1), 7–18. doi:10.1109/JSAC.2004.837352

Zhou, J., Leppanen, T., Harjula, E., Ylianttila, M., Ojala, T., & Yu, C., & Jin, H. (2013). CloudThings: A common architecture for integrating the Internet of Things with Cloud Computing. *Proceedings of the 2013 IEEE 17th International Conference on Computer Supported Cooperative Work in Design (CSCWD).* doi:10.1109/CSCWD.2013.6581037

Zhou, J., Leppänen, T., Harjula, M. E., Ylianttila, O. T., Yu, C., Jin, H., & Tianruo, Y. L. (2011). Cloud Things: A Common Architecture for Integrating the Internet of Things with Cloud Computing. *IEEE 17th International Conference on Computer Supported Cooperative Work in Design.*

Zhou, L., & Chao, H. C. (2011). Multimedia traffic security architecture for the Internet of Things. *IEEE Network,* 25(3), 35–40. doi:10.1109/MNET.2011.5772059

Zikopoulos, P., & Eaton, C. (2011). *Understanding big data: Analytics for enterprise class hadoop and streaming data.* McGraw-Hill Osborne Media.

Zwass, V. (2016). *Information System.* Encyclopedia Britannica, Inc. Retrieved from: https://www.britannica.com/topic/information-system

About the Contributors

Pradeep Tomar is working as faculty member in the School of Information and Communication Technology, Gautam Buddha University, Greater Noida, INDIA since 2009. Dr. Tomar earned Ph.D. from Department of Computer Science & Applications, M. D. University, Rohtak, Haryana, INDIA. Before joining Gautam Buddha University he worked as Software Engineer in a multi-national company, Noida and lecturer in M. D. University, Rohtak, Haryana and Kurukshetra University Kurukshetra, Haryana. Dr. Tomar has good teaching, research and software development experience as well as vast administrative experience at university level on various posts like research coordinator, examination coordinator, admission coordinator, programme coordinator, time table coordinators, proctor and hostel warden. Presently he is also working as a Treasurer in CSI, Noida Chapter. Dr. Tomar is also a member of IEEE, IEEE Computer Society, Computer Society of India (CSI), Indian Society for Technical Education (ISTE), Indian Science Congress Association (ISCA), International Association of Computer Science and Information Technology (IACSIT) and International Association of Engineering (IAENG). He served as a reviewer of journals and conferences and worked as advisory board members in national and international conferences. Dr. Tomar has qualified the National Eligibility Test (NET) for Lecturership in Computer Applications in 2003, Microsoft Certified Professional (MCP) in 2008, SUN Certified JAVA Programmer (SCJP) for the JAVA platform, standard edition 5.0 in 2008 and qualified the IBM Certified Database Associate - DB2 9 Fundamentals in 2010. Two books "Teaching of Mathematics" and "Communication and Information Technology" at national levels have been authored by Dr. Tomar. Dr. Tomar has been awarded with Bharat Jyoti Award by India International Friendship Society in the field of Technology in 2012. He has been awarded for the Best Computer Faculty award by Govt. of Pondicherry and ASDF society. His biography is published in Who's Who Reference Asia, Volume II. Several technical sessions in national and international conferences had been chaired by Dr. Tomar and he delivered expert talks in FDP, workshops, national and international conferences. Three conferences have been organized by

Dr. Tomar: one national conference with COMMUNE group and two international conferences, in which one international ICIAICT 2012 was organized with CSI, Noida Chapter and second international conference 2012 EPPICTM was organized in collaboration with MTMI, USA, University of Maryland Eastern Shore, USA and Frostburg State University, USA at School of Information and Communication Technology, Gautam Buddha University, Greater Noida, INDIA. Apart from teaching, researches in the areas of software engineering are being guided by Dr. Tomar. He has also contributed more than 65 papers/articles in national/international journals and conferences. His major current research interest is in Component-Based Software Engineering (CBSE) and IoT.

Gurjit Kaur, a bright scholar, gold medalist throughout including B.Tech and M.Tech and president awardee has spent over 13 years of her academic career towards research and teaching in the field of Electronics and Communication. She is having distinction of receiving a Gold medal by former President of India Dr. A. P. J. Abdul Kalam for being overall topper of the Punjab Technical University, Jalandhar by securing 82% marks. She has been a topper throughout her academic career. She earned her Ph.D. degree from Panjab University, Chandigarh in 2010 and her M. Tech from PEC University of Technology, Chandigarh in 2003 with distinction. Presently Dr Kaur is working as an Assistant Professor in the School of Information and Communication Technology, Gautam Buddha University, Greater Noida, India. Her research interests include Optical CDMA, Wireless Communication system, high-speed interconnect and IOT. Her name has been listed in Marquis Who's Who in Science and Technology, USA. She has published more than 70 papers in journals and conferences. She has authored one book on Optical Communication, and one book chapter on WiMax of Florida Atlantic University, published by CRC Press.

* * *

Sourav Banerjee is pursuing PhD in Computer Science and Engineering from University of Kalyani. He completed M.Tech in Computer Sc. & Engg in the year 2006 from University of Kalyani. He is presently working as an Assistant Professor in the Dept. of Computer Sc & Engg at Kalyani Government Engineering College. He is a member of IEEE, ACM, MIR Lab, IAENG.

Jai Prakash Bhati is working as Assistant Professor in Department of Computer Science and Engineering, School of Engineering and Technology, Noida International University, Greater Noida, Uttar Pradesh, India since August 2013. He has earned his master's degree, M.Tech. (Specialization in Intelligent Systems and Robotics) from School of Information and Communication Technology, Gautam

Buddha University, Greater Noida, U.P., India. Prior to his masters he has worked in various domains like ERP, technical support and software development around four years. Also he has worked as a guest faculty in the School of Information and Communication Technology, Gautam Buddha University, Greater Noida, U.P., India Apart from teaching experience he has administrative experience at university level on various posts like examination coordinator, registration coordinator, course coordinator, University Tech Fest coordinator, training and placement coordinator, sports event coordinator, academic tour coordinator. Mr. Bhati has organized and coordinate many workshops, seminars and quiz competitions in university. He has been member of organizing committee for national and international conferences at university level. Mr. Bhati has also contributed 03 papers in national/international journals and conferences. He is serving as reviewer for various national and international journals. His areas of interest are artificial intelligence, expert systems, soft computing, artificial neural network, Big Data, Cloud and DBMS.

Bala Chandra Mohan works in SCOPE school in VIT university Vellore. Completed PhD from Anna University. published research paper in scopus indexed journals with very good citations.

Akash Chowdhury has pursued the Bachelor of Technology Degree in Computer Science and Engineering from Institute of Science and Technology, India (2013-2017). He is currently pursuing the Master of Technology Degree in Distributed And Mobile Computing from Jadavpur University. He is the author of various book chapters and research articles. His present research interests include Cloud Computing, Internet of Things (IoT), Cloud Robotics, Distributed Systems, Mobile Computing and Communications and Mobile Cloud Computing.

Govind P. Gupta received his PhD degree from Indian Institute of Technology, Roorkee, India, in 2014. He is currently an Assistant Professor in the Department of Information Technology at National Institute of Technology, Raipur, India. His current research interests include Integration of Internet of Things (IoT) with Cloud Computing, Security issues with IoT, Software-defined Networking, Wireless Sensor Networks, and Big Data Processing. He is a professional member of the ACM, IEEE and CSI.

Swati Jaiswal is currently working as an Assistant Professor in Sinhgad Technical Education Society, Lonavala. She has completed her M.Tech in 2012 and currently pursuing her Ph.D from VIT Vellore. She has published 8 papers in international journal and one book chapter.

Jayashree K. is an Engineer by qualification, having done her Doctorate in the area of Web services Fault Management from Anna University, Chennai and Masters in Embedded System Technologies from Anna University and Bachelors in Computer Science and Engineering from Madras University. She is presently Associate Professor in the Department of Computer Science and Engineering at Rajalakshmi Engineering College, affiliated to Anna University Chennai. Her areas of interest include Web services, Cloud Computing, Data Mining and distributed computing. She is a member of ACM, CSI.

Saravanan K. is working as an Assistant professor, Department of Computer Science & Engineering at Anna University, Regional Campus, Tirunelveli. He received his master degree in M.E Software engineering in the year 2007 and B.E degree in Computer Science & Engineering. He has done doctoral degree on Cloud computing in Anna University, Chennai. His research interests include Cloud computing, Software engineering, Web Technology, Semantic Web and Big data analytics. He published papers in 9 international conferences and 16 international journals. He is an active researcher and academician.

Jagdeep Kaur is working as Assistant Professor in Computer Science and Engineering Department, The NorthCap University, Gurugram, Haryana, India. She has completed her Ph.D. in Computer science and Engineering from School of Information and Communication Technology, Gautam Budhha University,Greater Noida,UP, India. She holds a Bachelor of Technology (B.Tech.) degree in Computer Science and Engineering from BCET, Gurdaspur, Punjab, India (2003). She obtained her Master of Technology degree in Computer Science from Department of Computer Science and Engineering, Punjabi University, Patiala India (2005). Her research interests include Component Based Software Engineering, Software Reuse, Software Testing and IoT.

Deepak Kedia has been working as an Associate Professor in the Dept. of Electronics & Communication Engineering at GJUS&T, Hisar (Haryana)-India. He has 15 years of experience in teaching and research. He received a Gold Medal in B.Tech (Electronics & Communication Engineering) for standing first and did his M.Tech in Telecommunication Systems Engineering from IIT, Kharagpur. He obtained his doctoral degree in 2011 on the topic "Multicarrier CDMA". His research areas include Wireless mobile communication, Spread Spectrum, CDMA, OFDM and Internet of Things.

Swastik Mukherjee has pursued the Bachelor of Technology Degree in Computer Science and Engineering from Institute of Science and Technology, India (2013-2017). He is currently pursuing the Master of Technology Degree in Distributed And Mobile Computing from Jadavpur University. He is the author of various book chapters and research articles. His present research interests include Cloud Computing, Internet of Things (IoT), Cloud Robotics, Distributed Systems, Mobile Computing and Communications and Mobile Cloud Computing.

Srinivasan P. received M.C.A degree from Periyar University and Ph.D. from Anna University, India in 2014. He is currently working as an Associate Professor in Vellore Insitute of Technology, Vellore. Research interest includes Cloud Compting, Wireless Networks, Smart and Pervasive Computing, IoT and Machine Learning . Published various papers in International journals and conferences. Has 12 years of teaching experience in reputed engineering colleges in Tamil Nadu and Karnataka. Coordinated and attended various Faculty Developments Programmes and International conferences.

Yaman Parasher is currently a Masters student in Electronics and Communication Engineering Department, Gautam Buddha University, Greater Noida, India. He also worked in the Incubation Center for Medical Electronics at Indian Institute of Technology Patna as a Pre-Incubatee, since 2016. His research interests include Internet of Things, Wireless Sensor Networks, Biomedical Signal Processing, Embedded Systems Design, and Fabrication.

Babu R. is a Research Scholar in Anna University. He has completed his Masters in Software Engineering with a merit of 2nd rank in the University and Bachelors in Computer Science and Engineering from Rajalakshmi Engineering College affiliated to Anna University. His areas of interest include Web Services, Service Oriented Architecture, Cloud Computing, Big Data Analytics and Internet of Things. He is a life member of CSI and served as a Management Committee Member for two years. He has received Active Participation Award – Youth from CSI. He also received Faculty Excellence Award from Infosys in Faculty Enablement Program for two successive years.

Chithambaramani R. is a Research Scholar in Anna University. He has completed his Masters in Software Engineering and Bachelors in Computer Science and Engineering from Rajalakshmi Engineering College. His areas of interest include Web Services, Service Oriented Architecture and Cloud Computing. He is a member of CSI.

Deepak Saini is the Artificial Intelligence SME for Sapient Consulting and is currently responsible for driving technology innovation, leading various initiatives for developing powerful Text Analytics Accelerators for clients, and supporting sales & delivery. He completed his Masters in Computer Applications in 2001 and since then over a period of 16 years, he has been involved in designing and developing large scale Data Analytics solutions both on premise and cloud. In his most recent role, he is responsible for leading the architecture & delivery of AI enabled Question Answering Systems based on unstructured text for a leading Investment Bank. He is mostly interested in Information Retrieval and Natural Language Processing (NLP) topics like search, text categorization, document summarization, relations extraction, entity linking, linked data, graph evolution, etc.

Jasmine Saini has done her Ph.D. in the area of Gyro-Traveling Wave Tubes. She has done her M.E. from Thapar University, Patiala in 2004 and she joined the Department of Electronics and Communications Engineering, JUIT Waknaghat. Since December 2006, she is working as Assistant Professor in the Department of Electronics and Communications Engineering, JIIT Noida. During her teaching career, she has taught various subjects. She is engaged in research and development in the field of microstrip antennas, travelling wave tubes, IoT, etc. She has published papers in several International journals of high repute. Besides she has presented papers in several national and International conferences/seminars.

Supriya Sarkar is pursuing a PhD from VIT University Vellore. Completed ME from RGTU technical university with 8.5 CGPA. Published 7 research papers in the field of computer engineering and software.

Meghna Sharma is currently working as Assistant Professor (Selection Grade) in The NorthCap University, Gurgaon . She is B.E (CSE) and M.Tech (CSE) and is currently pursuing her PhD from YMCA Univeristy, Faridabad in the area of data mining .Her total teaching and research experience is more than 15 years. She is a recipient of the Science Award conferred by the Government of Haryana in 2007. Her area of interests are Data Mining, Machine Learning, Data Analytics, Internet of Things.

Aditya Pratap Singh received his PhD degree from Gautam Buddha University, Greater Noida, INDIA. He has obtained Master of Computer Application degree from Uttar Pradesh Technical University, Lucknow in 2003. He is working as assistant professor in the Department of MCA at Ajay Kumar Garg Engineering College, Ghaziabad, India. Before joining Ajay Kumar Garg Engineering College, he worked as programmer in Edge Solutions, Noida and as lecturer in Graphic Era

University, Dehradun, Uttarakhand. He has good experience in teaching, research and administrative experience at College level. His current research interests are in component-based software engineering and software measurement. He has presented his work in several national and international Journal and conferences. He has served in program committee relating to national conferences on cyber security issues.

Garima Singh is working as Research Scholar at Indira Gandhi Delhi Technical University for Women, Delhi. She obtained her B.E. degree in Electronics and Communication Engineering from Sharda University in 2013 and M.E. (Electronics and Communication) from Jaypee Institute of Information and Technology in 2015. She has been the topper throughout her academic carrier and has the distinction of receiving an A? for her M.E. thesis. Her professional experience and research are in the area of Cognitive Radio, Cooperative Communication, Optical and Wireless Communication System. She has several publications in International Journals and conferences.

Prabhjot Singh holds an undergraduate degree from National Institute of Technology, Jalandhar in the field of Instrumentation and Control Engineering. His masters is from Carnegie Mellon University, world's premier institute, in Software Engineering and Development Management. Thereafter he joined Salesforce Inc., world's top most innovative company as listed by Forbes, in their R&D department at Silicon Valley and is currently working as Lead Software Engineer. At Salesforce, he focused his research in the fields of Cloud Computing and Software Architecture design along with gaining his expertise on complex big data technologies like Hadoop, HBase, Machine Learning, Neural Networks. In parallel, he has authored book chapters, research papers and patents, alongside expanding his breadth in various other areas. He got Pragmatic Marketing Level VI certified, and then pursued High-Tech Product Management and Marketing and High Impact Leadership from University of California, Berkley. He is currently pursuing Innovation and Entrepreneurship Certificate from Stanford University and dreams to open his own startup utilizing the breadth of experience and innovation his experience till now.

Marcus Tanque is a highly-regarded technology strategist and an author with proven skills in business/data analytics, corporate security/engineering strategies, policies. He also has vested skills in artificial intelligence, cyber security practices, governance, enterprise infrastructure & management and diverse IT consulting practices. Dr. Tanque has a repertoire of technical competencies in assorted consultative functions for the government, public and private sectors. His natural entrepreneurial flair coupled with unparalleled contributions to academic, federal, and industry customers is of significance. Dr. Tanque has supported mission-critical business and technology projects: IT engineering, program/project management, systems security, machine learning, cyber security operations, artificial intelligence, big data analytics, information & communications technology as well as cloud-based solutions. Dr. Tanque holds a Ph.D. in Information Technology with a dual specialization in Information Assurance & Security; and a Masters in Information Systems Engineering.

Dimpal Tomar is working as Assistant Professor in Department of Computer Science and Engineering, School of Engineering and Technology, Noida International University, Greater Noida, U.P., India since September 2014. She has earned his master's degree M.Tech. (Specialization in Software Engineering) from School of Information and Communication Technology, Gautam Buddha University, Greater Noida, U.P., India. Ms. Dimpal has good teaching experience as well as administrative experience at university level on various posts like examination coordinator, Computer lab coordinator, course coordinator, University Fest coordinator. Also she has worked as a guest faculty in School of School of Information and Communication Technology, Gautam Buddha University, Greater Noida, U.P., India. Ms. Dimpal has coordinator many workshops, seminars and quiz competitions. She has been member of organizing committee for international conference at university level. Ms. Dimpal has also contributed 02 papers in national/international journals and conferences. His areas of interest are Data Structures, DBMS, Compiler, Construction, Analysis and Design of Algorithms.

Satvik Vats is PhD-Research Scholar in Department of Computer Science and Engineering, Birla Institute of Technology, Mesra-Ranchi (Deemed University), Jharkhand, India since January 2017. He has earned his master's degree, M.Tech. (Specialization in Software Engineering) from School of Engineering and Technology, Sharda University, Greater Noida, U.P., India. He is actively involved in the research field of Big Data Analytics and Machine Learning. He has published various books and papers in International refereed Journals and prestigious conferences. Presently, he is working on "Hybrid Approach of Frequent Item-sets Mining and Machine learning Techniques such as recommender system, supervised and unsupervised learning with integration of Big Data analytics concept.

Index

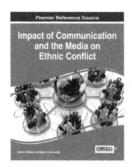

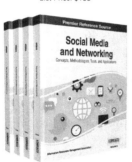
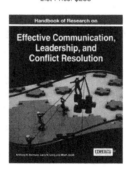

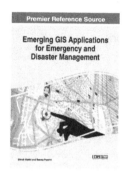

Printed in the United States
By Bookmasters